Forbes®
TOP COMPANIES

Forbes®

TOP COMPANIES

The Forbes® Annual Review of Today's Leading Businesses

Edited and with an Introduction by
Jonathan T. Davis

John Wiley & Sons, Inc.

New York • Chichester • Weinheim • Brisbane • Singapore • Toronto

This text is printed on acid-free paper.

This publication is designed to provide accurate and
authoritative information in regard to the subject
matter covered. It is sold with the understanding that
the publisher is not engaged in rendering legal, accounting,
or other professional services. If legal advice or other
expert assistance is required, the services of a competent
professional person should be sought.

ISBN 0471-17749-0 (paper)

Printed in the United States of America

10 9 8 7 6 5 4 3 2 1

Contents

Introduction

Of the hundred largest companies in 1917, only a handful, a dozen or so, are alive today. This economy is always changing. Companies, industries that are doing well today may not be doing well tomorrow . . . It's this changing economy that is the constant theme . . .

—Steve Forbes, 1987

Which American companies rank highest in sales . . . profits . . . assets . . . market value . . . productivity? What are the largest foreign companies? The best small companies? The largest privately owned companies?

Each year, the editors of *Forbes* magazine compile the most definitive listings of the top companies in the United States and the rest of the world.

In Forbes *Top Companies,* these lists are, for the first time, published together in a single volume. Finally, the manager, investor and entrepreneur have a handy, reliable source of statistical information about the world's leading business enterprises.

The value of Forbes *Top Companies* as a reference tool is so obvious as not to need further elaboration. (Doubters are invited to skip directly to the body of the book and prove this point to themselves.) Still, a description of the contents is in order.

The most widely known compilation in the book is the Forbes 500s, perhaps because it is sometimes confused with a similarly titled feature published by another magazine. In 1995, *Forbes* top editor, James W. Michaels, clarified the difference between their list and the Forbes 500s:

"*[Fortune]* uses sales volume as the only criterion for listing. Recognizing that sales volume alone cannot measure a company's importance, *Forbes* uses four criteria: net profits, market value, sales and assets. Because of its narrow criteria *Fortune*'s 500 omits such important Forbes 500s companies as Genentech, Duracell International, Newmont Mining, Boston Scientific. Though none of these has huge sales, each ranks among the most important U.S. businesses in terms of profits or market value or assets."

The difference between the Forbes 500s and Fortune 500 had, in years past, been even more pronounced. Originally the other magazine's editors drew a distinction between "industrial" and service businesses. This approach resulted in the omission from the *Fortune* list of such corporate giants as AT&T, Citicorp and Sears. Finally, in 1995, Fortune abandoned this increasingly irrelevant distinction.

For foreign companies—which now account for 60% of the world's stock market capitalization—*Forbes* compiles the International 500, arranged within geographic regions and ranked according to revenues. But, again on the belief that more than one yardstick is necessary to take the measure of a business, *Forbes* has created the World Super 50, a composite ranking based on the same four criteria used for the domestic 500s.

In business, size matters, but it isn't everything. For investors the bottom line is, literally, the bottom line: profitability and growth are what count. That's why *Forbes* has also been keeping tabs on up-and-comers. In the 200 Best Small Companies, *Forbes* ranks the (relatively) small, young companies that create new jobs and make the American economy the most dynamic in the world.

In the Private 500, *Forbes* ranks the largest privately owned businesses in America. "Private" doesn't mean "small." If Cargill, number one on the private list with sales of $56 billion, were a publicly held company, it would rank ninth on the Forbes Sales 500, behind General Electric and Mobil, but ahead of Sears, Roebuck and Philip Morris.

Because Forbes *Top Companies* is composed primarily of lists and tables, it is not the sort of book that any well-balanced individual would attempt to read through, start to finish. Yet, it isn't the sort of book that should sit on the shelf, like a telephone directory, consulted only when the need for a particular scrap of information arises. *Top Companies* is more like a dictionary: you may pick it up with a specific inquiry in mind but, before you know it, you've spent much more time than you intended, flipping among the cross-references.

In all, Forbes *Top Companies* reports on nearly 2,000 enterprises, thus providing as detailed a snapshot of capitalistic success as you are likely to find anywhere. It is worth bearing in mind, however, that it is a snapshot. Steve Forbes's observation, that the top companies in 1917 had almost all been displaced by 1987, is likely to be true 70 years hence of today's top companies. In capitalism, change is—to repeat the cliché—the only constant.

As the editor of this book and its companion volume, Forbes *Richest People,* I feel obliged to point out that the real work on this project was done by the writers and editors whose by-lines appear in these pages. In addition, it is hard to imagine any of the lists coming into existence without the guiding hand of Jim Michaels, whom I have quoted previously. I would also like to thank Greg Zorthian, Fred Maynor, Laura Santry, Ann Mintz and, especially, Barbara Strauch at *Forbes,* as well as Myles Thompson, Jacqueline Urinyi, and Janice Weisner at Wiley, for the contributions they have made to the development and publication of these books.

One final observation, not on any particular company or list, but on capitalism itself:

While Forbes *Top Companies* reports the results of competition within the capitalist system, history is likely to record that the greatest competition of the twentieth century was not between business enterprises, nor even between countries, but between two competing economic orders—capitalism and communism—based on vastly different views of human nature.

Ten years ago, when Soviet missiles were still targeted on American cities and the Berlin Wall still stood, I asked the late Malcolm Forbes, Sr. whether he thought, in the long run, communism would continue to pose a threat to capitalism. His prescient answer bears repeating.

"Nobody believes anymore that the greatest good for the greatest number comes from a communist society. It isn't an ideological argument. [Communism] just doesn't work. When everything belongs to everybody, nobody gets to enjoy it except the bureaucrat in charge of it. . . ."

"There is no freedom if there is no free enterprise. And that is the gut of capitalism."

Amen.

The Forbes 500s
Leading American Companies

Downsizing and restructuring notwithstanding, big business hired more people in 1995 than it laid off.

ERIC S. HARDY

Data compiled April, 1996.

Standard political oration: We must crack down on big business because it is restructuring hundreds of thousands of Americans out of jobs. Fact: At the end of 1995 the Forbes 500s companies provided full-time jobs for the equivalent of 20.4 million people. That is 240,000 more than big companies toted up in our directory a year before. This uptick in employment reversed a three-year trend of declining employment.

Employment gains unaccompanied by gains in output are bad news, not good news. Well, this is good news. Output is rising faster than job totals. Productivity gains are particularly visible in wholesaling and retailing. The staff of drugstore chain Walgreen went from 36,000 to 65,000 in the last ten years, while profits per employee (in inflation-adjusted dollars) rose 46%. Not just shareholders enjoy this bounty. Consumers benefit mightily from computerized inventory tracking.

What do you make of the fact that McDonald's employed 197,500 full-time-equivalent workers in 1995, a 12% increase from five years earlier? If you are a pessimist, we are becoming a nation of hamburger-flippers. If you are an optimist, the economy is strong. As middle-income families become more prosperous, they spend more of their income on conveniences like fast food. Are those low-wage hamburger flippers laid-off steelworkers? Only in Labor Secretary Reich's imagination. Most of them are teenagers or young people in their first jobs.

Much is made of the 175,000 jobs shed by IBM between 1985 and 1995. But look at the gains at Intel (employment up 73%, to 40,500, in ten years) and Seagate Technology (up 1,260%, from 4,700 to 64,000, in ten years). The fact is that high tech is creating more jobs than it is eliminating.

It's an obvious fact, but few people grasp it: The more profit an employee contributes, the more eager the employer is to employ him or her. The 1991 Forbes 500 survey listed 4,800 Microsoft employees; the average worker

1

contributed an inflation-adjusted $86,000 to Microsoft's 1990 profits. Microsoft now has nearly four times as many employees, with each person contributing $102,000 in profits. Netscape Communications didn't even exist in 1991; it's on the list now (by dint of market value), with 400 people.

Take health care. When the media mention health care, the phrase is usually coupled with the term "crisis." But think of the jobs created by our growing spending on medicine. In 1995 the 54 Forbes 500s health care companies employed 1.25 million people, a 17% increase over the number employed by 52 health care companies in the prior year's directory. That's 200,000 additional jobs—net.

One success story in the health care business is HBO & Co., which provides detailed cost and clinical analysis for hospitals. HBO provided jobs for about 2,000 people ten years ago; now HBO's payroll stands at 3,000, and the company's shares are worth $3.9 billion. HBO added workers, not because it is goodhearted, but because it paid to do so.

Restructuring is destroying jobs? The rising stock market does not reflect the fortunes of the average American? Consider these facts before you fall for those clichés: The number of people employed, 132 million, is 14% higher than a decade ago. The unemployment rate is near its low for the last 20 years.

But not all regions have fared equally well. There have been some shifts in headquarters location for companies that qualify for the Forbes 500s. In the past ten years first-place California gained 20 Forbes 500s companies. Other states with healthy gains include Alabama and Georgia. Not all of the Sunbelt saw dramatic increases in the number of new large companies, however. Texas, despite the relative decline in the energy industry, picked up one company.

The Grand Totals

The Forbes 500 companies make a significant contribution to the economy, accounting for about 1 in 6 non-government workers. The combined sales figures, however, cannot be compared with GDP because sales don't directly measure value added.

Category	1995 total	Change over 1994	15-year growth rate*
Sales 500	$4.5 trillion	10.0%	4.5%
Profits 500	285.0 billion	13.7	5.2
Assets 500	10.6 trillion	9.7	8.0
Market value 500	5.0 trillion	33.2	11.3
Total employment of 787 companies	20.4 million	1.2	−0.7

*annualized

THE SUPER 100

Rank 1995	Company	WHERE THEY RANK			
		Sales	Net profits	Assets	Market value
1	General Electric	7	2	6	1
1	General Motors	1	1	7	7
3	Exxon	3	3	24	4
4	Ford Motor	2	6	4	25
5	International Business Machines	6	5	30	8
5	Philip Morris Cos	10	4	39	5
7	Citicorp	17	8	3	24
8	Wal-Mart Stores	4	14	56	12
9	AT&T	5	454	26	3
10	Chase Manhattan	22	12	2	36
11	El du Pont de Nemours	11	10	57	17
11	Procter & Gamble	14	13	76	11
13	Hewlett-Packard	16	16	82	13
14	Mobil	8	20	52	18
15	American International Group	23	18	14	20
16	BankAmerica	33	15	5	40
16	Federal National Mortgage Assn	30	22	1	30
18	Coca-Cola	43	11	151	2
19	Merck	50	9	90	6
20	Johnson & Johnson	40	19	124	9
21	PepsiCo	19	38	83	14
22	Chrysler	9	23	40	47
23	GTE	35	17	58	22
24	Amoco	20	29	72	29
24	Intel	56	7	130	15

(Continued)

3

The Super 100 (Cont.)

Rank 1995	Company	Sales	Net profits	Assets	Market value
			WHERE THEY RANK		
26	Motorola	21	34	96	32
27	Allstate	28	27	33	60
28	NationsBank	55	26	9	56
29	Travelers Group	46	32	18	57
30	Merrill Lynch	31	56	11	125
31	American Express	53	40	20	46
32	Dow Chemical	34	24	92	49
33	Chevron	18	73	63	28
34	BellSouth	44	40	67	26
35	Loews	48	35	34	133
36	First Union	106	42	15	69
37	Bristol-Myers Squibb	73	33	169	21
38	JP Morgan & Co	71	48	10	77
39	Sears, Roebuck	13	64	66	58
40	Ameritech	77	25	101	37
41	Bell Atlantic	76	30	86	39
42	Texaco	12	105	85	50
43	Columbia/HCA Healthcare	45	61	112	44
43	SBC Communications	88	28	100	34
45	Federal Home Loan Mortgage	125	58	13	80
46	American Home Products	80	37	106	35
47	Banc One	133	49	25	79
48	Walt Disney	95	44	149	16
49	Eastman Kodak	63	50	159	43
50	Atlantic Richfield	59	45	87	61
51	First Chicago NBD	105	53	17	99
52	Boeing	37	185	99	38
53	International Paper	36	52	88	114
54	Pfizer	117	39	187	23
55	Minnesota Mining & Manufacturing	75	67	166	42
56	Abbott Laboratories	118	36	240	33
57	McDonald's	121	43	147	27
58	Sara Lee	41	81	192	70
59	Nynex	79	60	79	55
60	Berkshire Hathaway	277	106	71	19
60	Caterpillar	57	54	135	85
62	Norwest	155	69	32	97
63	Cigna	39	330	22	139
63	Microsoft	159	31	244	10
65	Southern Co	129	57	70	74

(Continued)

The Super 100 *(Cont.)*

Rank 1995	Company	Sales	Net profits	Assets	Market value
			WHERE THEY RANK		
66	Home Depot	60	104	283	45
67	Wells Fargo	237	63	43	104
68	United Technologies	29	95	140	87
69	Eli Lilly	180	21	161	31
70	First Interstate Bancorp	261	78	38	98
70	Xerox	51	*	80	83
72	Lockheed Martin	27	113	129	75
73	AlliedSignal	67	79	190	71
74	JC Penney	32	82	133	106
75	Bank of New York	229	75	41	120
76	MCI Communications	61	134	118	59
77	Morgan Stanley Group	103	124	12	165
78	Pacific Gas & Electric	124	46	77	119
79	General Re	166	83	60	102
80	Emerson Electric	112	72	231	62
80	RJR Nabisco	58	119	69	136
82	ITT Hartford Group	94	131	23	231
83	Sprint	86	70	150	95
84	Anheuser-Busch Cos	111	76	227	65
85	Aetna Life & Casualty	84	279	29	142
86	Viacom	98	316	75	84
87	U S West Communications Group	126	51	137	81
88	Fleet Financial Group	153	122	28	113
88	Texas Instruments	83	59	243	121
90	Rockwell International	78	92	197	94
91	Compaq Computer	65	90	269	111
92	KeyCorp	201	89	35	143
93	Union Pacific	157	71	117	82
94	Dean Witter Discover & Co	151	80	55	138
95	ConAgra	24	140	183	112
96	Raytheon	97	87	230	93
97	May Department Stores	102	94	221	91
98	Aluminum Co of America	92	88	173	110
99	Archer Daniels Midland	85	85	214	126
99	Monsanto	134	99	215	63

*Not on 500 list

THE SALES 500

General Motors takes first place for the eleventh straight year, maintaining its lead over Ford.

RONALD BOONE JR.

A lackluster economy? Hardly. Over half of America's 500 largest corporations ranked by sales had double-digit sales growth in 1995. Only 11% suffered a decline. The combined revenues of the Forbes Sales 500: $4.5 trillion, up 10% from a year ago.

The lone company to lose its spot among the top ten was Sears, Roebuck, which was displaced by Chrysler Corp. This isn't because Sears is falling apart, however. Rather, Sears is breaking apart: Allstate now has its own entry at position 28.

Winners

RANK '95	'94	Company	Sales ($mil)	% change
356	■	Comcast	3,363	144.5
331	■	Applied Materials	3,596	97.0
299	485	Micron Technology	3,972	90.8
166	279	General Re	7,210	87.9
428	■	UtiliCorp United	2,799	84.8

■ Not on 500 list in 1994.

Comcast rose to the top in sales growth in 1995 by dint of its acquisition of QVC early last year.

Losers

RANK '95	'94	Company	Sales ($mil)	% change
250	112	Baxter International	5,048	−45.9
453	272	Chiquita Brands Intl	2,566	−35.2
412	247	Masco	2,972	−34.5
192	122	Westinghouse	6,296	−28.8
324	209	WR Grace	3,666	−28.0

As in the case of Baxter International, a large sales decline often stems from discontinued operations.

The Forbes Sales 500

RANK '95	'94	Company	Sales ($ mil)	% change	RANK '95	'94	Company	Sales ($ mil)	% change
1	1	General Motors	168,829	9.0	46	34	Travelers Group	17,624	−4.6
2	2	Ford Motor	137,137	6.8	47	47	Fleming Cos	17,502	11.1
3	3	Exxon	107,893	8.2	48	72	Loews	17,219	39.9
4	4	Wal-Mart Stores	93,627	13.5	49	46	AMR	16,910	4.8
5	5	AT&T	79,609	6.0	50	54	Merck	16,681	11.4
6	6	IBM	71,940	12.3	51	38	Xerox	16,611	−6.9
7	7	General Electric	70,028	16.5	52	44	Supervalu	16,530	1.0
8	8	Mobil	64,767	9.8	53	51	American Express	16,445	8.2
9	11	Chrysler	53,195	1.9	54	49	Safeway	16,398	4.9
10	10	Philip Morris Cos	53,139	−1.2	55	64	NationsBank	16,327	24.5
11	13	du Pont de Nemours	36,508	7.2	56	86	Intel	16,202	40.6
12	14	Texaco	35,551	9.3	57	56	Caterpillar	16,072	12.2
13	9	Sears, Roebuck	34,925	5.8	58	50	RJR Nabisco	16,008	4.2
14	16	Procter & Gamble	34,923	10.6	59	53	Atlantic Richfield	15,819	5.2
15	12	Kmart	34,654	1.0	60	71	Home Depot	15,470	24.0
16	19	Hewlett-Packard	33,503	25.9	61	61	MCI Communication	15,265	14.4
17	15	Citicorp	31,690	0.1	62	129	Federated Dept Strs	15,049	81.0
18	17	Chevron	31,322	3.2	63	60	Eastman Kodak	14,980	10.5
19	18	PepsiCo	30,421	6.8	64	57	UAL	14,943	7.1
20	20	Amoco	27,066	3.9	65	93	Compaq Computer	14,755	35.8
21	26	Motorola	27,037	21.5	66	59	Digital Equipment	14,440	4.8
22	■	Chase Manhattan	26,220	9.8	67	66	AlliedSignal	14,346	11.9
23	25	American Intl Group	25,874	15.3	68	63	McDonnell Douglas	14,332	8.8
24	21	ConAgra	24,651	1.9	69	67	Georgia-Pacific	14,292	12.2
25	23	Kroger	23,938	4.3	70	94	Lehman Bros Holding	14,281	32.1
26	28	Dayton Hudson	23,516	10.3	71	82	JP Morgan & Co	13,838	16.1
27	24	Lockheed Martin	22,853	−0.2	72	■	Kimberly-Clark	13,789	15.1
28	■	Allstate	22,793	6.2	73	81	Bristol-Myers Squibb	13,767	14.9
29	30	United Technologies	22,624	8.8	74	65	McKesson	13,582	4.3
30	33	Federal Natl Mort	22,249	19.8	75	52	Minn Mining & Mfg	13,460	−10.7
31	37	Merrill Lynch	21,513	18.0	76	58	Bell Atlantic	13,430	−2.6
32	29	JC Penney	21,419	1.6	77	70	Ameritech	13,428	6.8
33	43	BankAmerica	20,386	24.0	78	90	Rockwell Intl	13,420	20.4
34	31	Dow Chemical	20,200	0.9	79	62	Nynex	13,407	0.9
35	32	GTE	19,957	2.2	80	120	American Home Prod	13,376	49.2
36	55	International Paper	19,797	32.3	81	75	Phillips Petroleum	13,368	9.5
37	27	Boeing	19,515	−11.0	82	73	Goodyear	13,166	7.1
38	41	Price/Costco	18,982	11.4	83	99	Texas Instruments	13,128	27.3
39	35	Cigna	18,955	3.1	84	39	Aetna Life & Cas	12,978	−25.9
40	48	Johnson & Johnson	18,842	19.8	85	76	Archer Daniels	12,971	6.5
41	42	Sara Lee	18,335	10.0	86	69	Sprint	12,765	6.5
42	36	American Stores	18,309	−0.3	87	85	Sysco	12,722	10.1
43	45	Coca-Cola	18,018	11.4	88	84	SBC Communications	12,670	9.0
44	40	BellSouth	17,886	6.2	89	78	IBP	12,668	4.9
45	91	Columbia/HCA	17,695	59.0	90	83	Albertson's	12,585	5.8

■ Not on 500 list in 1994

(Continued)

The Forbes Sales 500 *(Cont.)*

RANK '95	'94	Company	Sales ($ mil)	% change	RANK '95	'94	Company	Sales ($ mil)	% change
91	87	Winn-Dixie Stores	12,567	10.6	136	169	Salomon	8,933	42.3
92	104	Alcoa	12,500	26.2	137	77	Tenneco	8,899	−26.9
93	79	Delta Air Lines	12,250	1.6	138	140	Bergen Brunswig	8,841	15.8
94	■	ITT Hartford Group	12,150	9.4	139	151	Johnson Controls	8,659	21.2
95	95	Walt Disney	12,128	14.1	140	145	CPC International	8,431	13.6
96	97	Weyerhaeuser	11,788	13.4	141	127	Edison International	8,405	0.7
97	103	Raytheon	11,716	17.0	142	■	ITT Industries	8,382	15.0
98	149	Viacom	11,689	58.7	143	139	Sun Co	8,370	8.7
99	106	Ashland	11,495	19.5	144	142	Colgate-Palmolive	8,358	10.2
100	108	Apple Computer	11,378	19.1	145	135	Whirlpool	8,347	3.0
101	101	USX-Marathon	11,163	9.3	146	143	Bankers Trust NY	8,309	10.7
102	74	May Dept Stores	10,952	−10.4	147	131	Woolworth	8,224	−0.8
103	111	Morgan Stanley	10,797	15.2	148	136	Food Lion	8,211	3.5
104	109	Walgreen	10,682	12.2	149	156	Cardinal Health	8,180	18.5
105	■	First Chicago NBD	10,681	25.2	150	147	Time Warner	8,067	9.1
106	■	First Union	10,583	20.2	151	160	Dean Witter Discover	7,934	20.2
107	110	Deere & Co	10,520	12.0	152	150	Limited	7,881	7.7
108	107	CSX	10,504	9.3	153	■	Fleet Finl Group	7,875	16.4
109	100	Coastal	10,448	2.3	154	158	Dana	7,787	15.1
110	113	Occidental Petroleum	10,423	12.9	155	179	Norwest	7,582	25.7
111	80	Anheuser-Busch Cos	10,340	3.1	156	154	Campbell Soup	7,581	9.3
112	121	Emerson Electric	10,294	15.9	157	138	Union Pacific	7,486	−4.0
113	134	Alco Standard	10,272	24.5	158	152	USAir Group	7,474	6.8
114	102	WMX Technologies	10,248	1.5	159	203	Microsoft	7,419	40.9
115	118	TRW	10,172	11.9	160	185	Stone Container	7,351	27.9
116	98	Great A&P Tea	10,101	−2.2	161	161	Amerada Hess	7,302	10.6
117	132	Pfizer	10,021	21.0	162	167	Tosco	7,284	14.4
118	116	Abbott Laboratories	10,012	9.4	163	163	Equitable Cos	7,274	12.8
119	115	Federal Express	10,005	8.9	164	157	Unocal	7,235	4.8
120	105	Textron	9,973	3.0	165	183	Reynolds Metals	7,213	22.7
121	128	McDonald's	9,795	17.7	166	279	General Re	7,210	87.9
122	88	Melville	9,689	−14.1	167	173	Aflac	7,191	17.7
123	124	Fluor	9,644	13.6	168	■	Pharmacia & Upjohn	7,095	4.0
124	96	Pacific G&E	9,622	−7.9	169	174	Lowe's Cos	7,075	15.8
125	153	Federal Home Loan	9,519	36.2	170	168	PPG Industries	7,058	11.5
126	■	U S West Commun	9,484	3.4	171	164	Warner-Lambert	7,040	9.7
127	123	Toys 'R' Us	9,427	7.8	172	162	Kellogg	7,004	6.7
128	119	Enron	9,189	2.3	173	201	Champion Intl	6,972	31.1
129	130	Southern Co	9,180	10.6	174	170	Unicom	6,910	10.1
130	117	Northwest Airlines	9,085	−0.6	175	178	Eaton	6,822	12.7
131	114	Pacific Telesis	9,042	−2.1	176	159	Northrop Grumman	6,818	1.6
132	141	HJ Heinz	8,997	18.2	177	197	James River Corp Va	6,800	25.5
133	137	Banc One	8,971	14.2	178	175	Gillette	6,795	11.9
134	133	Monsanto	8,962	8.3	179	180	Coca-Cola Enterprise	6,773	12.7
135	126	Marriott Intl	8,961	6.5	180	187	Eli Lilly	6,764	18.4

■ Not on 500 list in 1994

(Continued)

The Forbes Sales 500 *(Cont.)*

Rank '95	'94	Company	Sales ($ mil)	% change	Rank '95	'94	Company	Sales ($ mil)	% change
181	177	Honeywell	6,731	11.1	226	225	St Paul Cos	5,410	15.1
182	210	Circuit City Stores	6,686	31.6	227	206	FoxMeyer Health	5,393	4.3
183	155	Lincoln National	6,633	−4.4	228	257	Rite Aid	5,369	26.1
184	252	Best Buy	6,589	52.3	229	258	Bank of New York	5,327	25.3
185	166	Consolidated Edison	6,537	2.6	230	271	PaineWebber Group	5,320	34.2
186	218	RR Donnelley & Sons	6,512	33.2	231	255	Office Depot	5,313	24.5
187	221	American General	6,495	34.2	232	223	Corning	5,313	11.4
188	176	USX-US Steel	6,456	6.4	233	306	Dell Computer	5,296	52.4
189	200	Sun Microsystems	6,390	19.5	234	228	Consol Freightways	5,281	12.8
190	191	Navistar Intl	6,358	13.2	235	125	General Mills	5,262	3.3
191	■	ITT	6,346	33.3	236	220	Genuine Parts	5,262	8.3
192	122	Westinghouse	6,296	−28.8	237	215	Wells Fargo	5,246	5.7
193	181	Entergy	6,274	5.2	238	224	Cummins Engine	5,245	10.7
194	146	Unisys	6,202	−16.2	239	267	AMP	5,227	29.8
195	213	Burlington Santa Fe	6,183	23.8	240	■	American Standard	5,221	17.1
196	195	Loral	6,179	13.5	241	237	Mead	5,179	13.6
197	182	Pub Svc Enterprise	6,164	4.2	242	226	Ryder System	5,167	10.3
198	227	PNC Bank	6,110	6.0	243	232	Household Intl	5,144	11.8
199	199	Transamerica	6,101	13.9	244	260	Rhone-Poulenc Rorer	5,142	23.2
200	188	Chubb	6,089	6.6	245	230	Schering-Plough	5,104	9.6
201	198	KeyCorp	6,054	12.7	246	263	Boise Cascade	5,074	22.6
202	250	NIKE	5,961	36.9	247	212	Vons Cos	5,071	1.5
203	172	Quaker Oats	5,954	−4.1	248	214	VF	5,062	1.8
204	231	Arrow Electronics	5,919	27.3	249	248	Crown Cork & Seal	5,054	13.5
205	193	Dillard Dept Stores	5,918	6.7	250	112	Baxter International	5,048	−45.9
206	229	Browning-Ferris Inds	5,917	26.5	251	251	Eastman Chemical	5,040	16.4
207	144	American Brands	5,905	−21.2	252	289	Revco DS	5,034	37.2
208	219	Union Carbide	5,888	21.0	253	■	Tele-Com-TCI	5,022	NA
209	216	Tandy	5,839	18.1	254	234	Panhandle Eastern	4,968	8.3
210	184	Southland	5,825	1.0	255	256	Case	4,937	15.8
211	189	Continental Airlines	5,825	2.7	256	275	Lyondell Petrochem	4,936	28.0
212	192	Ralston Purina	5,804	15.5	257	233	Cooper Industries	4,886	6.5
213	211	Merisel	5,802	27.7	258	222	Bethlehem Steel	4,868	1.0
214	204	Dresser Industries	5,775	10.0	259	244	Paccar	4,848	8.0
215	202	Tyson Foods	5,732	8.5	260	281	Tyco International	4,843	26.7
216	240	Ingersoll-Rand	5,729	27.1	261	259	First Interstate Bncp	4,828	13.7
217	186	Halliburton	5,699	3.4	262	■	AmeriSource Health	4,822	9.2
218	194	American Electric	5,670	3.0	263	282	Avnet	4,798	25.8
219	190	Texas Utilities	5,639	−0.4	264	241	Inland Steel Inds	4,781	6.3
220	196	FPL Group	5,592	3.1	265	242	Eckerd	4,772	7.8
221	284	United HealthCare	5,511	51.0	266	205	Black & Decker	4,766	−9.2
222	270	Seagate Technology	5,493	38.3	267	333	Lear Seating	4,714	49.8
223	253	Manpower	5,484	27.6	268	245	Duke Power	4,677	4.2
224	217	Dun & Bradstreet	5,415	10.6	269	397	Tenet Healthcare	4,671	71.5
225	238	Bank of Boston	5,411	19.0	270	266	Bindley Western Inds	4,670	15.8

■ Not on 500 list in 1994

(Continued)

The Forbes Sales 500 *(Cont.)*

Rank '95	Rank '94	Company	Sales ($ mil)	% change	Rank '95	Rank '94	Company	Sales ($ mil)	% change
271	235	Norfolk Southern	4,668	1.9	316	294	Central & So West	3,735	3.1
272	243	Dominion Resources	4,652	3.6	317	302	Safeco	3,723	5.2
273	300	Humana	4,605	28.8	318	296	Hershey Foods	3,691	2.3
274	273	Mellon Bank	4,514	14.1	319	285	Conrail	3,686	−1.3
275	268	FMC	4,510	12.4	320	269	Houston Industries	3,680	−8.0
276	254	Avon Products	4,492	5.3	321	339	Barnett Banks	3,680	18.8
277	276	Berkshire Hathaway	4,488	16.6	322	400	Gateway 2000	3,676	36.1
278	277	TJX Cos	4,448	15.7	323	■	NGC	3,666	13.2
279	332	HF Ahmanson	4,398	34.2	324	209	WR Grace	3,666	−28.0
280	286	Gap	4,395	18.1	325	467	WorldCom	3,640	63.9
281	322	Bear Stearns Cos	4,383	32.7	326	331	Mattel	3,639	13.5
282	239	LTV	4,283	−5.4	327	304	DTE Energy	3,636	3.3
283	313	Union Camp	4,212	24.0	328	■	American Finl Group	3,630	72.6
284	265	PECO Energy	4,186	3.6	329	317	Owens Corning	3,612	7.8
285	323	Phelps Dodge	4,185	27.2	330	312	Fina	3,607	5.4
286	354	Quantum	4,174	38.3	331	■	Applied Materials	3,596	97.0
287	307	Illinois Tool Works	4,152	20.0	332	301	Dial	3,575	0.8
288	293	UNUM	4,123	13.8	333	364	Great Western Finl	3,566	21.5
289	283	Stop & Shop Cos	4,116	8.6	334	326	Pitney Bowes	3,555	8.7
290	274	Nordstrom	4,114	5.6	335	■	Circle K	3,544	−0.2
291	340	Computer Sciences	4,100	32.9	336	350	Universal	3,525	15.5
292	328	Jefferson Smurfit	4,093	26.6	337	367	US Healthcare	3,518	20.9
293	■	First Data	4,081	34.7	338	462	SCI Systems	3,514	56.3
294	330	FHP International	4,021	25.1	339	311	Harris	3,507	2.2
295	264	Service Merchandise	4,019	−0.8	340	325	Reebok International	3,481	6.1
296	280	Gannett	4,007	4.8	341	337	Morton International	3,475	11.5
297	290	Waban	3,978	9.0	342	336	Intelligent Electron	3,475	11.1
298	343	PacifiCare Health	3,974	29.5	343	261	Aon	3,466	−16.6
299	485	Micron Technology	3,972	90.8	344	358	Nucor	3,462	16.3
300	262	Niagara Mohawk Pwr	3,917	−5.7	345	363	Temple-Inland	3,461	17.8
301	347	Sallie Mae	3,917	28.1	346	329	USF&G	3,459	7.4
302	299	Air Prods & Chems	3,892	8.7	347	368	National City	3,450	18.7
303	295	CMS Energy	3,890	7.5	348	320	Penn Traffic	3,448	3.9
304	303	Rohm & Haas	3,884	9.9	349	315	Times Mirror	3,448	2.7
305	356	Willamette Inds	3,874	28.8	350	381	Turner Broadcasting	3,437	22.4
306	288	Giant Food	3,861	4.5	351	335	Fred Meyer	3,429	9.6
307	291	General Public Utils	3,805	4.3	352	377	Parker Hannifin	3,427	21.2
308	278	Dole Food	3,804	8.7	353	324	Litton Industries	3,412	3.9
309	297	Owens-Illinois	3,790	5.4	354	305	PacifiCorp	3,401	−3.0
310	413	Oracle	3,777	44.3	355	362	Providian	3,388	14.5
311	310	Marsh & McLennan	3,770	9.8	356	■	Comcast	3,363	144.5
312	359	Wachovia	3,755	26.4	357	■	Trans World Airlines	3,317	−2.7
313	292	Northeast Utilities	3,749	2.9	358	352	Consol Natural Gas	3,307	8.9
314	341	Dover	3,746	21.4	359	444	First Bank System	3,297	38.8
315	327	SunTrust Banks	3,740	15.0	360	411	Turner	3,281	24.4

■ Not on 500 list in 1994

(Continued)

The Forbes Sales 500 *(Cont.)*

RANK '95	RANK '94	Company	Sales ($ mil)	% change	RANK '95	RANK '94	Company	Sales ($ mil)	% change
361	388	Westvaco	3,280	18.3	406	407	Whitman	2,947	10.8
362	353	WW Grainger	3,277	8.4	407	379	Mercantile Stores	2,944	4.4
363	338	Sherwin-Williams	3,274	5.6	408	415	Diamond Shamrock	2,937	12.7
364	■	Allmerica Financial	3,239	1.3	409	391	McGraw-Hill Cos	2,935	6.3
365	360	Beverly Enterprises	3,229	8.7	410	387	Baltimore G&E	2,935	5.5
366	386	Cyprus Amax Mineral	3,207	15.0	411	438	York International	2,930	21.0
367	■	Darden Restaurants	3,200	2.7	412	247	Masco	2,927	-34.5
368	495	Asarco	3,198	57.4	413	392	Alumax	2,926	6.2
369	433	Computer Associates	3,196	30.2	414	■	US Bancorp	2,917	11.0
370	355	Spiegel	3,184	5.6	415	430	Echlin	2,911	17.3
371	412	Automatic Data	3,166	20.2	416	348	Reliance Group	2,906	-4.6
372	■	Richfood Holdings	3,155	NA	417	383	American President	2,896	3.7
373	369	Mapco	3,152	8.6	418	376	Nash Finch	2,889	2.0
374	334	Southern Pacific Rail	3,151	0.3	419	419	Southwest Airlines	2,873	10.8
375	365	Reader's Digest Assn	3,151	7.4	420	385	Shaw Industries	2,870	2.9
376	408	Olin	3,150	18.5	421	427	CoreStates Financial	2,868	14.9
377	399	Praxair	3,146	16.0	422	421	Republic New York	2,860	11.7
378	425	CompUSA	3,135	24.4	423	404	Hasbro	2,858	7.0
379	373	Avery Dennison	3,114	9.0	424	■	Williams Cos	2,856	63.1
380	422	Comerica	3,113	21.7	425	■	Conseco	2,855	66.4
381	361	Alltel	3,110	5.0	426	351	Louisiana-Pacific	2,843	-6.5
382	384	WellPoint Health	3,107	11.3	427	443	Engelhard	2,840	19.0
383	■	Estee Lauder Cos	3,095	13.9	428	■	UtiliCorp United	2,799	84.8
384	469	Tech Data	3,087	27.6	429	374	Fleetwood Enterprise	2,795	-2.0
385	357	Smith's Food & Drug	3,084	3.4	430	414	Dean Foods	2,765	5.9
386	344	Long Island Lighting	3,075	0.3	431	394	Caldor	2,764	3.6
387	318	Centex	3,074	-8.3	432	416	Becton Dickinson	2,759	6.2
388	■	Staples	3,068	53.4	433	409	Knight-Ridder	2,752	3.9
389	346	General Dynamics	3,067	0.3	434	396	PP&L Resources	2,752	1.0
390	371	Yellow	3,057	6.6	435	454	Health Systems Intl	2,732	18.5
391	389	Florida Progress	3,056	10.3	436	428	Baker Hughes	2,725	9.6
392	437	MicroAge	3,047	25.7	437	431	Ultramar	2,714	9.7
393	465	Foster Wheeler	3,042	36.1	438	455	Sonoco Products	2,706	17.7
394	402	Brunswick	3,041	12.6	439	■	Foundation Health	2,703	42.7
395	342	Hormel Foods	3,040	-1.3	440	447	Kelly Services	2,690	13.9
396	314	Maytag	3,040	-9.9	441	450	Natl Semiconductor	2,681	15.6
397	366	Cinergy	3,031	3.7	442	■	Cisco Systems	2,668	73.2
398	■	Valero Energy	3,020	64.3	443	395	Payless Cashways	2,651	-3.1
399	349	Harcourt General	3,013	-1.0	444	434	Allegheny Power	2,648	8.0
400	440	Progressive	3,012	24.7	445	423	Longs Drug Stores	2,644	3.4
401	370	Carolina Power & Lt	3,007	4.5	446	375	Columbia Gas System	2,635	-7.0
402	457	Boatmen's Bancshs	2,996	30.6	447	426	Stanley Works	2,624	4.5
403	441	Owens & Minor	2,976	24.2	448	418	Ball	2,592	-0.1
404	382	NorAm Energy	2,965	5.8	449	429	No States Power	2,587	4.0
405	401	National Steel	2,954	9.4	450	405	Flagstar Cos	2,571	-3.5

■ Not on 500 list in 1994

(Continued)

The Forbes Sales 500 (Cont.)

RANK '95	RANK '94	Company	Sales ($ mil)	% change	RANK '95	RANK '94	Company	Sales ($ mil)	% change
451	458	Hannaford Bros	2,568	12.1	476	456	Fruit of the Loom	2,403	4.6
452	442	Teledyne	2,568	7.4	477	477	Beneficial	2,398	12.2
453	272	Chiquita Brands Intl	2,566	−35.2	478	432	Pennzoil	2,385	−3.6
454	■	MBNA	2,565	38.4	479	460	Varity	2,375	4.7
455	480	Maxxam	2,565	21.2	480	436	Caremark Intl	2,374	−2.1
456	390	Provident Cos	2,555	−7.5	481	■	U S West Media	2,374	24.4
457	■	OfficeMax	2,543	38.1	482	488	Great Lakes Chemical	2,361	14.3
458	461	Olsten	2,519	11.4	483	■	IMC Global	2,360	37.3
459	439	Centerior Energy	2,516	3.9	484	453	AST Research	2,348	1.6
460	486	Newell Co	2,498	20.4	485	472	Rubbermaid	2,344	8.1
461	■	Silicon Graphics	2,497	38.1	486	406	Pacific Enterprises	2,343	−12.0
462	479	Trinity Industries	2,474	16.2	487	■	Harnischfeger Inds	2,335	40.7
463	■	Golden West Finl	2,470	29.1	488	■	Vencor	2,324	14.3
464	445	Ohio Edison	2,466	4.1	489	■	Grand Union	2,312	−5.3
465	■	Caliber System	2,448	5.2	490	489	PHH	2,304	11.9
466	■	State Street Boston	2,446	29.7	491	■	Roadway Express	2,289	5.4
467	459	USG	2,444	6.7	492	482	Dow Jones	2,284	9.2
468	■	Solectron	2,435	36.4	493	463	New England Electric	2,272	1.3
469	493	General Instrument	2,432	19.4	494	■	Commercial Metals	2,268	23.9
470	■	Western Digital	2,430	27.9	495	473	Tandem Computers	2,263	4.4
471	478	Advanced Micro	2,430	13.8	496	■	US Industries	2,262	−18.7
472	378	Hercules	2,427	−14.0	497	■	Omnicom Group	2,258	28.5
473	449	Intl Multifoods	2,412	3.4	498	498	AK Steel Holding	2,257	11.9
474	448	New York Times	2,409	2.2	499	435	Hechinger	2,253	−8.0
475	470	BF Goodrich	2,409	9.5	500	484	Comdisco	2,246	7.7

■ Not on 500 list in 1994

THE PROFITS 500

For the second year in a row General Motors was America's most profitable corporation.

ROBERT J. SHERWOOD

General Motors may still be struggling to improve its product line, but its $7 billion in net income was the most ever reported by any firm in this survey. Imagine what this behemoth could earn if it could get its car-building costs under control. Ford, burdened with new-car launch costs, suffered a 22% profits setback, losing second place to General Electric.

Winners

RANK			NET PROFITS	
'95	'94	Company	'95 ($mil)	'94 ($mil)
333	▪	Tyson Foods	210.2	5.7
284	▪	Jefferson Smurfit	247.0	12.3
91	▪	Champion Intl	771.8	63.3
418	▪	Foundation Health	156.1	13.0
355	▪	American Finl Group	190.4	18.9

▪ Not on 500 list in 1994.

Tyson benefited from weak chicken-feed prices; Jefferson Smurfit and Champion, from firm pulp prices.

Losers

RANK			Net profits ($mil)	% change
'95	'94	Company		
454	6	AT&T	139.0	−97.0
431	123	Toys 'R' Us	148.1	−72.2
382	114	Colgate-Palmolive	172.0	−70.4
458	161	McKesson	137.0	−66.2
326	104	Bankers Trust NY	215.0	−65.0

A costly restructuring knocked AT&T out of the top ten, and almost off the Profits 500 list.

15

Overall it was a banner year for American industry. The combined net income for the Forbes Profits 500 in 1995 was $284 billion, 14% higher than in 1994. According to IBES Inc., 1996 should be even better; analysts predict a 17% gain for the 500 this year.

Technology profits may have peaked with the slowing of the personal computer boom. But Intel moved into the top ten, and IBM continued its recovery.

Wiring-products maker Hubbell, Delmarva Power & Light and American Greetings are among this year's drop-offs.

The Forbes Profits 500

Rank '95	'94	Company	Net profits ($mil)	% change	Cash flow ($mil)	Cash flow rank '95	Rank '95	'94	Company	Net profits ($mil)	% change	Cash flow ($mil)	Cash flow rank '95
1	1	General Motors	6,932.5	22.5	19,032	1	31	38	Microsoft	1,838.0	40.6	2,121	51
2	4	General Electric	6,573.0	39.1	8,154	5	32	36	Travelers Group	1,834.0	38.3	2,138	49
3	3	Exxon	6,470.0	26.9	11,856	2	33	22	Bristol-Myers Squibb	1,812.0	−1.6	2,260	44
4	5	Philip Morris Cos	5,478.0	15.9	7,149	6	34	30	Motorola	1,781.0	14.2	3,712	25
5	9	IBM	4,178.0	38.3	9,780	3	35	234	Loews	1,765.7	500.0+	1,766	64
6	2	Ford Motor	4,139.0	−22.0	9,339	4	36	32	Abbott Laboratories	1,688.7	11.3	2,255	45
7	16	Intel	3,566.2	55.8	4,936	12	37	31	American Home Prod	1,680.4	10.0	2,360	42
8	8	Citicorp	3,464.0	1.2	4,149	18	38	25	PepsiCo	1,606.0	−10.0	3,346	31
9	10	Merck	3,335.2	11.3	4,002	22	39	39	Pfizer	1,572.9	21.1	1,947	54
10	11	du Pont de Nemours	3,293.0	20.8	6,136	8	40	35	American Express	1,564.0	13.3	1,931	55
11	13	Coca-Cola	2,986.0	16.9	3,440	29	40	19	BellSouth	1,564.0	−27.6	5,019	10
12	■	Chase Manhattan	2,970.0	19.5	3,836	23	42	■	First Union	1,430.2	3.9	1,976	53
13	15	Procter & Gamble	2,835.0	16.7	4,136	19	43	43	McDonald's	1,427.3	16.6	2,124	50
14	12	Wal-Mart Stores	2,740.0	2.2	4,040	21	44	44	Walt Disney	1,393.7	13.8	3,390	30
15	17	BankAmerica	2,664.0	22.4	3,644	26	45	62	Atlantic Richfield	1,376.0	49.7	3,334	32
16	23	Hewlett-Packard	2,621.0	43.0	3,776	24	46	55	Pacific G&E	1,338.9	32.9	2,788	39
17	14	GTE	2,537.9	4.0	6,213	7	47	241	Williams Cos	1,318.2	409.2	1,688	65
18	18	American Intl Group	2,510.4	15.4	3,245	34	48	45	JP Morgan & Co	1,296.0	6.7	1,543	73
19	21	Johnson & Johnson	2,403.0	19.8	3,260	33	49	56	Banc One	1,277.9	27.1	1,583	72
20	26	Mobil	2,376.0	35.1	6,124	9	50	70	Eastman Kodak	1,252.0	52.1	2,168	47
21	41	Eli Lilly	2,290.9	78.1	2,845	38	51	■	U S West Commun	1,184.0	3.0	3,226	35
22	20	Federal Natl Mort	2,155.6	0.7	2,156	48	52	152	International Paper	1,153.0	166.9	2,184	46
23	7	Chrysler	2,121.0	−42.9	4,341	15	53	■	First Chicago NBD	1,150.0	−5.8	1,424	84
24	59	Dow Chemical	2,078.0	121.5	3,520	28	54	58	Caterpillar	1,136.0	19.0	1,818	62
25	47	Ameritech	2,007.6	71.5	4,185	17	55	160	Houston Industries	1,124.0	175.8	1,631	67
26	28	NationsBank	1,950.2	15.4	2,349	43	56	54	Merrill Lynch	1,114.0	9.6	1,481	77
27	■	Allstate	1,904.0	293.6	1,904	57	57	57	Southern Co	1,103.0	11.5	2,361	41
28	29	SBC Communications	1,889.3	14.6	4,059	20	58	53	Federal Home Loan	1,091.0	6.2	1,091	114
29	24	Amoco	1,862.0	4.1	4,656	13	59	89	Texas Instruments	1,088.0	57.5	1,844	58
30	34	Bell Atlantic	1,861.8	32.8	4,489	14	60	74	Nynex	1,069.5	34.9	3,636	27

■ Not on 500 list in 1994. D-P: Deficit to profit.

(Continued)

The Forbes Profits 500 (Cont.)

Rank '95	Rank '94	Company	Net profits ($mil)	% change	Cash flow ($mil)	Cash flow rank '95	Rank '95	Rank '94	Company	Net profits ($mil)	% change	Cash flow ($mil)	Cash flow rank '95
61	80	Columbia/HCA	1,064.0	42.8	2,045	52	104	107	Home Depot	731.5	21.0	913	141
62	48	Pacific Telesis	1,048.0	−7.7	2,912	37	105	63	Texaco	728.0	−20.0	3,113	36
63	68	Wells Fargo	1,032.0	22.7	1,304	93	106	130	Berkshire Hathaway	725.2	46.6	801	154
64	42	Sears, Roebuck	1,025.0	19.6	1,656	66	107	323	Quaker Oats	724.0	274.9	922	139
65	192	Georgia-Pacific	1,018.0	212.3	1,843	59	108	82	Consolidated Edison	723.9	−1.4	1,180	104
65	112	Micron Technology	1,018.0	72.8	1,294	94	109	101	Duke Power	714.5	11.8	1,389	88
67	37	Minn Mining & Mfg	976.0	−26.2	1,835	60	110	95	Norfolk Southern	712.7	6.7	1,126	109
68	144	Limited	961.5	114.5	1,247	96	111	124	Chubb	696.6	31.8	750	165
69	71	Norwest	956.0	19.4	1,268	95	112	150	Mellon Bank	691.0	59.6	962	132
70	64	Sprint	946.1	5.2	2,413	40	113	49	Lockheed Martin	682.0	−35.4	1,603	69
71	119	Union Pacific	946.0	73.3	1,588	71	114	94	Pub Svc Enterprise	662.3	−2.5	1,412	86
72	69	Emerson Electric	934.8	11.9	1,359	90	115	180	Unicom	659.5	85.8	1,609	68
73	27	Chevron	930.0	−45.1	4,330	16	116	110	Baxter International	649.0	8.9	985	128
74	167	Union Carbide	925.0	137.8	1,231	98	117	116	HJ Heinz	647.6	15.3	1,001	126
75	79	Bank of New York	914.0	22.0	1,112	111	118	191	Cisco Systems	633.9	94.3	704	177
76	52	Anheuser-Busch Cos	886.6	−12.6	1,452	82	119	77	RJR Nabisco	627.0	−17.9	1,798	63
77	61	Schering-Plough	886.6	−3.8	1,044	122	120	98	CSX	618.0	−5.2	1,218	101
78	84	First Interstate Bncp	885.1	20.7	1,081	116	121	115	Goodyear	611.0	7.8	1,046	121
79	78	AlliedSignal	875.0	15.3	1,487	75	122	■	Fleet Finl Group	610.0	−28.1	1,070	118
80	81	Dean Witter Discover	856.4	15.6	926	138	123	155	PECO Energy	609.7	42.9	1,184	103
81	240	Sara Lee	856.0	229.2	1,473	78	124	163	Morgan Stanley	609.0	54.2	737	168
82	50	JC Penney	838.0	−20.7	1,179	105	125	75	WMX Technologies	603.9	−23.0	1,482	76
83	96	General Re	824.9	24.0	825	150	126	121	Wachovia	602.5	11.8	693	182
84	87	Gillette	823.5	17.9	1,072	117	127	165	Pitney Bowes	583.1	48.2	855	147
85	100	Archer Daniels	810.3	25.9	1,221	99	128	158	First Bank System	568.1	35.3	714	174
86	111	Weyerhaeuser	799.0	35.7	1,420	85	129	125	SunTrust Banks	565.5	8.2	699	180
87	109	Raytheon	792.5	32.8	1,164	107	130	262	Applied Materials	559.9	131.2	657	189
88	145	Alcoa	790.5	78.4	1,521	74	131	188	Eastman Chemical	559.0	66.4	867	146
89	67	KeyCorp	789.2	−7.5	1,012	124	131	■	ITT Hartford Group	559.0	−11.6	644	194
90	65	Compaq Computer	789.0	−9.0	1,003	125	133	126	FPL Group	553.3	6.7	1,471	79
91	■	Champion Intl	771.8	500.0+	1,243	97	134	72	MCI Communication	548.0	−31.1	1,915	56
92	99	Rockwell Intl	769.3	18.5	1,366	89	135	128	American General	544.9	6.3	615	201
93	127	PPG Industries	767.6	49.2	1,119	110	136	83	American Brands	543.1	−26.0	801	155
94	76	May Dept Stores	755.0	−3.5	1,088	115	137	147	Bank of Boston	541.0	22.4	751	164
95	113	United Technologies	750.0	28.2	1,594	70	138	199	Amgen	537.7	68.2	622	199
96	229	Phelps Dodge	746.6	175.5	970	131	139	132	Barnett Banks	533.3	9.3	768	159
97	91	Campbell Soup	746.3	8.4	1,056	120	140	135	ConAgra	533.0	11.7	921	140
98	88	Warner-Lambert	739.5	6.6	942	136	141	129	American Electric	529.9	6.0	1,108	112
99	92	Edison International	739.0	8.6	1,826	61	142	146	St Paul Cos	521.2	17.7	612	203
99	103	Monsanto	739.0	18.8	1,337	92	143	141	Enron	519.7	14.6	951	134
101	■	Pharmacia & Upjohn	738.7	−11.4	1,219	100	144	173	Oracle	518.6	38.5	706	176
102	142	Tenneco	735.0	62.6	1,184	102	145	345	Willamette Inds	514.8	189.8	764	161
103	97	Deere & Co	733.9	12.0	992	127	146	185	CPC International	512.1	48.4	835	148

■ Not on 500 list in 1994. D-P: Deficit to profit.

(Continued)

The Forbes Profits 500 (Cont.)

Rank '95	'94	Company	Net profits ($mil)	% change	Cash flow ($mil)	Cash flow rank '95	Rank '95	'94	Company	Net profits ($mil)	% change	Cash flow ($mil)	Cash flow rank '95
147	■	Occidental Petroleum	511.0	D-P	1,464	80	190	166	US Healthcare	380.7	-2.7	414	284
148	178	NIKE	510.1	43.5	610	204	191	200	Browning-Ferris Inds	378.0	20.2	949	135
149	■	Delta Air Lines	510.0	D-P	1,133	108	192	■	UAL	378.0	390.9	1,102	113
150	136	PacifiCorp	505.0	7.9	971	130	193	■	Tenet Healthcare	375.9	D-P	659	187
151	86	Kellogg	490.3	-30.5	749	166	194	202	Carolina Power & Lt	372.6	19.0	819	152
152	186	Entergy	484.6	41.8	1,175	106	195	291	Bear Stearns Cos	371.2	71.7	436	273
153	182	Lincoln National	482.2	37.8	542	227	196	257	Air Prods & Chems	370.5	51.2	761	162
154	150	Textron	479.0	10.6	894	144	197	162	Sallie Mae	366.3	-9.1	366	316
155	138	Gannett	477.3	2.5	687	184	198	242	Mattel	357.8	39.9	491	248
156	154	Transamerica	470.5	10.1	777	158	199	181	Rhone-Poulenc Rorer	356.5	1.6	582	213
157	133	Phillips Petroleum	469.0	-3.1	1,406	87	200	228	Alltel	354.6	30.5	764	160
158	153	National City	465.1	8.3	574	218	201	198	Gap	354.0	10.6	551	225
159	159	Albertson's	465.0	11.4	716	173	202	235	MBNA	353.1	32.4	430	276
160	■	Salomon	457.0	D-P	570	220	203	■	Boise Cascade	351.9	D-P	593	209
161	175	Household Intl	453.2	23.3	717	172	204	194	Equitable Cos	350.2	8.1	350	328
162	251	CoreStates Financial	452.2	81.8	518	237	205	85	Mead	350.0	-50.5	587	211
163	458	Union Camp	451.1	284.8	739	167	206	210	Aflac	349.1	19.2	349	329
164	267	HF Ahmanson	450.9	90.0	549	226	207	324	Cinergy	347.2	81.6	627	196
165	244	Sun Microsystems	446.5	74.8	726	169	208	368	Case	346.0	109.7	476	252
166	190	TRW	446.2	34.1	956	133	209	207	Providian	345.3	14.8	387	297
167	■	Stone Container	444.5	D-P	816	153	210	209	Northwest Airlines	342.1	15.8	700	178
168	370	General Public Utils	440.1	168.9	879	145	211	222	Loral	339.2	22.7	594	208
169	■	Digital Equipment	430.5	D-P	937	137	212	195	Baltimore G&E	338.0	4.4	717	171
170	168	UST Inc	429.8	10.9	459	265	213	219	Honeywell	333.6	19.6	627	197
171	174	AMP	427.3	15.7	789	157	214	225	Hercules	332.8	21.4	465	260
172	134	Dominion Resources	425.0	-11.1	1,059	119	215	211	Walgreen	330.5	13.3	462	263
173	177	Automatic Data	422.0	17.5	610	205	216	■	US Bancorp	329.0	29.2	458	267
174	179	Boatmen's Bancshs	418.8	17.9	559	223	217	250	Safeway	328.3	31.2	658	188
175	169	Comerica	413.4	6.7	506	239	218	249	EMC	326.8	30.4	380	301
176	106	PNC Bank	408.1	-54.2	577	216	219	237	Morton International	326.3	23.4	499	242
177	157	DTE Energy	405.9	4.0	907	142	220	259	PP&L Resources	322.7	49.4	753	163
178	170	Marsh & McLennan	402.9	5.5	538	230	221	266	General Dynamics	321.0	34.9	359	321
179	176	Aon	402.8	11.9	561	222	222	102	Dun & Bradstreet	320.8	-49.0	795	156
180	164	Central & So West	402.0	2.0	827	149	223	321	Novell	320.3	65.3	416	282
181	226	Medtronic	400.2	46.6	521	236	224	232	Kroger	318.9	18.6	643	195
182	189	Eaton	399.0	19.8	680	186	225	205	Ohio Edison	317.2	4.5	644	193
183	201	Safeco	399.0	26.9	451	269	226	184	American Stores	316.8	-8.2	721	170
184	253	Seagate Technology	394.0	58.8	650	191	227	197	Union Electric	314.1	-2.1	573	219
185	66	Boeing	393.0	-54.1	1,426	83	228	149	Dayton Hudson	311.0	-28.3	905	143
186	287	Lyondell Petrochem	389.0	74.4	475	255	229	213	Genuine Parts	309.2	7.1	352	326
186	447	Reynolds Metals	389.0	219.6	700	179	230	283	Panhandle Eastern	303.6	34.8	583	212
188	221	Illinois Tool Works	387.6	39.5	540	229	231	206	Long Island Lighting	303.3	0.5	589	210
189	139	General Mills	385.6	56.0	579	214	232	313	USX-US Steel	303.0	50.7	621	200

■ Not on 500 list in 1994. D-P: Deficit to profit.

(Continued)

The Forbes Profits 500 *(Cont.)*

RANK '95	'94	Company	Net profits ($mil)	% change	Cash flow ($mil)	Cash flow rank '95	RANK '95	'94	Company	Net profits ($mil)	% change	Cash flow ($mil)	Cash flow rank '95
233	420	Lehman Bros Holding	301.0	126.3	403	288	276	■	Freeport Copper	253.6	94.7	378	304
234	204	Advanced Micro	300.5	−1.6	563	221	277	305	Paccar	252.8	23.6	325	343
235	233	RR Donnelley & Sons	298.8	11.2	697	181	278	■	Northrop Grumman	252.0	500.0+	535	231
236	413	Westvaco	296.5	116.3	530	234	279	137	Aetna Life & Cas	251.7	−46.2	427	278
237	220	Great Lakes Chemical	295.6	6.1	406	287	280	224	Progressive	250.5	−8.7	271	391
238	238	Rohm & Haas	292.0	10.6	534	232	281	281	Intl Flavors & Frags	248.8	10.1	290	370
239	187	Republic New York	288.6	−15.1	362	319	282	347	Niagara Mohawk Pwr	248.0	40.1	600	206
240	276	Dana	288.1	26.2	534	233	283	303	State Street Boston	247.1	19.1	358	323
241	258	Fifth Third Bancorp	287.7	17.7	306	362	284	■	Jefferson Smurfit	247.0	500.0+	400	291
242	214	United HealthCare	286.0	−0.8	380	302	285	315	Marriott Intl	246.9	23.5	376	307
243	306	Ralston Purina	285.3	77.9	494	245	286	288	Duracell Intl	245.6	11.2	341	336
244	215	Northeast Utilities	282.4	−1.5	692	183	287	261	Huntington Bancshs	244.5	0.8	313	356
245	■	Cytec Industries	282.2	403.3	372	311	288	285	Winn-Dixie Stores	243.0	8.5	471	258
246	332	Hershey Foods	281.9	53.0	416	283	289	■	Summit Bancorp	242.9	51.3	287	374
247	381	UNUM	281.1	81.7	281	382	290	299	Reader's Digest Assn	240.3	15.4	287	373
248	425	Temple-Inland	281.0	114.5	506	240	291	290	Allegheny Power	239.7	9.1	496	243
249	■	Cooper Industries	280.6	−4.2	499	241	292	493	Parker Hannifin	239.3	124.1	368	314
250	334	IBP	280.1	53.7	373	310	293	295	Florida Progress	238.9	12.7	598	207
251	243	Franklin Resources	279.6	9.4	321	348	294	318	Fluor	238.9	20.2	395	295
252	212	Federal Express	279.5	−4.0	983	129	295	480	LSI Logic	238.1	119.0	373	308
253	311	Dover	278.3	37.5	386	298	296	282	Premark Intl	237.6	5.4	371	313
254	263	Tribune	278.2	14.9	399	293	297	■	Alumax	237.4	408.4	347	332
255	260	No States Power	275.8	13.3	648	192	298	289	First of America Bk	236.7	7.3	306	360
256	280	Nucor	274.5	21.1	448	271	299	■	Kansas City Southern	236.7	125.6	312	358
257	265	Jefferson-Pilot	273.9	14.5	274	390	300	274	Golden West Finl	234.5	1.8	256	400
258	396	Tyco International	273.0	85.2	413	285	301	338	Wisconsin Energy	234.0	29.4	475	256
259	394	Dell Computer	272.0	82.3	309	359	302	343	Halliburton	233.8	35.7	478	250
260	239	MBIA	271.4	4.3	281	383	303	403	Enova	233.5	62.7	524	235
261	271	Coastal	270.4	16.3	652	190	304	351	Silicon Graphics	231.4	26.6	351	327
262	296	Ingersoll-Rand	270.3	28.0	450	270	305	■	Owens Corning	231.0	212.2	356	325
263	227	AK Steel Holding	268.6	−1.4	343	333	306	■	Consolidated Papers	229.2	164.3	322	347
264	■	WorldCom	267.7	D-P	579	215	307	302	Firstar	228.9	10.2	279	384
265	269	Sysco	266.8	13.5	402	289	308	312	Cincinnati Financial	227.4	13.0	237	419
266	193	Conrail	264.0	−18.5	557	224	309	308	McGraw-Hill Cos	227.1	11.8	459	266
267	270	Becton Dickinson	262.7	11.8	471	259	310	■	Sun Co	227.0	134.0	575	217
268	309	Praxair	262.0	29.1	541	228	311	286	Lowe's Cos	226.0	1.1	380	303
269	248	Great Western Finl	261.0	3.9	377	305	312	■	Price/Costco	224.9	D-P	371	312
270	442	Unocal	260.0	109.7	1,342	91	313	■	Continental Airlines	224.0	D-P	477	251
271	■	Bowater	258.2	D-P	432	274	313	246	Cummins Engine	224.0	−11.4	367	315
272	236	Natl Semiconductor	257.5	−3.0	481	249	315	273	Wm Wrigley Jr	223.7	−2.9	268	393
273	264	Avon Products	256.5	6.4	315	353	316	382	Conseco	222.5	44.1	426	279
274	433	Black & Decker	254.9	100.1	462	264	316	474	Viacom	222.5	102.3	1,043	123
275	336	Green Tree Financial	254.0	40.1	267	394	318	320	Newell Co	222.5	13.8	324	346

■ Not on 500 list in 1994.   D-P: Deficit to profit.   *(Continued)*

The Forbes Profits 500 *(Cont.)*

Rank '95	'94	Company	Net profits ($mil)	% change	Cash flow ($mil)	Cash flow rank '95	Rank '95	'94	Company	Net profits ($mil)	% change	Cash flow ($mil)	Cash flow rank '95
319	304	Dresser Industries	221.1	6.8	430	275	362	356	Pacific Enterprises	185.0	7.6	428	277
320	307	Centerior Energy	220.5	8.3	626	198	363	435	LTV	184.8	45.4	437	272
321	335	Northern Trust	220.0	20.7	298	364	364	424	Service Corp Intl	183.6	40.1	282	381
322	■	Alco Standard	218.7	159.6	334	340	365	340	Southwest Airlines	182.6	1.8	357	324
323	■	Bay Networks	218.3	114.9	282	380	366	300	Pioneer Hi-Bred Intl	182.4	–12.4	257	398
324	375	Mercantile Bancorp	216.8	34.7	252	405	367	328	Western Resources	181.7	–3.1	365	317
325	353	FMC	215.6	24.3	465	261	368	■	Cabot	181.3	87.6	276	388
326	104	Bankers Trust NY	215.0	–65.0	349	330	369	387	Circuit City Stores	181.0	19.1	259	397
327	359	SunAmerica	213.9	25.2	214	442	370	294	WellPoint Health	180.0	–15.6	202	460
328	392	Old Republic Intl	212.7	40.8	213	443	371	363	Crestar Financial	179.8	6.3	238	418
329	284	Tandy	212.0	–5.5	304	363	372	■	Bethlehem Steel	179.6	123.1	464	262
330	117	Cigna	211.0	–61.9	211	449	373	360	Public Service Colo	178.9	5.0	324	345
331	410	First USA	210.5	51.7	306	361	374	477	Southern National	178.1	–24.8	228	427
332	325	Clorox	210.2	10.4	318	352	375	369	Nipsco Industries	175.5	7.0	377	306
333	■	Tyson Foods	210.2	500.0+	424	280	376	434	AmSouth Bancorp	175.0	37.4	224	435
334	272	USF&G	209.4	–9.8	234	421	377	■	Gateway 2000	173.0	80.2	211	447
335	378	Whirlpool	209.0	32.3	491	247	378	398	Regions Financial	172.8	18.5	193	470
336	377	MGIC Investment	207.6	30.1	216	438	379	447	Hilton Hotels	172.8	42.0	315	354
337	■	Union Bank	207.3	227.8	256	401	380	418	Charles Schwab	172.6	27.5	241	413
338	292	American Natl Ins	206.4	–4.1	224	433	381	386	Food Lion	172.4	12.7	319	350
339	316	New England Electric	204.8	2.7	475	254	382	114	Colgate-Palmolive	172.0	–70.4	472	257
340	342	CMS Energy	204.0	14.0	681	185	383	465	Avnet	171.5	50.0	212	444
341	491	Mallinckrodt Group	203.1	89.8	339	338	384	362	Harcourt General	170.7	0.8	343	334
342	471	Arrow Electronics	202.5	81.0	238	417	385	379	DQE	170.6	8.8	402	290
343	366	Johnson Controls	201.6	19.8	495	244	386	440	Mirage	169.9	36.2	277	386
344	329	Sherwin-Williams	200.7	7.5	279	385	387	372	Meridian Bancorp	169.8	4.8	225	432
345	314	Pinnacle West	199.6	–0.5	476	253	388	■	Asarco	169.1	164.1	288	371
346	354	SouthTrust	199.0	15.0	246	408	389	■	Owens-Illinois	169.1	116.0	407	286
347	326	New York State E&G	196.7	4.8	381	300	390	346	So New Eng Telecom	168.8	–5.0	515	238
348	278	AMR	196.0	–14.0	1,455	81	391	390	Scana	168.3	45.8	386	299
349	■	Countrywide Credit	195.7	121.4	196	469	392	406	Ambac	167.6	18.8	172	481
350	■	Marshall & Ilsley	193.3	104.8	240	414	393	■	Southland	167.6	82.2	334	339
351	405	Sonat	192.9	36.4	492	246	394	358	Knight-Ridder	167.4	–2.1	319	349
352	371	DSC Communications	192.7	18.5	295	366	395	247	Dillard Dept Stores	167.2	–33.6	359	321
353	156	Burlington Santa Fe	192.0	–54.9	712	175	396	■	3Com	167.1	D-P	230	424
354	355	Washington Mutual	190.6	10.6	215	439	397	140	Apple Computer	167.0	–63.5	298	365
355	■	American Finl Group	190.4	500.0+	238	416	398	■	Vulcan Materials	166.2	69.7	277	387
356	361	Washington Post	190.1	12.0	287	372	399	310	Nordstrom	165.1	–18.6	293	367
357	348	Humana	190.0	8.0	260	395	400	397	First Tennessee Natl	164.9	12.7	200	461
358	337	Dow Jones	189.6	4.6	396	294	401	427	Harris	164.8	25.9	339	337
359	432	WW Grainger	186.7	46.0	255	402	402	245	Reebok International	164.8	–35.2	203	455
360	446	Georgia Gulf	186.5	52.7	219	437	403	380	DPL	164.7	6.3	284	377
361	385	TECO Energy	186.1	21.5	361	320	404	429	Sonoco Products	164.5	26.7	290	368

■ Not on 500 list in 1994. D-P: Deficit to profit.   *(Continued)*

The Forbes Profits 500 (Cont.)

Rank '95	'94	Company	Net profits ($mil)	% change	Cash flow ($mil)	Cash flow rank '95	Rank '95	'94	Company	Net profits ($mil)	% change	Cash flow ($mil)	Cash flow rank '95
405	373	Cabletron Systems	164.4	1.5	190	472	448	■	American Standard	141.8	D-P	285	376
406	■	Terra Industries	163.9	191.4	230	426	449	■	Gaylord Container	141.5	D-P	208	450
407	500	ReliaStar Financial	163.7	55.8	174	479	450	■	Estee Lauder Cos	141.2	16.8	185	476
408	■	IMC Global	163.6	126.6	313	357	451	■	Thermo Electron	140.1	35.5	225	431
409	456	CUC International	163.4	38.9	200	462	452	486	Omnicom Group	140.0	29.4	214	441
410	■	Navistar Intl	162.9	83.4	247	407	453	■	Olin	139.9	54.1	282	379
411	■	Teledyne	162.0	D-P	232	423	454	6	AT&T	139.0	–97.0	4,984	11
412	■	Supervalu	161.0	206.0	373	309	455	488	Molex	139.0	29.5	253	403
413	402	Citizens Utilities	159.5	10.8	318	351	456	454	Engelhard	137.5	16.6	203	456
414	■	Teradyne	159.3	124.5	202	457	457	482	BayBanks	137.4	26.8	165	488
415	■	Oryx Energy	158.0	D-P	456	268	458	161	McKesson	137.0	–66.2	206	452
416	223	VF	157.3	–42.7	325	344	459	496	Advanta	136.7	28.9	147	496
417	399	Brown-Forman	157.2	8.3	200	463	460	461	Star Banc	136.6	17.2	170	482
418	■	Foundation Health	156.1	500.0+	212	445	461	293	New York Times	135.9	–36.3	275	389
419	341	Hasbro	155.6	–13.2	285	375	462	452	Puget Sound P&L	135.7	13.0	243	409
420	384	Ryder System	155.4	1.2	819	151	463	■	Analog Devices	135.7	63.7	202	458
421	■	Rite Aid	155.2	500.0+	270	392	464	■	Union Planters	135.4	131.0	170	484
422	422	AG Edwards	153.8	16.4	184	477	465	463	Leggett & Platt	134.9	16.9	202	459
423	■	Nalco Chemical	153.7	58.3	243	410	466	393	Signet Banking	133.8	–10.7	164	489
424	349	Lubrizol	151.6	–13.6	226	429	467	■	Whitman	133.5	29.4	242	411
425	388	Illinova	151.6	–0.1	342	335	468	444	EW Scripps	133.4	8.7	200	464
426	492	First Colony	151.4	41.7	197	467	469	■	Computer Sciences	133.3	27.8	363	318
427	395	Unitrin	150.6	1.5	151	495	470	■	King World Prods	133.1	71.9	134	499
428	344	Beneficial	150.5	–15.3	199	466	471	■	Office Depot	132.4	26.1	197	468
429	416	Echlin	150.3	10.5	230	425	472	■	AirTouch Commun	131.9	34.5	348	331
430	438	AutoZone	149.4	19.6	206	454	473	■	Transatlantic Holding	131.9	29.7	132	500
431	123	Toys 'R' Us	148.1	–72.2	333	342	474	473	Sigma-Aldrich	131.7	19.3	173	480
432	450	Equifax	147.7	22.7	224	434	475	457	First Empire State	131.0	11.7	157	492
433	■	ITT	147.0	98.6	400	291	476	■	MidAmerican Energy	130.8	0.1	333	341
434	487	Inland Steel Inds	146.8	36.7	290	369	477	464	Interpublic Group	129.8	12.6	207	451
435	■	Read-Rite	146.6	252.6	226	428	478	466	Illinois Central	129.8	14.0	164	490
436	441	Genentech	146.4	17.7	206	453	479	■	Lafarge	129.6	60.7	224	436
437	439	BanPonce	146.4	17.3	211	448	480	■	St Jude Medical	129.4	63.3	170	485
438	■	Allmerica Financial	146.0	197.3	146	497	481	498	Pall	129.3	22.4	177	478
439	■	U S West Media	145.0	–47.5	394	296	482	462	AGCO	129.1	11.8	157	491
440	475	Frontier	144.8	31.7	314	355	483	414	Circus Circus	128.9	–5.4	225	430
441	■	Varian Associates	144.1	63.0	200	465	484	364	Integra Financial	128.4	–24.0	170	483
442	275	Litton Industries	143.7	–37.0	242	412	485	411	Baker Hughes	128.2	–7.5	283	378
443	479	Avery Dennison	143.7	31.4	252	404	486	■	Manpower	128.0	52.6	156	493
444	■	Sterling Chemicals	143.7	220.1	187	473	487	430	Brunswick	127.2	–1.4	248	406
445	231	Torchmark	143.2	–46.7	153	494	488	■	Liz Claiborne	126.9	53.2	166	487
446	■	Rayonier	142.3	103.3	238	415	489	■	James River Corp Va	126.4	D-P	612	202
447	415	Old Kent Financial	141.8	4.2	191	471	490	■	OfficeMax	125.8	314.2	167	486

■ Not on 500 list in 1994. D-P: Deficit to profit.

(Continued)

The Forbes Profits 500

RANK '95	'94	Company	Net profits ($mil)	% change	Cash flow ($mil)	Cash flow rank '95	RANK '95	'94	Company	Net profits ($mil)	% change	Cash flow ($mil)	Cash flow rank '95
491	401	Varity	125.5	-13.3	214	440	496	297	Armstrong World Ind	123.3	-41.4	259	396
492	443	Oklahoma G&E	125.3	1.2	257	399	497	■	Mercantile Stores	123.2	17.9	212	446
493	350	Cyprus Amax Mineral	124.0	-29.1	420	281	498	■	Southwestern PS	122.7	25.7	185	475
494	■	Hibernia	123.9	46.3	146	498	499	■	Kansas City P&L	122.6	17.0	234	420
495	252	General Instrument	123.8	-50.2	234	422	500	■	Manville	122.0	86.5	186	474

■ Not on 500 list in 1994. D-P: Deficit to profit.

THE ASSETS 500

*The Forbes Assets 500 controlled $10.6 trillion,
a gain of 9.7% over the prior year.*

CECILY J. FLUKE

When steel and railroads defined big business, assets were a good measure of corporate power. Nowadays the picture is a little more complicated. Financial assets account for most of the top positions in this ranking.

For the second year the leader of the pack is Federal National Mortgage, with $317 billion, in mostly financial assets. The largest industrial company on this year's list is Ford Motor—but only 16% of its assets are plant, equipment and inventory. Ford also does vehicle financing and equipment leasing.

Winners

RANK '95	'94	Company	Assets ($mil)	% change
343	■	Cox Communications	5,555	196.3
138	299	Jefferson-Pilot	16,478	168.4
263	481	Tenet Healthcare	8,141	146.4
123	253	Burlington Northern Santa Fe	18,269	140.6
306	471	WorldCom	6,552	135.5

■ Not on 500 list in 1994.

Jefferson-Pilot's assets rose 168%, largely by dint of two life insurers it acquired.

Losers

RANK '95	'94	Company	Assets ($mil)	% change
80	57	Xerox	25,969	−32.7
143	104	Pacific Telesis	15,841	−21.3
367	287	Sun Co	5,184	−19.8
265	211	American Brands	8,021	−18.1
342	276	OnBancorp	5,567	−17.2

Shareholders of four of these five companies hope smaller, restructured companies will be more prosperous.

Banks, already the dominant sector on the Assets 500, are becoming more dominant as they consolidate. That's how they downsize: Two big banks merge, then fire a few thousand workers. The same pressure to streamline often has the opposite effect on piles of industrial assets. AT&T and ITT aim to become more efficient by dividing into smaller pieces or shedding assets. Xerox posted the biggest asset loss, a drop of 33% to $26 billion, as it continued its exodus from financial services.

The Forbes Assets 500

Rank '95	Rank '94	Company	Sales ($ mil)	% change	Rank '95	Rank '94	Company	Sales ($ mil)	% change
1	1	Federal Natl Mort	316,550	16.2	36	42	Lincoln National	63,258	28.2
2	■	Chase Manhattan	303,989	6.5	37	46	American General	61,153	32.1
3	2	Citicorp	256,853	2.5	38	35	First Interstate Bncp	58,071	4.0
4	3	Ford Motor	243,283	10.9	39	39	Philip Morris Cos	53,811	2.2
5	4	BankAmerica	232,446	7.9	40	41	Chrysler	53,756	8.5
6	6	General Electric	228,035	17.3	41	43	Bank of New York	53,720	9.9
7	5	General Motors	217,079	9.3	42	36	HF Ahmanson	50,530	−5.9
8	7	Salomon	188,428	9.1	43	37	Wells Fargo	50,316	−5.7
9	9	NationsBank	187,298	10.4	44	38	Sallie Mae	50,002	−5.6
10	11	JP Morgan & Co	184,879	19.3	45	54	Transamerica	47,945	18.7
11	10	Merrill Lynch	176,857	8.0	46	47	Bank of Boston	47,397	6.2
12	13	Morgan Stanley	143,753	23.2	47	48	SunTrust Banks	46,471	8.8
13	17	Federal Home Loan	137,181	29.2	48	60	PaineWebber Group	45,671	27.4
14	15	American Intl Group	134,136	17.3	49	55	Wachovia	44,981	14.8
15	■	First Union	131,880	16.2	50	50	Great Western Finl	44,587	5.6
16	12	Lehman Bros Holding	129,000	1.6	51	53	Republic New York	43,882	6.9
17	■	First Chicago NBD	122,002	8.2	52	51	Mobil	42,138	1.4
18	14	Travelers Group	114,475	−0.7	53	52	Barnett Banks	41,554	0.7
19	21	Equitable Cos	113,749	20.2	54	56	Mellon Bank	40,646	5.2
20	20	American Express	107,405	10.7	55	75	Dean Witter Discover	38,208	19.9
21	19	Bankers Trust NY	104,002	7.2	56	65	Wal-Mart Stores	37,900	15.5
22	26	Cigna	95,903	11.4	57	58	du Pont de Nemours	37,312	1.1
23	■	ITT Hartford Group	93,855	22.3	58	49	GTE	37,019	−12.9
24	25	Exxon	91,296	3.9	59	67	National City	36,199	12.7
25	24	Banc One	90,454	1.7	60	71	General Re	35,946	21.5
26	28	AT&T	88,884	12.1	61	64	Comerica	35,470	6.1
27	30	Bear Stearns Cos	86,019	28.7	62	68	Golden West Finl	35,118	10.8
28	■	Fleet Finl Group	84,432	4.2	63	61	Chevron	34,330	−0.2
29	22	Aetna Life & Cas	84,324	−10.5	64	82	First Bank System	33,874	29.2
30	27	IBM	80,292	−1.0	65	74	Boatmen's Bancshs	33,704	16.5
31	33	PNC Bank	73,404	−5.2	66	23	Sears, Roebuck	33,130	−11.2
32	34	Norwest	72,134	21.6	67	62	BellSouth	31,880	−7.3
33	■	Allstate	70,029	14.1	68	■	US Bancorp	31,794	3.9
34	40	Loews	68,891	34.4	69	69	RJR Nabisco	31,518	0.4
35	31	KeyCorp	66,339	−0.7	70	79	Southern Co	30,554	13.0

■ Not on 500 list in 1994. NA: Not available.   (*Continued*)

The Forbes Assets 500 *(Cont.)*

RANK '95	'94	Company	Sales ($ mil)	% change	RANK '95	'94	Company	Sales ($ mil)	% change
71	98	Berkshire Hathaway	29,929	40.3	116	124	Union Bank	19,518	16.4
72	73	Amoco	29,845	1.8	117	131	Union Pacific	19,446	22.0
73	72	CoreStates Financial	29,621	1.0	118	127	MCI Communication	19,301	17.9
74	63	Household Intl	29,219	−14.9	119	137	Firstar	19,168	26.9
75	76	Viacom	29,026	2.7	120	132	Safeco	18,768	18.0
76	78	Procter & Gamble	28,215	3.2	121	117	WMX Technologies	18,695	6.6
77	77	Pacific G&E	26,850	−3.4	122	147	Crestar Financial	18,303	30.6
78	88	Providian	26,839	13.7	123	253	Burlington Santa Fe	18,269	140.6
79	70	Nynex	26,220	−12.8	124	134	Johnson & Johnson	17,873	14.1
80	57	Xerox	25,969	−32.7	125	143	SunAmerica	17,844	20.7
81	95	State Street Boston	25,785	18.7	126	111	Occidental Petroleum	17,815	−1.0
82	103	Hewlett-Packard	25,753	27.6	127	■	Allmerica Financial	17,758	11.5
83	84	PepsiCo	25,452	2.7	128	122	AmSouth Bancorp	17,739	5.7
84	102	Aflac	25,338	24.9	129	114	Lockheed Martin	17,648	−2.2
85	83	Texaco	24,937	−2.2	130	149	Intel	17,504	26.7
86	87	Bell Atlantic	24,157	−0.5	131	197	Conseco	17,298	60.0
87	86	Atlantic Richfield	23,999	−2.3	132	126	Pub Svc Enterprise	17,171	2.7
88	113	International Paper	23,977	34.4	133	129	JC Penney	17,102	5.6
89	92	Edison International	23,946	6.9	134	141	Fifth Third Bancorp	17,053	14.0
90	93	Merck	23,832	9.0	135	128	Caterpillar	16,830	3.6
91	85	First of America Bk	23,600	−3.9	136	201	Westinghouse	16,752	57.7
92	80	Dow Chemical	23,582	−11.2	137	■	U S West Commun	16,585	4.0
93	90	Unicom	23,247	0.5	138	299	Jefferson-Pilot	16,478	168.4
94	99	Textron	23,172	10.7	139	120	Provident Cos	16,301	−4.9
95	101	Chubb	22,997	11.0	140	135	United Technologies	15,958	2.1
96	118	Motorola	22,801	30.0	141	178	Mercantile Bancorp	15,934	30.2
97	91	Entergy	22,266	−1.5	142	133	American Electric	15,902	1.2
98	123	Time Warner	22,132	32.4	143	104	Pacific Telesis	15,841	−21.3
99	97	Boeing	22,098	3.0	144	145	Beneficial	15,693	9.4
100	81	SBC Communications	22,003	−15.4	145	168	BanPonce	15,675	22.7
101	105	Ameritech	21,943	10.0	146	207	ReliaStar Financial	15,519	49.7
102	■	Tele-Com-TCI	21,900	NA	147	155	McDonald's	15,400	13.3
103	110	Washington Mutual	21,633	17.2	148	121	Kmart	15,397	−9.6
104	■	Summit Bancorp	21,537	0.3	149	150	Walt Disney	15,276	10.7
105	100	Texas Utilities	21,536	3.1	150	142	Sprint	15,089	14.2
106	96	American Home Prod	21,363	−1.4	151	148	Coca-Cola	15,041	8.4
107	116	SouthTrust	20,787	17.9	152	138	PECO Energy	14,961	−0.9
108	231	Southern National	20,493	3.2	153	416	American Finl Group	14,954	41.7
109	106	Dime Bancorp	20,327	3.5	154	162	UNUM	14,788	12.7
110	115	Huntington Bancshs	20,255	14.0	155	139	Meridian Bancorp	14,758	−2.0
111	109	Northern Trust	19,934	7.4	156	269	GreenPoint Financial	14,670	110.9
112	175	Columbia/HCA	19,892	22.2	157	151	USF&G	14,651	6.4
113	112	Aon	19,736	10.1	158	125	Glendale Federal Bk	14,640	−12.6
114	119	St Paul Cos	19,657	12.3	159	140	Eastman Kodak	14,477	−3.3
115	107	AMR	19,600	0.6	160	158	Deere & Co	14,447	7.2

■ Not on 500 list in 1994. NA: Not available.   *(Continued)*

The Forbes Assets 500 *(Cont.)*

RANK '95	'94	Company	Sales ($ mil)	% change	RANK '95	'94	Company	Sales ($ mil)	% change
161	144	Eli Lilly	14,413	−0.7	206	209	Union Planters	11,277	12.6
162	152	Integra Financial	14,346	4.3	207	193	DTE Energy	11,131	1.3
163	146	Cal Fed Bancorp	14,321	1.0	208	164	Signet Banking	11,013	−14.8
164	242	Federated Dept Strs	14,295	15.5	209	202	Norfolk Southern	10,905	3.0
165	154	CSX	14,282	4.1	210	208	Central Fidelity Bks	10,811	7.5
166	157	Minn Mining & Mfg	14,183	5.1	211	224	First Colony	10,721	17.9
167	185	PacifiCorp	14,015	18.3	212	204	Coastal	10,659	1.2
168	153	Consolidated Edison	13,950	1.6	213	200	Centerior Energy	10,643	−0.5
169	165	Bristol-Myers Squibb	13,929	7.9	214	214	Archer Daniels	10,640	10.5
170	156	Dominion Resources	13,903	2.5	215	227	Monsanto	10,611	19.3
171	196	Central & So West	13,869	27.1	216	249	Charles Schwab	10,552	33.3
172	167	Regions Financial	13,709	6.8	217	203	Northeast Utilities	10,545	−0.4
173	169	Alcoa	13,643	10.4	218	342	Williams Cos	10,495	100.8
174	■	Charter One Finl	13,579	−6.5	219	179	McDonnell Douglas	10,466	−14.3
175	173	Tenneco	13,451	7.2	220	223	Compass Bancshares	10,262	12.5
176	166	Duke Power	13,358	3.9	221	216	May Dept Stores	10,122	6.9
177	171	Marshall & Ilsley	13,343	5.8	222	194	USX-Marathon	10,109	−7.7
178	182	Standard Federal	13,276	9.9	223	215	Digital Equipment	10,015	4.1
179	163	Weyerhaeuser	13,253	1.9	224	219	Reliance Group	9,988	6.6
180	183	Enron	13,239	10.6	225	220	Unocal	9,891	5.9
181	212	MBNA	13,229	36.8	226	221	General Public Utils	9,870	7.2
182	172	Bancorp Hawaii	13,207	4.9	227	192	Anheuser-Busch Cos	9,837	3.0
183	174	ConAgra	13,176	5.3	228	222	Goodyear	9,790	7.3
184	181	First Security	13,035	7.3	229	247	Equitable of Iowa	9,780	22.8
185	177	Temple-Inland	12,764	4.2	230	258	Raytheon	9,740	31.7
186	■	Liberty Financial Cos	12,749	16.2	231	230	Emerson Electric	9,733	11.5
187	191	Pfizer	12,729	14.7	232	251	First American	9,682	24.8
188	187	Dayton Hudson	12,570	7.5	233	275	Comcast	9,580	41.7
189	160	Long Island Lighting	12,484	−5.5	234	246	Commerce Bancshs	9,574	19.1
190	190	AlliedSignal	12,465	10.1	235	217	Star Banc	9,573	1.9
191	170	FPL Group	12,459	−1.3	236	226	Champion Intl	9,543	6.5
192	184	Sara Lee	12,389	3.5	237	218	PP&L Resources	9,492	1.3
193	199	Georgia-Pacific	12,335	15.0	238	213	Niagara Mohawk Pwr	9,478	−1.8
194	■	First Data	12,218	44.9	239	210	Baxter International	9,437	−5.6
195	206	First Tennessee Natl	12,077	14.8	240	233	Abbott Laboratories	9,413	10.4
196	198	BayBanks	12,064	12.0	241	235	Torchmark	9,346	11.2
197	180	Rockwell Intl	12,027	−1.3	242	239	Western National	9,314	11.9
198	195	Old Kent Financial	12,003	9.7	243	266	Texas Instruments	9,215	31.9
199	189	Delta Air Lines	11,998	5.4	244	307	Microsoft	9,106	52.8
200	188	Phillips Petroleum	11,978	4.7	245	229	Coca-Cola Enterprise	9,064	3.7
201	205	First Empire State	11,956	13.6	246	234	Roosevelt Finl Group	9,013	6.9
202	176	Houston Industries	11,820	−3.9	247	408	Rhone-Poulenc Rorer	8,987	106.0
203	186	UAL	11,728	−0.3	248	225	Ohio Edison	8,824	−1.9
204	■	Pharmacia & Upjohn	11,461	4.7	249	292	Countrywide Credit	8,658	55.2
205	■	Kimberly-Clark	11,439	−8.9	250	■	ITT	8,630	72.2

■ Not on 500 list in 1994. NA: Not available.

(Continued)

The Forbes Assets 500 *(Cont.)*

RANK '95	'94	Company	Sales ($ mil)	% change	RANK '95	'94	Company	Sales ($ mil)	% change
251	260	HJ Heinz	8,618	17.6	296	273	USAir Group	6,955	2.2
252	■	U S West Media	8,615	16.5	297	285	People's Bank	6,862	5.8
253	284	First Commerce	8,531	30.1	298	280	Union Electric	6,754	2.0
254	282	Toys 'R' Us	8,437	12.4	299	303	Federal Express	6,693	9.1
255	238	Conrail	8,424	1.2	300	296	TIG Holdings	6,683	9.3
256	245	Northwest Airlines	8,412	4.2	301	■	Astoria Financial	6,620	42.6
257	244	Baltimore G&E	8,317	2.1	302	313	Commercial Federal	6,594	13.7
258	241	Coast Savings Finl	8,252	0.7	303	293	Old Republic Intl	6,594	5.3
259	240	Carolina Power & Lt	8,227	0.2	304	336	Campbell Soup	6,576	21.6
260	250	First Virginia Banks	8,222	4.5	305	324	Apple Computer	6,553	18.4
261	243	Cinergy	8,220	0.9	306	471	WorldCom	6,552	135.5
262	259	CMS Energy	8,143	10.3	307	286	USX-US Steel	6,521	0.6
263	481	Tenet Healthcare	8,141	146.4	308	446	Gannett	6,504	75.4
264	283	Sovereign Bancorp	8,078	23.1	309	289	Allegheny Power	6,447	1.3
265	211	American Brands	8,021	–18.1	310	264	Stone Container	6,399	–8.7
266	265	USLife	7,931	13.2	311	310	Mercantile Bkshs	6,349	6.9
267	302	Synovus Finl	7,928	29.6	312	327	Gillette	6,340	15.4
268	257	Pitney Bowes	7,845	6.0	313	294	WR Grace	6,298	1.1
269	297	Compaq Computer	7,818	26.8	314	281	UMB Financial	6,281	–4.8
270	278	American Re	7,814	17.0	315	358	Union Carbide	6,256	24.4
271	279	Whirlpool	7,800	17.2	316	308	No States Power	6,229	4.6
272	237	Amerada Hess	7,756	–7.0	317	468	United HealthCare	6,216	78.1
273	256	Reynolds Metals	7,740	3.7	318	335	Provident Bncp	6,205	14.7
274	268	John Alden Financial	7,696	10.5	319	338	Cyprus Amax Mineral	6,196	14.6
275	348	Service Corp Intl	7,664	48.5	320	311	PPG Industries	6,194	5.1
276	298	Colgate-Palmolive	7,642	24.4	321	341	First Natl Nebraska	6,111	16.1
277	272	Browning-Ferris Inds	7,634	11.0	322	380	Cincinnati Financial	6,109	29.0
278	255	Panhandle Eastern	7,627	1.6	323	325	Warner-Lambert	6,101	10.3
279	254	First Hawaiian	7,565	0.4	324	288	Cooper Industries	6,064	5.3
280	317	CPC International	7,502	32.3	325	262	Columbia Gas System	6,057	–15.5
281	291	First Citizens Bcshs	7,384	16.6	326	345	Air Prods & Chems	6,034	16.4
282	263	American Stores	7,363	4.7	327	349	Deposit Guaranty	6,026	17.4
283	315	Home Depot	7,354	27.3	328	305	Corning	5,987	–0.6
284	295	First USA	7,324	18.2	329	360	Ryder System	5,894	17.5
285	330	MBIA	7,267	33.2	330	318	TRW	5,890	4.5
286	248	James River Corp Va	7,259	–8.4	331	■	ITT Industries	5,864	5.1
287	355	TCF Financial	7,240	–7.7	332	367	Loral	5,830	18.5
288	300	Protective Life	7,231	18.0	333	316	Florida Progress	5,791	1.3
289	290	Hibernia	7,196	13.6	334	368	PHH	5,742	17.4
290	306	American Natl Ins	7,140	19.8	335	314	Bethlehem Steel	5,700	–1.4
291	267	Potomac Electric	7,118	2.2	336	350	Dana	5,694	11.4
292	261	Unisys	7,113	–2.9	337	397	AirTouch Commun	5,648	25.8
293	312	Finova Group	7,037	20.6	338	365	Zions Bancorp	5,621	13.9
294	309	Ashland	7,035	18.2	339	322	Illinova	5,610	0.6
295	271	Pinnacle West	6,997	1.3	340	346	Hawaiian Electric	5,604	8.3

■ Not on 500 list in 1994. NA: Not available.   *(Continued)*

The Forbes Assets 500 *(Cont.)*

RANK '95	'94	Company	Sales ($ mil)	% change	RANK '95	'94	Company	Sales ($ mil)	% change
341	366	FirstMerit	5,597	13.7	386	■	Computer Associates	4,882	62.5
342	276	OnBancorp	5,567	−17.2	387	353	Sumitomo Bank Calif	4,856	−4.3
343	■	Cox Communications	5,555	196.3	388	405	Eastman Chemical	4,854	10.9
344	332	Black & Decker	5,545	2.1	389	425	Washington Federal	4,843	19.5
345	329	Dun & Bradstreet	5,516	0.9	390	376	Union Camp	4,838	1.3
346	344	Western Resources	5,491	5.8	391	356	Quaker Oats	4,824	54.0
347	351	First Financial	5,471	7.2	392	419	Old National Bncp	4,823	16.1
348	357	Case	5,469	8.3	393	363	Continental Airlines	4,821	4.8
349	■	Nextel Commun	5,467	94.6	394	395	Unitrin	4,819	5.4
350	304	Northrop Grumman	5,455	−9.8	395	430	Ralston Purina	4,806	23.1
351	456	Ingersoll-Rand	5,454	51.6	396	392	Dillard Dept Stores	4,779	4.4
352	339	Owens-Illinois	5,439	2.3	397	420	Southern Pacific Rail	4,749	14.4
353	326	Consol Natural Gas	5,418	−1.8	398	401	Riggs National	4,733	6.9
354	399	RR Donnelley & Sons	5,385	20.9	399	■	Prudential Reinsur	4,678	15.2
355	321	LTV	5,380	−3.7	400	389	Enova	4,670	0.6
356	378	Wilmington Trust	5,372	13.3	401	409	Schering-Plough	4,665	7.8
357	406	First Commercial	5,361	22.6	402	388	Downey Financial	4,656	0.1
358	386	Progressive	5,353	14.5	403	410	Boise Cascade	4,656	8.4
359	413	Centura Banks	5,326	25.6	404	421	Phelps Dodge	4,646	12.4
360	411	Ambac	5,309	23.7	405	414	Dresser Industries	4,623	9.1
361	354	Dauphin Deposit	5,297	4.5	406	■	Valley Natl Bancorp	4,586	22.5
362	394	Limited	5,267	15.2	407	402	Wisconsin Energy	4,561	3.5
363	331	Pacific Enterprises	5,259	−3.4	408	403	Scana	4,534	3.2
364	375	Crown Cork & Seal	5,235	9.5	409	497	Advanta	4,524	45.3
365	359	Safeway	5,194	3.4	410	■	MidAmerican Energy	4,524	2.4
366	352	New England Electric	5,191	2.1	411	443	AMP	4,505	19.5
367	287	Sun Co	5,184	−19.8	412	448	Tyson Foods	4,498	21.7
368	441	Alco Standard	5,142	36.1	413	■	Fremont General	4,477	46.0
369	387	Leucadia National	5,136	9.8	414	400	DQE	4,459	0.7
370	343	New York State E&G	5,114	−2.1	415	398	Kellogg	4,415	−1.2
371	■	Life Partners Group	5,092	41.9	416	424	Turner Broadcasting	4,395	7.9
372	■	CCB Financial	5,090	7.8	417	429	Paccar	4,391	11.8
373	384	Keystone Finl	5,075	7.8	418	371	Mead	4,373	−10.1
374	382	Alltel	5,073	7.6	419	415	Public Service Colo	4,354	3.5
375	374	Navistar Intl	5,067	5.7	420	396	Supervalu	4,339	−3.6
376	369	Honeywell	5,060	3.6	421	435	Marsh & McLennan	4,330	13.0
377	362	Comdisco	5,058	1.3	422	482	Asarco	4,327	31.5
378	385	Eaton	5,053	7.9	423	381	Pennzoil	4,308	−8.7
379	383	Kroger	5,045	7.2	424	426	Westvaco	4,305	7.1
380	370	Collective Bncp	5,029	3.3	425	476	FMC	4,301	28.3
381	377	Trustmark	4,993	4.8	426	391	Fleming Cos	4,297	−6.8
382	390	Magna Group	4,947	6.7	427	439	Interpublic Group	4,260	12.3
383	■	Long Island Bancorp	4,935	6.9	428	440	Dial	4,225	11.8
384	372	Price/Costco	4,925	11.0	429	431	BOK Financial	4,222	8.3
385	432	Johnson Controls	4,885	25.4	430	438	Cullen/Frost Bankers	4,200	10.7

■ Not on 500 list in 1994. NA: Not available.

(Continued)

The Forbes Assets 500 *(Cont.)*

RANK '95	RANK '94	Company	Sales ($ mil)	% change	RANK '95	RANK '94	Company	Sales ($ mil)	% change
431	373	Burlington Resources	4,165	−13.4	466	455	Boston Edison	3,644	0.8
432	■	City National	4,158	38.0	467	■	NIKE	3,643	22.9
433	418	FirstFed Financial	4,140	−0.4	468	■	Micron Technology	3,642	86.1
434	454	Albertson's	4,136	14.2	469	■	CNB Bancshares	3,629	37.0
435	465	Praxair	4,134	17.4	470	458	WR Berkley	3,619	1.0
436	457	Alleghany	4,123	14.9	471	■	Illinois Tool Works	3,613	40.0
437	422	St Paul Bancorp	4,117	−0.4	472	■	Freeport Copper	3,582	17.8
438	452	GATX	4,043	10.7	473	■	Center Financial	3,580	16.9
439	450	Citizens Bncp	4,040	9.5	474	492	Tyco International	3,559	11.7
440	490	Marriott Intl	4,018	25.3	475	474	Inland Steel Inds	3,558	6.1
441	428	Nipsco Industries	4,000	1.4	476	436	Host Marriott	3,557	5.7
442	444	Ohio Casualty	3,980	6.5	477	499	Lowe's Cos	3,556	14.5
443	379	Melville	3,962	−16.3	478	■	Omnicom Group	3,528	23.7
444	459	Citizens Utilities	3,918	9.6	479	■	IMC Global	3,522	31.6
445	433	Rohm & Haas	3,916	1.4	480	■	American Standard	3,520	11.5
446	470	Transatlantic Holding	3,899	12.8	481	319	General Mills	3,516	NA
447	498	UtiliCorp United	3,886	24.9	482	500	Walgreen	3,512	13.2
448	472	RCSB Financial	3,871	13.0	483	464	Sonat	3,511	−0.5
449	■	Life USA Holding	3,868	26.2	484	417	Woolworth	3,506	−16.0
450	451	One Valley Bncp WV	3,858	5.0	485	480	TECO Energy	3,473	4.9
451	449	Maxxam	3,832	3.8	486	■	Tele & Data Systems	3,469	24.3
452	■	Seagate Technology	3,830	25.8	487	■	Citizens Banking	3,464	28.1
453	412	Times Mirror	3,817	−10.5	488	462	Portland General	3,448	−3.1
454	479	United Carolina Bcsh	3,786	13.6	489	478	VF	3,447	3.3
455	404	Masco	3,779	−13.9	490	■	Willamette Inds	3,414	12.5
456	■	Thermo Electron	3,745	24.0	491	491	American Water Work	3,403	6.1
457	■	Automatic Data	3,728	29.1	492	■	Fluor	3,398	22.1
458	■	Colonial BancGroup	3,725	34.6	493	495	New York Times	3,377	7.6
459	484	Associated Banc-Cp	3,698	12.6	494	■	Fulton Financial	3,335	8.2
460	■	Natl Commerce Bncp	3,695	22.9	495	487	DPL	3,323	2.8
461	466	McKesson	3,674	4.8	496	■	Sysco	3,311	9.9
462	460	NorAm Energy	3,666	2.9	497	■	Quick & Reilly Group	3,311	16.0
463	483	Horace Mann	3,662	11.5	498	■	North Fork Bancorp	3,303	21.5
464	453	Ogden	3,653	0.2	499	■	BancorpSouth	3,302	31.1
465	340	Halliburton	3,647	−1.9	500	■	Fidelity Federal Bank	3,299	−11.1

■ Not on 500 list in 1994. NA: Not available.

THE MARKET VALUE 500

America's 500 most valuable companies are worth $5 trillion, roughly $1.2 trillion higher than the previous year.

JOHN H. CHRISTY

You could own all these companies for $5 trillion. What would that $5 trillion buy you? Combined earnings of $266 billion. Thus, the big stocks trade at 19 times earnings—not outlandish, but not exactly cheap, either. The market's average ratio of price to earnings over the past 68 years has been 14.

General Electric, with $126 billion in common-stock market value, is the most highly valued company in the world. (Japan's NTT is second, with $113 billion.) Second place in the U.S. goes to Atlanta-based Coca-Cola, which sold $18 billion worth of soft drinks and soft-drink syrup last year as its market value climbed 37% to $101 billion.

The computer industry fared well on Wall Street. With $61 billion in capitalization, Microsoft joins the top 10. Close behind are Hewlett-Packard, now ranked 13th, and Intel, 15th. In 1991 Oracle Corp's capitalization was $1.2 billion; it is now $21 billion, good enough for the 51st position. Since 1994 Digital Equipment has returned to profitability, and its market value has more than doubled, to $9.9 billion. Given the recent slowdown in the computer business, many hardware and software companies will have a tough time maintaining these handsome valuations.

Among the big gainers: Boston Scientific, a maker of medical devices, whose market value climbed 250%, to $8.2 billion. The airline industry was also on the rebound. Northwest Airlines' market value rose 133%, UAL's 123%, Southwest Airlines' 86% and AMR's 48%.

31

Winners

RANK			Market	
'95	'94	Company	value ($mil)	% change
229	■	Ascend Communications	5,573	500.0+
216	■	US Robotics	5,858	337.7
401	■	FORE Systems	3,000	307.7
233	■	HealthSouth	5,484	297.8
261	■	HFS	4,895	284.4

■ Not on 500 list in 1994.

As users rushed to get online, US Robotics, a modem manufacturer, saw its market value quadruple.

Losers

RANK			Market	
'95	'94	Company	value ($mil)	% change
278	136	Novell	4,571	–33.0
498	299	Advanced Micro Devices	2,328	–29.7
380	228	Apple Computer	3,200	–24.6
372	237	General Instrument	3,240	–20.9
420	279	Harrah's Entertainment	2,839	–20.8

Stocks that missed the rally in technology: Advanced Micro Devices, Novell, and Apple Computer.

Only 35 stocks on the list lost market value, and many of these losers are retailers. Wal-Mart fell out of the top ten, and Kmart's capitalization slid 15%. Bausch & Lomb, Cummins Engine, National Semiconductor, Niagara Mohawk Power and Woolworth are among the stocks that fell off this list.

The Forbes Market Value 500

RANK			Market		RANK			Market	
'95	'94	Company	value ($ mil)	% change	'95	'94	Company	value ($ mil)	% change
1	1	General Electric	126,238	36.4	16	26	Walt Disney	47,040	63.5
2	4	Coca-Cola	101,147	36.5	17	13	du Pont de Nemours	45,134	14.7
3	2	AT&T	98,122	18.6	18	14	Mobil	44,191	24.9
4	3	Exxon	98,118	21.1	19	29	Berkshire Hathaway	43,880	67.8
5	7	Philip Morris Cos	79,138	46.5	20	17	American Intl Group	43,687	31.9
6	6	Merck	76,342	39.0	21	18	Bristol-Myers Squibb	42,692	30.0
7	10	General Motors	69,947*	54.3	22	16	GTE	40,475	22.0
8	8	IBM	65,664	35.2	23	27	Pfizer	40,068	48.5
9	12	Johnson & Johnson	60,882	51.5	24	48	Citicorp	37,805	123.8
10	11	Microsoft	60,811	49.6	25	28	Ford Motor	37,668	43.0
11	9	Procter & Gamble	57,058	19.8	26	25	BellSouth	36,033	23.1
12	5	Wal-Mart Stores	54,530	–2.6	27	31	McDonald's	35,862	47.2
13	22	Hewlett-Packard	50,929	66.1	28	21	Chevron	35,807	14.4
14	20	PepsiCo	49,152	55.8	29	23	Amoco	34,872	15.2
15	15	Intel	48,336	44.7	30	36	Federal Natl Mort	34,260	64.0

■ Not on 500 list in 1994. NA: Not available.
* Includes Class E and Class H stock.

(Continued)

The Forbes Market Value 500 (Cont.)

RANK '95	'94	Company	Market value ($ mil)	% change	RANK '95	'94	Company	Market value ($ mil)	% change
31	38	Eli Lilly	33,527	67.0	76	61	AirTouch Commun	15,089	10.5
32	19	Motorola	32,897	1.0	77	72	JP Morgan & Co	15,027	32.6
33	24	Abbott Laboratories	32,229	9.0	78	65	WMX Technologies	14,916	13.6
34	30	SBC Communications	31,142	20.4	79	73	Banc One	14,807	35.0
35	35	American Home Prod	30,939	35.6	80	81	Federal Home Loan	14,571	41.1
36	■	Chase Manhattan	30,668	82.0	81	■	U S West Commun	14,566	NA
37	33	Ameritech	30,115	26.6	82	74	Union Pacific	14,443	31.7
38	47	Boeing	27,858	64.6	83	71	Xerox	14,423	16.5
39	34	Bell Atlantic	26,919	15.9	84	50	Viacom	14,372	−14.3
40	44	BankAmerica	26,868	51.6	85	82	Caterpillar	13,968	35.3
41	92	Cisco Systems	26,861	186.2	86	80	Warner-Lambert	13,951	32.2
42	32	Minn Mining & Mfg	26,588	10.9	87	108	United Technologies	13,502	65.5
43	45	Eastman Kodak	25,293	42.8	88	116	Medtronic	13,287	70.3
44	52	Columbia/HCA	24,018	29.4	89	■	Tele-Com-TCI	12,963	NA
45	37	Home Depot	23,602	13.9	90	88	HJ Heinz	12,635	30.1
46	51	American Express	23,370	45.0	91	99	May Dept Stores	12,551	42.8
47	58	Chrysler	23,314	63.5	92	184	Burlington Santa Fe	12,461	134.7
48	41	Gillette	23,117	26.1	93	97	Raytheon	12,426	39.0
49	39	Dow Chemical	22,272	17.8	94	101	Rockwell Intl	12,410	45.1
50	49	Texaco	21,562	28.0	95	83	Sprint	12,407	22.3
51	57	Oracle	21,275	48.3	96	91	Baxter International	12,371	31.3
52	■	Kimberly-Clark	21,271	47.8	97	118	Norwest	12,258	57.8
53	56	Schering-Plough	21,122	46.7	98	159	First Interstate Bncp	12,168	107.2
54	■	Pharmacia & Upjohn	21,089	137.1	99	■	First Chicago NBD	12,152	22.1
55	46	Nynex	21,080	23.3	100	94	Automatic Data	11,690	28.7
56	60	NationsBank	20,296	47.2	101	89	Colgate-Palmolive	11,566	20.1
57	70	Travelers Group	19,861	59.9	102	79	General Re	11,550	8.9
58	■	Sears, Roebuck	19,573	NA	103	170	NIKE	11,405	106.9
59	59	MCI Communication	19,294	39.7	104	107	Wells Fargo	11,349	38.7
60	■	Allstate	18,513	50.7	105	67	Pacific Telesis	11,289	−11.6
61	43	Atlantic Richfield	18,091	0.8	106	86	JC Penney	11,228	12.9
62	55	Emerson Electric	17,896	23.3	107	112	United HealthCare	11,107	37.7
63	103	Monsanto	17,733	108.2	108	141	Deere & Co	11,029	65.3
64	84	Computer Associates	17,570	73.3	109	98	Norfolk Southern	10,905	22.5
65	53	Anheuser-Busch Cos	17,120	15.4	110	137	Alcoa	10,679	58.8
66	54	Time Warner	17,073	16.6	111	104	Compaq Computer	10,613	25.1
67	66	Kellogg	16,632	26.9	112	124	ConAgra	10,441	39.9
68	100	Amgen	16,507	89.4	113	■	Fleet Finl Group	10,312	38.3
69	■	First Union	16,393	32.1	114	96	International Paper	10,245	13.2
70	64	Sara Lee	15,974	20.7	115	93	Phillips Petroleum	10,223	11.6
71	75	AlliedSignal	15,906	46.4	116	147	McDonnell Douglas	10,162	58.3
72	■	First Data	15,743	47.8	117	95	Dun & Bradstreet	10,121	12.6
73	68	Campbell Soup	15,588	23.9	118	110	CPC International	10,065	24.1
74	63	Southern Co	15,483	15.5	119	77	Pacific G&E	9,988	−6.2
75	78	Lockheed Martin	15,094	41.8	120	160	Bank of New York	9,955	70.4

■ Not on 500 list in 1994. NA: Not available.

(Continued)

The Forbes Market Value 500 (Cont.)

RANK '95	RANK '94	Company	Market value ($ mil)	% change	RANK '95	RANK '94	Company	Market value ($ mil)	% change
121	109	Texas Instruments	9,943	22.6	166	188	Westinghouse	7,524	46.7
122	165	PNC Bank	9,940	74.6	167	130	Toys 'R' Us	7,442	5.8
123	113	Duke Power	9,884	23.3	168	132	Edison International	7,375	6.3
124	205	Digital Equipment	9,859	110.9	169	146	Consolidated Edison	7,313	12.7
125	115	Merrill Lynch	9,769	22.3	170	172	Pitney Bowes	7,310	32.8
126	85	Archer Daniels	9,696	–3.6	171	277	3Com	7,297	101.1
127	■	U S West Media	9,682	NA	172	166	Mellon Bank	7,277	28.4
128	123	Gannett	9,629	28.8	173	144	American General	7,263	10.4
129	102	Tenneco	9,621	12.6	174	131	US Healthcare	7,182	2.9
130	114	Albertson's	9,542	19.3	175	187	Ralston Purina	7,125	38.6
131	106	CSX	9,499	15.5	176	■	ITT	7,111	NA
132	117	AMP	9,349	20.1	177	174	Hercules	7,069	29.3
133	162	Loews	9,279	59.8	178	206	AMR	6,920	48.1
134	125	PPG Industries	9,237	25.3	179	179	Wm Wrigley Jr	6,902	28.8
135	87	General Mills	9,204	NA	180	265	Bay Networks	6,824	80.3
136	119	RJR Nabisco	9,110	17.6	181	242	Federated Dept Strs	6,805	69.4
137	120	Weyerhaeuser	9,060	18.3	182	204	Honeywell	6,785	44.6
138	126	Dean Witter Discover	9,036	24.1	183	156	Marsh & McLennan	6,779	12.4
139	173	Cigna	8,988	64.0	184	128	Micron Technology	6,754	–5.4
140	129	Texas Utilities	8,836	24.2	185	152	Dominion Resources	6,748	8.0
141	111	Enron	8,736	8.0	186	183	Unicom	6,717	26.0
142	149	Aetna Life & Cas	8,658	36.6	187	216	Hershey Foods	6,624	49.0
143	133	KeyCorp	8,570	23.5	188	225	Halliburton	6,624	54.8
144	306	Sun Microsystems	8,409	162.0	189	207	Textron	6,622	43.4
145	169	Rhone-Poulenc Rorer	8,339	49.8	190	224	MBNA	6,543	52.6
146	135	Chubb	8,278	20.5	191	233	Household Intl	6,484	56.5
147	186	First Bank System	8,276	60.3	192	140	Georgia-Pacific	6,449	–3.7
148	393	Boston Scientific	8,249	250.4	193	177	Air Prods & Chems	6,426	19.0
149	248	WorldCom	8,198	107.0	194	230	Union Carbide	6,415	52.5
150	145	Occidental Petroleum	8,137	24.3	195	260	Alco Standard	6,362	67.1
151	278	Loral	8,090	124.3	196	139	Pub Svc Enterprise	6,332	–5.5
152	161	Walgreen	7,969	36.7	197	143	Browning-Ferris Inds	6,312	–4.6
153	121	Corning	7,932	3.7	198	229	Marriott Intl	6,282	49.3
154	189	Illinois Tool Works	7,917	54.8	199	164	Genentech	6,276	9.3
155	212	Gap	7,913	74.2	200	158	UST Inc	6,269	5.7
156	153	SunTrust Banks	7,909	26.9	201	256	Crown Cork & Seal	6,238	59.6
157	134	Unocal	7,884	14.7	202	208	Applied Materials	6,213	34.8
158	182	Goodyear	7,868	47.4	203	200	Entergy	6,178	30.1
159	203	WR Grace	7,819	66.3	204	197	Dayton Hudson	6,054	22.5
160	127	American Brands	7,793	8.1	205	196	Sysco	6,052	22.2
161	154	Wachovia	7,590	22.8	206	215	Conrail	6,034	37.1
162	157	American Electric	7,559	26.5	207	■	Freeport Copper	5,969	31.7
163	150	FPL Group	7,558	20.8	208	192	Duracell Intl	5,913	16.8
164	191	Mattel	7,541	48.4	209	■	Seagate Technology	5,888	225.2
165	190	Morgan Stanley	7,527	47.7	210	232	CUC International	5,888	41.3

■ Not on 500 list in 1994. NA: Not available.   (Continued)

The Forbes Market Value 500 (Cont.)

RANK '95	RANK '94	Company	Market value ($ mil)	% change	RANK '95	RANK '94	Company	Market value ($ mil)	% change
211	246	Avon Products	5,883	48.1	256	307	Boatmen's Bancshs	5,000	55.9
212	261	Turner Broadcasting	5,880	54.5	257	185	Reader's Digest Assn	4,977	-5.9
213	275	Safeway	5,877	61.4	258	218	Amerada Hess	4,952	12.4
214	244	Fluor	5,865	46.9	259	■	Frontier	4,922	44.9
215	168	PECO Energy	5,862	5.3	260	238	National City	4,912	21.1
216	■	US Robotics	5,858	337.7	261	■	HFS	4,895	284.4
217	■	Cox Communications	5,842	NA	262	■	US Bancorp	4,854	22.7
218	227	Barnett Banks	5,775	35.3	263	254	DTE Energy	4,843	23.3
219	219	TRW	5,773	31.8	264	356	Sallie Mae	4,801	78.0
220	180	Alltel	5,773	7.8	265	243	Masco	4,772	19.1
221	176	PacifiCorp	5,757	6.6	266	314	EMC	4,770	54.6
222	223	CoreStates Financial	5,746	33.7	267	171	Kmart	4,708	-14.5
223	210	Eastman Chemical	5,713	25.3	268	■	America Online	4,708	236.6
224	234	Morton International	5,680	37.8	269	449	Northwest Airlines	4,707	132.6
225	178	RR Donnelley & Sons	5,677	5.2	270	390	Parametric Tech	4,702	97.9
226	181	Lowe's Cos	5,672	6.1	271	273	Rohm & Haas	4,679	28.0
227	258	Aon	5,629	45.7	272	316	Kroger	4,665	52.1
228	290	Fifth Third Bancorp	5,612	63.3	273	193	Burlington Resources	4,636	-8.1
229	■	Ascend Commun	5,573	500.0+	274	255	Eaton	4,628	18.1
230	209	Central & So West	5,534	21.0	275	214	Quaker Oats	4,617	3.1
231	■	ITT Hartford Group	5,519	NA	276	239	Equitable Cos	4,617	14.2
232	201	USX-Marathon	5,497	16.0	277	395	Chiron	4,590	96.0
233	■	HealthSouth	5,484	297.8	278	136	Novell	4,571	-33.0
234	361	Service Corp Intl	5,453	108.1	279	347	Charles Schwab	4,568	63.6
235	251	Tyco International	5,452	38.5	280	175	Rubbermaid	4,541	-16.6
236	325	Praxair	5,446	83.5	281	270	Champion Intl	4,535	23.4
237	194	Houston Industries	5,432	8.2	282	226	St Paul Cos	4,535	6.1
238	163	Intl Flavors & Frags	5,424	-6.4	283	272	AutoZone	4,521	23.5
239	283	Newmont Mining	5,420	54.5	284	317	Franklin Resources	4,510	47.2
240	199	Genuine Parts	5,410	12.0	285	301	Comerica	4,500	38.4
241	202	Nucor	5,401	14.8	286	308	Ingersoll-Rand	4,498	40.8
242	291	Dover	5,399	57.3	287	296	Hilton Hotels	4,496	34.7
243	365	Thermo Electron	5,331	106.5	288	387	Southwest Airlines	4,494	85.8
244	266	Becton Dickinson	5,328	41.6	289	259	Cinergy	4,494	17.0
245	231	Winn-Dixie Stores	5,324	27.5	290	359	Green Tree Financial	4,492	68.6
246	310	Bank of Boston	5,310	68.6	291	267	Phelps Dodge	4,485	19.6
247	142	Limited	5,279	-20.7	292	■	Tele-Com-Liberty	4,471	NA
248	236	Bankers Trust NY	5,278	28.5	293	285	McGraw-Hill Cos	4,453	27.3
249	262	Lincoln National	5,274	38.7	294	284	Safeco	4,410	25.9
250	264	Dresser Industries	5,198	36.8	295	298	Panhandle Eastern	4,399	32.6
251	250	Transamerica	5,186	31.7	296	318	Pioneer Hi-Bred Intl	4,394	43.4
252	344	Williams Cos	5,136	82.8	297	241	Great Lakes Chemical	4,361	8.3
253	322	Cabletron Systems	5,066	67.4	298	300	Clorox	4,348	33.2
254	385	Informix	5,020	107.2	299	252	Aflac	4,342	10.3
255	247	Carolina Power & Lt	5,019	26.4	300	245	Whirlpool	4,324	8.4

■ Not on 500 list in 1994. NA: Not available.

(Continued)

The Forbes Market Value 500 *(Cont.)*

Rank '95	Rank '94	Company	Market value ($ mil)	% change	Rank '95	Rank '94	Company	Market value ($ mil)	% change
301	257	Newell Co	4,323	10.7	346	338	Molex	3,544	23.7
302	286	American Stores	4,320	24.0	347	309	WW Grainger	3,504	10.9
303	302	UNUM	4,288	32.0	348	■	Netscape Commun	3,483	NA
304	304	Tenet Healthcare	4,260	32.3	349	350	Cincinnati Financial	3,482	25.3
305	400	Tellabs	4,174	79.6	350	343	Interpublic Group	3,460	23.1
306	352	Dillard Dept Stores	4,140	50.3	351	440	Linear Technology	3,439	67.5
307	274	Tribune	4,136	13.5	352	■	IMC Global	3,425	130.0
308	324	Coastal	4,133	38.4	353	358	Allegheny Power	3,425	27.6
309	351	Baker Hughes	4,113	48.6	354	397	EW Scripps	3,421	46.5
310	410	Mirage	4,109	86.2	355	■	Cascade Commun	3,404	267.2
311	■	Estee Lauder Cos	4,091	NA	356	321	Ohio Edison	3,395	11.9
312	288	Providian	4,081	18.4	357	249	DSC Communications	3,381	−14.6
313	263	Comcast	4,066	6.9	358	398	Dana	3,378	44.7
314	336	Delta Air Lines	4,043	40.2	359	444	Analog Devices	3,376	65.8
315	289	Consol Natural Gas	4,036	17.3	360	405	MGIC Investment	3,371	48.9
316	211	Cooper Industries	4,018	−11.9	361	339	Knight-Ridder	3,353	18.1
317	303	Nordstrom	4,008	24.2	362	320	WellPoint Health	3,346	10.2
318	434	Times Mirror	4,003	91.9	363	399	Huntington Bancshs	3,327	42.8
319	271	Union Electric	3,996	9.1	364	420	Circus Circus	3,324	53.6
320	372	Computer Sciences	3,976	57.1	365	467	Firstar	3,313	46.4
321	408	MFS Communication	3,975	78.3	366	377	Anadarko Petroleum	3,293	32.0
322	268	Federal Express	3,972	7.9	367	330	No States Power	3,272	12.4
323	198	Silicon Graphics	3,943	−19.5	368	425	First USA	3,268	53.2
324	292	Baltimore G&E	3,909	15.2	369	312	Harcourt General	3,268	5.1
325	281	Dow Jones	3,897	10.5	370	280	Tyson Foods	3,261	−7.7
326	253	Humana	3,890	−1.1	371	345	Willamette Inds	3,258	16.1
327	383	State Street Boston	3,872	59.5	372	237	General Instrument	3,240	−20.9
328	360	Southern Pacific Rail	3,864	45.5	373	386	Black & Decker	3,230	33.5
329	276	Salomon	3,859	6.1	374	341	Progressive	3,217	13.5
330	■	HBO & Co	3,854	173.7	375	366	MBIA	3,212	24.5
331	■	Case	3,795	117.1	376	367	Republic New York	3,208	24.7
332	293	General Public Utils	3,795	13.5	377	349	Washington Post	3,205	15.3
333	348	Jefferson-Pilot	3,783	35.8	378	■	Guidant	3,202	134.5
334	■	Nextel Commun	3,780	155.6	379	355	Premark Intl	3,200	18.5
335	319	PP&L Resources	3,766	23.4	380	228	Apple Computer	3,200	−24.6
336	326	General Dynamics	3,747	26.9	381	454	Omnicom Group	3,196	59.4
337	353	Coca-Cola Enterprise	3,728	36.1	382	337	Florida Progress	3,185	11.0
338	327	Reynolds Metals	3,713	25.7	383	370	Kerr-McGee	3,179	25.2
339	333	Sherwin-Williams	3,712	28.0	384	269	Office Depot	3,178	−13.6
340	335	Price/Costco	3,686	27.7	385	364	Westvaco	3,175	22.6
341	213	H&R Block	3,683	−18.2	386	■	Summit Bancorp	3,174	35.6
342	311	LSI Logic	3,653	17.3	387	334	Torchmark	3,156	9.3
343	282	Melville	3,630	3.3	388	376	Pall	3,149	26.2
344	305	VF	3,589	11.7	389	340	IVAX	3,142	10.8
345	287	Union Camp	3,551	3.0	390	■	Dell Computer	3,117	78.6

■ Not on 500 list in 1994. NA: Not available.

(Continued)

The Forbes Market Value 500 *(Cont.)*

RANK '95	RANK '94	Company	Market value ($ mil)	% change	RANK '95	RANK '94	Company	Market value ($ mil)	% change
391	379	Great Western Finl	3,103	26.6	436	331	Food Lion	2,718	−6.4
392	346	Hasbro	3,078	9.9	437	■	Regions Financial	2,715	70.6
393	495	Staples	3,063	68.2	438	421	FMC	2,714	25.6
394	332	Wisconsin Energy	3,048	5.1	439	391	Manpower	2,708	14.2
395	413	Western Atlas	3,039	38.3	440	448	Scana	2,704	33.6
396	382	USX-US Steel	3,027	23.9	441	■	Paychex	2,689	99.8
397	■	PanAmSat	3,025	NA	442	438	Premier Industrial	2,682	29.7
398	■	Oxford Health Plans	3,009	111.7	443	497	ALZA	2,640	45.4
399	475	Northern Trust	3,006	58.2	444	■	SunAmerica	2,638	76.9
400	396	Northrop Grumman	3,004	28.4	445	402	Deluxe	2,625	13.9
401	■	FORE Systems	3,000	307.7	446	432	HF Ahmanson	2,619	25.1
402	484	PacifiCare Health	2,976	58.2	447	■	Xilinx	2,617	65.4
403	■	ITT Industries	2,971	NA	448	403	Brown-Forman	2,613	13.9
404	■	Raychem	2,968	66.3	449	457	CMS Energy	2,612	30.5
405	407	Potomac Electric	2,962	32.7	450	■	Liz Claiborne	2,607	129.5
406	363	Sonat	2,962	14.3	451	■	360° Commun	2,597	NA
407	362	Engelhard	2,946	14.7	452	419	Dial	2,595	19.6
408	■	BMC Software	2,946	78.5	453	378	Cyprus Amax Mineral	2,592	5.2
409	392	Circuit City Stores	2,944	24.6	454	■	Harris	2,578	47.7
410	453	Sigma-Aldrich	2,932	46.1	455	384	Homestake Mining	2,565	5.6
411	374	Equifax	2,926	16.4	456	388	Enova	2,564	6.0
412	430	Beneficial	2,919	38.5	457	■	Atmel	2,562	60.2
413	435	Avery Dennison	2,918	40.6	458	■	Dole Food	2,559	57.9
414	409	Golden West Finl	2,914	31.7	459	■	Vencor	2,542	35.1
415	460	Johnson Controls	2,910	46.1	460	■	Paging Network	2,535	49.3
416	431	Cardinal Health	2,901	37.9	461	373	Temple-Inland	2,525	0.2
417	297	Tandy	2,886	−13.3	462	■	StrataCom	2,523	79.5
418	427	First of America Bk	2,879	35.7	463	468	Lyondell Petrochem	2,520	29.9
419	■	Meridian Bancorp	2,871	64.5	464	401	Adobe Systems	2,520	8.4
420	279	Harrah's Entertain	2,839	−20.8	465	437	So New Eng Telecom	2,513	21.4
421	423	New York Times	2,808	30.4	466	354	Citizens Utilities	2,508	−7.6
422	414	Parker Hannifin	2,790	27.6	467	412	Consolidated Papers	2,503	13.8
423	389	TECO Energy	2,787	17.0	468	478	Manor Care	2,500	32.0
424	■	Altera	2,785	126.4	469	■	UAL	2,496	122.9
425	433	Bear Stearns Cos	2,782	33.0	470	442	Sonoco Products	2,495	22.1
426	■	Southern National	2,777	35.0	471	411	DPL	2,467	11.9
427	315	Mead	2,773	−9.9	472	■	Healthsource	2,464	80.0
428	369	Mallinckrodt Group	2,773	9.0	473	357	Northeast Utilities	2,462	−8.4
429	429	Tele & Data Systems	2,765	31.0	474	487	Allergan	2,452	32.8
430	■	Harley-Davidson	2,741	56.2	475	■	McKesson	2,450	46.8
431	■	US Satellite Broad	2,739	NA	476	■	Qualcomm	2,449	44.1
432	■	PeopleSoft	2,731	165.1	477	450	Hillenbrand Inds	2,444	21.1
433	329	Louisiana-Pacific	2,728	−7.1	478	■	Stanley Works	2,443	37.6
434	470	St Jude Medical	2,724	41.2	479	499	Mercury Finance	2,438	34.4
435	428	Rite Aid	2,722	28.5	480	417	Stryker	2,434	12.1

■ Not on 500 list in 1994. NA: Not available.   *(Continued)*

The Forbes Market Value 500 *(Cont.)*

RANK '95	'94	Company	Market value ($ mil)	% change	RANK '95	'94	Company	Market value ($ mil)	% change
481	447	Lehman Bros Holding	2,433	20.2	491	485	Pinnacle West	2,374	27.8
482	472	Whitman	2,430	27.1	492	■	Crestar Financial	2,360	47.7
483	465	Ashland	2,425	23.7	493	451	Arrow Electronics	2,354	16.9
484	■	Mercantile Bancorp	2,417	43.2	494	■	Synovus Finl	2,347	82.3
485	458	Marshall & Ilsley	2,414	20.7	495	381	Gaylord Entertain	2,335	−4.5
486	■	SouthTrust	2,406	41.9	496	■	Armstrong World Ind	2,334	38.9
487	439	New England Electric	2,394	16.5	497	■	Intuit	2,334	54.5
488	455	James River Corp Va	2,389	19.3	498	299	Advanced Micro	2,328	−29.7
489	■	Kohl's	2,387	51.0	499	375	Mylan Labs	2,314	−7.4
490	■	Sundstrand	2,385	57.8	500	■	General Nutrition Cos	2,312	127.3

■ Not on 500 list in 1994. NA: Not available.

JOBS
AND PRODUCTIVITY

Surprise: Despite all the talk about downsizing, America's largest corporations added to their payrolls last year.

SHLOMO Z. REIFMAN

For most of the past decade and a half, employment at Forbes 500s companies has been shrinking, even while their sales have been rising. Big corporations have simply learned to make better use of their workers.

The year 1995 saw an interruption in that long-running trend. The 787 companies listed in one or more of our rankings employed 20.4 million people at year-end, a bit more than a 1% gain from 1994. The payroll growth didn't hurt productivity: Combined sales for these companies gained 10% from the previous year, a good 7% after inflation. Combined profits were up 12%.

The moral is pretty clear: We don't need laws against downsizing to create jobs; we need a strong economy.

Which industries were the most productive in terms of sales and profits per worker? Generally those that use more capital. Productivity varies widely from industry to industry. Measured by sales per employee, the most productive sector is energy-international oils, with a median $1.2 million. The least productive is restaurant chains, with $44,400.

A diversified group of companies in the natural gas business takes first place in terms of profits per employee. The five companies in this group have median profits per employee of $74,200. The least productive group comprises the six firms in travel & transport-shipping, in which the median company earned only $500 per employee.

To find a company on the tables below, first check the address directory for the industry group for the firm.

Jobs and Productivity 500 Table

Rank Company	Profits	PER EMPLOYEE ($000) Sales (rank)	PER EMPLOYEE ($000) Assets (rank)	Employees (000)
AEROSPACE & DEFENSE				
1 General Dynamics	13.3	127.5 (11)	131.6 (9)	100.2
2 Raytheon	11.9	175.6 (6)	146.0 (6)	77.2
3 Loral	11.7	213.8 (2)	201.7 (3)	11.2
4 AlliedSignal	9.9	163.0 (7)	141.6 (8)	106.5
5 Textron	8.7	181.3 (3)	421.3 (1)	56.0
6 Sundstrand	8.6	160.1 (8)	173.2 (4)	13.1
7 Northrop Grumman	6.6	177.7 (5)	142.2 (7)	39.6
8 Litton Industries	4.9	117.3 (12)	89.4 (12)	50.7
9 United Technologies	4.4	132.3 (10)	93.3 (11)	197.0
10 Lockheed Martin	4.0	135.2 (9)	104.4 (10)	174.5
11 Boeing	3.6	178.4 (4)	202.0 (2)	161.7
12 McDonnell Douglas	−6.4	221.6 (1)	161.8 (5)	124.6
Industry medians	**7.6**	**169.3**	**144.1**	
BUSINESS—ENVIRONMENTAL & WASTE				
1 Thermo Electron	11.4	179.2 (1)	304.0 (1)	9.5
2 Browning-Ferris Inds	9.5	147.9 (2)	190.8 (3)	25.4
3 WMX Technologies	8.5	144.7 (3)	264.1 (2)	52.0
Industry medians	**9.5**	**147.9**	**264.1**	
BUSINESS—SERVICES				
1 Comdisco	50.7	1,074.6 (1)	2,420.1 (1)	1.9
2 H&R Block	24.3	391.8 (5)	263.7 (4)	3.5
3 WW Grainger	17.7	310.7 (6)	157.7 (6)	8.1
4 Automatic Data	16.9	126.6 (8)	149.1 (7)	20.0
5 Manpower	16.1	689.8 (2)	190.9 (5)	7.0
6 PHH	16.0	472.2 (4)	1,176.6 (2)	4.3
7 Paychex	14.1	90.8 (12)	63.0 (13)	3.4
8 Kelly Services	13.4	517.3 (3)	138.2 (8)	3.9
9 Olsten	10.8	301.7 (7)	106.8 (9)	7.8
10 Equifax	10.4	114.2 (10)	78.0 (11)	14.1
11 Computer Sciences	4.1	124.6 (9)	77.1 (12)	20.6
12 Ogden	0.2	48.6 (13)	81.2 (10)	42.5
13 First Data	−2.3	111.8 (11)	334.7 (3)	36.5
Industry medians	**14.1**	**301.7**	**149.1**	
BUSINESS—SUPPLIES				
1 Pitney Bowes	19.3	117.5 (5)	259.3 (2)	30.7
2 Minn Mining & Mfg	13.9	191.6 (4)	201.9 (3)	88.6
3 Avery Dennison	9.3	201.5 (2)	127.1 (5)	19.0
4 Alco Standard	6.5	306.2 (1)	153.3 (4)	18.0
5 Deluxe	4.6	97.5 (6)	67.9 (6)	17.1
6 Xerox	−5.5	192.3 (3)	300.6 (1)	110.3
Industry medians	**7.9**	**192.0**	**177.6**	

Jobs and Productivity 500 Table *(Cont.)*

		PER EMPLOYEE ($000)		Employees
Rank Company	Profits	Sales (rank)	Assets (rank)	(000)
CAPITAL GOODS—ELECTRICAL EQUIPMENT				
1 General Electric	30.0	319.8 (1)	1,041.3 (1)	295.0
2 Premier Industrial	25.5	192.4 (2)	126.7 (4)	5.2
3 Emerson Electric	11.8	130.5 (6)	123.4 (5)	73.7
4 Rockwell Intl	10.0	173.7 (3)	155.6 (3)	105.3
5 Teledyne	9.0	142.7 (4)	89.2 (7)	34.2
6 Honeywell	6.6	133.4 (5)	100.3 (6)	62.8
7 American Standard	3.5	128.9 (7)	86.9 (8)	40.5
8 Westinghouse	0.2	80.9 (8)	215.3 (2)	115.8
Industry medians	**9.5**	**138.1**	**125.1**	
CAPITAL GOODS—HEAVY EQUIPMENT				
1 AGCO	22.3	367.5 (1)	374.1 (2)	4.1
2 Deere & Co	21.7	311.1 (2)	427.2 (1)	38.7
3 Case	21.2	302.9 (3)	335.5 (3)	17.0
4 Caterpillar	20.9	296.2 (4)	310.2 (4)	59.7
5 Tenneco	12.8	154.8 (6)	233.9 (5)	91.0
6 Harnischfeger Inds	7.2	161.6 (5)	175.2 (6)	12.2
7 Ingersoll-Rand	7.0	148.7 (8)	141.6 (7)	32.7
8 Trinity Industries	6.6	149.9 (7)	86.0 (8)	14.7
Industry medians	**16.9**	**228.9**	**272.1**	
CAPITAL GOODS—OTHER INDUSTRIAL EQUIPMENT				
1 Illinois Tool Works	19.0	204.0 (1)	177.5 (1)	17.1
2 Dover	11.5	155.0 (3)	110.4 (3)	20.3
3 Tyco International	8.0	142.4 (4)	104.7 (5)	14.3
4 Parker Hannifin	7.8	112.0 (7)	76.5 (7)	31.0
5 Cooper Industries	6.9	120.3 (6)	149.4 (2)	40.7
6 Stanley Works	3.0	132.6 (5)	84.4 (6)	17.8
7 York International	−5.5	167.9 (2)	110.4 (3)	14.9
Industry medians	**7.8**	**142.4**	**110.4**	
CHEMICALS—DIVERSIFIED				
1 Union Carbide	78.6	500.6 (1)	531.8 (1)	37.7
2 Dow Chemical	44.6	433.3 (2)	505.9 (2)	62.1
3 Hercules	33.5	244.2 (6)	250.8 (6)	21.6
4 du Pont de Nemours	31.1	344.4 (3)	352.0 (4)	144.9
5 Monsanto	25.5	309.7 (5)	366.7 (3)	41.6
6 PPG Industries	24.6	226.2 (8)	198.5 (7)	35.3
7 Rohm & Haas	24.5	325.3 (4)	327.9 (5)	13.0
8 Olin	10.8	244.2 (6)	176.1 (9)	15.3
9 FMC	9.9	207.3 (9)	197.7 (8) 24.0	
Industry medians	**25.5**	**309.7**	**327.9**	

(Continued)

Jobs and Productivity 500 Table (Cont.)

Rank Company	Profits	PER EMPLOYEE ($000) Sales (rank)	Assets (rank)	Employees (000)
CHEMICALS—SPECIALIZED				
1 Georgia Gulf	162.9	944.6 (2)	443.1 (4)	1.2
2 Lyondell Petrochem	155.7	1,976.0 (1)	1,043.2 (1)	2.2
3 Sterling Chemicals	119.7	817.6 (3)	509.4 (3)	1.2
4 Cytec Industries	56.4	252.0 (12)	258.8 (12)	5.0
5 Intl Flavors & Frags	53.9	312.1 (7)	332.7 (8)	4.2
6 Terra Industries	49.5	668.8 (4)	563.8 (2)	3.3
7 Cabot	38.2	388.5 (5)	363.8 (7)	5.8
8 Great Lakes Chemical	36.0	287.9 (8)	301.1 (10)	5.3
9 Lubrizol	33.2	364.7 (6)	327.1 (9)	5.1
10 Eastman Chemical	31.8	286.3 (9)	275.8 (11)	17.8
11 Air Prods & Chems	26.4	277.0 (10)	429.5 (5)	14.1
12 Nalco Chemical	25.6	202.1 (14)	228.0 (14)	5.7
13 Morton International	23.6	251.8 (13)	207.9 (16)	9.1
14 Sigma-Aldrich	23.5	171.2 (18)	175.7 (18)	4.0
15 IMC Global	17.8	256.6 (11)	382.8 (6)	6.0
16 Praxair	14.6	174.8 (17)	229.7 (13)	17.3
17 Sherwin-Williams	11.0	180.2 (16)	117.8 (19)	16.6
18 BF Goodrich	8.8	180.6 (15)	186.7 (17)	11.9
19 WR Grace	−11.0	124.0 (19)	213.0 (15)	50.9
Industry medians	**31.8**	**277.0**	**301.1**	
COMPUTERS & COMMUNICATIONS—MAJOR SYSTEMS				
1 Compaq Computer	50.2	939.0 (1)	497.5 (1)	10.3
2 Silicon Graphics	36.7	395.9 (6)	359.1 (4)	4.4
3 Dell Computer	33.6	653.8 (3)	265.2 (5)	6.7
4 Teradyne	32.9	245.8 (12)	211.3 (9)	4.8
5 Sun Microsystems	30.8	440.7 (5)	225.4 (7)	10.8
6 Hewlett-Packard	25.7	328.6 (8)	252.6 (6)	93.5
7 Gateway 2000	25.2	535.4 (4)	163.7 (11)	4.5
8 IBM	18.8	323.2 (9)	360.7 (3)	378.5
9 Apple Computer	10.5	714.5 (2)	411.5 (2)	14.5
10 Tandem Computers	8.8	268.6 (10)	213.8 (8)	10.2
11 Digital Equipment	7.0	234.0 (13)	162.3 (12)	124.9
12 Raychem	6.8	168.7 (14)	152.9 (14)	11.3
13 Harris	6.2	131.9 (16)	113.1 (15)	34.3
14 SCI Systems	4.7	266.5 (11)	96.2 (16)	12.0
15 Unisys	−14.9	148.2 (15)	170.0 (10)	78.8
16 AST Research	−39.7	356.1 (7)	160.1 (13)	7.0
Industry medians	**14.7**	**325.9**	**212.6**	
COMPUTERS & COMMUNICATIONS—PERIPHERALS				
1 Cisco Systems	194.1	817.1 (4)	724.6 (1)	2.4
2 Micron Technology	150.5	587.1 (5)	538.3 (2)	5.2

Jobs and Productivity 500 Table *(Cont.)*

Rank Company	Profits	PER EMPLOYEE ($000) Sales (rank)	Assets (rank)	Employees (000)
COMPUTERS & COMMUNICATIONS-PERIPHERALS				
3 EMC	94.7	556.9 (8)	506.0 (3)	2.8
4 Intel	88.1	400.3 (13)	432.5 (7)	23.4
5 Linear Technology	83.3	242.9 (18)	331.7 (14)	1.0
6 Applied Materials	65.7	422.3 (11)	380.7 (11)	5.6
7 LSI Logic	61.5	327.1 (14)	477.3 (4)	3.4
8 3Com	54.4	583.4 (6)	408.3 (9)	2.5
9 Bay Networks	52.7	416.9 (12)	344.7 (13)	3.0
10 Atmel	46.5	259.6 (17)	376.4 (12)	2.4
11 Tellabs	42.8	235.3 (20)	204.5 (20)	2.5
12 US Robotics	39.9	455.1 (10)	311.1 (15)	2.4
13 Cabletron Systems	31.0	201.8 (23)	177.7 (21)	0.8
14 Arrow Electronics	29.8	870.5 (3)	397.2 (10)	6.1
15 FORE Systems	27.8	229.5 (21)	461.6 (6)	0.9
16 Advanced Micro	24.5	198.1 (24)	247.1 (18)	11.9
17 Analog Devices	23.8	177.9 (25)	229.7 (19)	5.4
18 Varian Associates	21.8	239.5 (19)	144.5 (23)	6.6
19 Avnet	19.1	533.1 (9)	273.6 (16)	8.0
20 Texas Instruments	18.8	226.5 (22)	159.0 (22)	72.1
21 Molex	14.1	135.8 (27)	141.2 (24)	6.5
22 Natl Semiconductor	12.4	129.0 (28)	125.2 (26)	32.5
23 Western Digital	11.9	317.8 (15)	118.4 (28)	6.6
24 AMP	11.4	139.8 (26)	120.4 (27)	24.6
25 Solectron	11.2	276.5 (16)	139.5 (25)	8.8
26 Tech Data	8.8	1,262.4 (2)	426.9 (8)	1.8
27 Quantum	7.6	574.5 (7)	260.7 (17)	0.6
28 Read-Rite	7.1	52.1 (30)	45.4 (30)	20.8
29 Seagate Technology	6.1	85.5 (29)	59.6 (29)	35.8
30 Merisel	−2.9	1,835.4 (1)	464.6 (5)	2.8
Industry medians	**26.2**	**297.2**	**292.4**	
COMPUTERS & COMMUNICATIONS-SOFTWARE				
1 Altera	112.2	518.9 (2)	924.5 (1)	0.8
2 Microsoft	102.1	411.9 (4)	505.6 (5)	4.8
3 Xilinx	89.6	533.1 (1)	687.5 (2)	1.0
4 Parametric Tech	54.0	262.9 (9)	296.6 (10)	1.2
5 BMC Software	52.8	298.2 (6)	407.4 (7)	1.3
6 Adobe Systems	48.1	392.6 (5)	455.6 (6)	0.4
7 Novell	42.9	265.7 (8)	315.2 (9)	2.3
8 Informix	38.8	261.0 (10)	248.3 (12)	2.0
9 PeopleSoft	29.5	228.5 (11)	315.4 (8)	1.0
10 Oracle	27.0	197.0 (12)	144.1 (14)	5.5
11 America Online	1.8	287.3 (7)	279.6 (11)	2.5

(Continued)

Jobs and Productivity 500 Table *(Cont.)*

Rank Company	Profits	PER EMPLOYEE ($000) Sales (rank)	Assets (rank)	Employees (000)
COMPUTERS & COMMUNICATIONS—SOFTWARE				
12 Intuit	−1.6	179.4 (14)	186.6 (13)	2.7
13 Netscape Commun	−7.8	181.7 (13)	512.9 (4)	0.4
14 Computer Associates	−14.4	423.3 (3)	646.6 (3)	6.6
Industry medians	**40.9**	**276.5**	**361.4**	
COMPUTERS & COMMUNICATIONS—TELECOMMUNICATIONS				
1 Ascend Commun	145.6	712.3 (2)	1,597.4 (3)	0.2
2 PanAmSat	115.4	764.2 (1)	9,465.9 (1)	0.2
3 Cascade Commun	78.2	414.9 (4)	344.2 (17)	0.3
4 StrataCom	64.6	408.6 (5)	363.8 (14)	0.8
5 WorldCom	35.7	485.3 (3)	873.6 (4)	5.4
6 Citizens Utilities	35.2	236.1 (13)	865.5 (6)	1.7
7 DSC Communications	34.2	252.3 (11)	330.9 (20)	4.7
8 SBC Communications	32.0	214.6 (14)	372.6 (13)	66.5
9 Ameritech	31.1	208.3 (15)	340.4 (19)	76.6
10 Bell Atlantic	27.8	200.3 (16)	360.3 (15)	80.4
11 GTE	23.4	183.8 (24)	340.9 (18)	156.0
12 U S West Commun	23.2	185.5 (23)	324.5 (21)	51.1
13 Alltel	22.0	193.2 (22)	315.1 (23)	10.0
14 Pacific Telesis	20.9	180.0 (27)	315.3 (22)	67.1
15 Frontier	20.7	306.0 (7)	301.0 (25)	4.3
16 AirTouch Commun	20.3	249.0 (12)	868.9 (5)	5.3
17 Sprint	19.5	262.9 (10)	310.8 (24)	42.2
18 So New Eng Telecom	17.9	194.9 (21)	288.8 (27)	12.5
19 Tele & Data Systems	17.8	163.3 (28)	593.7 (8)	4.8
20 BellSouth	17.4	199.1 (17)	354.8 (16)	101.6
21 Nynex	15.7	196.7 (20)	384.6 (11)	94.6
22 Qualcomm	13.6	180.5 (26)	379.4 (12)	2.5
23 Motorola	13.0	197.4 (19)	166.4 (30)	104.5
24 MCI Communication	12.7	354.2 (6)	447.9 (10)	21.9
25 General Instrument	10.1	197.7 (18)	187.1 (29)	11.2
26 AT&T	0.5	263.7 (9)	294.4 (26)	278.6
27 360ì Commun	−0.5	265.1 (8)	626.8 (7)	3.1
28 Paging Network	−10.2	149.0 (29)	283.2 (28)	4.0
29 MFS Communication	−82.9	180.6 (25)	578.1 (9)	2.2
30 Nextel Commun	−128.2	86.7 (30)	2,663.0 (2)	2.1
Industry medians	**20.5**	**204.3**	**357.6**	
CONSTRUCTION—BUILDERS				
1 Centex	7.3	480.7 (2)	364.6 (1)	4.9
2 Fluor	5.9	236.7 (4)	83.4 (4)	21.1
3 Foster Wheeler	2.3	250.0 (3)	228.1 (3)	8.5

Jobs and Productivity 500 Table *(Cont.)*

	PER EMPLOYEE ($000)			Employees
Rank Company	Profits	Sales (rank)	Assets (rank)	(000)
CONSTRUCTION—BUILDERS				
4 Turner	0.5	1,281.3 (1)	309.6 (2)	3.1
Industry medians	**4.1**	**365.4**	**268.9**	
CONSTRUCTION—BUILDING MATERIALS				
1 Manville	16.3	185.5 (2)	329.9 (1)	17.5
2 Owens Corning	13.4	208.8 (1)	188.5 (2)	18.4
3 Masco	−12.3	81.5 (3)	105.3 (3)	41.8
Industry medians	**13.4**	**185.5**	**188.5**	
CONSTRUCTION—CEMENT & GYPSUM				
1 Vulcan Materials	24.4	214.3 (2)	178.3 (2)	6.6
2 Lafarge	19.8	225.3 (1)	262.3 (1)	7.9
3 USG	−2.6	197.1 (3)	152.4 (3)	12.7
Industry medians	**19.8**	**214.3**	**178.3**	
CONSUMER DURABLES—APPLIANCES				
1 Black & Decker	8.7	162.9 (3)	189.6 (1)	41.0
2 Whirlpool	4.9	197.7 (1)	184.7 (2)	37.8
3 Maytag	−0.8	167.2 (2)	116.9 (3)	25.1
Industry medians	**4.9**	**167.2**	**184.7**	
CONSUMER DURABLES—AUTOMOBILES & TRUCKS				
1 Chrysler	18.9	472.8 (1)	477.8 (2)	109.9
2 Paccar	17.6	336.7 (4)	304.9 (5)	12.3
3 Ford Motor	11.9	395.2 (3)	701.1 (1)	381.4
4 Navistar Intl	10.5	410.3 (2)	327.0 (3)	14.1
5 General Motors	9.8	238.1 (5)	306.2 (4)	761.4
Industry medians	**11.9**	**395.2**	**327.0**	
CONSUMER DURABLES—AUTOMOTIVE PARTS				
1 Genuine Parts	14.1	240.3 (1)	103.9 (6)	16.0
2 Varity	12.4	234.5 (2)	181.2 (1)	10.5
3 Cummins Engine	9.0	210.2 (3)	122.5 (3)	25.0
4 Eaton	7.7	132.5 (10)	98.1 (8)	37.7
5 Goodyear	6.9	148.3 (8)	110.3 (4)	107.7
6 Dana	6.8	183.6 (4)	134.3 (2)	37.0
6 TRW	6.8	155.7 (6)	90.1 (9)	75.0
8 Echlin	6.4	124.4 (11)	87.6 (10)	17.3
9 Johnson Controls	3.5	151.9 (7)	85.7 (11)	43.1
10 Lear Seating	3.3	164.0 (5)	106.5 (5)	21.6
11 ITT Industries	0.4	144.5 (9)	101.1 (7)	58.0
Industry medians	**6.8**	**155.7**	**103.9**	

(Continued)

Jobs and Productivity 500 Table *(Cont.)*

		PER EMPLOYEE ($000)		Employees
Rank Company	Profits	Sales (rank)	Assets (rank)	(000)
CONSUMER DURABLES—HOME FURNISHINGS				
1 Armstrong World Ind	10.8	183.4 (1)	189.2 (1)	25.2
2 Newell Co	10.3	116.2 (5)	136.3 (2)	10.6
3 Premark Intl	9.9	92.2 (7)	103.0 (4)	25.4
4 Leggett & Platt	8.3	126.3 (3)	74.7 (6)	14.5
5 Rubbermaid	4.3	166.8 (2)	120.4 (3)	8.7
6 Shaw Industries	2.6	116.4 (4)	67.5 (7)	12.7
7 US Industries	–1.0	108.0 (6)	83.2 (5)	20.9
Industry medians	**8.3**	**116.4**	**103.0**	
CONSUMER DURABLES—RECREATION EQUIPMENT				
1 Harley-Davidson	24.7	296.8 (1)	219.9 (1)	6.3
2 Brunswick	6.1	145.9 (3)	113.2 (2)	22.9
3 Fleetwood Enterprise	4.4	155.3 (2)	77.4 (3)	12.0
Industry medians	**6.1**	**155.3**	**113.2**	
CONSUMER NONDURABLES—PERSONAL PRODUCTS				
1 Clorox	44.7	442.3 (1)	395.6 (1)	5.4
2 Duracell Intl	30.3	269.1 (4)	321.4 (3)	7.7
3 Procter & Gamble	28.6	352.0 (2)	284.4 (4)	84.1
4 Gillette	24.8	205.0 (8)	191.3 (8)	30.4
5 Estee Lauder Cos	14.3	312.6 (3)	184.5 (9)	9.9
6 Service Corp Intl	9.1	82.3 (11)	381.9 (2)	9.8
7 Avon Products	8.2	144.4 (9)	66.0 (11)	29.8
8 Colgate-Palmolive	4.6	224.1 (6)	204.9 (6)	24.8
9 James River Corp Va	4.2	223.7 (7)	238.8 (5)	34.4
10 Kimberly-Clark	0.6	243.7 (5)	202.2 (7)	56.6
11 Dial	0.0	114.0 (10)	134.7 (10)	29.3
Industry medians	**9.1**	**224.1**	**204.9**	
CONSUMER NONDURABLES—PHOTOGRAPHY & TOYS				
1 Mattel	15.2	154.8 (3)	114.7 (3)	11.8
2 Eastman Kodak	13.0	155.3 (2)	150.1 (2)	136.1
3 Hasbro	12.0	219.9 (1)	201.3 (1)	7.7
Industry medians	**13.0**	**155.3**	**150.1**	
CONSUMER NONDURABLES—WEARING APPAREL				
1 NIKE	35.8	418.6 (2)	255.8 (1)	4.3
2 Reebok International	24.5	518.5 (1)	246.6 (2)	3.1
3 Liz Claiborne	16.5	269.8 (3)	172.3 (3)	5.8
4 VF	2.4	76.7 (4)	52.2 (5)	42.4
5 Fruit of the Loom	–6.4	67.3 (5)	81.8 (4)	26.9
Industry medians	**16.5**	**269.8**	**172.3**	

Jobs and Productivity 500 Table *(Cont.)*

		PER EMPLOYEE ($000)		Employees
Rank Company	Profits	Sales (rank)	Assets (rank)	(000)
ELECTRIC UTILITIES—NORTH CENTRAL				
1 Ohio Edison	63.6	494.3 (1)	1,768.7 (1)	6.8
2 DPL	60.4	460.1 (2)	1,218.0 (8)	2.9
3 Kansas City P&L	52.5	379.1 (9)	1,233.4 (7)	2.9
4 Union Electric	50.4	337.6 (15)	1,084.5 (11)	7.1
5 Wisconsin Energy	50.2	380.1 (8)	979.1 (12)	5.7
6 DTE Energy	48.2	431.9 (4)	1,322.4 (4)	10.0
7 Western Resources	43.4	375.3 (11)	1,310.7 (5)	4.6
8 DQE	42.0	300.2 (16)	1,097.2 (10)	4.3
9 Nipsco Industries	39.9	391.5 (6)	909.2 (14)	4.7
10 Cinergy	39.7	347.0 (13)	941.0 (13)	5.3
11 Illinova	38.3	415.0 (5)	1,418.4 (3)	4.3
12 No States Power	36.4	341.1 (14)	821.4 (16)	7.5
13 Unicom	36.1	378.5 (10)	1,273.3 (6)	18.4
14 MidAmerican Energy	32.9	433.4 (3)	1,137.4 (9)	4.0
15 Centerior Energy	32.5	370.3 (12)	1,566.8 (2)	8.8
16 American Electric	27.8	297.2 (17)	833.4 (15)	22.7
17 CMS Energy	20.4	388.1 (7)	812.5 (17)	9.6
Industry medians	**39.9**	**379.1**	**1,137.4**	
ELECTRIC UTILITIES—NORTHEAST				
1 PECO Energy	75.0	514.6 (3)	1,839.0 (2)	11.1
2 Pub Svc Enterprise	56.7	527.5 (2)	1,469.4 (4)	13.2
3 Long Island Lighting	52.1	528.6 (1)	2,145.8 (1)	6.4
4 New York State E&G	47.3	483.6 (4)	1,230.9 (6)	4.6
5 PP&L Resources	45.8	390.5 (11)	1,347.1 (5)	8.1
6 Consolidated Edison	43.2	390.2 (12)	832.7 (15)	19.6
7 General Public Utils	42.2	365.1 (13)	947.1 (12)	12.8
8 New England Electric	41.7	462.6 (5)	1,057.0 (9)	5.6
9 Allegheny Power	40.4	446.7 (6)	1,087.6 (8)	5.9
10 Baltimore G&E	40.3	349.8 (14)	991.3 (11)	9.2
11 Northeast Utilities	31.5	417.9 (9)	1,175.6 (7)	8.3
12 Boston Edison	28.7	415.5 (10)	929.8 (13)	4.7
13 Niagara Mohawk Pwr	27.6	435.1 (7)	1,052.7 (10)	11.7
14 American Water Work	23.7	206.6 (15)	876.0 (14)	4.0
15 Potomac Electric	20.2	418.9 (8)	1,523.6 (3)	5.2
Industry medians	**41.7**	**418.9**	**1,087.6**	
ELECTRIC UTILITIES—SOUTH CENTRAL				
1 Houston Industries	110.2	361.0 (6)	1,159.4 (4)	13.3
2 Southwestern PS	56.0	388.7 (5)	882.2 (6)	2.2
3 Central & So West	50.4	468.2 (2)	1,738.4 (2)	8.4
4 Oklahoma G&E	44.9	467.2 (3)	988.5 (5)	3.8

(Continued)

Jobs and Productivity 500 Table *(Cont.)*

Rank Company	Profits	PER EMPLOYEE ($000) Sales (rank)	Assets (rank)	Employees (000)
ELECTRIC UTILITIES—SOUTH CENTRAL				
5 Entergy	33.5	434.3 (4)	1,541.1 (3)	13.3
6 Texas Utilities	−12.3	500.6 (1)	1,911.9 (1)	15.2
Industry medians	**47.7**	**450.8**	**1,350.3**	
ELECTRIC UTILITIES—SOUTHEAST				
1 Carolina Power & Lt	49.5	399.1 (4)	1,092.1 (2)	8.1
2 FPL Group	47.1	476.2 (1)	1,060.9 (3)	19.0
3 TECO Energy	42.2	315.6 (5)	787.3 (7)	4.5
4 Duke Power	41.8	273.7 (8)	781.8 (8)	19.7
5 Dominion Resources	39.8	435.1 (2)	1,300.5 (1)	13.1
6 Scana	37.7	303.3 (6)	1,016.5 (4)	4.4
7 Southern Co	36.3	302.2 (7)	1,005.7 (5)	30.4
8 Florida Progress	32.8	419.5 (3)	795.0 (6)	7.7
Industry medians	**40.8**	**357.4**	**1,011.1**	
ELECTRIC UTILITIES—WEST				
1 Pacific G&E	63.8	458.2 (3)	1,278.6 (5)	26.2
2 Puget Sound P&L	62.1	539.7 (1)	1,496.1 (2)	2.5
3 Enova	53.8	431.2 (4)	1,076.6 (7)	4.2
4 Edison International	45.3	514.9 (2)	1,466.9 (3)	17.0
5 PacifiCorp	39.6	266.8 (8)	1,099.4 (6)	16.0
6 Public Service Colo	36.0	424.8 (5)	876.5 (9)	6.6
7 Portland General	31.8	385.9 (6)	1,352.7 (4)	3.5
8 Pinnacle West	27.9	233.2 (9)	977.2 (8)	8.4
9 Hawaiian Electric	22.9	382.8 (7)	1,655.5 (1)	3.2
Industry medians	**39.6**	**424.8**	**1,278.6**	
ENERGY—INTEGRATED GAS				
1 NGC	89.6	3,542.0 (1)	1,838.1 (1)	1.0
2 Pacific Enterprises	22.6	286.4 (4)	642.9 (3)	43.1
3 NorAm Energy	9.6	436.0 (3)	539.1 (5)	6.8
4 Consol Natural Gas	3.0	466.9 (2)	765.0 (2)	7.5
5 Columbia Gas System	−43.4	264.6 (5)	608.1 (4)	10.8
Industry medians	**9.6**	**436.0**	**642.9**	
ENERGY—INTERNATIONAL OILS				
1 Exxon	77.0	1,284.4 (1)	1,086.9 (1)	104.0
2 Mobil	43.6	1,189.5 (3)	773.9 (3)	67.6
3 Amoco	43.4	630.2 (5)	694.9 (5)	54.1
4 Texaco	25.1	1,228.0 (2)	861.4 (2)	38.1
5 Chevron	21.0	705.6 (4)	773.4 (4)	54.5
Industry medians	**43.4**	**1,189.5**	**773.9**	

Jobs and Productivity 500 Table *(Cont.)*

Rank Company	Profits	PER EMPLOYEE ($000) Sales (rank)	Assets (rank)	Employees (000)
ENERGY—OILFIELD SERVICES				
1 Baker Hughes	8.6	182.3 (2)	215.6 (1)	21.5
2 Dresser Industries	7.3	190.4 (1)	152.4 (3)	32.3
3 Western Atlas	7.0	155.1 (3)	173.5 (2)	13.6
4 Halliburton	4.1	100.2 (4)	64.1 (4)	71.2
Industry medians	**7.2**	**168.7**	**163.0**	
ENERGY—OTHER ENERGY				
1 Oryx Energy	131.7	845.0 (5)	1,388.3 (4)	2.8
2 Atlantic Richfield	60.9	700.0 (8)	1,061.9 (5)	27.0
3 Fina	38.2	1,320.1 (3)	910.6 (7)	3.8
4 Valero Energy	36.0	1,819.2 (2)	1,732.9 (3)	1.8
5 Occidental Petroleum	27.7	564.3 (12)	964.5 (6)	54.5
6 Phillips Petroleum	26.2	746.8 (7)	669.2 (13)	22.1
7 Tosco	22.0	2,081.2 (1)	571.4 (14)	1.7
8 Unocal	20.3	564.4 (11)	771.6 (10)	17.4
9 Anadarko Petroleum	19.5	401.5 (17)	2,097.2 (2)	0.8
10 UtiliCorp United	17.0	595.4 (10)	826.8 (8)	4.7
11 Sun Co	16.5	606.7 (9)	375.8 (17)	21.3
12 Ultramar	16.4	934.4 (4)	678.6 (12)	3.0
13 Mapco	12.2	514.3 (14)	374.2 (18)	6.2
14 Diamond Shamrock	7.5	467.3 (16)	357.3 (19)	5.1
15 Ashland	2.4	357.0 (19)	218.5 (20)	35.6
16 USX-Marathon	−3.9	531.2 (13)	481.0 (15)	21.0
17 Kerr-McGee	−6.6	379.2 (18)	680.4 (11)	7.3
18 Pennzoil	−30.1	235.5 (20)	425.2 (16)	11.2
19 Amerada Hess	−41.2	762.7 (6)	810.1 (9)	9.6
20 Burlington Resources	−153.6	479.1 (15)	2,287.1 (1)	5.1
Industry medians	**16.8**	**579.9**	**726.0**	
ENERGY—OTHER GAS				
1 Williams Cos	145.3	314.7 (5)	1,156.6 (4)	4.3
2 Sonat	96.3	993.6 (2)	1,753.1 (2)	5.2
3 Enron	74.2	1,312.7 (1)	1,891.3 (1)	6.6
4 Panhandle Eastern	58.1	950.2 (3)	1,458.9 (3)	6.0
5 Coastal	17.0	657.1 (4)	670.4 (5)	13.5
Industry medians	**74.2**	**950.2**	**1,458.9**	
ENTERTAINMENT & INFORMATION—ADVERTISING & PUBLISHING				
1 Reader's Digest Assn	38.8	508.3 (1)	342.1 (1)	7.4
2 Washington Post	27.7	250.1 (2)	252.1 (4)	6.2
3 Tribune	26.5	213.8 (4)	313.2 (2)	16.6
4 Dow Jones	17.6	212.5 (5)	241.8 (5)	9.7

(Continued)

Jobs and Productivity 500 Table *(Cont.)*

Rank Company	Profits	PER EMPLOYEE ($000) Sales (rank)	Assets (rank)	Employees (000)
ENTERTAINMENT & INFORMATION—ADVERTISING & PUBLISHING				
5 EW Scripps	16.1	124.1 (12)	199.5 (10)	10.0
6 McGraw-Hill Cos	14.8	190.7 (7)	201.6 (8)	13.8
7 Gannett	14.7	123.1 (13)	199.8 (9)	36.7
8 Harcourt General	12.6	222.2 (3)	222.9 (7)	24.9
9 New York Times	10.8	192.0 (6)	269.1 (3)	10.5
10 Knight-Ridder	8.0	131.2 (10)	143.3 (13)	21.1
11 Omnicom Group	7.9	127.2 (11)	198.7 (11)	15.3
12 RR Donnelley & Sons	7.5	164.0 (8)	135.6 (14)	26.8
13 Interpublic Group	6.9	115.3 (14)	225.4 (6)	15.8
14 Dun & Bradstreet	6.6	112.1 (15)	114.2 (15)	68.3
15 Times Mirror	−17.1	149.3 (9)	165.3 (12)	29.1
Industry medians	**12.6**	**164.0**	**201.6**	
ENTERTAINMENT & INFORMATION—BROADCASTING & MOVIES				
1 King World Prods	309.5	1,370.3 (2)	1,716.6 (2)	0.4
2 Walt Disney	20.5	178.4 (9)	224.6 (11)	49.5
3 Turner Broadcasting	17.1	572.9 (3)	732.6 (6)	3.6
4 Gaylord Entertain	16.9	110.1 (12)	170.6 (12)	6.2
5 Cox Communications	15.2	199.6 (8)	834.7 (4)	6.7
6 U S West Media	14.3	233.6 (6)	847.7 (3)	10.2
7 Viacom	4.1	213.6 (7)	530.4 (8)	5.0
8 Tele-Com-TCI	−0.8	156.9 (10)	684.4 (7)	32.0
9 Time Warner	−2.1	135.8 (11)	372.6 (10)	38.1
10 Comcast	−3.2	285.0 (4)	811.9 (5)	3.1
11 Tele-Com-Liberty	−4.1	234.9 (5)	442.7 (9)	6.1
12 US Satellite Broad	−1,251.8	1,478.4 (1)	2,048.9 (1)	0.1
Industry medians	**9.2**	**223.6**	**708.5**	
FINANCIAL SERVICES—BROKERAGE				
1 Morgan Stanley	64.6	1,145.2 (2)	15,247.5 (3)	6.9
2 Quick & Reilly Group	61.9	450.0 (6)	3,626.8 (6)	0.9
3 Salomon	52.5	1,026.2 (3)	21,646.0 (1)	8.9
4 Bear Stearns Cos	49.6	585.9 (4)	11,498.3 (4)	5.8
5 Lehman Bros Holding	37.3	1,770.5 (1)	15,993.1 (2)	8.9
6 Merrill Lynch	24.8	479.1 (5)	3,938.9 (5)	40.0
7 Charles Schwab	22.0	226.4 (8)	1,344.2 (8)	2.9
8 Marsh & McLennan	15.1	141.5 (9)	162.5 (10)	24.0
9 AG Edwards	14.1	122.8 (10)	233.3 (9)	10.4
10 PaineWebber Group	5.0	330.7 (7)	2,838.7 (7)	12.8
Industry medians	**31.1**	**464.6**	**3,782.9**	
FINANCIAL SERVICES—LEASE & FINANCE				
1 MBIA	743.6	1,266.4 (3)	19,910.8 (3)	0.2

Jobs and Productivity 500 Table (Cont.)

Rank Company	Profits	PER EMPLOYEE ($000) Sales (rank)	Assets (rank)	Employees (000)
FINANCIAL SERVICES—LEASE & FINANCE				
2 Federal Natl Mort	634.0	6,543.8 (1)	93,102.9 (1)	2.5
3 Ambac	378.3	687.0 (6)	11,984.8 (4)	0.5
4 Federal Home Loan	335.7	2,928.9 (2)	42,209.5 (2)	2.0
5 MGIC Investment	203.7	606.4 (7)	1,839.8 (12)	1.1
6 Finova Group	105.3	843.1 (4)	7,590.6 (6)	0.8
7 Green Tree Financial	104.3	275.8 (13)	978.7 (18)	1.9
8 First USA	79.0	486.9 (8)	2,748.2 (7)	1.8
9 Sallie Mae	75.2	804.4 (5)	10,269.4 (5)	2.3
10 Mercury Finance	67.6	212.3 (18)	1,003.6 (17)	1.4
11 Advanta	65.7	375.8 (9)	2,174.1 (10)	1.7
12 Franklin Resources	65.0	199.2 (20)	516.5 (20)	1.9
13 Countrywide Credit	51.5	338.3 (12)	2,279.5 (9)	4.1
14 Travelers Group	36.7	352.5 (11)	2,289.5 (8)	23.5
15 MBNA	34.9	253.4 (16)	1,306.6 (15)	8.3
16 Household Intl	31.7	359.7 (10)	2,043.0 (11)	14.6
17 Dean Witter Discover	28.9	268.1 (15)	1,290.9 (16)	26.0
18 American Express	21.9	230.4 (17)	1,504.7 (14)	107.2
19 Beneficial	17.2	274.1 (14)	1,793.5 (13)	7.5
19 GATX	17.2	210.8 (19)	691.1 (19)	3.9
Industry medians	**66.7**	**356.1**	**2,108.6**	
FINANCIAL SERVICES—MULTINATIONAL BANKS				
1 JP Morgan & Co	79.3	847.2 (1)	11,318.7 (1)	13.6
2 Republic New York	55.6	550.4 (3)	8,446.9 (2)	4.1
3 Citicorp	41.3	377.5 (4)	3,059.6 (6)	93.5
4 Chase Manhattan	39.5	348.8 (5)	4,043.8 (4)	75.2
5 BankAmerica	32.9	251.7 (8)	2,869.7 (7)	55.6
6 First Chicago NBD	32.5	301.7 (6)	3,446.7 (5)	35.4
7 Bank of Boston	29.9	298.6 (7)	2,616.0 (8)	18.1
8 Bankers Trust NY	15.0	581.1 (2)	7,273.4 (3)	13.6
Industry medians	**36.2**	**363.2**	**3,745.3**	
FINANCIAL SERVICES—REGIONAL BANKS				
1 North Fork Bancorp	60.6	294.3 (7)	3,832.1 (5)	0.9
2 Bank of New York	59.2	344.8 (4)	3,476.8 (9)	14.4
3 Collective Bncp	55.1	383.3 (3)	5,238.9 (3)	0.9
4 Riggs National	54.9	233.0 (28)	2,957.8 (17)	2.4
5 Wells Fargo	52.9	268.8 (12)	2,577.7 (36)	20.7
6 Fifth Third Bancorp	49.0	251.7 (17)	2,902.1 (20)	4.0
7 Valley Natl Bancorp	48.2	259.9 (15)	3,530.3 (8)	1.3
8 Provident Bncp	43.8	316.7 (6)	3,783.8 (6)	1.5
9 First Bank System	42.9	249.2 (18)	2,560.2 (37)	9.5

(Continued)

Jobs and Productivity 500 Table *(Cont.)*

Rank Company	Profits	Per Employee ($000) Sales (rank)	Assets (rank)	Employees (000)
FINANCIAL SERVICES—REGIONAL BANKS				
10 Natl Commerce Bncp	42.5	260.3 (14)	3,201.9 (12)	1.1
11 City National	42.1	217.4 (40)	3,584.1 (7)	2.3
12 Wilmington Trust	38.8	217.9 (38)	2,317.6 (47)	1.9
13 Wachovia	38.1	237.7 (25)	2,847.1 (22)	13.7
14 First Financial	38.0	274.4 (10)	3,252.7 (11)	1.6
14 Roosevelt Finl Group	38.0	524.0 (1)	7,593.1 (1)	1.2
16 Mercantile Bkshs	36.9	196.4 (51)	2,245.1 (51)	2.7
17 Hibernia	36.5	181.4 (67)	2,122.8 (66)	3.4
18 Star Banc	36.1	224.5 (34)	2,533.3 (39)	3.6
19 Northern Trust	33.6	272.2 (11)	3,044.2 (15)	5.8
20 Mercantile Bancorp	33.0	213.0 (45)	2,427.2 (42)	4.4
21 NationsBank	32.9	275.5 (9)	3,160.5 (13)	27.7
22 First Interstate Bncp	32.4	176.9 (74)	2,127.4 (63)	35.5
23 First Union	32.0	236.8 (26)	2,951.4 (18)	44.7
24 Comerica	31.9	239.9 (23)	2,733.3 (29)	6.7
25 Summit Bancorp	31.7	224.6 (32)	2,812.7 (24)	6.4
26 CoreStates Financial	31.5	200.0 (49)	2,066.0 (72)	13.1
26 OnBancorp	31.5	325.2 (5)	3,928.8 (4)	1.5
28 Huntington Bancshs	31.1	217.8 (39)	2,579.5 (35)	6.0
29 Signet Banking	30.8	263.2 (13)	2,531.1 (40)	6.4
30 First American	30.1	213.3 (44)	2,828.4 (23)	3.7
30 First Empire State	30.1	247.9 (19)	2,749.7 (27)	2.7
32 CCB Financial	29.8	224.6 (32)	2,623.6 (34)	1.6
33 Central Fidelity Bks	29.3	236.6 (27)	3,006.4 (16)	3.2
33 Centura Banks	29.3	222.0 (36)	2,690.1 (32)	1.9
33 Union Bank	29.3	219.0 (37)	2,758.0 (26)	7.3
33 Zions Bancorp	29.3	186.4 (61)	2,025.5 (75)	2.1
37 SunTrust Banks	29.1	192.7 (54)	2,394.0 (43)	19.9
38 AmSouth Bancorp	28.8	247.6 (20)	2,915.2 (19)	5.1
39 Bancorp Hawaii	28.5	244.2 (21)	3,092.2 (14)	3.9
40 Mellon Bank	28.4	185.8 (62)	1,672.7 (91)	16.5
41 Regions Financial	28.1	191.7 (55)	2,232.7 (53)	4.1
42 Dauphin Deposit	27.8	184.5 (63)	2,244.6 (52)	1.7
43 Fulton Financial	27.7	160.7 (88)	2,023.5 (76)	1.5
44 Old Kent Financial	27.6	213.6 (43)	2,338.9 (45)	4.6
45 Barnett Banks	27.3	188.2 (58)	2,125.3 (64)	18.2
46 Compass Bancshares	27.2	209.6 (46)	2,533.9 (38)	2.5
47 BOK Financial	27.0	201.2 (48)	2,317.2 (48)	1.8
47 Trustmark	27.0	184.5 (63)	2,259.1 (49)	2.0
49 KeyCorp	26.9	206.0 (47)	2,257.4 (50)	9.0
50 Banc One	26.7	187.5 (59)	1,890.4 (83)	18.6
50 Crestar Financial	26.7	226.5 (31)	2,719.6 (30)	6.0
50 Meridian Bancorp	26.7	215.0 (42)	2,320.8 (46)	5.8

Jobs and Productivity 500 Table *(Cont.)*

Rank Company	Profits	Per employee ($000) Sales (rank)	Assets (rank)	Employees (000)
FINANCIAL SERVICES—REGIONAL BANKS				
53 Keystone Finl	26.5	178.9 (70)	2,192.1 (55)	2.3
54 Associated Banc-Cp	26.3	178.9 (70)	2,084.5 (68)	1.7
55 SouthTrust	26.2	223.2 (35)	2,740.5 (28)	4.6
56 Deposit Guaranty	25.9	176.4 (75)	2,149.1 (60)	2.4
57 First Hawaiian	25.5	217.2 (41)	2,509.0 (41)	2.3
57 Union Planters	25.5	187.3 (60)	2,123.8 (65)	2.5
59 United Carolina Bcsh	25.4	190.2 (56)	2,178.2 (57)	1.8
60 Integra Financial	25.0	237.8 (24)	2,795.4 (25)	4.0
61 One Valley Bncp WV	24.9	162.2 (87)	1,955.5 (80)	2.0
62 Boatmen's Bancshs	24.5	175.3 (76)	1,971.7 (79)	8.4
63 Marshall & Ilsley	24.1	168.0 (81)	1,662.1 (92)	6.0
64 BayBanks	23.9	177.4 (72)	2,100.9 (67)	5.7
64 Firstar	23.9	181.6 (66)	2,001.1 (77)	6.8
66 Cullen/Frost Bankers	23.8	177.1 (73)	2,163.9 (58)	1.8
67 First Tennessee Natl	23.7	189.2 (57)	1,732.2 (88)	3.9
68 Old National Bncp	23.6	180.2 (68)	2,203.1 (54)	1.9
69 Commerce Bancshs	23.3	165.2 (85)	2,069.1 (71)	3.7
70 Norwest	23.2	184.4 (65)	1,754.3 (87)	18.2
71 Southern National	23.1	230.5 (29)	2,661.4 (33)	2.2
72 First Natl Nebraska	22.6	228.3 (30)	1,682.9 (90)	3.2
72 National City	22.6	168.0 (81)	1,762.6 (86)	15.5
74 First Virginia Banks	22.3	132.8 (94)	1,646.0 (93)	4.5
74 US Bancorp	22.3	198.0 (50)	2,157.7 (59)	9.8
76 Colonial BancGroup	22.2	172.6 (78)	2,136.1 (61)	1.7
77 Magna Group	22.1	170.2 (80)	2,131.6 (62)	2.4
78 First Commercial	21.7	150.9 (91)	2,042.3 (74)	2.3
79 CNB Bancshares	21.5	193.4 (53)	2,189.9 (56)	1.7
80 Citizens Bncp	21.0	174.6 (77)	2,347.3 (44)	1.9
81 BancorpSouth	20.8	166.6 (84)	1,938.9 (82)	1.7
82 State Street Boston	19.8	196.3 (52)	2,069.3 (70)	7.9
83 Fleet Finl Group	19.6	253.6 (16)	2,719.2 (31)	31.1
84 BanPonce	19.2	168.0 (81)	2,058.5 (73)	7.0
85 Synovus Finl	18.8	156.9 (90)	1,300.5 (95)	5.0
86 First of America Bk	18.1	163.5 (86)	1,801.4 (85)	10.1
87 Citizens Banking	17.8	146.6 (93)	1,834.7 (84)	1.7
88 First Commerce	17.7	172.0 (79)	1,986.7 (78)	2.6
89 PNC Bank	16.1	240.5 (22)	2,889.9 (21)	18.1
90 First Security	15.8	157.5 (89)	1,720.5 (89)	4.5
91 First Citizens Bcshs	15.0	148.8 (92)	1,950.3 (81)	3.6
92 Charter One Finl	14.1	473.8 (2)	5,636.7 (2)	2.4
93 UMB Financial	13.4	128.6 (95)	1,612.3 (94)	2.8
94 FirstMerit	9.5	179.4 (69)	2,069.7 (69)	2.3

(Continued)

Jobs and Productivity 500 Table *(Cont.)*

Rank Company	Profits	PER EMPLOYEE ($000) Sales (rank)	Assets (rank)	Employees (000)
FINANCIAL SERVICES—REGIONAL BANKS				
95 Sumitomo Bank Calif	−72.7	282.6 (8)	3,301.1 (10)	1.7
Industry medians	**27.0**	**201.2**	**2,317.2**	
FINANCIAL SERVICES—THRIFT INSTITUTIONS				
1 Washington Federal	141.6	674.4 (1)	8,805.1 (1)	0.5
2 GreenPoint Financial	63.0	429.3 (10)	8,599.3 (2)	1.4
3 Golden West Finl	56.2	592.0 (3)	8,417.6 (4)	2.7
4 Astoria Financial	53.2	521.0 (4)	7,761.0 (5)	0.9
5 HF Ahmanson	52.9	515.4 (5)	5,922.4 (9)	10.8
6 Washington Mutual	43.6	372.1 (15)	4,952.7 (15)	2.0
7 Sovereign Bancorp	43.3	397.9 (13)	6,195.0 (8)	1.1
8 Commercial Federal	42.7	437.3 (9)	5,763.9 (10)	1.0
9 Cal Fed Bancorp	42.5	487.0 (6)	6,509.4 (7)	5.3
10 Standard Federal	40.8	338.3 (16)	4,532.5 (16)	2.3
11 Long Island Bancorp	37.1	304.9 (17)	4,105.6 (17)	1.2
12 St Paul Bancorp	33.6	288.8 (18)	3,804.7 (18)	1.0
13 People's Bank	29.2	250.2 (19)	2,823.8 (21)	2.5
14 RCSB Financial	25.6	217.6 (22)	2,622.9 (22)	1.6
15 Downey Financial	23.4	376.1 (14)	5,162.2 (14)	1.0
16 Glendale Federal Bk	22.1	446.5 (8)	5,761.6 (11)	6.2
17 Dime Bancorp	21.2	484.8 (7)	6,923.2 (6)	3.5
18 Coast Savings Finl	20.9	426.4 (11)	5,245.8 (12)	2.0
19 Center Financial	17.9	225.6 (21)	2,832.6 (20)	1.3
20 Great Western Finl	17.4	237.5 (20)	2,968.7 (19)	13.4
21 TCF Financial	14.8	177.4 (23)	1,734.5 (23)	2.4
22 FirstFed Financial	13.5	642.8 (2)	8,570.9 (3)	0.3
23 Fidelity Federal Bank	−109.0	399.6 (12)	5,212.4 (13)	0.6
Industry medians	**33.6**	**399.6**	**5,245.8**	
FOOD DISTRIBUTORS—FOOD WHOLESALERS				
1 Richfood Holdings	12.7	1,157.5 (1)	205.0 (1)	2.7
2 Sysco	9.5	452.7 (2)	117.8 (2)	19.2
3 Supervalu	3.7	380.0 (4)	99.7 (4)	40.4
4 Nash Finch	1.9	307.3 (5)	54.7 (5)	11.1
5 Fleming Cos	1.0	419.7 (3)	103.0 (3)	22.9
Industry medians	**3.7**	**419.7**	**103.0**	
FOOD DISTRIBUTORS—RESTAURANT CHAINS				
1 McDonald's	7.2	49.6 (1)	78.0 (1)	177.0
2 Darden Restaurants	0.8	44.4 (2)	29.0 (2)	72.0
3 Flagstar Cos	−0.6	28.6 (3)	16.7 (3)	109.0
Industry medians	**0.8**	**44.4**	**29.0**	

Jobs and Productivity 500 Table *(Cont.)*

Rank Company	Profits	Per employee ($000) Sales (rank)	Assets (rank)	Employees (000)
FOOD DISTRIBUTORS—SUPERMARKETS & CONVENIENCE STORES				
1 Albertson's	7.4	200.8 (6)	66.0 (9)	56.5
2 Southland	6.5	224.9 (2)	80.4 (5)	31.4
3 Hannaford Bros	5.5	203.0 (5)	76.0 (6)	15.0
4 Giant Food	4.0	151.4 (11)	56.9 (11)	26.1
5 American Stores	3.7	216.2 (3)	86.9 (4)	167.1
6 Food Lion	3.6	172.0 (10)	55.4 (12)	44.0
7 Safeway	2.9	146.4 (12)	46.4 (14)	112.3
8 Winn-Dixie Stores	2.8	144.7 (13)	31.0 (15)	97.5
9 Vons Cos	2.3	174.9 (9)	75.4 (7)	34.5
10 Great A&P Tea	2.0	353.6 (1)	102.5 (2)	95.5
10 Stop & Shop Cos	2.0	122.9 (14)	66.1 (8)	30.5
12 Circle K	1.7	177.2 (7)	51.5 (13)	20.0
13 Kroger	1.6	122.1 (15)	25.7 (16)	170.0
14 Penn Traffic	−1.5	121.0 (16)	63.2 (10)	23.5
15 Smith's Food & Drug	−2.3	175.2 (8)	95.8 (3)	15.2
16 Grand Union	−14.1	208.9 (4)	112.4 (1)	11.2
Industry medians	**2.6**	**175.1**	**66.1**	
FOOD, DRINK & TOBACCO—BEVERAGES				
1 Coca-Cola	91.9	554.4 (1)	462.8 (1)	22.5
2 Anheuser-Busch Cos	37.0	431.0 (2)	410.0 (2)	46.0
3 Brown-Forman	22.6	218.8 (3)	192.4 (4)	5.5
4 Whitman	8.3	183.5 (5)	147.2 (5)	15.1
5 PepsiCo	3.4	64.0 (6)	53.5 (6)	287.0
6 Coca-Cola Enterprise	2.6	215.0 (4)	287.7 (3)	20.0
Industry medians	**15.5**	**216.9**	**240.1**	
FOOD, DRINK & TOBACCO—FOOD PROCESSORS				
1 Archer Daniels	54.6	874.4 (1)	717.3 (1)	11.0
2 Quaker Oats	41.8	344.2 (5)	278.8 (5)	30.0
3 General Mills	39.0	532.5 (2)	355.8 (2)	9.9
4 Pioneer Hi-Bred Intl	37.3	318.3 (6)	313.4 (3)	4.3
5 Kellogg	32.5	464.7 (3)	292.9 (4)	17.3
6 Wm Wrigley Jr	31.3	245.4 (11)	153.7 (9)	5.8
7 Hershey Foods	20.7	270.4 (10)	207.4 (6)	12.3
8 Campbell Soup	17.0	173.2 (16)	150.2 (11)	52.7
9 HJ Heinz	15.3	213.2 (13)	204.2 (7)	36.8
10 CPC International	10.8	178.6 (15)	158.9 (8)	34.2
11 Hormel Foods	10.5	302.5 (8)	122.8 (13)	8.2
12 Ralston Purina	8.9	181.7 (14)	150.5 (10)	56.2
13 IBP	8.8	395.9 (4)	63.4 (19)	29.5
14 ConAgra	5.9	271.3 (9)	145.0 (12)	75.0

(Continued)

Jobs and Productivity 500 Table *(Cont.)*

Rank Company	Profits	PER EMPLOYEE ($000) Sales (rank)	Assets (rank)	Employees (000)
FOOD, DRINK & TOBACCO—FOOD PROCESSORS				
15 Sara Lee	5.7	123.0 (17)	83.1 (16)	104.8
16 Dean Foods	5.3	234.3 (12)	116.6 (14)	8.2
17 Intl Multifoods	4.0	318.1 (7)	109.8 (15)	9.1
18 Tyson Foods	3.5	95.7 (18)	75.1 (17)	43.0
19 Dole Food	2.8	88.5 (19)	56.8 (20)	48.0
20 Chiquita Brands Intl	0.4	65.0 (20)	66.4 (18)	45.0
Industry medians	**10.7**	**257.9**	**150.4**	
FOOD, DRINK & TOBACCO—TOBACCO				
1 UST Inc	105.3	318.5 (3)	192.2 (5)	3.6
2 Loews	69.5	677.9 (1)	2,712.2 (1)	26.9
3 Philip Morris Cos	34.7	336.3 (2)	340.6 (3)	161.6
4 American Brands	17.6	191.1 (5)	259.6 (4)	48.2
5 RJR Nabisco	8.6	218.4 (4)	430.0 (2)	55.0
6 Universal	1.5	117.5 (6)	68.3 (6)	20.0
Industry medians	26.2	268.5	300.1	
FOREST PRODUCTS—PACKAGING				
1 Gaylord Container	34.5	259.5 (2)	233.3 (3)	4.1
2 Temple-Inland	18.5	227.7 (5)	839.7 (1)	12.9
3 Stone Container	16.2	267.3 (1)	232.7 (4)	32.3
4 Jefferson Smurfit	15.1	249.6 (3)	169.7 (6)	16.6
5 Sonoco Products	9.1	149.5 (7)	116.9 (8)	14.8
6 Owens-Illinois	6.0	133.5 (8)	191.5 (5)	27.8
7 Crown Cork & Seal	3.3	225.9 (6)	234.0 (2)	16.0
8 Ball	−1.6	229.9 (4)	143.0 (7)	13.4
Industry medians	**12.1**	**228.8**	**212.1**	
FOREST PRODUCTS—PAPER & LUMBER				
1 Rayonier	50.8	450.2 (1)	588.5 (1)	2.8
2 Bowater	44.9	348.0 (2)	505.8 (2)	5.1
3 Consolidated Papers	42.0	289.4 (8)	354.3 (4)	4.7
4 Willamette Inds	40.5	304.5 (5)	268.4 (10)	9.8
5 Champion Intl	31.7	286.1 (9)	391.6 (3)	29.1
6 Union Camp	24.3	226.7 (12)	260.5 (12)	19.9
7 Mead	22.4	331.0 (3)	279.4 (8)	21.7
8 Georgia-Pacific	21.5	302.5 (6)	261.1 (11)	59.8
9 Weyerhaeuser	21.0	309.8 (4)	348.3 (5)	42.9
10 Westvaco	20.8	230.4 (11)	302.4 (7)	15.0
11 Boise Cascade	20.4	294.7 (7)	270.4 (9)	19.7
12 International Paper	14.8	254.9 (10)	308.7 (6)	66.3
13 Louisiana-Pacific	−3.8	210.6 (13)	207.8 (13)	13.0
Industry medians	**22.4**	**294.7**	**302.4**	

Jobs and Productivity 500 Table *(Cont.)*

Rank Company	Profits	PER EMPLOYEE ($000) Sales (rank)	Assets (rank)	Employees (000)
HEALTH—DRUGS				
1 Amgen	140.4	506.5 (7)	635.2 (4)	0.6
2 Mylan Labs	89.0	308.8 (9)	462.7 (10)	1.2
3 Eli Lilly	88.6	261.7 (12)	557.5 (6)	29.1
4 Merck	72.0	359.9 (8)	514.2 (9)	35.7
5 ALZA	53.9	242.8 (14)	697.3 (3)	0.7
6 Genentech	52.5	307.3 (10)	720.8 (2)	1.8
7 Schering-Plough	43.2	249.0 (13)	227.5 (19)	20.5
8 Bristol-Myers Squibb	37.7	286.5 (11)	289.9 (17)	53.5
9 Pfizer	37.4	238.3 (15)	302.7 (15)	42.3
10 Abbott Laboratories	33.9	200.8 (18)	188.8 (21)	42.4
11 American Home Prod	24.1	191.8 (21)	306.3 (14)	50.5
12 Cardinal Health	22.6	2,045.1 (2)	525.4 (8)	3.4
13 Pharmacia & Upjohn	21.4	205.6 (17)	332.2 (13)	34.5
14 Warner-Lambert	20.3	192.9 (20)	167.2 (22)	34.4
15 Mallinckrodt Group	19.7	216.3 (16)	273.0 (18)	9.0
16 Bindley Western Inds	19.1	5,449.4 (1)	985.0 (1)	0.4
17 Bergen Brunswig	14.8	1,975.7 (3)	542.1 (7)	3.8
18 AmeriSource Health	14.5	1,928.9 (4)	405.8 (11)	2.5
19 IVAX	14.2	155.8 (23)	165.2 (23)	7.3
20 Rhone-Poulenc Rorer	13.5	194.0 (19)	339.1 (12)	16.0
21 McKesson	11.2	1,113.3 (6)	301.2 (16)	14.3
22 FoxMeyer Health	−3.8	1,904.2 (5)	570.5 (5)	5.3
23 Chiron	−74.3	159.6 (22)	216.2 (20)	0.6
Industry medians	**22.6**	**261.7**	**339.1**	
HEALTH—HEALTH CARE SERVICES				
1 US Healthcare	82.3	760.8 (4)	360.5 (4)	1.9
2 WellPoint Health	48.0	828.6 (3)	714.5 (1)	3.2
3 Health Systems Intl	32.6	993.5 (1)	441.3 (3)	2.6
4 PacifiCare Health	28.0	958.2 (2)	354.1 (5)	3.2
5 United HealthCare	20.5	395.1 (6)	445.6 (2)	8.2
6 Oxford Health Plans	17.6	593.4 (5)	204.6 (9)	3.0
7 Foundation Health	15.8	273.9 (10)	213.2 (8)	7.5
8 Humana	14.6	354.2 (7)	221.4 (6)	9.3
9 Healthsource	13.8	286.9 (9)	214.4 (7)	4.1
10 Tenet Healthcare	6.4	79.6 (13)	138.7 (12)	45.3
11 Columbia/HCA	4.7	78.1 (14)	87.8 (15)	140.5
12 Manor Care	4.3	51.3 (16)	65.6 (16)	23.0
13 HealthSouth	3.3	64.4 (15)	121.6 (14)	24.2
14 FHP International	1.8	309.3 (8)	180.8 (11)	14.0
15 Vencor	0.1	38.1 (18)	31.4 (17)	61.0
16 Beverly Enterprises	−0.1	39.1 (17)	30.4 (18)	94.0

(Continued)

Jobs and Productivity 500 Table *(Cont.)*

Rank Company	Profits	PER EMPLOYEE ($000) Sales (rank)	Assets (rank)	Employees (000)
HEALTH—HEALTH CARE SERVICES				
17 HBO & Co	–8.5	167.8 (12)	181.2 (10)	3.0
18 Caremark Intl	–11.5	235.7 (11)	125.5 (13)	8.5
Industry medians	**10.1**	**280.4**	**192.9**	
HEALTH—MEDICAL SUPPLIES				
1 St Jude Medical	56.7	317.1 (2)	445.2 (1)	0.5
2 Medtronic	37.4	195.3 (5)	208.4 (8)	6.5
3 Johnson & Johnson	29.3	230.1 (3)	218.2 (6)	82.7
4 Guidant	20.3	187.0 (7)	212.3 (7)	5.0
5 Pall	19.9	138.7 (12)	169.8 (10)	6.3
6 Stryker	19.7	197.1 (4)	193.2 (9)	3.7
7 Baxter International	19.1	148.7 (11)	278.0 (3)	64.7
8 Becton Dickinson	14.3	150.4 (10)	160.3 (11)	18.7
9 Allergan	13.3	195.1 (6)	240.6 (5)	6.6
10 Hillenbrand Inds	9.1	164.1 (8)	310.1 (2)	9.3
11 Boston Scientific	1.2	157.2 (9)	152.7 (12)	2.6
12 Corning	–1.2	126.5 (13)	142.6 (13)	28.1
13 Owens & Minor	–3.6	960.2 (1Ï)	276.7 (4)	2.1
Industry medians	**19.1**	**187.0**	**212.3**	
INSURANCE—DIVERSIFIED				
1 American Intl Group	74.9	772.4 (1)	4,004.1 (2)	33.3
2 Safeco	53.2	496.4 (3)	2,502.4 (3)	8.6
3 Lincoln National	50.1	689.3 (2)	6,573.6 (1)	16.7
4 Old Republic Intl	39.0	311.4 (7)	1,210.5 (7)	4.9
5 Horace Mann	30.8	308.6 (8)	1,525.9 (6)	2.5
6 Unitrin	20.2	194.0 (9)	646.0 (9)	8.2
7 Leucadia National	17.9	342.7 (6)	1,170.6 (8)	3.2
8 Aetna Life & Cas	7.2	371.8 (5)	2,415.7 (4)	46.3
9 Cigna	4.5	407.3 (4)	2,060.9 (5)	50.6
Industry medians	**30.8**	**371.8**	**2,060.9**	
INSURANCE—LIFE & HEALTH				
1 SunAmerica	186.0	975.9 (6)	15,516.8 (3)	1.0
2 Equitable of Iowa	176.5	1,590.1 (4)	20,333.5 (2)	4.8
3 First Colony	154.7	1,694.0 (3)	10,950.6 (5)	0.9
4 Aflac	86.5	1,782.1 (2)	6,279.6 (9)	3.1
5 Conseco	68.4	877.5 (7)	5,315.8 (12)	0.7
6 Protective Life	64.8	743.9 (12)	6,112.8 (10)	1.1
7 ReliaStar Financial	58.9	751.9 (11)	5,582.4 (11)	3.0
8 Jefferson-Pilot	57.0	326.8 (21)	3,430.8 (17)	4.1
9 Life USA Holding	54.4	777.2 (10)	11,018.6 (4)	0.4
10 USLife	50.2	828.4 (8)	3,776.4 (16)	2.1

Jobs and Productivity 500 Table *(Cont.)*

Rank Company	Profits	Per employee ($000) Sales (rank)	Assets (rank)	Employees (000)
INSURANCE—LIFE & HEALTH				
11 Torchmark	49.6	716.6 (13)	3,239.4 (18)	6.0
12 Liberty Financial Cos	48.0	667.0 (14)	8,284.2 (8)	1.5
13 Life Partners Group	47.6	993.6 (5)	9,428.9 (6)	0.5
14 American Natl Ins	45.2	322.2 (22)	1,564.1 (22)	7.5
15 Transamerica	44.4	575.6 (16)	4,523.1 (14)	16.9
16 UNUM	39.9	584.8 (15)	2,097.6 (21)	4.8
17 American General	38.6	460.5 (19)	4,335.5 (15)	12.4
18 Providian	38.3	375.8 (20)	2,976.8 (19)	9.0
19 Provident Cos	36.1	797.0 (9)	5,084.6 (13)	5.6
20 Western National	29.2	2,278.8 (1)	37,254.0 (1)	0.2
21 Equitable Cos	26.0	540.8 (17)	8,457.8 (7)	13.4
22 Aon	22.4	192.5 (23)	1,096.4 (23)	9.0
23 John Alden Financial	1.9	484.3 (18)	2,230.7 (20)	3.4
Industry medians	**48.0**	**743.9**	**5,315.8**	
INSURANCE—PROPERTY & CASUALTY				
1 Transatlantic Holding	501.4	4,430.3 (1)	14,825.0 (1)	0.3
2 General Re	249.2	2,177.7 (2)	10,856.6 (2)	2.4
3 Cincinnati Financial	103.3	752.6 (6)	2,777.0 (7)	1.7
4 Chubb	63.3	553.6 (10)	2,090.6 (11)	9.9
5 TIG Holdings	51.9	824.2 (5)	2,937.6 (6)	2.8
6 Allstate	42.0	503.1 (11)	1,545.8 (14)	45.3
7 Fremont General	41.7	566.1 (9)	2,743.5 (8)	1.5
8 St Paul Cos	41.4	429.3 (13)	1,560.0 (13)	12.2
9 USF&G	35.5	586.2 (8)	2,483.2 (10)	12.6
10 Progressive	32.3	388.4 (15)	690.3 (19)	6.2
11 Berkshire Hathaway	30.9	191.0 (20)	1,273.6 (16)	20.0
12 ITT Hartford Group	28.0	607.5 (7)	4,692.8 (5)	20.0
13 Ohio Casualty	25.8	378.5 (16)	1,030.1 (18)	5.2
14 American Finl Group	22.3	424.5 (14)	1,749.0 (12)	16.1
15 WR Berkley	22.0	368.9 (17)	1,306.4 (15)	2.5
16 Allmerica Financial	21.6	479.8 (12)	2,630.8 (9)	6.8
17 Reliance Group	10.2	324.0 (18)	1,113.5 (17)	9.1
18 Alleghany	9.2	192.0 (19)	443.4 (20)	5.5
19 Prudential Reinsur	1.4	1,731.5 (3)	8,537.1 (3)	0.5
20 American Re	−72.7	1,497.8 (4)	6,512.0 (4)	1.2
Industry medians	**31.6**	**528.4**	**2,286.9**	
METALS—NONFERROUS METALS				
1 Phelps Dodge	48.4	271.4 (5)	301.3 (7)	13.7
2 Newmont Mining	40.2	226.9 (8)	632.6 (3)	2.8
3 Freeport Copper	32.9	238.2 (7)	465.1 (5)	7.7

(Continued)

Jobs and Productivity 500 Table *(Cont.)*

Rank Company	Profits	PER EMPLOYEE ($000) Sales (rank)	Assets (rank)	Employees (000)
METALS—NONFERROUS METALS				
4 Engelhard	25.2	519.7 (1)	301.1 (8)	7.5
5 Asarco	22.3	420.8 (2)	569.3 (4)	9.2
6 Alumax	16.8	206.5 (10)	221.3 (10)	14.0
7 Homestake Mining	16.4	388.0 (3)	716.3 (1)	2.1
8 Reynolds Metals	13.1	243.7 (6)	261.5 (9)	30.8
9 Cyprus Amax Mineral	12.8	331.4 (4)	640.3 (2)	8.4
10 Alcoa	12.0	189.1 (11)	206.4 (11)	63.7
11 Maxxam	4.8	215.6 (9)	322.0 (6)	11.2
Industry medians	**16.8**	**243.7**	**322.0**	
METALS—STEEL				
1 AK Steel Holding	45.7	384.1 (3)	360.0 (3)	6.2
2 Nucor	45.4	572.2 (1)	379.5 (1)	5.5
3 USX-US Steel	14.5	309.7 (5)	312.8 (4)	21.3
4 LTV	12.4	288.4 (7)	362.3 (2)	36.7
5 National Steel	11.0	307.5 (6)	277.7 (6)	9.6
6 Inland Steel Inds	9.5	310.3 (4)	230.9 (7)	20.2
7 Bethlehem Steel	9.2	249.6 (8)	292.3 (5)	29.6
8 Commercial Metals	8.0	428.5 (2)	146.5 (8)	5.3
Industry medians	**11.7**	**310.0**	**302.6**	
RETAILING—APPAREL				
1 Limited	15.0	122.7 (2)	82.0 (2)	65.5
2 Gap	6.2	76.4 (5)	40.7 (5)	24.5
3 Nordstrom	4.7	117.5 (3)	82.8 (1)	29.0
4 TJX Cos	0.6	92.7 (4)	57.2 (4)	25.0
5 Melville	−9.6	151.2 (1)	61.8 (3)	110.1
Industry medians	**4.7**	**117.5**	**61.8**	
RETAILING—CONSUMER ELECTRONICS				
1 Circuit City Stores	5.8	215.7 (5)	101.6 (5)	14.0
2 CompUSA	5.5	435.8 (3)	122.6 (4)	7.2
3 Tandy	4.8	131.5 (6)	61.3 (6)	3.9
4 Best Buy	3.0	355.2 (4)	148.7 (3)	15.2
5 MicroAge	−0.6	1,596.2 (2)	305.2 (2)	1.4
6 Intelligent Electron	−16.3	2,990.2 (1)	769.6 (1)	0.7
Industry medians	**3.9**	**395.5**	**135.7**	
RETAILING—DEPARTMENT STORES				
1 May Dept Stores	8.2	119.7 (6)	110.6 (4)	115.5
2 Mercantile Stores	6.5	155.0 (3)	109.2 (5)	23.5
3 Kohl's	6.4	169.7 (1)	70.9 (7)	11.4
4 Dillard Dept Stores	4.4	156.4 (2)	126.3 (1)	31.8

Jobs and Productivity 500 Table *(Cont.)*

Rank Company	Profits	PER EMPLOYEE ($000) Sales (rank)	Assets (rank)	Employees (000)
RETAILING—DEPARTMENT STORES				
5 JC Penney	4.1	105.3 (7)	84.0 (6)	197.0
6 Sears, Roebuck	3.7	127.0 (5)	120.5 (3)	480.0
7 Federated Dept Strs	0.6	130.4 (4)	123.9 (2)	89.5
Industry medians	**4.4**	**130.4**	**110.6**	
RETAILING—DRUG & DISCOUNT				
1 Walgreen	5.1	164.3 (2)	54.0 (7)	47.8
2 Rite Aid	4.2	146.3 (6)	76.1 (2)	30.0
2 Wal-Mart Stores	4.2	144.4 (7)	58.4 (6)	299.0
4 Eckerd	2.9	147.0 (5)	47.4 (10)	32.8
4 Longs Drug Stores	2.9	167.4 (1)	54.0 (7)	14.7
6 Revco DS	2.4	157.3 (3)	70.7 (3)	18.0
7 Dayton Hudson	1.5	115.3 (10)	61.6 (5)	157.0
8 Fred Meyer	1.1	127.0 (8)	61.9 (4)	21.4
9 Caldor	0.0	153.6 (4)	78.6 (1)	18.0
10 Kmart	−1.7	115.5 (9)	51.3 (9)	369.0
11 Woolworth	−1.9	95.1 (11)	40.5 (11)	140.0
Industry medians	**2.4**	**146.3**	**58.4**	
RETAILING—HOME IMPROVEMENT				
1 Home Depot	11.9	252.4 (1)	120.0 (1)	22.3
2 Lowe's Cos	5.5	172.4 (4)	86.6 (2)	15.4
3 Waban	4.2	231.4 (2)	77.5 (4)	12.8
4 Hechinger	−6.0	173.3 (3)	84.6 (3)	10.0
5 Payless Cashways	−7.2	145.1 (5)	73.6 (5)	18.3
Industry medians	**4.2**	**173.3**	**84.6**	
RETAILING—HOME SHOPPING				
1 CUC International	16.3	141.5 (3)	114.1 (2)	7.3
2 Service Merchandise	1.8	144.5 (2)	69.8 (3)	21.5
3 Spiegel	−0.7	225.8 (1)	161.3 (1)	11.2
Industry medians	**1.8**	**144.5**	**114.1**	
RETAILING—SPECIALTY RETAILERS				
1 AutoZone	9.4	122.6 (6)	81.5 (6)	17.4
2 Staples	8.9	372.3 (2)	170.2 (1)	9.6
3 OfficeMax	8.7	175.0 (4)	109.3 (5)	14.5
4 General Nutrition Cos	8.1	99.1 (7)	80.4 (7)	8.5
5 Price/Costco	6.1	511.3 (1)	132.7 (3)	33.8
6 Office Depot	6.0	241.8 (3)	115.2 (4)	18.8
7 Toys 'R' Us	2.6	165.5 (5)	148.1 (2)	38.0
Industry medians	**8.1**	**175.0**	**115.2**	

(Continued)

Jobs and Productivity 500 Table *(Cont.)*

Rank Company	Profits	PER EMPLOYEE ($000) Sales (rank)	Assets (rank)	Employees (000)
TRAVEL & TRANSPORT—AIRLINES				
1 Southwest Airlines	9.9	156.3 (6)	177.2 (4)	8.3
2 Delta Air Lines	8.4	201.8 (2)	197.7 (1)	60.3
3 Northwest Airlines	7.7	204.6 (1)	189.5 (2)	43.8
4 Continental Airlines	6.6	172.8 (4)	143.1 (7)	38.3
5 UAL	4.9	195.5 (3)	153.5 (6)	74.0
6 Federal Express	3.0	106.2 (9)	71.0 (9)	80.9
7 USAir Group	2.7	170.8 (5)	159.0 (5)	51.8
8 AMR	1.8	153.7 (7)	178.2 (3)	92.9
9 Trans World Airlines	−10.0	145.5 (8)	129.5 (8)	22.8
Industry medians	**4.9**	**170.8**	**159.0**	
TRAVEL & TRANSPORT—HOTELS & GAMING				
1 HFS	39.2	203.2 (2)	567.6 (2)	2.0
2 Mirage	11.6	90.8 (4)	122.3 (4)	15.7
3 Circus Circus	6.7	67.6 (6)	115.1 (5)	11.3
4 ITT	4.7	201.5 (3)	274.0 (3)	31.5
5 Harrah's Entertain	4.1	80.9 (5)	85.4 (6)	26.9
6 Hilton Hotels	3.6	33.1 (8)	63.8 (7)	38.5
7 Marriott Intl	1.4	52.3 (7)	23.4 (8)	164.7
8 Host Marriott	−77.5	605.0 (1)	4,446.3 (1)	219.5
Industry medians	**4.4**	**85.9**	**118.7**	
TRAVEL & TRANSPORT—RAILROAD				
1 Illinois Central	39.8	197.5 (2)	430.9 (2)	3.3
2 Kansas City Southern	38.5	126.0 (8)	331.6 (6)	7.8
3 Norfolk Southern	26.4	172.7 (4)	403.4 (3)	32.0
4 Union Pacific	19.1	151.2 (7)	392.8 (4)	48.3
5 CSX	13.0	221.8 (1)	301.6 (7)	51.4
6 Conrail	11.2	156.8 (6)	358.3 (5)	27.8
7 Burlington Santa Fe	5.6	179.5 (3)	530.4 (1)	32.9
8 Southern Pacific Rail	−0.2	169.9 (5)	256.0 (8)	18.5
Industry medians	**16.1**	**171.3**	**375.6**	
TRAVEL & TRANSPORT—SHIPPING				
1 American President	5.7	546.4 (1)	354.5 (1)	4.9
2 Ryder System	3.5	118.0 (3)	134.6 (2)	41.3
3 Consol Freightways	1.4	128.7 (2)	67.0 (3)	41.1
4 Roadway Express	−0.5	86.4 (6)	26.9 (6)	26.5
5 Yellow	−0.9	87.3 (5)	41.0 (5)	28.9
6 Caliber System	−1.1	101.2 (4)	57.4 (4)	24.2
Industry medians	**0.5**	**109.6**	**62.2**	

CROSS-INDEX OF RANKINGS

This cross-index tells you where the 787 companies are to be found in the rankings for sales, profits, assets and market value.

Big companies are getting bigger. When the first Forbes 500s Directory came in 1969, it took $255 million to get on the sales list, $14 million for profits, $416 million for assets and $280 million for market value. Corresponding minimums for this year's rankings: $2.2 billion, $122 million, $3.3 billion and $2.3 billion. Back out inflation and you still have a near doubling of what it means to be big.

The ranking table that follows shows where to find a company on each of the four 500-company rankings. There are 275 companies that make all four of the lists. The other 512 appear three or fewer times.

Rankings 500 Table

| WHERE THEY RANK: 1995 | | | | | | | | |
Sales	Net profits	Assets	Market value	Company	Sales ($mil)	Net profits ($mil)	Assets ($mil)	Market value ($mil)
118	36	240	33	**Abbott Laboratories**	10,012	1,688.7	9,413	32,229
■	■	■	464	**Adobe Systems**	762	93.5	885	2,520
471	234	■	498	**Advanced Micro Devices**	2,430	300.5	3,031	2,328
■	459	409	■	**Advanta**	782	136.7	4,524	1,941
84	279	29	142	**Aetna Life & Casualty**	12,978	251.7	84,324	8,658
167	206	84	299	**Aflac**	7,191	349.1	25,338	4,342
■	482	■	■	**AGCO**	2,125	129.1	2,163	1,399
279	164	42	446	**HF Ahmanson**	4,398	450.9	50,530	2,619

■ Not on 500 list.

Continued

63

Rankings 500 Table *(Cont.)*

WHERE THEY RANK: 1995					Sales ($mil)	Net profits ($mil)	Assets ($mil)	Market value ($mil)
Sales	Net profits	Assets	Market value	Company				
302	196	326	193	Air Products & Chemicals	3,892	370.5	6,034	6,426
■	472	337	76	AirTouch Communications	1,619	131.9	5,648	15,089
498	263	■	■	AK Steel Holding	2,257	268.6	2,116	1,028
90	159	434	130	Albertson's	12,585	465.0	4,136	9,542
113	322	368	195	Alco Standard	10,272	218.7	5,142	6,362
■	■	436	■	Alleghany	1,785	85.3	4,123	1,394
444	291	309	353	Allegheny Power System	2,648	239.7	6,447	3,425
■	■	■	474	Allergan	1,067	72.5	1,316	2,452
67	79	190	71	AlliedSignal	14,346	875.0	12,465	15,906
364	438	127	■	Allmerica Financial	3,239	146.0	17,758	1,272
28	27	33	60	Allstate	22,793	1,904.0	70,029	18,513
381	200	374	220	Alltel	3,110	354.6	5,073	5,773
■	■	■	424	Altera	402	86.9	716	2,785
413	297	■	■	Alumax	2,926	237.4	3,135	1,562
92	88	173	110	Aluminum Co of America	12,500	790.5	13,643	10,679
■	■	■	443	ALZA	326	72.4	937	2,640
■	392	360	■	Ambac	304	167.6	5,309	1,639
161	■	272	258	Amerada Hess	7,302	−394.4	7,756	4,952
■	■	■	268	America Online	713	4.4	694	4,708
207	136	265	160	American Brands	5,905	543.1	8,021	7,793
218	141	142	162	American Electric Power	5,670	529.9	15,902	7,559
53	40	20	46	American Express	16,445	1,564.0	107,405	23,370
328	355	153	■	American Financial Group[1]	3,630	190.4	14,954	1,796
187	135	37	173	American General	6,495	544.9	61,153	7,263
80	37	106	35	American Home Products	13,376	1,680.4	21,363	30,939
23	18	14	20	American International Group	25,874	2,510.4	134,136	43,687
■	338	290	■	American National Insurance	1,471	206.4	7,140	1,801
417	■	■	■	American President Cos Ltd	2,896	30.3	1,879	549
■	■	270	■	American Re	1,797	−87.2	7,814	1,841
240	448	480	■	American Standard Cos	5,221	141.8	3,520	2,206
42	226	282	302	American Stores	18,309	316.8	7,363	4,320
■	■	491	■	American Water Works	803	92.1	3,403	1,285
262	■	■	■	AmeriSource Health	4,822	36.2	1,015	698
77	25	101	37	Ameritech	13,428	2,007.6	21,943	30,115
■	138	■	68	Amgen	1,940	537.7	2,433	16,507
20	29	72	29	Amoco	27,066	1,862.0	29,845	34,872
239	171	411	132	AMP	5,227	427.3	4,505	9,349
49	348	115	178	AMR	16,910	196.0	19,600	6,920
■	376	128	■	AmSouth Bancorporation	1,507	175.0	17,739	2,205
■	■	■	366	Anadarko Petroleum	434	21.0	2,267	3,293
■	463	■	359	Analog Devices	1,014	135.7	1,309	3,376
111	76	227	65	Anheuser-Busch Cos	10,340	886.6	9,837	17,120
343	179	113	227	Aon	3,466	402.8	19,736	5,629
100	397	305	380	Apple Computer	11,378	167.0	6,553	3,200
331	130	■	202	Applied Materials	3,596	559.9	3,243	6,213

Rankings 500 Table *(Cont.)*

WHERE THEY RANK: 1995					Sales ($mil)	Net profits ($mil)	Assets ($mil)	Market value ($mil)
Sales	Net profits	Assets	Market value	Company				
85	85	214	126	Archer Daniels Midland	12,971	810.3	10,640	9,696
■	496	■	496	Armstrong World Industries	2,085	123.3	2,150	2,334
204	342	■	493	Arrow Electronics	5,919	202.5	2,701	2,354
368	388	422	■	Asarco	3,198	169.1	4,327	1,426
■	■	■	229	Ascend Communications	150	30.6	335	5,573
99	■	294	483	Ashland	11,495	76.0	7,035	2,425
■	■	459	■	Associated Banc-Corp	317	46.7	3,698	602
484	■	■	■	AST Research	2,348	−262.1	1,056	262
■	■	301	■	Astoria Financial	444	45.4	6,620	565
5	454	26	3	AT&T	79,609	139.0	88,884	98,122
59	45	87	61	Atlantic Richfield	15,819	1,376.0	23,999	18,091
■	■	■	457	Atmel	634	113.7	920	2,562
371	173	457	100	Automatic Data Processing	3,166	422.0	3,728	11,690
■	430	■	283	AutoZone	1,943	149.4	1,292	4,521
379	443	■	413	Avery Dennison	3,114	143.7	1,964	2,918
263	383	■	■	Avnet	4,798	171.5	2,462	2,068
276	273	■	211	Avon Products	4,492	256.5	2,053	5,883
436	485	■	309	Baker Hughes	2,725	128.2	3,223	4,113
448	■	■	■	Ball	2,592	−18.6	1,613	911
410	212	257	324	Baltimore Gas & Electric	2,935	338.0	8,317	3,909
133	49	25	79	Banc One	8,971	1,277.9	90,454	14,807
■	■	182	■	Bancorp Hawaii	1,043	121.8	13,207	1,417
■	■	499	■	BancorpSouth	284	35.5	3,302	478
225	137	46	246	Bank of Boston	5,411	541.0	47,397	5,310
229	75	41	120	Bank of New York	5,327	914.0	53,720	9,955
33	15	5	40	BankAmerica	20,386	2,664.0	232,446	26,868
146	326	21	248	Bankers Trust New York	8,309	215.0	104,002	5,278
■	437	145	■	BanPonce	1,279	146.4	15,675	1,459
321	139	53	218	Barnett Banks	3,680	533.3	41,554	5,775
250	116	239	96	Baxter International	5,048	649.0	9,437	12,371
■	323	■	180	Bay Networks	1,728	218.3	1,429	6,824
■	457	196	■	BayBanks	1,019	137.4	12,064	2,005
281	195	27	425	Bear Stearns Cos	4,383	371.2	86,019	2,782
432	267	■	244	Becton Dickinson	2,759	262.7	2,941	5,328
76	30	86	39	Bell Atlantic	13,430	1,861.8	24,157	26,919
44	40	67	26	BellSouth	17,886	1,564.0	31,880	36,033
477	428	144	412	Beneficial	2,398	150.5	15,693	2,919
138	■	■	■	Bergen Brunswig	8,841	66.0	2,426	979
■	■	470	■	WR Berkley	1,022	60.9	3,619	973
277	106	71	19	Berkshire Hathaway	4,488	725.2	29,929	43,880
184	■	■	■	Best Buy	6,589	56.3	2,758	779
258	372	335	■	Bethlehem Steel	4,868	179.6	5,700	1,523
365	■	■	■	Beverly Enterprises	3,229	−8.1	2,506	1,122
270	■	■	■	Bindley Western Industries	4,670	16.4	844	189

■ Not on 500 list.   [1]Formerly American Premier Group.

Continued

Rankings 500 Table *(Cont.)*

WHERE THEY RANK: 1995				Company	Sales ($mil)	Net profits ($mil)	Assets ($mil)	Market value ($mil)
Sales	Net profits	Assets	Market value					
266	274	344	373	Black & Decker	4,766	254.9	5,545	3,230
■	■	■	341	H&R Block	1,528	94.8	1,029	3,683
■	■	■	408	BMC Software	397	70.2	542	2,946
402	174	65	256	Boatmen's Bancshares	2,996	418.8	33,704	5,000
37	185	99	38	Boeing	19,515	393.0	22,098	27,858
246	203	403	■	Boise Cascade	5,074	351.9	4,656	2,017
■	■	429	■	BOK Financial	367	49.2	4,222	429
■	■	466	■	Boston Edison	1,629	112.3	3,644	1,269
■	■	■	148	Boston Scientific	1,107	8.4	1,075	8,249
■	271	■	■	Bowater	2,001	258.2	2,908	1,564
73	33	169	21	Bristol-Myers Squibb	13,767	1,812.0	13,929	42,692
■	417	■	448	Brown-Forman	1,520	157.2	1,337	2,613
206	191	277	197	Browning-Ferris Industries	5,917	378.0	7,634	6,312
394	487	■	■	Brunswick	3,041	127.2	2,361	2,259
195	353	123	92	Burlington Northern Santa Fe[2]	6,183	192.0	18,269	12,461
■	■	431	273	Burlington Resources	873	−279.6	4,165	4,636
■	405	■	253	Cabletron Systems	1,070	164.4	942	5,066
■	368	■	■	Cabot	1,845	181.3	1,728	2,234
■	■	163	■	Cal Fed Bancorp[3]	1,072	93.6	14,321	769
431	■	■	■	Caldor	2,764	0.6	1,415	72
465	■	■	■	Caliber System	2,448	−27.2	1,389	1,713
156	97	304	73	Campbell Soup	7,581	746.3	6,576	15,588
149	■	■	416	Cardinal Health	8,180	90.3	2,102	2,901
480	■	■	■	Caremark International	2,374	−116.3	1,264	2,271
401	194	259	255	Carolina Power & Light	3,007	372.6	8,227	5,019
■	■	■	355	Cascade Communications	135	25.4	112	3,404
255	208	348	331	Case	4,937	346.0	5,469	3,795
57	54	135	85	Caterpillar	16,072	1,136.0	16,830	13,968
■	■	372	■	CCB Financial	436	57.9	5,090	763
■	■	473	■	Center Financial	285	22.6	3,580	271
459	320	213	■	Centerior Energy	2,516	220.5	10,643	1,184
387	■	■	■	Centex	3,074	46.5	2,332	820
316	180	171	230	Central & South West	3,735	402.0	13,869	5,534
■	■	210	■	Central Fidelity Banks	851	105.4	10,811	1,357
■	■	359	■	Centura Banks	440	58.0	5,326	750
173	91	236	281	Champion International	6,972	771.8	9,543	4,535
■	■	174	■	Charter One Financial	1,141	34.0	13,579	1,487
22	12	2	36	Chase Manhattan	26,220	2,970.0	303,989	30,668
18	73	63	28	Chevron	31,322	930.0	34,330	35,807
453	■	■	■	Chiquita Brands International	2,566	16.8	2,623	848
■	■	■	277	Chiron	1,101	−512.5	1,490	4,590
9	23	40	47	Chrysler	53,195	2,121.0	53,756	23,314
200	111	95	146	Chubb	6,089	696.6	22,997	8,278
39	330	22	139	Cigna	18,955	211.0	95,903	8,988
■	308	322	349	Cincinnati Financial	1,656	227.4	6,109	3,482

Rankings 500 Table *(Cont.)*

WHERE THEY RANK: 1995					Sales ($mil)	Net profits ($mil)	Assets ($mil)	Market value ($mil)
Sales	Net profits	Assets	Market value	Company				
397	207	261	289	Cinergy	3,031	347.2	8,220	4,494
335	■	■	■	Circle K	3,544	33.4	1,031	729
182	369	■	409	Circuit City Stores	6,686	181.0	3,150	2,944
■	483	■	364	Circus Circus Enterprises	1,300	128.9	2,212	3,324
442	118	■	41	Cisco Systems	2,668	633.9	2,366	26,861
17	8	3	24	Citicorp	31,690	3,464.0	256,853	37,805
■	■	439	■	Citizens Bancorp	300	36.1	4,040	448
■	■	487	■	Citizens Banking	277	33.6	3,464	420
■	413	444	466	Citizens Utilities	1,069	159.5	3,918	2,508
■	■	432	■	City National	252	48.8	4,158	560
■	332	■	298	Clorox	2,079	210.2	1,859	4,348
303	340	262	449	CMS Energy	3,890	204.0	8,143	2,612
■	■	469	■	CNB Bancshares	320	35.7	3,629	505
■	■	258	■	Coast Savings Financial	671	32.8	8,252	530
109	261	212	308	Coastal	10,448	270.4	10,659	4,133
43	11	151	2	Coca-Cola	18,018	2,986.0	15,041	101,147
179	■	245	337	Coca-Cola Enterprises	6,773	82.0	9,064	3,728
144	382	276	101	Colgate-Palmolive	8,358	172.0	7,642	11,566
■	■	380	■	Collective Bancorp	368	52.9	5,029	507
■	■	458	■	Colonial BancGroup	301	38.8	3,725	430
446	■	325	■	Columbia Gas System	2,635	−432.3	6,057	2,134
45	61	112	44	Columbia/HCA Healthcare	17,695	1,064.0	19,892	24,018
356	■	233	313	Comcast	3,363	−37.8	9,580	4,066
500	■	377	■	Comdisco	2,246	106.0	5,058	1,064
380	175	61	285	Comerica	3,113	413.4	35,470	4,500
■	■	234	■	Commerce Bancshares	764	107.6	9,574	1,303
■	■	302	■	Commercial Federal	500	48.9	6,594	565
494	■	■	■	Commercial Metals	2,268	42.4	775	414
65	90	269	111	Compaq Computer	14,755	789.0	7,818	10,613
■	■	220	■	Compass Bancshares	849	110.3	10,262	1,214
378	■	■	■	CompUSA	3,135	39.8	882	1,034
369	■	386	64	Computer Associates Intntl.	3,196	−108.6	4,882	17,570
291	469	■	320	Computer Sciences	4,100	133.3	2,536	3,976
24	140	183	112	ConAgra	24,651	533.0	13,176	10,441
319	266	255	206	Conrail	3,686	264.0	8,424	6,034
425	316	131	■	Conseco	2,855	222.5	17,298	1,403
185	108	168	169	Consolidated Edison	6,537	723.9	13,950	7,313
234	■	■	■	Consolidated Freightways	5,281	57.4	2,750	1,180
358	■	353	315	Consolidated Natural Gas	3,307	21.3	5,418	4,036
■	306	■	467	Consolidated Papers	1,579	229.2	1,933	2,503
211	313	393	■	Continental Airlines	5,825	224.0	4,821	1,407
257	249	324	316	Cooper Industries	4,886	280.6	6,064	4,018
421	162	73	222	CoreStates Financial	2,868	452.2	29,621	5,746
232	■	328	153	Corning	5,313	−50.8	5,987	7,932

■ Not on 500 list.   ²Formerly Burlington Northern.   ³Formerly California Federal Bank.

Continued

Rankings 500 Table *(Cont.)*

Sales	Net profits	Assets	Market value	Company	Sales ($mil)	Net profits ($mil)	Assets ($mil)	Market value ($mil)
■	349	249	■	Countrywide Credit Industries	1,285	195.7	8,658	2,096
■	■	343	217	Cox Communications	1,328	101.2	5,555	5,842
140	146	280	118	CPC International	8,431	512.1	7,502	10,065
■	371	122	492	Crestar Financial	1,525	179.8	18,303	2,360
249	■	364	201	Crown Cork & Seal	5,054	74.9	5,235	6,238
108	120	165	131	CSX	10,504	618.0	14,282	9,499
■	409	■	210	CUC International	1,415	163.4	1,141	5,888
■	■	430	■	Cullen/Frost Bankers	344	46.3	4,200	540
238	313	■	■	Cummins Engine	5,245	224.0	3,056	1,663
366	493	319	453	Cyprus Amax Minerals	3,207	124.0	6,196	2,592
■	245	■	■	Cytec Industries	1,260	282.2	1,294	1,453
154	240	336	358	Dana	7,787	288.1	5,694	3,378
367	■	■	■	Darden Restaurants	3,200	58.0	2,089	2,108
■	■	361	■	Dauphin Deposit	435	65.6	5,297	910
26	228	188	204	Dayton Hudson	23,516	311.0	12,570	6,054
430	■	■	■	Dean Foods	2,765	62.3	1,376	1,038
151	80	55	138	Dean Witter Discover & Co	7,934	856.4	38,208	9,036
107	103	160	108	Deere & Co	10,520	733.9	14,447	11,029
233	259	■	390	Dell Computer	5,296	272.0	2,148	3,117
93	149	199	314	Delta Air Lines	12,250	510.0	11,998	4,043
■	■	■	445	Deluxe	1,858	87.0	1,295	2,625
■	■	327	■	Deposit Guaranty	495	72.6	6,026	891
332	■	428	452	Dial	3,575	1.1	4,225	2,595
408	■	■	■	Diamond Shamrock	2,937	47.3	2,245	908
66	169	223	124	Digital Equipment	14,440	430.5	10,015	9,859
205	395	396	306	Dillard Department Stores	5,918	167.2	4,779	4,140
■	■	109	■	Dime Bancorp	1,423	62.2	20,327	1,097
95	44	149	16	Walt Disney	12,128	1,393.7	15,276	47,040
308	■	■	458	Dole Food	3,804	119.8	2,442	2,559
272	172	170	185	Dominion Resources	4,652	425.0	13,903	6,748
186	235	354	225	RR Donnelley & Sons	6,512	298.8	5,385	5,677
314	253	■	242	Dover	3,746	278.3	2,667	5,399
34	24	92	49	Dow Chemical	20,200	2,078.0	23,582	22,272
492	358	■	325	Dow Jones	2,284	189.6	2,599	3,897
■	■	402	■	Downey Financial	339	21.1	4,656	386
■	403	495	471	DPL	1,255	164.7	3,323	2,467
■	385	414	■	DQE	1,220	170.6	4,459	2,162
214	319	405	250	Dresser Industries	5,775	221.1	4,623	5,198
■	352	■	357	DSC Communications	1,422	192.7	1,865	3,381
327	177	207	263	DTE Energy	3,636	405.9	11,131	4,843
11	10	57	17	EI du Pont de Nemours	36,508	3,293.0	37,312	45,134
268	109	176	123	Duke Power	4,677	714.5	13,358	9,884
224	222	345	117	Dun & Bradstreet	5,415	320.8	5,516	10,121
■	286	■	208	Duracell International	2,180	245.6	2,604	5,913
251	131	388	223	Eastman Chemical	5,040	559.0	4,854	5,713

Rankings 500 Table (Cont.)

WHERE THEY RANK: 1995								
Sales	Net profits	Assets	Market value	Company	Sales ($mil)	Net profits ($mil)	Assets ($mil)	Market value ($mil)
63	50	159	43	Eastman Kodak	14,980	1,252.0	14,477	25,293
175	182	378	274	Eaton	6,822	399.0	5,053	4,628
415	429	■	■	Echlin	2,911	150.3	2,049	2,179
265	■	■	■	Eckerd	4,772	93.0	1,539	1,634
141	99	89	168	Edison International[4]	8,405	739.0	23,946	7,375
■	422	■	■	AG Edwards	1,341	153.8	2,549	1,545
■	218	■	266	EMC	1,921	326.8	1,746	4,770
112	72	231	62	Emerson Electric	10,294	934.8	9,733	17,896
427	456	■	407	Engelhard	2,840	137.5	1,646	2,946
■	303	400	456	Enova[5]	1,871	233.5	4,670	2,564
128	143	180	141	Enron	9,189	519.7	13,239	8,736
193	152	97	203	Entergy	6,274	484.6	22,266	6,178
■	432	■	411	Equifax	1,623	147.7	1,109	2,926
163	204	19	276	Equitable Cos	7,274	350.2	113,749	4,617
■	■	229	■	Equitable of Iowa Cos	765	84.9	9,780	1,156
383	450	■	311	Estee Lauder Cos	3,095	141.2	1,826	4,091
3	3	24	4	Exxon	107,893	6,470.0	91,296	98,118
119	252	299	322	Federal Express	10,005	279.5	6,693	3,972
125	58	13	80	Federal Home Loan Mortgage	9,519	1,091.0	137,181	14,571
30	22	1	30	Federal National Mortgage Assn	22,249	2,155.6	316,550	34,260
62	■	164	181	Federated Department Stores	15,049	74.6	14,295	6,805
294	■	■	■	FHP International	4,021	23.1	2,350	1,319
■	■	500	■	Fidelity Federal Bank	253	−69.0	3,299	223
■	241	134	228	Fifth Third Bancorp	1,479	287.7	17,053	5,612
330	■	■	■	Fina	3,607	104.4	2,488	1,498
■	■	293	■	Finova Group	782	97.6	7,037	1,420
■	■	232	■	First American Corp	730	103.1	9,682	1,285
359	128	64	147	First Bank System	3,297	568.1	33,874	8,276
105	53	17	99	First Chicago NBD	10,681	1,150.0	122,002	12,152
■	■	281	■	First Citizens BancShares	563	56.9	7,384	632
■	426	211	■	First Colony	1,658	151.4	10,721	1,171
■	■	253	■	First Commerce	738	76.0	8,531	1,236
■	■	357	■	First Commercial	396	56.9	5,361	861
293	■	194	72	First Data	4,081	−84.2	12,218	15,743
■	475	201	■	First Empire State	1,078	131.0	11,956	1,524
■	■	347	■	First Financial Corp	462	64.0	5,471	598
■	■	279	■	First Hawaiian	655	77.0	7,565	856
261	78	38	98	First Interstate Bancorp	4,828	885.1	58,071	12,168
■	■	321	■	First National of Nebraska	829	82.2	6,111	1,492
■	298	91	418	First of America Bank	2,143	236.7	23,600	2,879
■	■	184	■	First Security	1,193	120.0	13,035	2,080
■	400	195	■	First Tennessee National	1,319	164.9	12,077	2,137
106	42	15	69	First Union	10,583	1,430.2	131,880	16,393
■	331	284	368	First USA	1,298	210.5	7,324	3,268

■ Not on 500 list.   [4]Formerly SCEcorp.   [5]Formerly San Diego Gas & Electric.

Continued

Rankings 500 Table *(Cont.)*

WHERE THEY RANK: 1995					Sales ($mil)	Net profits ($mil)	Assets ($mil)	Market value ($mil)
Sales	Net profits	Assets	Market value	Company				
■	■	260	■	First Virginia Banks	664	111.6	8,222	1,358
■	307	119	365	Firstar	1,740	228.9	19,168	3,313
■	■	433	■	FirstFed Financial	310	6.5	4,140	158
■	■	341	■	FirstMerit	485	25.7	5,597	1,080
450	■	■	■	Flagstar Cos	2,571	−55.7	1,501	143
153	122	28	113	Fleet Financial Group	7,875	610.0	84,432	10,312
429	■	■	■	Fleetwood Enterprises	2,795	80.0	1,394	1,146
47	■	426	■	Fleming Cos	17,502	42.0	4,297	637
391	293	333	382	Florida Progress	3,056	238.9	5,791	3,185
123	294	492	214	Fluor	9,644	238.9	3,398	5,865
275	325	425	438	FMC	4,510	215.6	4,301	2,714
148	381	■	436	Food Lion	8,211	172.4	2,645	2,718
2	6	4	25	Ford Motor	137,137	4,139.0	243,283	37,668
■	■	■	401	FORE Systems	198	24.0	398	3,000
393	■	■	■	Foster Wheeler	3,042	28.5	2,776	1,857
439	418	■	■	Foundation Health	2,703	156.1	2,104	2,094
227	■	■	■	FoxMeyer Health	5,393	−10.9	1,616	268
220	133	191	163	FPL Group	5,592	553.3	12,459	7,558
■	251	■	284	Franklin Resources	857	279.6	2,221	4,510
■	276	472	207	Freeport-McMoRan Copper & Gold	1,834	253.6	3,582	5,969
■	■	413	■	Fremont General	924	68.0	4,477	600
■	440	■	259	Frontier	2,144	144.8	2,109	4,922
476	■	■	■	Fruit of the Loom	2,403	−227.3	2,920	1,957
■	■	494	■	Fulton Financial	265	45.6	3,335	574
296	155	308	128	Gannett	4,007	477.3	6,504	9,629
280	201	■	155	Gap	4,395	354.0	2,343	7,913
322	377	■	■	Gateway 2000	3,676	173.0	1,124	2,087
■	■	438	■	GATX	1,233	100.8	4,043	912
■	449	■	■	Gaylord Container	1,064	141.5	957	548
■	■	■	495	Gaylord Entertainment	707	108.4	1,096	2,335
■	436	■	199	Genentech	857	146.4	2,011	6,276
389	221	■	336	General Dynamics	3,067	321.0	3,164	3,747
7	2	6	1	General Electric	70,028	6,573.0	228,035	126,238
469	495	■	372	General Instrument	2,432	123.8	2,301	3,240
235	189	481	135	General Mills	5,262	385.6	3,516	9,204
1	1	7	7	General Motors	168,829	6,932.5	217,079	69,947
■	■	■	500	General Nutrition Cos	846	69.1	686	2,312
307	168	226	332	General Public Utilities	3,805	440.1	9,870	3,795
166	83	60	102	General Re	7,210	824.9	35,946	11,550
236	229	■	240	Genuine Parts	5,262	309.2	2,274	5,410
■	360	■	■	Georgia Gulf	1,082	186.5	507	1,373
69	65	193	192	Georgia-Pacific	14,292	1,018.0	12,335	6,449
306	■	■	■	Giant Food	3,861	102.2	1,451	1,898
178	84	312	48	Gillette	6,795	823.5	6,340	23,117
■	■	158	■	Glendale Federal Bank FSB	1,134	56.2	14,640	662

Rankings 500 Table *(Cont.)*

WHERE THEY RANK: 1995								
Sales	Net profits	Assets	Market value	Company	Sales ($mil)	Net profits ($mil)	Assets ($mil)	Market value ($mil)
463	300	62	414	**Golden West Financial**	2,470	234.5	35,118	2,914
475	■	■	■	**BF Goodrich**	2,409	118.0	2,490	2,032
82	121	228	158	**Goodyear Tire & Rubber**	13,166	611.0	9,790	7,868
324	■	313	159	**WR Grace**	3,666	−325.9	6,298	7,819
362	359	■	347	**WW Grainger**	3,277	186.7	1,663	3,504
489	■	■	■	**Grand Union**	2,312	−155.8	1,244	53
116	■	■	■	**Great Atlantic & Pacific Tea**	10,101	57.2	2,928	1,075
482	237	■	297	**Great Lakes Chemical**	2,361	295.6	2,469	4,361
333	269	50	391	**Great Western Financial**	3,566	261.0	44,587	3,103
■	275	■	290	**Green Tree Financial**	672	254.0	2,384	4,492
■	■	156	■	**GreenPoint Financial**[6]	732	107.5	14,670	1,475
35	17	58	22	**GTE**	19,957	2,537.9	37,019	40,475
■	■	■	378	**Guidant**	931	101.1	1,057	3,202
217	302	465	188	**Halliburton**	5,699	233.8	3,647	6,624
451	■	■	■	**Hannaford Bros**	2,568	70.2	962	1,153
399	384	■	369	**Harcourt General**	3,013	170.7	3,021	3,268
■	■	■	430	**Harley-Davidson**	1,351	112.5	1,001	2,741
487	■	■	■	**Harnischfeger Industries**	2,335	103.5	2,532	1,885
■	■	■	420	**Harrah's Entertainment**[7]	1,550	78.8	1,637	2,839
339	401	■	454	**Harris**	3,507	164.8	3,007	2,578
423	419	■	392	**Hasbro**	2,858	155.6	2,616	3,078
■	■	340	■	**Hawaiian Electric Industries**	1,296	77.5	5,604	1,053
■	■	■	330	**HBO & Co**	496	−25.2	535	3,854
435	■	■	■	**Health Systems International**	2,732	89.6	1,214	1,807
■	■	■	472	**Healthsource**	1,167	56.3	872	2,464
■	■	■	233	**HealthSouth**	1,557	78.9	2,940	5,484
499	■	■	■	**Hechinger**	2,253	−77.6	1,100	174
132	117	251	90	**HJ Heinz**	8,997	647.6	8,618	12,635
472	214	■	177	**Hercules**	2,427	332.8	2,493	7,069
318	246	■	187	**Hershey Foods**	3,691	281.9	2,831	6,624
16	16	82	13	**Hewlett-Packard**	33,503	2,621.0	25,753	50,929
■	■	■	261	**HFS**	413	79.7	1,153	4,895
■	494	289	■	**Hibernia**	615	123.9	7,196	1,193
■	■	■	477	**Hillenbrand Industries**	1,625	89.9	3,070	2,444
■	379	■	287	**Hilton Hotels**	1,590	172.8	3,060	4,496
60	104	283	45	**Home Depot**	15,470	731.5	7,354	23,602
■	■	■	455	**Homestake Mining**	716	30.3	1,322	2,565
181	213	376	182	**Honeywell**	6,731	333.6	5,060	6,785
■	■	463	■	**Horace Mann Educators**	741	73.9	3,662	729
395	■	■	■	**Hormel Foods**	3,040	105.6	1,234	1,956
■	■	476	■	**Host Marriott**	484	−62.0	3,557	2,056
243	161	74	191	**Household International**	5,144	453.2	29,219	6,484
320	55	202	237	**Houston Industries**	3,680	1,124.0	11,820	5,432
273	357	■	326	**Humana**	4,605	190.0	2,878	3,890

■ Not on 500 list.   [6]Formerly GP Financial.   [7]Formerly Promus Cos.

Continued

Rankings 500 Table (Cont.)

Sales	Net profits	Assets	Market value	Company	Sales ($mil)	Net profits ($mil)	Assets ($mil)	Market value ($mil)
■	287	110	363	Huntington Bancshares	1,710	244.5	20,255	3,327
89	250	■	■	IBP	12,668	280.1	2,028	2,286
■	478	■	■	Illinois Central	644	129.8	1,404	1,682
287	188	471	154	Illinois Tool Works	4,152	387.6	3,613	7,917
■	425	339	■	Illinova	1,641	151.6	5,610	2,091
483	408	479	352	IMC Global	2,360	163.6	3,522	3,425
■	■	■	254	Informix	709	105.3	674	5,020
216	262	351	286	Ingersoll-Rand	5,729	270.3	5,454	4,498
264	434	475	■	Inland Steel Industries	4,781	146.8	3,558	1,255
■	484	162	■	Integra Financial	1,220	128.4	14,346	2,205
56	7	130	15	Intel	16,202	3,566.2	17,504	48,336
342	■	■	■	Intelligent Electronics	3,475	−19.0	894	216
6	5	30	8	Intntl. Business Machines	71,940	4,178.0	80,292	65,664
■	281	■	238	Intntl. Flavors & Fragrances	1,439	248.8	1,534	5,424
473	■	■	■	Intntl. Multifoods	2,412	30.1	832	346
36	52	88	114	Intntl. Paper	19,797	1,153.0	23,977	10,245
■	477	427	350	Interpublic Group of Cos	2,180	129.8	4,260	3,460
■	■	■	497	Intuit	490	−4.5	510	2,334
191	433	250	176	ITT	6,346	147.0	8,630	7,111
94	131	23	231	ITT Hartford Group	12,150	559.0	93,855	5,519
142	■	331	403	ITT Industries	8,382	21.0	5,864	2,971
■	■	■	389	IVAX	1,260	114.8	1,335	3,142
177	489	286	488	James River Corp of Virginia	6,800	126.4	7,259	2,389
■	257	138	333	Jefferson-Pilot	1,569	273.9	16,478	3,783
292	284	■	■	Jefferson Smurfit	4,093	247.0	2,783	1,263
■	■	274	■	John Alden Financial	1,671	6.5	7,696	465
40	19	124	9	Johnson & Johnson	18,842	2,403.0	17,873	60,882
139	343	385	415	Johnson Controls	8,659	201.6	4,885	2,910
■	499	■	■	Kansas City Power & Light	886	122.6	2,883	1,524
■	299	■	■	Kansas City Southern Industries	775	236.7	2,040	1,809
172	151	415	67	Kellogg	7,004	490.3	4,415	16,632
440	■	■	■	Kelly Services	2,690	69.5	719	1,141
■	■	■	383	Kerr-McGee	1,801	−31.2	3,232	3,179
201	89	35	143	KeyCorp	6,054	789.2	66,339	8,570
■	■	373	■	Keystone Financial	414	61.3	5,075	846
72	■	205	52	Kimberly-Clark	13,789	33.2	11,439	21,271
■	470	■	■	King World Productions	589	133.1	738	1,551
15	■	148	267	Kmart	34,654	−520.0	15,397	4,708
433	394	■	361	Knight-Ridder	2,752	167.4	3,006	3,353
■	■	■	489	Kohl's	1,926	72.7	805	2,387
25	224	379	272	Kroger	23,938	318.9	5,045	4,665
■	479	■	■	Lafarge	1,472	129.6	1,714	1,290
267	■	■	■	Lear Seating	4,714	94.2	3,061	1,837
■	465	■	■	Leggett & Platt	2,059	134.9	1,218	2,042
70	233	16	481	Lehman Brothers Holdings	14,281	301.0	129,000	2,433

Rankings 500 Table *(Cont.)*

WHERE THEY RANK: 1995					Sales ($mil)	Net profits ($mil)	Assets ($mil)	Market value ($mil)
Sales	Net profits	Assets	Market value	Company				
■	■	369	■	Leucadia National	1,504	78.5	5,136	1,511
■	■	186	■	Liberty Financial Cos	1,027	73.9	12,749	865
■	■	371	■	Life Partners Group	537	25.7	5,092	565
■	■	449	■	Life USA Holding	273	19.1	3,868	161
180	21	161	31	Eli Lilly	6,764	2,290.9	14,413	33,527
152	68	362	247	Limited	7,881	961.5	5,267	5,279
183	153	36	249	Lincoln National	6,633	482.2	63,258	5,274
■	■	■	351	Linear Technology	328	112.5	448	3,439
353	442	■	■	Litton Industries	3,412	143.7	2,601	2,265
■	488	■	450	Liz Claiborne	2,082	126.9	1,329	2,607
27	113	129	75	Lockheed Martin	22,853	682.0	17,648	15,094
48	35	34	133	Loews	17,219	1,765.7	68,891	9,279
■	■	383	■	Long Island Bancorp	366	44.6	4,935	701
386	231	189	■	Long Island Lighting	3,075	303.3	12,484	2,039
445	■	■	■	Longs Drug Stores	2,644	46.2	854	923
196	211	332	151	Loral	6,179	339.2	5,830	8,090
426	■	■	433	Louisiana-Pacific	2,843	−51.7	2,805	2,728
169	311	477	226	Lowe's Cos	7,075	226.0	3,556	5,672
■	295	■	342	LSI Logic	1,268	238.1	1,850	3,653
282	363	355	■	LTV	4,283	184.8	5,380	1,380
■	424	■	■	Lubrizol	1,664	151.6	1,492	1,928
256	186	■	463	Lyondell Petrochemical	4,936	389.0	2,606	2,520
■	■	382	■	Magna Group	395	51.2	4,947	670
■	341	■	428	Mallinckrodt Group	2,228	203.1	2,812	2,773
■	■	■	468	Manor Care	1,262	105.9	1,614	2,500
223	486	■	439	Manpower	5,484	128.0	1,518	2,708
■	500	■	■	Manville[8]	1,392	122.0	2,474	1,566
373	■	■	■	Mapco	3,152	74.7	2,293	1,597
135	285	440	198	Marriott International	8,961	246.9	4,018	6,282
311	178	421	183	Marsh & McLennan Cos	3,770	402.9	4,330	6,779
■	350	177	485	Marshall & Ilsley	1,349	193.3	13,343	2,414
412	■	455	265	Masco	2,927	−441.7	3,779	4,772
326	198	■	164	Mattel	3,639	357.8	2,696	7,541
455	■	451	■	Maxxam	2,565	57.5	3,832	381
102	94	221	91	May Department Stores	10,952	755.0	10,122	12,551
396	■	■	■	Maytag	3,040	−15.0	2,125	2,158
■	260	285	375	MBIA	462	271.4	7,267	3,212
454	202	181	190	MBNA	2,565	353.1	13,229	6,543
121	43	147	27	McDonald's	9,795	1,427.3	15,400	35,862
68	■	219	116	McDonnell Douglas	14,332	−416.0	10,466	10,162
409	309	■	293	McGraw-Hill Cos	2,935	227.1	3,104	4,453
61	134	118	59	MCI Communications	15,265	548.0	19,301	19,294
74	458	461	475	McKesson	13,582	137.0	3,674	2,450
241	205	418	427	Mead	5,179	350.0	4,373	2,773

■Not on 500 list.   [8]To change name to Schuller.

Continued

Rankings 500 Table *(Cont.)*

WHERE THEY RANK: 1995					Sales	Net profits	Assets	Market value
Sales	Net profits	Assets	Market value	Company	($mil)	($mil)	($mil)	($mil)
▪	181	▪	88	Medtronic	2,090	400.2	2,230	13,287
274	112	54	172	Mellon Bank	4,514	691.0	40,646	7,277
122	▪	443	343	Melville	9,689	−615.2	3,962	3,630
▪	324	141	484	Mercantile Bancorporation	1,398	216.8	15,934	2,417
▪	▪	311	▪	Mercantile Bankshares	555	104.4	6,349	1,231
407	497	▪	▪	Mercantile Stores	2,944	123.2	2,075	2,128
50	9	90	6	Merck	16,681	3,335.2	23,832	76,342
▪	▪	▪	479	Mercury Finance	348	110.9	1,647	2,438
▪	387	155	419	Meridian Bancorp	1,367	169.8	14,758	2,871
213	▪	▪	▪	Merisel	5,802	−9.2	1,469	80
31	56	11	125	Merrill Lynch	21,513	1,114.0	176,857	9,769
351	▪	▪	▪	Fred Meyer	3,429	30.3	1,672	794
▪	▪	▪	321	MFS Communications	583	−267.9	1,867	3,975
▪	336	▪	360	MGIC Investment	618	207.6	1,875	3,371
392	▪	▪	▪	MicroAge	3,047	−1.1	583	135
299	65	468	184	Micron Technology	3,972	1,018.0	3,642	6,754
159	31	244	10	Microsoft	7,419	1,838.0	9,106	60,811
▪	476	410	▪	MidAmerican Energy	1,724	130.8	4,524	1,763
75	67	166	42	Minnesota Mining & Manufacturing	13,460	976.0	14,183	26,588
▪	386	▪	310	Mirage Resorts	1,331	169.9	1,792	4,109
8	20	52	18	Mobil	64,767	2,376.0	42,138	44,191
▪	455	▪	346	Molex	1,337	139.0	1,390	3,544
134	99	215	63	Monsanto	8,962	739.0	10,611	17,733
71	48	10	77	JP Morgan & Co	13,838	1,296.0	184,879	15,027
103	124	12	165	Morgan Stanley Group	10,797	609.0	143,753	7,527
341	219	▪	224	Morton International	3,475	326.3	2,869	5,680
21	34	96	32	Motorola	27,037	1,781.0	22,801	32,897
▪	▪	▪	499	Mylan Laboratories	409	117.8	613	2,314
▪	423	▪	▪	Nalco Chemical	1,215	153.7	1,370	2,089
418	▪	▪	▪	Nash Finch	2,889	17.4	514	177
347	158	59	260	National City	3,450	465.1	36,199	4,912
▪	▪	460	▪	National Commerce Bancorporation	300	49.0	3,695	698
441	272	▪	▪	National Semiconductor	2,681	257.5	2,602	2,031
405	▪	▪	▪	National Steel	2,954	105.4	2,668	655
55	26	9	56	NationsBank	16,327	1,950.2	187,298	20,296
190	410	375	▪	Navistar International	6,358	162.9	5,067	819
▪	▪	▪	348	Netscape Communications	81	−3.4	228	3,483
493	339	366	487	New England Electric System	2,272	204.8	5,191	2,394
▪	347	370	▪	New York State Electric & Gas	2,010	196.7	5,114	1,645
474	461	493	421	New York Times	2,409	135.9	3,377	2,808
460	318	▪	301	Newell Co	2,498	222.5	2,931	4,323
▪	▪	▪	239	Newmont Mining	636	112.6	1,774	5,420
▪	▪	349	334	Nextel Communications	178	−263.2	5,467	3,780
323	▪	▪	▪	NGC	3,666	92.7	1,902	1,271
300	282	238	▪	Niagara Mohawk Power	3,917	248.0	9,478	974

Rankings 500 Table *(Cont.)*

WHERE THEY RANK: 1995					Sales ($mil)	Net profits ($mil)	Assets ($mil)	Market value ($mil)
Sales	Net profits	Assets	Market value	Company				
202	148	467	103	NIKE	5,961	510.1	3,643	11,405
■	375	441	■	Nipsco Industries	1,722	175.5	4,000	2,253
404	■	462	■	NorAm Energy	2,965	65.5	3,666	1,125
290	399	■	317	Nordstrom	4,114	165.1	2,898	4,008
271	110	209	109	Norfolk Southern	4,668	712.7	10,905	10,905
■	■	498	■	North Fork Bancorporation	254	52.2	3,303	585
313	244	217	473	Northeast Utilities	3,749	282.4	10,545	2,462
449	255	316	367	Northern States Power	2,587	275.8	6,229	3,272
■	321	111	399	Northern Trust	1,782	220.0	19,934	3,006
176	278	350	400	Northrop Grumman	6,818	252.0	5,455	3,004
130	210	256	269	Northwest Airlines	9,085	342.1	8,412	4,707
155	69	32	97	Norwest	7,582	956.0	72,134	12,258
■	223	■	278	Novell	1,986	320.3	2,355	4,571
344	256	■	241	Nucor	3,462	274.5	2,296	5,401
79	60	79	55	Nynex	13,407	1,069.5	26,220	21,080
110	147	126	150	Occidental Petroleum	10,423	511.0	17,815	8,137
231	471	■	384	Office Depot	5,313	132.4	2,531	3,178
457	490	■	■	OfficeMax	2,543	125.8	1,588	2,007
■	■	464	■	Ogden	2,185	7.4	3,653	1,033
■	■	442	■	Ohio Casualty	1,462	99.7	3,980	1,301
464	225	248	356	Ohio Edison	2,466	317.2	8,824	3,395
■	492	■	■	Oklahoma Gas & Electric	1,302	125.3	2,755	1,570
■	447	198	■	Old Kent Financial	1,096	141.8	12,003	1,797
■	■	392	■	Old National Bancorp	394	51.7	4,823	836
■	328	303	■	Old Republic International	1,696	212.7	6,594	1,688
376	453	■	■	Olin	3,150	139.9	2,272	2,158
458	■	■	■	Olsten	2,519	90.5	892	1,997
497	452	478	381	Omnicom Group	2,258	140.0	3,528	3,196
■	■	342	■	OnBancorp	461	44.7	5,567	462
■	■	450	■	One Valley Bancorp of W. VA	320	49.1	3,858	537
310	144	■	51	Oracle	3,777	518.6	2,763	21,275
■	415	■	■	Oryx Energy	1,014	158.0	1,666	1,345
403	■	■	■	Owens & Minor	2,976	−11.3	858	351
329	305	■	■	Owens Corning	3,612	231.0	3,261	2,189
309	389	352	■	Owens-Illinois	3,790	169.1	5,439	1,890
■	■	■	398	Oxford Health Plans	1,765	52.4	609	3,009
259	277	417	■	Paccar	4,848	252.8	4,391	1,914
486	362	363	■	Pacific Enterprises	2,343	185.0	5,259	2,123
124	46	77	119	Pacific Gas & Electric	9,622	1,338.9	26,850	9,988
131	62	143	105	Pacific Telesis Group	9,042	1,048.0	15,841	11,289
298	■	■	402	PacifiCare Health Systems	3,974	116.0	1,468	2,976
354	150	167	221	PacifiCorp	3,401	505.0	14,015	5,757
■	■	■	460	Paging Network	646	−44.2	1,228	2,535
230	■	48	■	PaineWebber Group	5,320	80.8	45,671	2,051

■ Not on 500 list.

Continued

Rankings 500 Table *(Cont.)*

Sales	Net profits	Assets	Market value	Company	Sales ($mil)	Net profits ($mil)	Assets ($mil)	Market value ($mil)
				WHERE THEY RANK: 1995				
■	481	■	388	Pall	902	129.3	1,104	3,149
■	■	■	397	PanAmSat	116	17.5	1,439	3,025
254	230	278	295	Panhandle Eastern	4,968	303.6	7,627	4,399
■	■	■	270	Parametric Technology	441	90.6	497	4,702
352	292	■	422	Parker Hannifin	3,427	239.3	2,340	2,790
■	■	■	441	Paychex	311	48.4	216	2,689
443	■	■	■	Payless Cashways	2,651	−132.3	1,345	160
284	123	152	215	PECO Energy	4,186	609.7	14,961	5,862
348	■	■	■	Penn Traffic	3,448	−43.8	1,801	169
32	82	133	106	JC Penney	21,419	838.0	17,102	11,228
478	■	423	■	Pennzoil	2,385	−305.1	4,308	1,751
■	■	297	■	People's Bank	608	71.0	6,862	782
■	■	■	432	PeopleSoft	228	29.4	314	2,731
19	38	83	14	PepsiCo	30,421	1,606.0	25,452	49,152
117	39	187	23	Pfizer	10,021	1,572.9	12,729	40,068
168	101	204	54	Pharmacia & Upjohn	7,095	738.7	11,461	21,089
285	96	404	291	Phelps Dodge	4,185	746.6	4,646	4,485
490	■	334	■	PHH	2,304	78.1	5,742	925
10	4	39	5	Philip Morris Cos	53,139	5,478.0	53,811	79,138
81	157	200	115	Phillips Petroleum	13,368	469.0	11,978	10,223
■	345	295	491	Pinnacle West Capital	1,670	199.6	6,997	2,374
■	366	■	296	Pioneer Hi-Bred International	1,555	182.4	1,531	4,394
334	127	268	170	Pitney Bowes	3,555	583.1	7,845	7,310
198	176	31	122	PNC Bank	6,110	408.1	73,404	9,940
■	■	488	■	Portland General	984	81.0	3,448	1,524
■	■	291	405	Potomac Electric Power	1,957	94.4	7,118	2,962
434	220	237	335	PP&L Resources[9]	2,752	322.7	9,492	3,766
170	93	320	134	PPG Industries	7,058	767.6	6,194	9,237
377	268	435	236	Praxair	3,146	262.0	4,134	5,446
■	296	■	379	Premark International	2,213	237.6	2,471	3,200
■	■	■	442	Premier Industrial	866	114.8	570	2,682
38	312	384	340	Price/Costco	18,982	224.9	4,925	3,686
14	13	76	11	Procter & Gamble	34,923	2,835.0	28,215	57,058
400	280	358	374	Progressive	3,012	250.5	5,353	3,217
■	■	288	■	Protective Life	880	76.7	7,231	1,001
■	■	318	■	Provident Bancorp	519	71.9	6,205	908
456	■	139	■	Provident Cos[10]	2,555	115.6	16,301	1,499
355	209	78	312	Providian	3,388	345.3	26,839	4,081
■	■	399	■	Prudential Reinsurance Holdings	949	0.7	4,678	1,117
■	373	419	■	Public Service Co of Colorado	2,111	178.9	4,354	2,169
197	114	132	196	Public Service Enterprise Group	6,164	662.3	17,171	6,332
■	462	■	■	Puget Sound Power & Light	1,179	135.7	3,269	1,583
203	107	391	275	Quaker Oats	5,954	724.0	4,824	4,617
■	■	■	476	Qualcomm	457	34.3	961	2,449
286	■	■	■	Quantum	4,174	55.5	1,894	1,027

Rankings 500 Table *(Cont.)*

WHERE THEY RANK: 1995					Sales ($mil)	Net profits ($mil)	Assets ($mil)	Market value ($mil)
Sales	Net profits	Assets	Market value	Company				
■	■	497	■	**Quick & Reilly Group**	411	56.5	3,311	611
212	243	395	175	**Ralston Purina**	5,804	285.3	4,806	7,125
■	■	■	404	**Raychem**	1,602	64.4	1,452	2,968
■	446	■	■	**Rayonier**	1,260	142.3	1,648	1,078
97	87	230	93	**Raytheon**	11,716	792.5	9,740	12,426
■	■	448	■	**RCSB Financial**[11]	321	37.8	3,871	335
■	435	■	■	**Read-Rite**	1,083	146.6	944	882
375	290	■	257	**Reader's Digest Association**	3,151	240.3	2,121	4,977
340	402	■	■	**Reebok International**	3,481	164.8	1,656	2,151
■	378	172	437	**Regions Financial**	1,177	172.8	13,709	2,715
416	■	224	■	**Reliance Group Holdings**	2,906	91.4	9,988	922
■	407	146	■	**ReliaStar Financial**	2,090	163.7	15,519	1,640
422	239	51	376	**Republic New York**	2,860	288.6	43,882	3,208
252	■	■	■	**Revco DS**	5,034	77.2	2,261	1,867
165	186	273	338	**Reynolds Metals**	7,213	389.0	7,740	3,713
244	199	247	145	**Rhone-Poulenc Rorer**	5,142	356.5	8,987	8,339
372	■	■	■	**Richfood Holdings**	3,155	34.5	559	860
■	■	398	■	**Riggs National**	373	87.8	4,733	360
228	421	■	435	**Rite Aid**	5,369	155.2	2,792	2,722
58	119	69	136	**RJR Nabisco**	16,008	627.0	31,518	9,110
491	■	■	■	**Roadway Express**	2,289	−12.7	714	280
78	92	197	94	**Rockwell International**	13,420	769.3	12,027	12,410
304	238	445	271	**Rohm & Haas**	3,884	292.0	3,916	4,679
■	■	246	■	**Roosevelt Financial Group**	622	45.1	9,013	779
485	■	■	280	**Rubbermaid**	2,344	59.8	1,692	4,541
242	420	329	■	**Ryder System**	5,167	155.4	5,894	2,171
317	183	120	294	**Safeco**	3,723	399.0	18,768	4,410
54	217	365	213	**Safeway**	16,398	328.3	5,194	5,877
■	480	■	434	**St Jude Medical**	724	129.4	1,016	2,724
■	■	437	■	**St Paul Bancorp**	312	36.4	4,117	475
226	142	114	282	**St Paul Cos**	5,410	521.2	19,657	4,535
301	197	44	264	**Sallie Mae**	3,917	366.3	50,002	4,801
136	160	8	329	**Salomon**	8,933	457.0	188,428	3,859
41	81	192	70	**Sara Lee**	18,335	856.0	12,389	15,974
88	28	100	34	**SBC Communications**[12]	12,670	1,889.3	22,003	31,142
■	391	408	440	**Scana**	1,353	168.3	4,534	2,704
245	77	401	53	**Schering-Plough**	5,104	886.6	4,665	21,122
■	380	216	279	**Charles Schwab**	1,777	172.6	10,552	4,568
338	■	■	■	**SCI Systems**	3,514	62.3	1,269	1,047
■	468	■	354	**EW Scripps**	1,030	133.4	1,656	3,421
222	184	452	209	**Seagate Technology**	5,493	394.0	3,830	5,888
13	64	66	58	**Sears, Roebuck**	34,925	1,025.0	33,130	19,573
■	364	275	234	**Service Corp International**	1,652	183.6	7,664	5,453
295	■	■	■	**Service Merchandise**	4,019	50.3	1,941	561

■ Not on 500 list.   [9]Formerly Pennsylvania Power & Light.   [10]Formerly Provident Life & Accident.   [11]Formerly Rochester Community Savings Bank.   [12]Formerly Southwestern Bell.   *Continued*

Rankings 500 Table *(Cont.)*

WHERE THEY RANK: 1995								
Sales	Net profits	Assets	Market value	Company	Sales ($mil)	Net profits ($mil)	Assets ($mil)	Market value ($mil)
420	■	■	■	Shaw Industries	2,870	64.4	1,665	1,581
363	344	■	339	Sherwin-Williams	3,274	200.7	2,141	3,712
■	474	■	410	Sigma-Aldrich	960	131.7	985	2,932
■	466	208	■	Signet Banking	1,145	133.8	11,013	1,462
461	304	■	323	Silicon Graphics	2,497	231.4	2,265	3,943
385	■	■	■	Smith's Food & Drug Centers	3,084	−40.5	1,686	608
468	■	■	■	Solectron	2,435	98.3	1,229	2,169
■	351	483	406	Sonat	1,990	192.9	3,511	2,962
438	404	■	470	Sonoco Products	2,706	164.5	2,115	2,495
129	57	70	74	Southern Co	9,180	1,103.0	30,554	15,483
■	374	108	426	Southern National	1,775	178.1	20,493	2,777
■	390	■	465	Southern New England Telecomm.	1,839	168.8	2,724	2,513
374	■	397	328	Southern Pacific Rail	3,151	−3.4	4,749	3,864
210	393	■	■	Southland	5,825	167.6	2,081	1,358
■	346	107	486	SouthTrust	1,693	199.0	20,787	2,406
419	365	■	288	Southwest Airlines	2,873	182.6	3,256	4,494
■	498	■	■	Southwestern Public Service	853	122.7	1,935	1,309
■	■	264	■	Sovereign Bancorp	519	56.4	8,078	520
370	■	■	■	Spiegel	3,184	−9.5	2,274	1,118
86	70	150	95	Sprint	12,765	946.1	15,089	12,407
■	■	178	■	Standard Federal Bancorp	991	119.5	13,276	1,284
447	■	■	478	Stanley Works	2,624	59.1	1,670	2,443
388	■	■	393	Staples	3,068	73.7	1,403	3,063
■	460	235	■	Star Banc	849	136.6	9,573	1,839
466	283	81	327	State Street Boston	2,446	247.1	25,785	3,872
■	444	■	■	Sterling Chemicals	981	143.7	611	710
160	167	310	■	Stone Container	7,351	444.5	6,399	1,425
289	■	■	■	Stop & Shop Cos	4,116	68.6	2,215	1,343
■	■	■	462	StrataCom	332	52.5	295	2,523
■	■	■	480	Stryker	872	87.0	855	2,434
■	■	387	■	Sumitomo Bank of California	416	−106.9	4,856	414
■	289	104	386	Summit Bancorp	1,720	242.9	21,537	3,174
143	310	367	■	Sun Co	8,370	227.0	5,184	2,150
189	165	■	144	Sun Microsystems	6,390	446.5	3,268	8,409
■	327	125	444	SunAmerica	1,122	213.9	17,844	2,638
■	■	■	490	Sundstrand	1,473	79.0	1,593	2,385
315	129	47	156	SunTrust Banks	3,740	565.5	46,471	7,909
52	412	420	■	Supervalu	16,530	161.0	4,339	2,136
■	■	267	494	Synovus Financial	957	114.6	7,928	2,347
87	265	496	205	Sysco	12,722	266.8	3,311	6,052
495	■	■	■	Tandem Computers	2,263	74.3	1,801	1,042
209	329	■	417	Tandy	5,839	212.0	2,722	2,886
■	■	287	■	TCF Financial	740	61.7	7,240	1,255
384	■	■	■	Tech Data	3,087	21.5	1,044	574
■	361	485	423	TECO Energy	1,392	186.1	3,473	2,787

Rankings 500 Table *(Cont.)*

Where they rank: 1995					Sales	Net profits	Assets	Market value
Sales	Net profits	Assets	Market value	Company	($mil)	($mil)	($mil)	($mil)
■	■	■	292	Tele-Comm.-Liberty Media Grp.	1,433	−25.1	2,701	4,471
253	■	102	89	Tele-Comm.-TCI Group	5,022	−24.0	21,900	12,963
452	411	■	■	Teledyne	2,568	162.0	1,606	1,621
■	■	486	429	Telephone & Data Systems	954	104.0	3,469	2,765
■	■	■	305	Tellabs	635	115.6	552	4,174
345	248	185	461	Temple-Inland	3,461	281.0	12,764	2,525
269	193	263	304	Tenet Healthcare	4,671	375.9	8,141	4,260
137	102	175	129	Tenneco	8,899	735.0	13,451	9,621
■	414	■	■	Teradyne	1,191	159.3	1,024	1,522
■	406	■	■	Terra Industries	2,216	163.9	1,868	1,045
12	105	85	50	Texaco	35,551	728.0	24,937	21,562
83	59	243	121	Texas Instruments	13,128	1,088.0	9,215	9,943
219	■	105	140	Texas Utilities	5,639	−138.6	21,536	8,836
120	154	94	189	Textron	9,973	479.0	23,172	6,622
■	451	456	243	Thermo Electron	2,207	140.1	3,745	5,331
■	396	■	171	3Com	1,792	167.1	1,254	7,297
■	■	■	451	360° Communications	834	−1.7	1,973	2,597
■	■	300	■	TIG Holdings	1,875	118.0	6,683	1,854
150	■	98	66	Time Warner	8,067	−124.0	22,132	17,073
349	■	453	318	Times Mirror	3,448	−394.8	3,817	4,003
278	■	■	■	TJX Cos	4,448	29.6	2,746	1,892
■	445	241	387	Torchmark	2,067	143.2	9,346	3,156
162	■	■	■	Tosco	7,284	77.1	2,000	1,705
127	431	254	167	Toys 'R' Us	9,427	148.1	8,437	7,442
357	■	■	■	Trans World Airlines	3,317	−227.5	2,952	793
199	156	45	251	Transamerica	6,101	470.5	47,945	5,186
■	473	446	■	Transatlantic Holdings	1,165	131.9	3,899	1,552
46	32	18	57	Travelers Group	17,624	1,834.0	114,475	19,861
■	254	■	307	Tribune	2,245	278.2	3,288	4,136
462	■	■	■	Trinity Industries	2,474	109.2	1,420	1,423
■	■	381	■	Trustmark	408	59.8	4,993	751
115	166	330	219	TRW	10,172	446.2	5,890	5,773
360	■	■	■	Turner	3,281	1.3	793	48
350	■	416	212	Turner Broadcasting System	3,437	102.7	4,395	5,880
260	258	474	235	Tyco International	4,843	273.0	3,559	5,452
215	333	412	370	Tyson Foods	5,732	210.2	4,498	3,261
126	51	137	81	U S West Communications Group	9,484	1,184.0	16,585	14,566
481	439	252	127	U S West Media Group	2,374	145.0	8,615	9,682
64	192	203	469	UAL	14,943	378.0	11,728	2,496
437	■	■	■	Ultramar	2,714	47.6	1,971	1,267
■	■	314	■	UMB Financial	501	52.2	6,281	725
174	115	93	186	Unicom	6,910	659.5	23,247	6,717
■	337	116	■	Union Bank	1,550	207.3	19,518	1,947
283	163	390	345	Union Camp	4,212	451.1	4,838	3,551

■ Not on 500 list.

Continued

Rankings 500 Table *(Cont.)*

| WHERE THEY RANK: 1995 | | | | | Sales ($mil) | Net profits ($mil) | Assets ($mil) | Market value ($mil) |
Sales	Net profits	Assets	Market value	Company				
208	74	315	194	Union Carbide	5,888	925.0	6,256	6,415
■	227	298	319	Union Electric	2,103	314.1	6,754	3,996
157	71	117	82	Union Pacific	7,486	946.0	19,446	14,443
■	464	206	■	Union Planters	994	135.4	11,277	1,336
194	■	292	■	Unisys	6,202	−624.6	7,113	1,114
■	■	454	■	United Carolina Bancshares	331	44.2	3,786	537
221	242	317	107	United HealthCare	5,511	286.0	6,216	11,107
414	216	68	262	US Bancorp	2,917	329.0	31,794	4,854
337	190	■	174	US Healthcare	3,518	380.7	1,667	7,182
496	■	■	■	US Industries	2,262	−20.0	1,742	1,084
■	■	■	216	US Robotics	1,092	95.7	746	5,858
■	■	■	431	US Satellite Broadcasting	108	−91.4	150	2,739
29	95	140	87	United Technologies	22,624	750.0	15,958	13,502
■	427	394	■	Unitrin	1,447	150.6	4,819	1,848
336	■	■	■	Universal	3,525	43.7	2,050	951
164	270	225	157	Unocal	7,235	260.0	9,891	7,884
288	247	154	303	UNUM	4,123	281.1	14,788	4,288
158	■	296	■	USAir Group	7,474	119.3	6,955	1,126
346	334	157	■	USF&G	3,459	209.4	14,651	1,854
467	■	■	■	USG	2,444	−32.0	1,890	1,188
■	■	266	■	USLife	1,740	105.4	7,931	1,009
■	170	■	200	UST Inc	1,300	429.8	785	6,269
101	■	222	232	USX-Marathon	11,163	−83.0	10,109	5,497
188	232	307	396	USX-US Steel	6,456	303.0	6,521	3,027
428	■	447	■	UtiliCorp United	2,799	79.8	3,886	1,338
398	■	■	■	Valero Energy	3,020	59.8	2,877	1,083
■	■	406	■	Valley National Bancorp	338	62.6	4,586	911
■	441	■	■	Varian Associates	1,581	144.1	954	1,558
479	491	■	■	Varity	2,375	125.5	1,835	1,619
488	■	■	459	Vencor	2,324	8.4	1,912	2,542
248	416	489	344	VF	5,062	157.3	3,447	3,589
98	316	75	84	Viacom	11,689	222.5	29,026	14,372
247	■	■	■	Vons Cos	5,071	68.1	2,187	1,355
■	398	■	■	Vulcan Materials	1,461	166.2	1,216	1,945
297	■	■	■	Waban	3,978	73.0	1,332	855
312	126	49	161	Wachovia	3,755	602.5	44,981	7,590
4	14	56	12	Wal-Mart Stores	93,627	2,740.0	37,900	54,530
104	215	482	152	Walgreen	10,682	330.5	3,512	7,969
171	98	323	86	Warner-Lambert	7,040	739.5	6,101	13,951
■	■	389	■	Washington Federal	371	77.9	4,843	904
■	354	103	■	Washington Mutual	1,625	190.6	21,633	2,122
■	356	■	377	Washington Post	1,719	190.1	1,733	3,205
382	370	■	362	WellPoint Health Networks	3,107	180.0	2,679	3,346
237	63	43	104	Wells Fargo	5,246	1,032.0	50,316	11,349
■	■	■	395	Western Atlas	2,226	99.8	2,489	3,039

Rankings 500 Table *(Cont.)*

WHERE THEY RANK: 1995								
Sales	Net profits	Assets	Market value	Company	Sales ($mil)	Net profits ($mil)	Assets ($mil)	Market value ($mil)
470	■	■	■	Western Digital	2,430	90.8	906	852
■	■	242	■	Western National	570	7.3	9,314	998
■	367	346	■	Western Resources	1,572	181.7	5,491	1,870
192	■	136	166	Westinghouse Electric	6,296	15.0	16,752	7,524
361	236	424	385	Westvaco	3,280	296.5	4,305	3,175
96	86	179	137	Weyerhaeuser	11,788	799.0	13,253	9,060
145	335	271	300	Whirlpool	8,347	209.0	7,800	4,324
406	467	■	482	Whitman	2,947	133.5	2,363	2,430
305	145	490	371	Willamette Industries	3,874	514.8	3,414	3,258
424	47	218	252	Williams Cos	2,856	1,318.2	10,495	5,136
■	■	356	■	Wilmington Trust	505	90.0	5,372	1,104
91	288	■	245	Winn-Dixie Stores	12,567	243.0	2,691	5,324
■	301	407	394	Wisconsin Energy	1,770	234.0	4,561	3,048
114	125	121	78	WMX Technologies	10,248	603.9	18,695	14,916
147	■	484	■	Woolworth	8,224	−164.0	3,506	2,112
325	264	306	149	WorldCom[13]	3,640	267.7	6,552	8,198
■	315	■	179	Wm Wrigley Jr	1,755	223.7	1,099	6,902
51	■	80	83	Xerox	16,611	−472.0	25,969	14,423
■	■	■	447	Xilinx	520	87.4	671	2,617
390	■	■	■	Yellow	3,057	−30.1	1,435	316
411	■	■	■	York International	2,930	−96.1	1,927	2,073
■	■	338	■	Zions Bancorporation	517	81.3	5,621	1,040

■ Not on 500 list.   [13]Formerly LDDS Communications.

ADDRESSES

The following table lists the chief executive, principal business, address and telephone number of the 787 U.S. corporations that qualified for one or more of the ranking lists in this issue. The table also contains the World Wide Web address or E-mail address of many of these companies.

Abbott Laboratories 100 Abbott Park Road Abbott Park, IL 60064-3500 CEO: Duane L Burnham	Drugs 847-937-6100 Fax: 847-937-1511
Adobe Systems PO Box 7900 Mountain View, CA 94039-7900 CEO: John E Warnock	Computer software http://www.adobe.com 415-961-4400 Fax: 415-961-3769
Advanced Micro Devices PO Box 3453 Sunnyvale, CA 94088-3453 CEO: Walter J Sanders III	Computer peripherals http://www.amd.com 408-732-2400 Fax: 408-774-7010
Advanta 300 Welsh Road Horsham, PA 19044 CEO: Alex Hart	Lease & finance 215-657-4000 Fax: 215-784-8071

Aetna Life & Casualty
151 Farmington Avenue
Hartford, CT 06156-3224
CEO: Ronald E Compton

Diversified insurance
http://www.aetna.com
203-273-0123
Fax: 203-273-3971

Aflac
1932 Wynnton Road
Columbus, GA 31999
CEO: Daniel P Amos

Life & health insurance

706-323-3431
Fax: 706-324-6330

AGCO
4830 River Green Parkway
Duluth, GA 30136-2574
CEO: Robert J Ratliff

Heavy equipment

770-813-9200
Fax: 770-813-6118

HF Ahmanson
4900 Rivergrade Road
Irwindale, CA 91706
CEO: Charles R Rinehart

Thrift
http://www.investquest.com
818-814-7986
Fax: 818-814-5659

Air Products & Chemicals
7201 Hamilton Boulevard
Allentown, PA 18195-1501
CEO: Harold A Wagner

Specialty chemicals
http://www.airproducts.com
610-481-4911
Fax: 610-481-5900

AirTouch Communications
One California Street
San Francisco, CA 94111
CEO: Sam Ginn

Telecommunications

415-658-2000
Fax: 415-658-2034

AK Steel Holding
703 Curtis Street
Middletown, OH 45043-0001
CEO: Richard M Wardrop Jr

Steel

513-425-5000
Fax: 513-425-5613

Albertson's
PO Box 20
Boise, ID 83726
CEO: Gary G Michael

Supermarkets & convenience

208-385-6200
Fax: 208-385-6349

Alco Standard
PO Box 834
Valley Forge, PA 19482-0834
CEO: John E Stuart

Business supplies

610-296-8000
Fax: 610-296-8419

Alleghany
375 Park Avenue
New York, NY 10152
CEO: John J Burns Jr

Property & casualty ins

212-752-1356
Fax: 212-759-8149

Allegheny Power System
12 East 49th Street
New York, NY 10017-1028
CEO: Klaus Bergman

Electric util-NE
http://www.alleghenypower.com
212-752-2121
Fax: 212-836-4340

Allergan
PO Box 19534
Irvine, CA 92713-9534
CEO: William C Shepherd

Medical supplies

714-752-4500
Fax: 714-246-6987

AlliedSignal
PO Box 2245
Morristown, NJ 07962-2245
CEO: Lawrence A Bossidy

Aerospace & defense
http://www.alliedsignal.com
201-455-2000
Fax: 201-455-4807

Allmerica Financial
440 Lincoln Street
Worcester, MA 01653
CEO: John F O'Brien

Property & casualty ins

508-855-1000
Fax: 508-853-6332

Allstate
2775 Sanders Road
Northbrook, IL 60062-6127
CEO: Jerry D Choate

Property & casualty ins

847-402-5000
Fax: 847-402-0045

Alltel
One Allied Drive
Little Rock, AR 72202
CEO: Joe T Ford

Telecommunications

501-661-8000
Fax: 501-661-5444

Altera
2610 Orchard Parkway
San Jose, CA 95134-2020
CEO: Rodney Smith

Computer software
http://www.altera.com
408-894-7000

Alumax
5655 Peachtree Parkway
Norcross, GA 30092-2812
CEO: Allen Born

Nonferrous metals

770-246-6600
Fax: 770-246-6696

Aluminum Co of America
425 Sixth Avenue
Pittsburgh, PA 15219-1850
CEO: Paul H O'Neill

Nonferrous metals

412-553-4545
Fax: 412-553-4498

ALZA
PO Box 10950
Palo Alto, CA 94303-0802
CEO: Ernest Mario

Drugs
http://www.alza.com
415-494-5000
Fax: 415-494-5151

Ambac
One State Street Plaza
New York, NY 10004
CEO: Phillip B Lassiter

Lease & finance

212-668-0340
Fax: 212-509-9190

Amerada Hess
1185 Avenue of the Americas
New York, NY 10036
CEO: John B Hess

Miscellaneous energy

212-997-8500
Fax: 212-536-8390

America Online
8619 Westwood Center Drive
Vienna, VA 22182-2285
CEO: Stephen Case

Computer software

703-448-8700
Fax: 703-918-1101

American Brands
PO Box 811
Old Greenwich, CT 06870-0811
CEO: Thomas C Hays

Tobacco

203-698-5000
Fax: 203-637-2580

American Electric Power
1 Riverside Plaza
Columbus, OH 43215
CEO: E Linn Draper Jr

Electric util-NC

614-223-1500
Fax: 614-223-1599

American Express
American Express Tower
New York, NY 10285-4814
CEO: Harvey Golub

Lease & finance
http://www.americanexpress.com
212-640-2000
Fax: 212-640-3370

American Financial Group
One East Fourth Street
Cincinnati, OH 45202
CEO: Carl H Lindner

Property & casualty ins

513-579-2121
Fax: 513-579-0108

American General
PO Box 3247
Houston, TX 77019-3247
CEO: Harold S Hook

Life & health insurance

713-522-1111
Fax: 713-523-8531

American Home Products
Five Giralda Farms
Madison, NJ 07940
CEO: John R Stafford

Drugs

201-660-5000
Fax: 201-660-7178

American International Group
70 Pine Street
New York, NY 10270
CEO: Maurice R Greenberg

Diversified insurance
http://www.aig.com
212-770-7000

American National Insurance
One Moody Plaza
Galveston, TX 77550-7999
CEO: Robert L Moody

Life & health insurance

409-763-4661
Fax: 409-766-6663

American President Cos Ltd
1111 Broadway
Oakland, CA 94607
CEO: Timothy J Rhein

Shipping

510-272-8000
Fax: 510-272-8831

American Re
555 College Road East
Princeton, NJ 08543-5241
CEO: Paul H Inderbitzin

Property & casualty ins
http://www.iusweb.com/amre
609-243-4200
Fax: 609-243-4257

American Standard Cos
PO Box 6820
Piscataway, NJ 08855-6820
CEO: Emmanuel A Kampouris

Electrical equipment

908-980-6000

American Stores
PO Box 27447
Salt Lake City, UT 84127-0447
CEO: Victor L Lund

Supermarkets & convenience

801-539-0112
Fax: 801-531-0768

American Water Works
PO Box 1770
Voorhees, NJ 08043
CEO: George W Johnstone

Electric util-NE

609-346-8200
Fax: 609-346-8229

AmeriSource Health
PO Box 959
Valley Forge, PA 19482-0959
CEO: John F McNamara

Drugs

610-296-4480
Fax: 610-647-0141

Ameritech
30 South Wacker Drive
Chicago, IL 60606
CEO: Richard C Notebaert

Telecommunications
http://www.ameritech.com
312-750-5000
Fax: 312-207-0016

Amgen
1840 Dehavilland Drive
Thousand Oaks, CA 91320-1789
CEO: Gordon Binder

Drugs

805-447-1000
Fax: 805-447-1010

Amoco
PO Box 87703
Chicago, IL 60680-0703
CEO: H Laurance Fuller

International oil
http://www.amoco.com
312-856-6111
Fax: 312-856-2460

AMP
PO Box 3608
Harrisburg, PA 17105-3608
CEO: William J Hudson Jr

Computer peripherals
http://www.amp.com
717-564-0100
Fax: 717-780-6130

AMR
PO Box 619616
DFW Airport, TX 75261-9616
CEO: Robert L Crandall

Airline

817-963-1234
Fax: 817-967-9641

AmSouth Bancorporation
PO Box 11007
Birmingham, AL 35288
CEO: C Dowd Ritter

Regional bank
http://www.amsouth.com
205-320-7151
Fax: 205-326-4072

Anadarko Petroleum
PO Box 1330
Houston, TX 77251-1330
CEO: Robert J Allison Jr

Miscellaneous energy

713-875-1101
Fax: 713-874-3282

Analog Devices
One Technology Way
Norwood, MA 02062
CEO: Ray Stata

Computer peripherals

617-329-4700
Fax: 617-326-8703

Anheuser-Busch Cos
One Busch Place
St Louis, MO 63118-1852
CEO: August A Busch III

Beverages
http://www.budweiser.com
314-577-2000
Fax: 314-577-2900

Aon
123 North Wacker Drive
Chicago, IL 60606
CEO: Patrick G Ryan

Life & health insurance

312-701-3000
Fax: 312-701-3100

Apple Computer
1 Infinite Loop
Cupertino, CA 95014
CEO: Gilbert F Amelio

Computer systems
http://www.apple.com
408-996-1010
Fax: 408-974-4507

Applied Materials
3050 Bowers Avenue
Santa Clara, CA 95054
CEO: James C Morgan

Computer peripherals
http://www.appliedmaterials.co
408-727-5555
Fax: 408-748-5119

Archer Daniels Midland
PO Box 1470
Decatur, IL 62525
CEO: Dwayne O Andreas

Food processor

217-424-5200
Fax: 217-424-6196

Armstrong World Industries
PO Box 3001
Lancaster, PA 17604-3001
CEO: George A Lorch

Home furnishings & recreation

717-397-0611
Fax: 717-396-2408

Arrow Electronics
25 Hub Drive
Melville, NY 11747
CEO: Stephen P Kaufman

Computer peripherals

516-391-1300
Fax: 516-391-1640

Asarco
180 Maiden Lane
New York, NY 10038-4991
CEO: Richard de J Osborne

Nonferrous metals

212-510-2000
Fax: 212-510-1990

Ascend Communications
1275 Harbor Bay Parkway
Alameda, CA 94502
CEO: Mory Ejabat

Telecommunications

510-769-6001

Ashland
PO Box 391
Ashland, KY 41114
CEO: John R Hall

Miscellaneous energy

606-329-3333
Fax: 606-329-3559

Associated Banc-Corp
PO Box 13307
Green Bay, WI 54307-3307
CEO: Harry B Conlon

Regional bank

414-433-3166
Fax: 414-433-3261

AST Research
PO Box 57005
Irvine, CA 92619-7005
CEO: Ian Diery

Computer systems
http://www.ast.com
714-727-4141
Fax: 714-727-9355

Astoria Financial
One Astoria Federal Plaza
Lake Success, NY 11042-1085
CEO: George L Engelke Jr

Thrift

516-327-3000

AT&T
32 Avenue of the Americas
New York, NY 10013-2412
CEO: Robert E Allen

Telecommunications
http://www.att.com
212-387-5400
Fax: 212-387-5347

Atlantic Richfield
515 South Flower Street
Los Angeles, CA 90071-2201
CEO: Michael R Bowlin

Miscellaneous energy

213-486-3708
Fax: 213-486-8741

Atmel
2125 O'Nel Drive
San Jose, CA 95131
CEO: George Perlegos

Computer peripherals

408-441-0311
Fax: 408-436-4200

Automatic Data Processing
One ADP Boulevard
Roseland, NJ 07068-1728
CEO: Josh S Weston

Business services

201-994-5000
Fax: 201-994-5495

AutoZone
PO Box 2198
Memphis, TN 38101
CEO: Joseph R Hyde III

Specialty stores

901-495-6500
Fax: 901-495-8300

Avery Dennison
PO Box 7090
Pasadena, CA 91109-7090
CEO: Charles D Miller

Business supplies

818-304-2000
Fax: 818-792-7312

Avnet
80 Cutter Mill Road
Great Neck, NY 11021-3107
CEO: Leon Machiz

Computer peripherals
http://www.avnet.com
516-466-7000
Fax: 516-466-1203

Avon Products
9 West 57th Street
New York, NY 10019-2683
CEO: James E Preston

Personal products

212-546-6015
Fax: 212-546-7197

Baker Hughes
PO Box 4740
Houston, TX 77210-4740
CEO: James D Woods

Oilfield services
http://www.bhi-net.com
713-439-8600
Fax: 713-439-8699

Ball
PO Box 2407
Muncie, IN 47307-0407
CEO: George A Sissel

Packaging
http://www.ball.com
317-747-6100
Fax: 317-747-6813

Baltimore Gas & Electric
PO Box 1475
Baltimore, MD 21203-1475
CEO: Christian H Poindexter

Electric util-NE
http://www.bge.com
410-234-5000
Fax: 410-234-5367

Banc One
100 East Broad Street
Columbus, OH 43271
CEO: John B McCoy

Regional bank
http://www.bankone.com
614-248-5944
Fax: 614-248-5220

Bancorp Hawaii
PO Box 2900
Honolulu, HI 96846-9972
CEO: Lawrence M Johnson

Regional bank
http://www.boh.com/econ
808-847-8888

BancorpSouth
One Mississippi Plaza
Tupelo, MS 38801
CEO: Aubrey Burns Patterson

Regional bank

601-680-2000
Fax: 601-680-2006

Bank of Boston
100 Federal Street
Boston, MA 02110
CEO: Charles K Gifford

Multinational bank
http://www.bkb.com
617-434-2200
Fax: 617-434-6802

Bank of New York
48 Wall Street
New York, NY 10286
CEO: John Carter Bacot

Regional bank

212-495-1784

BankAmerica
PO Box 37000
San Francisco, CA 94137
CEO: David A Coulter

Multinational bank
http://www.bankamerica.com
415-622-3456
Fax: 415-622-9403

Bankers Trust New York
130 Liberty Street
New York, NY 10006
CEO: Frank N Newman

Multinational bank

212-250-2500
Fax: 212-669-1681

BanPonce
PO Box 362708
San Juan, PR 00936-2708
CEO: Richard L Carrion

Regional bank

809-765-9800
Fax: 809-754-9290

Barnett Banks
PO Box 40789
Jacksonville, FL 32203-0789
CEO: Charles E Rice

Regional bank

904-791-7720
Fax: 904-791-5191

Baxter International
One Baxter Parkway
Deerfield, IL 60015
CEO: Vernon R Loucks Jr

Medical supplies
http://www.fete.com
708-948-2000
Fax: 708-948-3080

Bay Networks
4401 Great American Parkway
Santa Clara, CA 95054
CEO: Andrew K Ludwick

Computer peripherals
http://www.baynetworks.com
408-988-2400
Fax: 409-988-5525

BayBanks
175 Federal Street
Boston, MA 02110
CEO: William M Crozier Jr

Regional bank
http://www.baybank.com
617-482-1040
Fax: 617-482-3182

Bear Stearns Cos
245 Park Avenue
New York, NY 10167
CEO: James E Cayne

Brokerage

212-272-2000
Fax: 212-272-4785

Becton Dickinson
1 Becton Drive
Franklin Lakes, NJ 07417-1880
CEO: Clateo Castellini

Medical supplies

201-847-6800
Fax: 201-847-6475

Bell Atlantic
1717 Arch Street
Philadelphia, PA 19103
CEO: Raymond W Smith

Telecommunications
http://www.ba.com
215-963-6000
Fax: 215-963-9029

BellSouth
1155 Peachtree Street NE
Atlanta, GA 30309-3610
CEO: John L Clendenin

Telecommunications
http://www.bellsouth.com
404-249-2000
Fax: 404-249-5597

Beneficial
301 North Walnut Street
Wilmington, DE 19801
CEO: Finn M W Caspersen

Lease & finance
http://www.beneficial.com
302-425-2500
Fax: 302-425-2512

Bergen Brunswig
4000 Metropolitan Drive
Orange, CA 92668-3510
CEO: Robert E Martini

Drugs

714-385-4000
Fax: 714-385-1442

WR Berkley
PO Box 2518
Greenwich, CT 06836-2518
CEO: William R Berkley

Property & casualty ins

203-629-3000
Fax: 203-629-3492

Berkshire Hathaway
1440 Kiewit Plaza
Omaha, NE 68131
CEO: Warren E Buffett

Property & casualty ins

402-346-1400

Best Buy
PO Box 9312
Minneapolis, MN 55440-9312
CEO: Richard M Schulze

Electronics stores

612-947-2000
Fax: 612-947-2422

Bethlehem Steel
1170 Eighth Avenue
Bethlehem, PA 18016-7699
CEO: Curtis H Barnette

Steel
http://www.bethsteel.com
610-694-2424
Fax: 610-694-5743

Beverly Enterprises
5111 Rogers Avenue
Fort Smith, AR 72919
CEO: David R Banks

Health care services

501-484-8412
Fax: 501-484-8917

Bindley Western Industries
10333 North Meridian Street
Indianapolis, IN 46290
CEO: William E Bindley

Drugs

317-298-9900
Fax: 317-580-9753

Black & Decker
701 East Joppa Road
Towson, MD 21286
CEO: Nolan D Archibald

Appliances

410-716-3900
Fax: 410-716-2933

H&R Block
4400 Main Street
Kansas City, MO 64111
CEO: Richard H Brown

Business services

816-753-6900
Fax: 816-753-8628

BMC Software
2101 Citywest Boulevard
Houston, TX 77042-2827
CEO: Max P Watson Jr

Computer software
http://www.bmc.com
713-918-8800
Fax: 713-918-8000

Boatmen's Bancshares
PO Box 236
St Louis, MO 63166-0236
CEO: Andrew B Craig III

Regional bank

314-466-6000
Fax: 314-466-7333

Boeing
PO Box 3707
Seattle, WA 98124-2207
CEO: Philip M Condit

Aerospace & defense
http://www.boeing.com
206-655-2608
Fax: 206-655-7004

Boise Cascade
PO Box 50
Boise, ID 83728-0001
CEO: George J Harad

Paper & lumber
http://www.bc.com
208-384-6161
Fax: 208-384-7189

BOK Financial
PO Box 2300
Tulsa, OK 74192
CEO: Stanley A Lybarger

Regional bank

918-588-6000
Fax: 918-588-6853

Boston Edison
800 Boylston Street
Boston, MA 02199-2599
CEO: Thomas J May

Electric util-NE

617-424-2000
Fax: 617-424-2605

Boston Scientific
One Boston Scientific Place
Natick, MA 01760-1537
CEO: Peter M Nicholas

Medical supplies

508-650-8000
Fax: 508-650-8955

Bowater
PO Box 1028
Greenville, SC 29602
CEO: Arnold M Nemirow

Paper & lumber

864-271-7733
Fax: 864-282-9594

Bristol-Myers Squibb
345 Park Avenue
New York, NY 10154-0037
CEO: Charles A Heimbold Jr

Drugs
http://www.bms.com
212-546-4000
Fax: 212-546-4020

Brown-Forman
PO Box 1080
Louisville, KY 40201-1080
CEO: Owsley Brown II

Beverages
http://www.brown-forman.com
502-585-1100
Fax: 502-774-7876

Browning-Ferris Industries
PO Box 3151
Houston, TX 77253
CEO: Bruce E Ranck

Environmental & waste

713-870-8100
Fax: 713-870-7844

Brunswick
1 North Field Court
Lake Forest, IL 60045-4811
CEO: Peter N Larson

Recreation equipment

847-735-4700
Fax: 847-735-4765

Burlington Northern Santa Fe
777 Main Street
Fort Worth, TX 76102-5384
CEO: Robert D Krebs

Railroad

817-333-2000
Fax: 817-333-2314

Burlington Resources
PO Box 4239
Houston, TX 77210-4239
CEO: Robert S Shackouls

Miscellaneous energy

713-624-9000
Fax: 713-624-9645

Cabletron Systems
PO Box 5005
Rochester, NH 03866-5005
CEO: S Robert Levine

Computer peripherals
http://www.cabletron.com
603-337-1402
Fax: 603-337-1457

Cabot
75 State Street
Boston, MA 02109-1806
CEO: Samuel W Bodman

Specialty chemicals

617-345-0100
Fax: 617-342-6242

Cal Fed Bancorp
5700 Wilshire Boulevard
Los Angeles, CA 90036
CEO: Edward G Harshfield

Thrift
http://calfed.com
213-932-4200
Fax: 213-930-9485

Caldor
20 Glover Avenue
Norwalk, CT 06856-5620
CEO: Don R Clarke

Drug & discount stores

203-846-1641
Fax: 203-849-2019

Caliber System
PO Box 5459
Akron, OH 44334
CEO: Daniel J Sullivan

Shipping

330-665-5646
Fax: 330-665-8853

Campbell Soup
Campbell Place
Camden, NJ 08103-1799
CEO: David W Johnson

Food processor

609-342-4800
Fax: 609-342-5299

Cardinal Health
5555 Glendon Court
Dublin, OH 43016
CEO: Robert D Walter

Drugs

614-717-5000
Fax: 614-717-6000

Caremark International
2215 Sanders Road
Northbrook, IL 60062
CEO: C A Lance Piccolo

Health care services
http://www.caremark.com
847-559-4700
Fax: 847-559-3905

Carolina Power & Light
PO Box 1551
Raleigh, NC 27602-1551
CEO: Sherwood H Smith Jr

Electric util-SE

919-546-6111
Fax: 919-546-7826

Cascade Communications
5 Carlisle Road
Westford, MA 01886
CEO: Daniel E Smith

Telecommunications
http://www.casc.com
508-692-2600

Case
700 State Street
Racine, WI 53404
CEO: Jean-Pierre Rosso

Heavy equipment

414-636-6011
Fax: 414-636-5043

Caterpillar
100 Northeast Adams Street
Peoria, IL 61629-1425
CEO: Donald V Fites

Heavy equipment

309-675-1000
Fax: 309-675-5815

CCB Financial
PO Box 931
Durham, NC 27702
CEO: Ernest C Roessler

Regional bank

919-683-7777
Fax: 919-683-7263

Center Financial
60 North Main Street
Waterbury, CT 06702
CEO: Robert J Narkis

Thrift

203-578-7000

Centerior Energy
PO Box 94661
Cleveland, OH 44101-4661
CEO: Robert J Farling

Electric util-NC
http://www.centerior.com
216-447-3100
Fax: 216-447-3240

Centex
PO Box 19000
Dallas, TX 75219
CEO: Laurence E Hirsch

Builder

214-559-6500
Fax: 214-559-6750

Central & South West
PO Box 660164
Dallas, TX 75266-0164
CEO: E R Brooks

Electric util-SC

214-777-1000
Fax: 214-777-1033

Central Fidelity Banks
PO Box 27602
Richmond, VA 23261
CEO: Lewis N Miller Jr

Regional bank

804-782-4000
Fax: 804-697-7260

Centura Banks
PO Box 1220
Rocky Mount, NC 27802
CEO: Robert R Mauldin

Regional bank
http://www.centura.com
919-977-4400
Fax: 919-977-4800

Champion International
One Champion Plaza
Stamford, CT 06921
CEO: Andrew C Sigler

Paper & lumber

203-358-7000
Fax: 203-358-2975

Charter One Financial
1215 Superior Avenue
Cleveland, OH 44114
CEO: Charles John Koch

Regional bank
http://www.charterone.com
216-566-5300
Fax: 216-566-1465

Chase Manhattan
270 Park Avenue
New York, NY 10017-2070
CEO: Walter V Shipley

Multinational bank

212-270-6000
Fax: 212-270-4240

Chevron
225 Bush Street
San Francisco, CA 94104-4289
CEO: Kenneth T Derr

International oil
http://www.chevron.com
415-894-7700
Fax: 415-894-7000

Chiquita Brands International
250 East Fifth Street
Cincinnati, OH 45202
CEO: Carl H Lindner Jr

Food processor

513-784-8011
Fax: 513-784-8030

Chiron
4560 Horton Street
Emeryville, CA 94608-2916
CEO: Edward E Penhoet

Drugs

415-655-8730
Fax: 510-601-3376

Chrysler
1000 Chrysler Drive
Auburn Hills, MI 48326-2766
CEO: Robert J Eaton

Autos & trucks
http://www.chryslercorp.com
810-576-5741
Fax: 810-512-1756

Chubb
PO Box 1615
Warren, NJ 07061-1615
CEO: Dean R O'Hare

Property & casualty ins

908-903-2000
Fax: 908-903-2003

Cigna
One Liberty Place
Philadelphia, PA 19192-1550
CEO: Wilson H Taylor

Diversified insurance

215-761-1000
Fax: 215-761-5504

Cincinnati Financial
PO Box 145496
Cincinnati, OH 45250-5496
CEO: Robert B Morgan

Property & casualty ins

513-870-2000
Fax: 513-870-2066

Cinergy
PO Box 960
Cincinnati, OH 45201-0960
CEO: James E Rogers

Electric util-NC

513-381-2000
Fax: 513-651-9196

Circle K
PO Box 52084
Phoenix, AZ 85072-2084
CEO: John F Antioco

Supermarkets & convenience

602-437-0600
Fax: 602-530-5147

Circuit City Stores
9950 Mayland Drive
Richmond, VA 23233
CEO: Richard L Sharp

Electronics stores

804-527-4000
Fax: 804-527-4164

Circus Circus Enterprises
PO Box 14967
Las Vegas, NV 89114-4967
CEO: Clyde T Turner

Hotels & gaming

702-734-0410
Fax: 702-794-3891

Cisco Systems
170 West Tasman Drive
San Jose, CA 95134-1706
CEO: John T Chambers

Computer peripherals
http://www.cisco.com
408-526-4000
Fax: 408-526-4100

Citicorp
399 Park Avenue
New York, NY 10043
CEO: John S Reed

Multinational bank

212-559-1000
Fax: 212-793-6457

Citizens Bancorp
14401 Sweitzer Lane
Laurel, MD 20707
CEO: Alfred H Smith Jr

Regional bank

301-206-6000
Fax: 301-206-6113

Citizens Banking
One Citizens Banking Center
Flint, MI 48502-2401
CEO: Charles R Weeks

Regional bank

810-766-7500
Fax: 810-766-6948

Citizens Utilities
PO Box 3801
Stamford, CT 06905
CEO: Leonard Tow

Telecommunications

203-329-8800
Fax: 203-329-4663

City National
400 North Roxbury Drive
Beverly Hills, CA 90210
CEO: Russell Goldsmith

Regional bank

310-888-6000
Fax: 310-888-6069

Clorox
1221 Broadway
Oakland, CA 94612-1888
CEO: G Craig Sullivan

Personal products
http://www.clorox.com
510-271-7000
Fax: 510-832-1463

CMS Energy
330 Town Center Drive
Dearborn, MI 48126
CEO: William T McCormick Jr

Electric util-NC

313-436-9200
Fax: 517-788-2186

CNB Bancshares
20 NW Third Street
Evansville, IN 47739-0001
CEO: H Lee Cooper

Regional bank
http://www.cnbe.com
812-464-3400
Fax: 812-464-3496

Coast Savings Financial
1000 Wilshire Boulevard
Los Angeles, CA 90017-2457
CEO: Ray Martin

Thrift

213-362-2000
Fax: 213-688-0837

Coastal
Nine Greenway Plaza
Houston, TX 77046-0995
CEO: David A Arledge

Other gas

713-877-1400
Fax: 713-877-6754

Coca-Cola
PO Drawer 1734
Atlanta, GA 30301
CEO: Roberto C Goizueta

Beverages

404-676-2121
Fax: 404-676-3434

Coca-Cola Enterprises
PO Box 723040
Atlanta, GA 31139-0040
CEO: Summerfield K Johnston Jr

Beverages
http://www.cokecce.com
770-989-3000

Colgate-Palmolive
300 Park Avenue
New York, NY 10022-7499
CEO: Reuben Mark

Personal products
http://www.colgate.com
212-310-2000
Fax: 212-310-3284

Collective Bancorp
PO Box 316
Egg Harbor, NJ 08215
CEO: Thomas H Hamilton

Regional bank

609-625-1110
Fax: 609-965-4381

Colonial BancGroup
PO Box 1108
Montgomery, AL 36101
CEO: Robert E Lowder

Regional bank
http://www.traveler.com/is/col
334-240-5000
Fax: 334-240-5345

Columbia Gas System
20 Montchanin Road
Wilmington, DE 19807-0020
CEO: Oliver G Richard III

Integrated gas
http://www.columbiaenergy.com
302-429-5000
Fax: 302-429-5596

Columbia/HCA Healthcare
One Park Plaza
Nashville, TN 37203
CEO: Richard L Scott

Health care services
http://www.columbia.net
615-327-9551
Fax: 615-320-2570

Comcast
1500 Market Street
Philadelphia, PA 19102-2148
CEO: Ralph J Roberts

Broadcasting & movies
http://www.comcast.com
215-665-1700
Fax: 215-981-7790

Comdisco
6111 North River Road
Rosemont, IL 60018
CEO: Jack Slevin

Business services
http://www.comdisco.com
847-698-3000
Fax: 847-518-5060

Comerica
PO Box 75000
Detroit, MI 48275-3230
CEO: Eugene A Miller

Regional bank
http://www.comerica.com
313-222-3300
Fax: 313-964-0638

Commerce Bancshares
PO Box 13686
Kansas City, MO 64199-3686
CEO: David W Kemper

Regional bank

816-234-2000
Fax: 816-234-2369

Commercial Federal
2120 South 72nd Street
Omaha, NE 68124
CEO: William A Fitzgerald

Thrift

402-554-9200
Fax: 402-390-5328

Commercial Metals
7800 Stemmons Freeway
Dallas, TX 75247
CEO: Stanley A Rabin

Steel

214-689-4300
Fax: 214-689-4320

Compaq Computer
PO Box 692000
Houston, TX 77269-2000
CEO: Eckhard Pfeiffer

Computer systems
http://www.compaq.com
713-370-0670
Fax: 713-514-1740

Compass Bancshares
15 South 20th Street
Birmingham, AL 35233
CEO: D Paul Jones Jr

Regional bank

205-933-3000
Fax: 205-715-7812

CompUSA
14951 North Dallas Parkway
Dallas, TX 75240
CEO: James F Halpin

Electronics stores
http://www.compusa.com
214-982-4000
Fax: 214-982-4276

Computer Associates International
One Computer Associates Plaza
Islandia, NY 11788-7000
CEO: Charles B Wang

Computer software
http://www.cai.com
516-342-5224
Fax: 516-342-5329

Computer Sciences
2100 East Grand Avenue
El Segundo, CA 90245
CEO: Van B Honeycutt

Business services
http://csc.com
310-615-0311
Fax: 310-322-9805

ConAgra
One ConAgra Drive
Omaha, NE 68102-5001
CEO: Philip B Fletcher

Food processor

402-595-4000

Conrail
PO Box 41417
Philadelphia, PA 19101-1417
CEO: David M LeVan

Railroad

215-209-2000
Fax: 215-209-4074

Conseco
PO Box 1911
Carmel, IN 46032
CEO: Stephen C Hilbert

Life & health insurance
http://www.conseco.com
317-817-6100
Fax: 317-817-6327

Consolidated Edison
4 Irving Place
New York, NY 10003
CEO: Eugene R McGrath

Electric util-NE

212-460-4600
Fax: 212-475-0734

Consolidated Freightways
3240 Hillview Avenue
Palo Alto, CA 94304-1297
CEO: Donald E Moffitt

Shipping

415-494-2900
Fax: 415-813-0160

Consolidated Natural Gas
CNG Tower
Pittsburgh, PA 15222-3199
CEO: George A Davidson Jr

Integrated gas

412-227-1000
Fax: 412-227-1304

Consolidated Papers
PO Box 8050
Wisconsin Rapids, WI 54495-8050
CEO: Patrick F Brennan

Paper & lumber

715-422-3111
Fax: 715-422-3203

Continental Airlines
PO Box 4607
Houston, TX 77210-4607
CEO: Gordon M Bethune

Airline

713-834-5000
Fax: 713-590-2150

Cooper Industries
PO Box 4446
Houston, TX 77210-4446
CEO: H John Riley Jr

Misc industrial equip

713-739-5400
Fax: 713-739-5555

CoreStates Financial
PO Box 7618
Philadelphia, PA 19101-7618
CEO: Terrence A Larsen

Regional bank

215-973-3100
Fax: 215-973-1761

Corning
One Riverfront Plaza
Corning, NY 14831
CEO: James R Houghton

Medical supplies
http://www.corning.com
607-974-9000
Fax: 607-974-8830

Countrywide Credit Industries
PO Box 7137
Pasadena, CA 91109-7137
CEO: David S Loeb

Lease & finance

818-304-8400
Fax: 818-584-2268

Cox Communications
1400 Lake Hearn Drive NE
Atlanta, GA 30319
CEO: James O Robbins

Broadcasting & movies
http://www.cox.com
404-843-5000
Fax: 404-843-5777

CPC International
PO Box 8000
Englewood Cliffs, NJ 07632-9976
CEO: Charles R Shoemate

Food processor
cpcintl@interramp.com
201-894-4000
Fax: 201-894-2186

Crestar Financial
PO Box 26665
Richmond, VA 23261-6665
CEO: Richard G Tilghman

Regional bank

804-782-5000
Fax: 804-782-7744

Crown Cork & Seal
9300 Aston Road
Philadelphia, PA 19136
CEO: William J Avery

Packaging

215-698-5100
Fax: 215-698-7050

CSX
PO Box 85629
Richmond, VA 23285-5629
CEO: John W Snow

Railroad
http://www.csx.com
804-782-1400
Fax: 804-782-1409

CUC International
PO Box 10049
Stamford, CT 06904-2049
CEO: Walter A Forbes

Home shopping

203-324-9261
Fax: 203-977-8501

Cullen/Frost Bankers
PO Box 1600
San Antonio, TX 78296
CEO: Thomas C Frost

Regional bank

210-220-4011
Fax: 210-220-9117

Cummins Engine
Box 3005
Columbus, IN 47202-3005
CEO: James A Henderson

Auto parts
http://www.cummins.com
812-377-5000
Fax: 812-377-3334

Cyprus Amax Minerals
PO Box 3299
Englewood, CO 80155-3299
CEO: Milton H Ward

Nonferrous metals

303-643-5000
Fax: 303-643-5269

Cytec Industries
5 Garret Mountain Plaza
West Paterson, NJ 07424
CEO: Daryl D Fry

Specialty chemicals

201-357-3100
Fax: 201-357-3088

Dana
PO Box 1000
Toledo, OH 43697
CEO: Southwood J Morcott

Auto parts
http://www.dana.com
419-535-4500
Fax: 419-535-4544

Darden Restaurants
5900 Lake Ellenor Drive
Orlando, FL 32809
CEO: Joe R Lee

Restaurant chain

407-245-4000

Dauphin Deposit
PO Box 2961
Harrisburg, PA 17105-2961
CEO: Christopher R Jennings

Regional bank

717-255-2121
Fax: 717-231-2632

Dayton Hudson
777 Nicollet Mall
Minneapolis, MN 55402
CEO: Robert J Ulrich

Drug & discount stores

612-370-6948
Fax: 612-370-6565

Dean Foods
3600 North River Road
Franklin Park, IL 60131
CEO: Howard M Dean
13.5

Food processor

847-625-6200
Fax: 847-671-8744

Dean Witter, Discover & Co
Two World Trade Center
New York, NY 10048
CEO: Philip J Purcell

Lease & finance

212-392-2222
Fax: 212-392-8404

Deere & Co
John Deere Road
Moline, IL 61265-8098
CEO: Hans W Becherer

Heavy equipment
http://www.90.deere.com
309-765-8000
Fax: 309-765-5682

Dell Computer
2214 West Braker Lane
Austin, TX 78758
CEO: Michael S Dell

Computer systems
http://www.dell.com
512-338-4400
Fax: 512-728-3653

Delta Air Lines
PO Box 20706
Atlanta, GA 30320-6001
CEO: Ronald W Allen

Airline

404-715-2600
Fax: 404-715-1400

Deluxe
PO Box 64235
St Paul, MN 55164-0235
CEO: John A Blanchard III

Business supplies

612-483-7111
Fax: 612-481-4477

Deposit Guaranty
PO Box 730
Jackson, MS 39205-0730
CEO: Emerson B Robinson Jr

Regional bank
http://www.dgb.com
601-354-8211
Fax: 601-354-8192

Dial
Dial Tower
Phoenix, AZ 85077
CEO: John W Teets

Personal products

602-207-4000
Fax: 602-207-5100

Diamond Shamrock
PO Box 696000
San Antonio, TX 78269-6000
CEO: Roger R Hemminghaus

Miscellaneous energy

210-641-6800
Fax: 210-641-8885

Digital Equipment
111 Powdermill Road
Maynard, MA 01754-2571
CEO: Robert B Palmer

Computer systems
http://www.digital.com
508-493-7182
Fax: 508-493-7374

Dillard Department Stores
PO Box 486
Little Rock, AR 72203
CEO: William T Dillard Sr

Department stores

501-376-5200
Fax: 501-376-5036

Dime Bancorp
589 Fifth Avenue
New York, NY 10017
CEO: James M Large Jr

Thrift

800-843-3463
Fax: 212-326-6169

Walt Disney
500 South Buena Vista Street
Burbank, CA 91521-0301
CEO: Michael D Eisner

Broadcasting & movies

818-560-1000
Fax: 818-559-7203

Dole Food
PO Box 5132
Westlake Village, CA 91359-5132
CEO: David H Murdock

Food processor
http://www.dolesaday.com
818-879-6600
Fax: 818-879-6618

Dominion Resources
PO Box 26532
Richmond, VA 23261
CEO: Thos E Capps

Electric util-SE
http://vapower.com
804-775-5700
Fax: 804-775-5819

RR Donnelley & Sons
77 West Wacker Drive
Chicago, IL 60601-1696
CEO: John R Walter

Advertising publishing

312-326-8000
Fax: 312-326-7706

Dover
280 Park Avenue
New York, NY 10017-1292
CEO: Thomas L Reece

Misc industrial equip

212-922-1640
Fax: 212-922-1656

Dow Chemical
2030 Dow Center
Midland, MI 48674
CEO: William S Stavropoulos

Diversified chemicals
http://www.dow.com
517-636-1000
Fax: 517-636-1830

Dow Jones
200 Liberty Street
New York, NY 10281
CEO: Peter R Kann

Advertising publishing

212-416-2000
Fax: 212-416-3299

Downey Financial
PO Box 6000
Newport Beach, CA 92658-6000
CEO: Stephen W Prough

Thrift

714-854-0300
Fax: 714-854-8162

DPL
Courthouse Plaza Southwest
Dayton, OH 45402
CEO: Peter H Forster

Electric util-NC

513-224-6000
Fax: 513-259-7147

DQE
PO Box 68
Pittsburgh, PA 15230-0068
CEO: Wesley W von Schack

Electric util-NC
http://www.dqe.com
412-393-6000
Fax: 412-393-4635

Dresser Industries
PO Box 718
Dallas, TX 75221-0718
CEO: William E Bradford

Oilfield services

214-740-6000
Fax: 214-740-6584

DSC Communications
1000 Coit Road
Plano, TX 75075-5813
CEO: James L Donald

Telecommunications

214-519-3000
Fax: 214-519-4289

DTE Energy
2000 Second Avenue
Detroit, MI 48226
CEO: John E Lobbia

Electric util-NC

313-235-8000
Fax: 313-237-9828

EI du Pont de Nemours
1007 Market Street
Wilmington, DE 19898
CEO: John A Krol

Diversified chemicals
http://www.dupont.com
302-774-1000

Duke Power
422 South Church Street
Charlotte, NC 28242-0001
CEO: William H Grigg

Electric util-SE
http://www.dukepower.com
704-594-0887
Fax: 704-382-8375

Dun & Bradstreet
187 Danbury Road
Wilton, CT 06897
CEO: Robert E Weissman

Advertising publishing
http://www.dnb.com
203-834-4200
Fax: 203-834-4262

Duracell International
Berkshire Corporate Park
Bethel, CT 06801
CEO: Charles R Perrin

Personal products
http://www.duracell.com
203-796-4000
Fax: 203-796-4096

Eastman Chemical
PO Box 511
Kingsport, TN 37662-5075
CEO: Earnest W Deavenport Jr

Specialty chemicals
http://www.eastman.com
423-229-2000
Fax: 423-229-1008

Eastman Kodak
343 State Street
Rochester, NY 14650-0910
CEO: George M C Fisher

Photography & toys

716-724-4000
Fax: 716-724-0663

Eaton
1111 Superior Avenue
Cleveland, OH 44114-2584
CEO: Stephen R Hardis

Auto parts

216-523-5000
Fax: 216-523-4787

Echlin
100 Double Beach Road
Branford, CT 06405
CEO: Frederick J Mancheski

Auto parts

203-481-5751
Fax: 203-481-6485

Eckerd
PO Box 4689
Clearwater, FL 34618
CEO: Frank Newman

Drug & discount stores

813-399-6000
Fax: 813-399-6369

Edison International
PO Box 999
Rosemead, CA 91770
CEO: John E Bryson

Electric util-W

818-302-1212
Fax: 818-302-2117

AG Edwards
One North Jefferson Avenue
St Louis, MO 63103
CEO: Benjamin F Edwards III

Brokerage

314-955-3000
Fax: 314-955-5547

EMC
35 Parkwood Drive
Hopkinton, MA 01748-9103
CEO: Michael C Ruettgers

Computer peripherals
http://www.emc.com
508-435-1000
Fax: 508-435-7954

Emerson Electric
PO Box 4100
St Louis, MO 63136
CEO: Charles F Knight

Electrical equipment

314-553-2000
Fax: 314-553-1605

Engelhard
101 Wood Avenue
Iselin, NJ 08830-0770
CEO: Orin R Smith

Nonferrous metals

908-205-6000
Fax: 908-906-0337

Enova
PO Box 1831
San Diego, CA 92112-4150
CEO: Stephen Baum

Electric util-W

619-696-2000
Fax: 619-696-1814

Enron
PO Box 1188
Houston, TX 77251-1188
CEO: Kenneth L Lay

Other gas

713-853-6161
Fax: 713-853-6790

Entergy
PO Box 61005
New Orleans, LA 70161
CEO: Edwin Lupberger

Electric util-SC

504-529-5262
Fax: 504-576-4269

Equifax
PO Box 4081
Atlanta, GA 30302
CEO: Daniel W McGlaughlin

Business services
http://www.equifax.com
404-885-8000
Fax: 404-888-5452

Equitable Cos
787 Seventh Avenue
New York, NY 10019
CEO: Joseph J Melone

Life & health insurance

212-554-1234
Fax: 212-554-2472

Equitable of Iowa Cos
PO Box 1635
Des Moines, IA 50306-1635
CEO: Frederick S Hubbell

Life & health insurance

515-245-6911
Fax: 515-245-6973

Estee Lauder Cos
767 Fifth Avenue
New York, NY 10153
CEO: Leonard A Lauder

Personal products

212-572-4200

Exxon
5959 Las Colinas Boulevard
Irving, TX 75039-2298
CEO: Lee R Raymond

International oil

214-444-1000
Fax: 214-444-1348

Federal Express
2005 Corporate Avenue
Memphis, TN 38132
CEO: Frederick W Smith

Airline

901-369-3600
Fax: 901-395-4928

Federal Home Loan Mortgage
8200 Jones Branch Drive
McLean, VA 22102
CEO: Leland C Brendsel

Lease & finance

703-903-2000
Fax: 703-903-2239

Federal National Mortgage Assn
3900 Wisconsin Avenue NW
Washington, DC 20016-2899
CEO: James A Johnson

Lease & finance
http://www.fanniemae.com
202-752-7000
Fax: 202-752-3808

Federated Department Stores
7 West Seventh Street
Cincinnati, OH 45202
CEO: Allen Questrom

Department stores

513-579-7000
Fax: 513-579-7555

FHP International
9900 Talbert Avenue
Fountain Valley, CA 92708-8000
CEO: Westcott W Price III

Health care services
http://www.fhp.com
714-963-7233
Fax: 714-378-5655

Fidelity Federal Bank
PO Box 1631
Glendale, CA 91209-1631
CEO: Richard M Greenwood

Thrift

818-549-3116
Fax: 818-549-3499

Fifth Third Bancorp
38 Fountain Square Plaza
Cincinnati, OH 45263
CEO: George A Schaefer Jr

Regional bank
http://www.53.com
513-579-5300
Fax: 513-579-5226

Fina
PO Box 2159
Dallas, TX 75221-2159
CEO: Ron W Haddock

Miscellaneous energy

214-750-2400
Fax: 214-750-2399

Finova Group
PO Box 2209
Phoenix, AZ 85002-2209
CEO: Samuel L Eichenfield

Lease & finance
http://www.finova.com
602-207-4900
Fax: 602-207-4099

First American Corp
First American Center
Nashville, TN 37237-0708
CEO: Dennis C Bottorff

Regional bank

615-748-2000
Fax: 615-748-2412

First Bank System
601 Second Avenue South
Minneapolis, MN 55402-4302
CEO: John F Grundhofer

Regional bank

612-973-1111
Fax: 612-973-4072

First Chicago NBD
One First National Plaza
Chicago, IL 60670
CEO: Verne G Istock

Multinational bank
http://www.fcnbd.com
312-732-4000
Fax: 312-732-6092

First Citizens BancShares
PO Box 27131
Raleigh, NC 27611-7131
CEO: Lewis R Holding

Regional bank
http://www.firstcitizens.com
919-755-7000
Fax: 919-755-2844

First Colony
901 East Byrd Street
Richmond, VA 23219
CEO: Bruce C Gottwald Jr

Life & health insurance
http://firstcolonylife.com
804-775-0300
Fax: 804-649-7030

First Commerce
201 St Charles Avenue
New Orleans, LA 70170
CEO: Ian Arnof

Regional bank

504-561-1371
Fax: 504-582-1014

First Commercial
PO Box 1471
Little Rock, AR 72203
CEO: Barnett Grace

Regional bank

501-371-7000
Fax: 501-371-7413

First Data
401 Hackensack Avenue
Hackensack, NJ 07601
CEO: Henry C Duques

Business services

201-525-4700
Fax: 201-342-0402

First Empire State
One M & T Plaza
Buffalo, NY 14240
CEO: Robert G Wilmers

Regional bank

716-842-5138
Fax: 716-842-5021

First Financial Corp
1305 Main Street
Stevens Point, WI 54481
CEO: John C Seramur

Regional bank

715-341-0400
Fax: 715-345-4139

First Hawaiian
PO Box 3200
Honolulu, HI 96847
CEO: Walter A Dods Jr

Regional bank
http://www.fhb.com
808-525-7000
Fax: 808-533-7844

First Interstate Bancorp
PO Box 54068
Los Angeles, CA 90054
CEO: William E B Siart

Regional bank

213-614-3001
Fax: 213-614-3741

First National of Nebraska
1620 Dodge Street
Omaha, NE 68102
CEO: John R Lauritzen

Regional bank

402-341-0500
Fax: 402-342-4332

First of America Bank
211 South Rose Street
Kalamazoo, MI 49007-5264
CEO: Daniel R Smith

Regional bank

616-376-9000
Fax: 616-376-7016

First Security
PO Box 30006
Salt Lake City, UT 84130-0006
CEO: Spencer F Eccles

Regional bank

801-246-6000
Fax: 801-359-6928

First Tennessee National
PO Box 84
Memphis, TN 38101
CEO: Ralph Horn

Regional bank

901-523-4444
Fax: 901-523-4354

First Union
One First Union Center
Charlotte, NC 28288-0013
CEO: Edward E Crutchfield

Regional bank
http://www.firstunion.com
704-374-6161
Fax: 704-374-3425

First USA
1601 Elm Street
Dallas, TX 75201
CEO: John C Tolleson

Lease & finance

214-849-2000
Fax: 214-849-3748

First Virginia Banks
6400 Arlington Boulevard
Falls Church, VA 22042-2336
CEO: Barry J Fitzpatrick

Regional bank

703-241-4000
Fax: 703-241-3090

Firstar
PO Box 532
Milwaukee, WI 53201
CEO: Roger L Fitzsimonds

Regional bank
http://www.firstar.com
414-765-4321
Fax: 414-765-6040

FirstFed Financial
401 Wilshire Boulevard
Santa Monica, CA 90401-1490
CEO: William S Mortensen

Thrift

310-319-6000
Fax: 310-319-6046

FirstMerit
III Cascade Plaza
Akron, OH 44308-1103
CEO: John R Cochran

Regional bank

216-996-6300
Fax: 216-384-7133

Flagstar Cos
203 East Main Street
Spartanburg, SC 29319-0001
CEO: James B Adamson

Restaurant chain

803-597-8000

Fleet Financial Group
One Federal Street
Boston, MA 02211
CEO: Terrence Murray

Regional bank

617-346-4000
Fax: 617-346-5477

Fleetwood Enterprises
PO Box 7638
Riverside, CA 92513-7638
CEO: John C Crean

Recreation equipment

909-351-3500
Fax: 909-351-3690

Fleming Cos
PO Box 26647
Oklahoma City, OK 73126-0647
CEO: Robert E Stauth

Food wholesaler
http://www.fleming.com
405-840-7200
Fax: 405-841-8149

Florida Progress
PO Box 14042
St Petersburg, FL 33733
CEO: Jack B Critchfield

Electric util-SE

813-824-6400
Fax: 813-824-6527

Fluor
3333 Michelson Drive
Irvine, CA 92730
CEO: Leslie G McCraw

Builder

714-975-2000
Fax: 714-975-5981

FMC
200 East Randolph Drive
Chicago, IL 60601
CEO: Robert N Burt

Diversified chemicals

312-861-6000
Fax: 312-861-6176

Food Lion
PO Box 1330
Salisbury, NC 28145-1330
CEO: Tom E Smith

Supermarkets & convenience
http://www.foodlion.com
704-633-8250
Fax: 704-639-1353

Ford Motor
PO Box 1899
Dearborn, MI 48121-1899
CEO: Alex J Trotman

Autos & trucks
http://www.ford.com/news
313-322-3000
Fax: 313-845-0570

FORE Systems
174 Thorn Hill Road
Warrendale, PA 15086-7535
CEO: Eric Cooper

Computer peripherals
http://www.fore.com
412-772-6600
Fax: 412-772-6500

Foster Wheeler
Perryville Corporate Park
Clinton, NJ 08809-4000
CEO: Richard J Swift

Builder

908-730-4000
Fax: 908-730-5300

Foundation Health
3400 Data Drive
Rancho Cordova, CA 95670
CEO: Daniel D Crowley

Health care services

916-631-5000
Fax: 916-631-5882

FoxMeyer Health
1220 Senlac Drive
Carrollton, TX 75006
CEO: Abbey J Butler

Drugs

214-446-4800
Fax: 214-446-4898

FPL Group
PO Box 14000
Juno Beach, FL 33408-0420
CEO: James L Broadhead

Electric util-SE

407-694-4696
Fax: 407-694-4718

Franklin Resources
PO Box 7777
San Mateo, CA 94403-7777
CEO: Charles B Johnson

Lease & finance

415-312-2000
Fax: 415-574-5012

Freeport-McMoRan Copper & Gold
1615 Poydras Street
New Orleans, LA 70112
CEO: James R Moffett

Nonferrous metals

504-582-4000

Fremont General
PO Box 2208
Santa Monica, CA 90407-2208
CEO: James A McIntyre

Property & casualty ins

310-315-5500
Fax: 310-315-5599

Frontier
180 South Clinton Avenue
Rochester, NY 14646-0700
CEO: Ronald L Bittner

Telecommunications
http://www.frontiercorp.com
716-777-1000
Fax: 716-325-4624

Fruit of the Loom
233 South Wacker Drive
Chicago, IL 60606
CEO: William Farley

Wearing apparel

312-876-1724
Fax: 312-993-1827

Fulton Financial
PO Box 4887
Lancaster, PA 17604
CEO: Rufus A Fulton Jr

Regional bank

717-291-2411
Fax: 717-295-2695

Gannett
1100 Wilson Boulevard
Arlington, VA 22234
CEO: John J Curley

Advertising publishing
http://www.gannett.com
703-284-6000
Fax: 703-276-5540

Gap
One Harrison Street
San Francisco, CA 94105
CEO: Millard Drexler

Apparel stores

415-952-4400
Fax: 415-896-0322

Gateway 2000
PO Box 2000
North Sioux City, SD 57049-2000
CEO: Theodore W Waitt

Computer systems
http://www.gw2k.com
605-232-2000
Fax: 605-232-2465

GATX
500 West Monroe Street
Chicago, IL 60661-3676
CEO: Ronald H Zech

Lease & finance
http://iw.zacks.com
312-621-6200
Fax: 312-621-6646

Gaylord Container
500 Lake Cook Road
Deerfield, IL 60015
CEO: Marvin A Pomerantz

Packaging

847-405-5500
Fax: 847-405-5628

Gaylord Entertainment
One Gaylord Drive
Nashville, TN 37214
CEO: Earl W Wendell

Broadcasting & movies

615-316-6000
Fax: 615-316-6555

Genentech
460 Point San Bruno Boulevard
South San Francisco, CA 94080
CEO: Arthur D Levinson

Drugs

415-225-1000
Fax: 415-225-6000

General Dynamics
3190 Fairview Park Drive
Falls Church, VA 22042-4523
CEO: James R Mellor

Aerospace & defense

703-876-3000
Fax: 703-876-3125

General Electric
3135 Easton Turnpike
Fairfield, CT 06431-0001
CEO: John F Welch Jr

Electrical equipment
http://www.ge.com
203-373-2211
Fax: 203-373-2884

General Instrument
8770 West Bryn Mawr Avenue
Chicago, IL 60631
CEO: Richard Friedland

Telecommunications

312-695-1000
Fax: 312-695-1001

General Mills
PO Box 1113
Minneapolis, MN 55440
CEO: Stephen W Sanger

Food processor

612-540-2311
Fax: 612-540-4576

General Motors
3044 West Grand Boulevard
Detroit, MI 48202-3091
CEO: John F Smith Jr

Autos & trucks

313-556-5000
Fax: 313-556-5108

General Nutrition Cos
921 Penn Avenue
Pittsburgh, PA 15222
CEO: William E Watts

Specialty stores

412-288-4600
Fax: 412-338-8900

General Public Utilities
100 Interpace Parkway
Parsippany, NJ 07054-1149
CEO: James R Leva

Electric util-NE

201-263-6500
Fax: 201-263-6393

General Re
PO Box 10351
Stamford, CT 06904-2351
CEO: Ronald E Ferguson

Property & casualty ins

203-328-5000
Fax: 203-328-6474

Genuine Parts
2999 Circle 75 Parkway
Atlanta, GA 30339
CEO: Larry L Prince

Auto parts

770-953-1700
Fax: 770-956-2211

Georgia Gulf
PO Box 105197
Atlanta, GA 30348
CEO: Jerry R Satrum

Specialty chemicals

770-395-4500
Fax: 770-395-4529

Georgia-Pacific
PO Box 105605
Atlanta, GA 30348-5605
CEO: Alston D Correll

Paper & lumber

404-652-4000
Fax: 404-230-1675

Giant Food
PO Box 1804
Washington, DC 20013
CEO: Pete L Manos

Supermarkets & convenience

301-341-4100
Fax: 301-618-4967

Gillette
Prudential Tower Building
Boston, MA 02199
CEO: Alfred M Zeien

Personal products

617-421-7000
Fax: 617-421-8214

Glendale Federal Bank FSB
PO Box 1709
Glendale, CA 91209
CEO: Stephen J Trafton

Thrift
http://www.glenfed.com
818-500-2000
Fax: 818-409-3296

Golden West Financial
1901 Harrison Street
Oakland, CA 94612
CEO: Marion O Sandler

Thrift

510-446-3420
Fax: 510-446-4137

BF Goodrich
3925 Embassy Parkway
Akron, OH 44333-1799
CEO: John D Ong

Specialty chemicals

216-374-2000
Fax: 216-374-4087

Goodyear Tire & Rubber
1144 East Market Street
Akron, OH 44316-0001
CEO: Samir F Gibara

Auto parts

216-796-2121
Fax: 216-796-2222

WR Grace
One Town Center Road
Boca Raton, FL 33486-1010
CEO: Albert J Costello

Specialty chemicals

407-362-2000
Fax: 407-362-2193

WW Grainger
455 Knightsbridge Parkway
Lincolnshire, IL 60069
CEO: Richard L Keyser

Business services
http://www.grainger.com
847-793-9030
Fax: 847-793-6452

Grand Union
201 Willowbrook Boulevard
Wayne, NJ 07470-0966
CEO: Joseph J McCaig

Supermarkets & convenience

201-890-6100
Fax: 201-890-6671

Great Atlantic & Pacific Tea
2 Paragon Drive
Montvale, NJ 07645
CEO: James Wood

Supermarkets & convenience

201-573-9700
Fax: 201-930-8332

Great Lakes Chemical
PO Box 2200
West Lafayette, IN 47906-0200
CEO: Robert B McDonald

Specialty chemicals

317-497-6100
Fax: 317-497-6234

Great Western Financial
9200 Oakdale Avenue
Chatsworth, CA 91311-6519
CEO: John F Maher

Thrift
http://www.gwf.com
818-775-3411
Fax: 818-775-3471

Green Tree Financial
345 Saint Peter Street
Saint Paul, MN 55102-1639
CEO: Lawrence M Coss

Lease & finance

612-293-3400
Fax: 612-293-3646

GreenPoint Financial
41-60 Main Street
Flushing, NY 11355-3820
CEO: Thomas S Johnson

Thrift

718-670-7600
Fax: 718-670-6064

GTE
One Stamford Forum
Stamford, CT 06904
CEO: Charles R Lee

Telecommunications
http://www.gte.com
203-965-2000
Fax: 203-965-3496

Guidant
PO Box 44906
Indianapolis, IN 46244
CEO: Ronald W Dollens

Medical supplies
http://www.gdt.com
317-971-2000
Fax: 317-971-2040

Halliburton
500 North Akard Street
Dallas, TX 75201-3391
CEO: Dick Cheney

Oilfield services

214-978-2600
Fax: 214-978-2611

Hannaford Bros
PO Box 1000
Portland, ME 04104
CEO: Hugh G Farrington

Supermarkets & convenience

207-883-2911
Fax: 207-885-3165

Harcourt General
27 Boylston Street
Chestnut Hill, MA 02167
CEO: Robert J Tarr Jr

Advertising publishing

617-232-8200
Fax: 617-739-1395

Harley-Davidson
PO Box 653
Milwaukee, WI 53201
CEO: Richard F Teerlink

Recreation equipment

414-342-4680
Fax: 414-935-4977

Harnischfeger Industries
PO Box 554
Milwaukee, WI 53201
CEO: Jeffery T Grade

Heavy equipment

414-671-4400
Fax: 414-797-6405

Harrah's Entertainment
1023 Cherry Road
Memphis, TN 38117-5423
CEO: Philip G Satre

Hotels & gaming

901-762-8600
Fax: 901-762-8637

Harris
1025 West Nasa Boulevard
Melbourne, FL 32919
CEO: Phillip W Farmer

Computer systems
http://www.harris.com
407-727-9100
Fax: 407-727-9646

Hasbro
1027 Newport Avenue
Pawtucket, RI 02862-0200
CEO: Alan G Hassenfeld

Photography & toys

401-431-8697
Fax: 401-431-8467

Hawaiian Electric Industries
PO Box 730
Honolulu, HI 96808-0730
CEO: Robert F Clarke

Electric util-W
http://www.hei.com
808-543-5662
Fax: 808-543-7966

HBO & Co
301 Perimeter Center North
Atlanta, GA 30346
CEO: Charles W McCall

Health care services
http://www.hboc.com
770-393-6000
Fax: 770-393-6092

Health Systems International
21600 Oxnard Street
Woodland Hills, CA 91367
CEO: Malik M Hasan

Health care services

800-474-6676
Fax: 818-593-8591

Healthsource
Two College Park Drive
Hooksett, NH 03106
CEO: Norman C Payson

Health care services

603-268-7000
Fax: 603-268-7908

HealthSouth
Two Perimeter Park South
Birmingham, AL 35243
CEO: Richard M Scrushy

Health care services

205-967-7116

Hechinger
3500 Pennsy Drive
Landover, MD 20785-1691
CEO: John W Hechinger Jr

Home improvement stores

301-341-1000
Fax: 301-341-0980

HJ Heinz
PO Box 57
Pittsburgh, PA 15230-0057
CEO: Anthony J F O'Reilly

Food processor

412-456-5700
Fax: 412-456-6128

Hercules
Hercules Plaza
Wilmington, DE 19894-0001
CEO: Thomas L Gossage

Diversified chemicals
jrapp@herc.com
302-594-5000
Fax: 302-594-5400

Hershey Foods
PO Box 810
Hershey, PA 17033-0810
CEO: Kenneth L Wolfe

Food processor
http://www.hersheys.com
717-534-6799
Fax: 717-534-7873

Hewlett-Packard
3000 Hanover Street
Palo Alto, CA 94304
CEO: Lewis E Platt

Computer systems
http://www.hp.com
415-857-2030
Fax: 415-857-7299

HFS
PO Box 278
Parsippany, NJ 07054-0278
CEO: Henry R Silverman

Hotels & gaming

201-428-9700
Fax: 201-428-6057

Hibernia
PO Box 61540
New Orleans, LA 70161
CEO: Stephen A Hansel

Regional bank

504-533-3333
Fax: 504-533-5841

Hillenbrand Industries
700 State Route 46 East
Batesville, IN 47006-8835
CEO: W August Hillenbrand

Medical supplies

812-934-7000
Fax: 812-934-7364

Hilton Hotels
9336 Civic Center Drive
Beverly Hills, CA 90210
CEO: Stephen F Bollenbach

Hotels & gaming

310-278-4321
Fax: 310-205-4001

Home Depot
2455 Paces Ferry Road
Atlanta, GA 30339-4024
CEO: Bernard Marcus

Home improvement stores

770-433-8211
Fax: 770-431-2685

Homestake Mining
650 California Street
San Francisco, CA 94108-2788
CEO: Harry M Conger

Nonferrous metals

415-981-8150
Fax: 415-397-5038

Honeywell
PO Box 524
Minneapolis, MN 55440-0524
CEO: Michael R Bonsignore

Electrical equipment
http://www.honeywell.com
612-951-1000
Fax: 612-951-2294

Horace Mann Educators
1 Horace Mann Plaza
Springfield, IL 62715-0001
CEO: Paul J Kardos

Diversified insurance

217-789-2500
Fax: 217-788-5161

Hormel Foods
1 Hormel Place
Austin, MN 55912-3680
CEO: Joel W Johnson

Food processor

507-437-5611
Fax: 507-437-5489

Host Marriott
10400 Fernwood Road
Bethesda, MD 20817-1109
CEO: Terence C Golden

Hotels & gaming

301-380-9000
Fax: 301-380-5067

Household International
2700 Sanders Road
Prospect Heights, IL 60070-2799
CEO: William F Aldinger III

Lease & finance

847-564-5000
Fax: 847-205-7452

Houston Industries
PO Box 4567
Houston, TX 77210
CEO: Don D Jordan

Electric util-SC

713-629-3000
Fax: 713-629-3129

Humana
PO Box 1438
Louisville, KY 40201-1438
CEO: David A Jones

Health care services
http://www.humana.com
502-580-1000
Fax: 502-580-3615

Huntington Bancshares
Huntington Center
Columbus, OH 43287
CEO: Frank Wobst

Regional bank
http://www.huntington.com
614-476-8300
Fax: 614-463-5284

IBP
PO Box 515
Dakota City, NE 68731
CEO: Robert L Peterson

Food processor

402-494-2061
Fax: 402-241-2946

Illinois Central
455 N Cityfront Plaza Drive
Chicago, IL 60611-5504
CEO: E Hunter Harrison

Railroad

312-755-7500
Fax: 312-755-7839

Illinois Tool Works
3600 West Lake Avenue
Glenview, IL 60025-5811
CEO: W James Farrell

Misc industrial equip

708-724-7500
Fax: 708-657-4392

Illinova
PO Box 511
Decatur, IL 62525-1805
CEO: Larry D Haab

Electric util-NC
http://www.illinova.com
217-424-6600
Fax: 217-424-7390

IMC Global
2100 Sanders Road
Northbrook, IL 60062-6146
CEO: Wendell F Bueche

Specialty chemicals

708-272-9200
Fax: 708-205-4805

Informix
4100 Bohannon Drive
Menlo Park, CA 94025
CEO: Phillip E White

Computer software
http://www.informix.com
415-926-6300
Fax: 415-926-6593

Ingersoll-Rand
200 Chestnut Ridge Road
Woodcliff Lake, NJ 07675
CEO: James E Perrella

Heavy equipment

201-573-0123
Fax: 201-573-3516

Inland Steel Industries
30 West Monroe Street
Chicago, IL 60603
CEO: Robert J Darnall

Steel
http://www.inland.com
312-346-0300
Fax: 312-899-3964

Integra Financial
Four PPG Place
Pittsburgh, PA 15222-5408
CEO: William F Roemer

Regional bank

412-644-7669
Fax: 412-644-6020

Intel
2200 Mission College Boulevard
Santa Clara, CA 95052-8119
CEO: Andrew S Grove

Computer peripherals
http://www.intel.com
408-765-8080
Fax: 408-765-1774

Intelligent Electronics
411 Eagleview Boulevard
Exton, PA 19341
CEO: Richard D Sanford

Electronics stores

610-458-5500
Fax: 610-458-6702

International Business Machines
Old Orchard Road
Armonk, NY 10504
CEO: Louis V Gerstner Jr

Computer systems

914-765-1900
Fax: 914-765-5099

International Flavors & Fragrances
521 West 57th Street
New York, NY 10019
CEO: Eugene P Grisanti

Specialty chemicals

212-765-5500
Fax: 212-708-7130

International Multifoods
Box 2942
Minneapolis, MN 55402-0942
CEO: Anthony Luiso

Food processor

612-340-3300
Fax: 612-340-3743

International Paper
Two Manhattanville Road
Purchase, NY 10577
CEO: John T Dillon

Paper & lumber

914-397-1500
Fax: 914-397-1691

Interpublic Group of Cos
1271 Avenue of the Americas
New York, NY 10020
CEO: Philip H Geier Jr

Advertising publishing

212-399-8000
Fax: 212-399-8130

Intuit
2535 Garcia Avenue
Mountain View, CA 94043
CEO: William V Campbell

Computer software
http://www.qfn.com
415-944-6000

ITT
1330 Avenue of the Americas
New York, NY 10019-5490
CEO: Rand V Araskog

Hotels & gaming

212-258-1000
Fax: 212-489-5196

ITT Hartford Group
Hartford Plaza
Hartford, CT 06115
CEO: Donald R Frahm

Property & casualty ins
http://www.itthartford.com
860-547-5000
Fax: 860-547-6097

ITT Industries
4 West Red Oak Lane
White Plains, NY 10604
CEO: D Travis Engen

Auto parts

914-641-2000
Fax: 914-696-2960

IVAX
8800 North West 36th Street
Miami, FL 33178-2404
CEO: Phillip Frost

Drugs

305-590-2200
Fax: 305-590-2609

James River Corp of Virginia
PO Box 2218
Richmond, VA 23218
CEO: Miles L Marsh

Personal products

804-644-5411
Fax: 804-649-4428

Jefferson-Pilot
PO Box 21008
Greensboro, NC 27420
CEO: David A Stonecipher

Life & health insurance
http://www.jpc.com
910-691-3000
Fax: 910-691-3311

Jefferson Smurfit
8182 Maryland Avenue
Clayton, MO 63105
CEO: James E Terrill

Packaging

314-746-1100
Fax: 314-746-1276

John Alden Financial
PO Box 020270
Miami, FL 33102-0270
CEO: Glendon E Johnson

Life & health insurance

305-715-2000
Fax: 305-715-1275

Johnson & Johnson
One Johnson & Johnson Plaza
New Brunswick, NJ 08933
CEO: Ralph S Larsen

Medical supplies
http://www.jnj.com
908-524-0400

Johnson Controls
PO Box 591
Milwaukee, WI 53201
CEO: James H Keyes

Auto parts

414-228-1200
Fax: 414-228-2077

Kansas City Power & Light
PO Box 418679
Kansas City, MO 64141-9679
CEO: Drue Jennings

Electric util-NC

816-556-2200
Fax: 816-556-2222

Kansas City Southern Industries
114 West 11th Street
Kansas City, MO 64105-1804
CEO: Landon H Rowland

Railroad

816-556-0303
Fax: 816-556-0192

Kellogg
PO Box 3599
Battle Creek, MI 49016-3599
CEO: Arnold G Langbo

Food processor

616-961-2000
Fax: 616-961-2871

Kelly Services
999 West Big Beaver Road
Troy, MI 48084
CEO: Terence E Adderley

Business services
http://www.kellyservices.com
810-362-4444
Fax: 810-244-4154

Kerr-McGee
PO Box 25861
Oklahoma City, OK 73125
CEO: Frank A McPherson

Miscellaneous energy

405-270-1313
Fax: 405-270-2991

KeyCorp
127 Public Square
Cleveland, OH 44114-1306
CEO: Robert W Gillespie

Regional bank

216-689-3000
Fax: 216-689-5115

Keystone Financial
PO Box 3660
Harrisburg, PA 17105-3660
CEO: Carl L Campbell

Regional bank

717-233-1555
Fax: 717-231-5759

Kimberly-Clark
PO Box 619100
Dallas, TX 75261-9100
CEO: Wayne R Sanders

Personal products

214-281-1200
Fax: 214-281-1490

King World Productions
1700 Broadway
New York, NY 10019-5963
CEO: Michael King

Broadcasting & movies

212-315-4000
Fax: 212-247-7674

Kmart
3100 West Big Beaver Road
Troy, MI 48084-3163
CEO: Floyd Hall

Drug & discount stores

810-643-1000
Fax: 810-643-5513

Knight-Ridder
One Herald Plaza
Miami, FL 33132-1693
CEO: P Anthony Ridder

Advertising publishing

305-376-3800
Fax: 305-995-8156

Kohl's
N54 W13600 Woodale Drive
Menomonee Falls, WI 53051
CEO: William S Kellogg

Department stores

414-783-5800
Fax: 414-783-5255

Kroger
1014 Vine Street
Cincinnati, OH 45202-1100
CEO: Joseph A Pichler

Supermarkets & convenience

513-762-4000

Lafarge
PO Box 4600
Reston, VA 22090
CEO: Michel Rose

Cement & gypsum

703-264-3600
Fax: 703-264-0634

Lear Seating
21557 Telegraph Road
Southfield, MI 48034
CEO: Kenneth L Way

Auto parts

810-746-1500
Fax: 810-746-1524

Leggett & Platt
No.1-Leggett Road
Carthage, MO 64836
CEO: Harry M Cornell Jr

Home furnishings & recreation

417-358-8131
Fax: 417-358-6045

Lehman Brothers Holdings
3 World Financial Center
New York, NY 10285
CEO: Richard S Fuld Jr

Brokerage

212-526-7000
Fax: 212-528-6075

Leucadia National
315 Park Avenue South
New York, NY 10010
CEO: Ian M Cumming

Diversified insurance

212-460-1900
Fax: 212-598-4869

Liberty Financial Cos
600 Atlantic Avenue
Boston, MA 02210-2214
CEO: Kenneth R Leibler

Life & health insurance
http://www.lib.com
617-722-6000
Fax: 617-742-8386

Life Partners Group
7887 East Belleview Avenue
Englewood, CO 80111
CEO: John Massey

Life & health insurance

303-779-1111

Life USA Holding
PO Box 59060
Minneapolis, MN 55459-0060
CEO: Robert W MacDonald

Life & health insurance

612-546-7386
Fax: 612-525-6000

Eli Lilly
Lilly Corporate Center
Indianapolis, IN 46285
CEO: Randall L Tobias

Drugs
http://www.lilly.com
317-276-2000
Fax: 317-276-2095

Limited
PO Box 16000
Columbus, OH 43216
CEO: Leslie H Wexner

Apparel stores

614-479-7000
Fax: 614-479-7079

Lincoln National
PO Box 1110
Fort Wayne, IN 46801
CEO: Ian M Rolland

Diversified insurance

219-455-2000
Fax: 219-455-2733

Linear Technology
1630 McCarthy Boulevard
Milpitas, CA 95035
CEO: Robert H Swanson Jr

Computer peripherals

408-432-1900
Fax: 408-434-0507

Litton Industries
21240 Burbank Boulevard
Woodland Hills, CA 91367-6675
CEO: John M Leonis

Aerospace & defense
http://www.littoncorp.com
818-598-5000
Fax: 818-598-3322

Liz Claiborne
1441 Broadway
New York, NY 10018
CEO: Paul R Charron

Wearing apparel

212-354-4900
Fax: 212-626-1800

Lockheed Martin
6801 Rockledge Drive
Bethesda, MD 20817
CEO: Norman R Augustine

Aerospace & defense
http://www.lmco.com
301-897-6000
Fax: 301-897-6083

Loews
667 Madison Avenue
New York, NY 10021-8087
CEO: Laurence A Tisch

Tobacco

212-545-2000
Fax: 212-545-2860

Long Island Bancorp
201 Old Country Road
Melville, NY 11747-2424
CEO: John J Conefry Jr

Thrift
http://www.lisb.com
215-547-2000

Long Island Lighting
175 East Old Country Road
Hicksville, NY 11801
CEO: William J Catacosinos

Electric util-NE
http://www.lilco.com
516-755-6650

Longs Drug Stores
PO Box 5222
Walnut Creek, CA 94596
CEO: Robert M Long

Drug & discount stores

510-937-1170
Fax: 510-210-6886

Loral
600 Third Avenue
New York, NY 10016
CEO: Bernard L Schwartz

Aerospace & defense

212-697-1105
Fax: 212-661-8988

Louisiana-Pacific
111 Southwest Fifth Avenue
Portland, OR 97204
CEO: Mark A Suwyn

Paper & lumber

503-221-0800
Fax: 503-796-0319

Lowe's Cos
Box 1111
No Wilkesboro, NC 28656-0001
CEO: Leonard G Herring

Home improvement stores
http://www.lowes.com
910-651-4000
Fax: 910-651-4766

LSI Logic
1551 McCarthy Boulevard
Milpitas, CA 95035
CEO: Wilfred J Corrigan

Computer peripherals
http://www.lsilogic.com
408-433-8000
Fax: 408-433-7715

LTV
PO Box 6778
Cleveland, OH 44101
CEO: David H Hoag

Steel

216-622-5000
Fax: 216-622-4578

Lubrizol
29400 Lakeland Boulevard
Wickliffe, OH 44092-2298
CEO: William G Bares

Specialty chemicals

216-943-4200
Fax: 216-943-9062

Lyondell Petrochemical
PO Box 3646
Houston, TX 77253-3646
CEO: Bob G Gower

Specialty chemicals

713-652-7200
Fax: 713-652-4151

Magna Group
1401 South Brentwood Boulevard
St Louis, MO 63144-1401
CEO: G Thomas Andes

Regional bank

314-963-2500
Fax: 314-963-2570

Mallinckrodt Group
7733 Forsyth Boulevard
St Louis, MO 63105
CEO: C Ray Holman

Drugs

314-854-5200
Fax: 314-854-5345

Manor Care
10750 Columbia Pike
Silver Spring, MD 20901
CEO: Stewart Bainum Jr

Health care services

301-681-9400
Fax: 301-905-4062

Manpower
PO Box 2053
Milwaukee, WI 53201
CEO: Mitchell S Fromstein

Business services

414-961-1000
Fax: 414-332-9213

Manville
PO Box 5108
Denver, CO 80217-5108
CEO: W Thomas Stephens

Building materials

303-978-2000
Fax: 303-978-2108

Mapco
PO Box 645
Tulsa, OK 74101-0645
CEO: James E Barnes

Miscellaneous energy

918-581-1800
Fax: 918-581-1534

Marriott International
Marriott Drive
Washington, DC 20058
CEO: J Willard Marriott Jr

Hotels & gaming

301-380-3000
Fax: 301-897-9014

Marsh & McLennan Cos
1166 Avenue of the Americas
New York, NY 10036-2774
CEO: A J C Smith

Brokerage

212-345-5000
Fax: 212-345-4810

Marshall & Ilsley
770 North Water Street
Milwaukee, WI 53202
CEO: James B Wigdale

Regional bank

414-765-7801
Fax: 414-765-7899

Masco
21001 Van Born Road
Taylor, MI 48180
CEO: Richard A Manoogian

Building materials

313-274-7400
Fax: 313-374-6666

Mattel
333 Continental Boulevard
El Segundo, CA 90245-5012
CEO: John W Amerman

Photography & toys

310-252-2000
Fax: 310-252-3671

Maxxam
PO Box 572887
Houston, TX 77257-2887
CEO: Charles E Hurwitz

Nonferrous metals

713-975-7600
Fax: 713-267-3703

May Department Stores
611 Olive Street
St Louis, MO 63101
CEO: David C Farrell

Department stores
http://maycompany.com
314-342-6300
Fax: 314-342-4461

Maytag
403 West Fourth Street North
Newton, IA 50208
CEO: Leonard A Hadley

Appliances

515-792-8000
Fax: 515-791-8376

MBIA
113 King Street
Armonk, NY 10504
CEO: David H Elliott

Lease & finance
75757.3673@compuserve.com
914-273-4545
Fax: 914-765-3163

MBNA
Wilmington, DE 19884-0786
CEO: Alfred Lerner

Lease & finance
302-453-9930
Fax: 302-456-8541

McDonald's
One Kroc Drive
Oak Brook, IL 60521-2278
CEO: Michael R Quinlan

Restaurant chain

708-575-3000
Fax: 708-575-5512

McDonnell Douglas
PO Box 516
St Louis, MO 63166-0516
CEO: Harry C Stonecipher

Aerospace & defense

314-232-0232
Fax: 314-234-3826

McGraw-Hill Cos
1221 Avenue of the Americas
New York, NY 10020-1095
CEO: Joseph L Dionne

Advertising publishing
http://www.mcgraw-hill.com
212-512-2000
Fax: 212-512-2305

MCI Communications
1801 Pennsylvania Avenue NW
Washington, DC 20006
CEO: Bert C Roberts Jr

Telecommunications

202-872-1600
Fax: 202-887-2967

McKesson
One Post Street
San Francisco, CA 94104
CEO: Alan Seelenfreund

Drugs

415-983-8300
Fax: 415-983-8826

Mead
Courthouse Plaza Northeast
Dayton, OH 45463
CEO: Steven C Mason

Paper & lumber

513-222-6323
Fax: 513-495-3021

Medtronic
7000 Central Avenue NE
Minneapolis, MN 55432-3576
CEO: William W George

Medical supplies
http://www.medtronic.com
612-574-4000
Fax: 612-574-4879

Mellon Bank
One Mellon Bank Center
Pittsburgh, PA 15258-0001
CEO: Frank V Cahouet

Regional bank
http://www.mellon.com
412-234-5000
Fax: 412-236-1662

Melville
One Theall Road
Rye, NY 10580
CEO: Stanley P Goldstein

Apparel stores

914-925-4000
Fax: 914-925-4052

Mercantile Bancorporation
PO Box 524
St Louis, MO 63166-0524
CEO: Thomas H Jacobsen

Regional bank

314-425-2525
Fax: 314-425-1286

Mercantile Bankshares
PO Box 1477
Baltimore, MD 21203
CEO: H Furlong Baldwin

Regional bank

410-237-5900
Fax: 410-237-5427

Mercantile Stores
9450 Seward Road
Fairfield, OH 45014-2230
CEO: David L Nichols

Department stores

513-881-8000
Fax: 513-881-8689

Merck
PO Box 100
Whitehouse Station, NJ 08889-0100
CEO: Raymond V Gilmartin

Drugs

908-423-1000

Mercury Finance
100 Field Drive
Lake Forest, IL 60045
CEO: John N Brincat

Lease & finance

847-295-8600
Fax: 847-295-8699

Meridian Bancorp
PO Box 1102
Reading, PA 19603
CEO: Samuel A McCullough

Regional bank

610-655-2000
Fax: 610-655-2492

Merisel
200 Continental Boulevard
El Segundo, CA 90245-0984
CEO: Dwight A Steffensen

Computer peripherals
http://www.merisel.com
310-615-3080
Fax: 310-615-1234

Merrill Lynch
World Financial Center
New York, NY 10281-1331
CEO: Daniel P Tully

Brokerage
http://ml.com
212-449-1000

Fred Meyer
PO Box 42121
Portland, OR 97242-0121
CEO: Robert G Miller

Drug & discount stores

503-232-8844
Fax: 503-797-5299

MFS Communications
3555 Farnam Street
Omaha, NE 68131
CEO: James Q Crowe

Telecommunications
http://www.mfsdatanet.com
402-977-5300
Fax: 402-977-5325

MGIC Investment
PO Box 488
Milwaukee, WI 53201
CEO: William H Lacy

Lease & finance
http://www.mgic.com
414-347-6480
Fax: 414-347-6802

MicroAge
PO Box 1920
Tempe, AZ 85280-1920
CEO: Jeffrey D McKeever

Electronics stores

602-804-2000
Fax: 602-929-2444

Micron Technology
PO Box 6
Boise, ID 83707-0006
CEO: Steven R Appleton

Computer peripherals

208-368-4000
Fax: 208-368-4435

Microsoft
One Microsoft Way
Redmond, WA 98052-6399
CEO: William H Gates

Computer software
http://www.microsoft.com
206-882-8080
Fax: 206-936-7329

MidAmerican Energy
PO Box 657
Des Moines, IA 50303-0657
CEO: Russell E Christiansen

Electric util-NC

515-281-2250
Fax: 515-242-4261

Minnesota Mining & Manufacturing
3M Center
St Paul, MN 55144-1000
CEO: Livio D DeSimone

Business supplies
http://www.mmm.com
612-733-1110
Fax: 612-733-9973

Mirage Resorts
PO Box 7777
Las Vegas, NV 89177-0777
CEO: Stephen A Wynn

Hotels & gaming

702-791-7111
Fax: 702-792-7676

Mobil
3225 Gallows Road
Fairfax, VA 22037-0001
CEO: Lucio A Noto

International oil
http://www.mobil.com
703-846-3000
Fax: 703-846-6002

Molex
2222 Wellington Court
Lisle, IL 60532-1682
CEO: Frederick A Krehbiel

Computer peripherals
http://www.molex.com
708-969-4550
Fax: 708-969-1352

Monsanto
800 North Lindbergh Boulevard
St Louis, MO 63167
CEO: Robert B Shapiro

Diversified chemicals
http://www.monsanto.com
314-694-1000
Fax: 314-694-7625

JP Morgan & Co
60 Wall Street
New York, NY 10260-0060
CEO: Douglas A Warner III

Multinational bank
http://www.jpmorgan.com
212-483-2323

Morgan Stanley Group
1585 Broadway
New York, NY 10036
CEO: Richard B Fisher

Brokerage
http://www.ms.com
212-761-4000
Fax: 212-761-7105

Morton International
100 North Riverside Plaza
Chicago, IL 60606-1596
CEO: S Jay Stewart

Specialty chemicals

312-807-2000
Fax: 312-807-2881

Motorola
1303 East Algonquin Road
Schaumburg, IL 60196
CEO: Gary L Tooker

Telecommunications

847-576-5000
Fax: 847-576-7653

Mylan Laboratories
1030 Century Building
Pittsburgh, PA 15222
CEO: Milan Puskar

Drugs

412-232-0100
Fax: 412-232-0123

Nalco Chemical
One Nalco Center
Naperville, IL 60563-1198
CEO: Edward J Mooney

Specialty chemicals

708-305-1000
Fax: 708-305-2900

Nash Finch
PO Box 355
Minneapolis, MN 55440-0355
CEO: Alfred N Flaten

Food wholesaler

612-832-0534
Fax: 612-844-1236

National City
1900 East Ninth Street
Cleveland, OH 44114-3484
CEO: David A Daberko

Regional bank

216-575-2000
Fax: 216-575-2983

National Commerce Bancorporation
One Commerce Square
Memphis, TN 38150
CEO: Thomas M Garrott

Regional bank

901-523-3434
Fax: 901-523-3120

National Semiconductor
PO Box 58090
Santa Clara, CA 95052-8090
CEO: Position vacant

Computer peripherals
http://www.national.com
408-721-5000
Fax: 408-739-9803

National Steel
4100 Edison Lakes Parkway
Mishawaka, IN 46545-3440
CEO: V John Goodwin

Steel

219-273-7000
Fax: 219-273-7477

NationsBank
NationsBank Corporate Center
Charlotte, NC 28255
CEO: Hugh L McColl Jr

Regional bank
http://www.nationsbank.com
704-386-5000
Fax: 704-386-4579

Navistar International
455 North Cityfront Plaza Dr
Chicago, IL 60611
CEO: John R Horne

Autos & trucks

312-836-2000
Fax: 312-836-2159

Netscape Communications
501 East Middlefield Road
Mountain View, CA 94043
CEO: James L Barksdale

Computer software
http://home.netscape.com
415-254-1900
Fax: 415-528-4124

New England Electric System
25 Research Drive
Westborough, MA 01582-0001
CEO: John W Rowe

Electric util-NE

508-389-2000
Fax: 508-389-3198

New York State Electric & Gas
PO Box 3287
Ithaca, NY 14852-3287
CEO: James A Carrigg

Electric util-NE
http://www.nyseg.com
607-347-4131
Fax: 607-347-2560

New York Times
229 West 43rd Street
New York, NY 10036-3959
CEO: Arthur Ochs Sulzberger

Advertising publishing

212-556-1234
Fax: 212-556-7389

Newell Co
29 East Stephenson Street
Freeport, IL 61032
CEO: William P Sovey

Home furnishings & recreation

815-235-4171
Fax: 608-365-8341

Newmont Mining
1700 Lincoln Street
Denver, CO 80203
CEO: Ronald C Cambre

Nonferrous metals

303-863-7414
Fax: 303-837-6034

Nextel Communications
201 Route 17 North
Rutherford, NJ 07070
CEO: Daniel F Akerson

Telecommunications

201-438-1400
Fax: 201-939-4888

NGC
13430 Northwest Freeway
Houston, TX 77040
CEO: C L Watson

Integrated gas

713-507-6400

Niagara Mohawk Power
300 Erie Boulevard West
Syracuse, NY 13202
CEO: William E Davis

Electric util-NE

315-474-1511

NIKE
One Bowerman Drive
Beaverton, OR 97005-6453
CEO: Philip H Knight

Wearing apparel

503-671-6453
Fax: 503-671-6300

Nipsco Industries
5265 Hohman Avenue
Hammond, IN 46320
CEO: Gary L Neale

Electric util-NC

219-853-5200
Fax: 219-647-6061

NorAm Energy
PO Box 2628
Houston, TX 77252-2628
CEO: T Milton Honea

Integrated gas
http://www.noram.com
713-654-5100
Fax: 713-654-5297

Nordstrom
1501 Fifth Avenue
Seattle, WA 98101-1603
CEO: Bruce A Nordstrom

Apparel stores

206-628-2111
Fax: 206-628-1135

Norfolk Southern
Three Commercial Place
Norfolk, VA 23510-2191
CEO: David R Goode

Railroad

804-629-2600
Fax: 804-629-2822

North Fork Bancorporation
275 Broad Hollow Road
Melville, NY 11747
CEO: John Adam Kanas

Regional bank

516-298-5000

Northeast Utilities
PO Box 270
Hartford, CT 06141-0270
CEO: Bernard M Fox

Electric util-NE

203-665-5000
Fax: 203-665-5884

Northern States Power
414 Nicollet Mall
Minneapolis, MN 55401-1927
CEO: James J Howard

Electric util-NC
http://www.nspco.com
612-330-5500
Fax: 612-330-7558

Northern Trust
50 South LaSalle Street
Chicago, IL 60675
CEO: William A Osborn

Regional bank
http://www.ntrs.com
312-630-6000
Fax: 312-630-6739

Northrop Grumman
1840 Century Park East
Los Angeles, CA 90067-2199
CEO: Kent Kresa

Aerospace & defense

310-553-6262
Fax: 310-201-3023

Northwest Airlines
5101 Northwest Drive
St Paul, MN 55111-3034
CEO: John H Dasburg

Airline

612-726-2111
Fax: 612-726-3139

Norwest
Norwest Center
Minneapolis, MN 55479-1062
CEO: Richard M Kovacevich

Regional bank

612-667-1234
Fax: 612-667-2206

Novell
1555 North Technology Way
Orem, UT 84057
CEO: Robert J Frankenberg

Computer software

801-429-7000
Fax: 801-222-4478

Nucor
2100 Rexford Road
Charlotte, NC 28211
CEO: John D Correnti

Steel

704-366-7000
Fax: 704-362-4208

Nynex
1095 Avenue of the Americas
New York, NY 10036
CEO: Ivan G Seidenberg

Telecommunications
http://www.nynex.com
212-370-7400
Fax: 212-921-2917

Occidental Petroleum
10889 Wilshire Boulevard
Los Angeles, CA 90024
CEO: Ray R Irani

Miscellaneous energy

310-208-8800
Fax: 310-443-6690

Office Depot
2200 Old Germantown Road
Delray Beach, FL 33445
CEO: David I Fuente

Specialty stores

407-278-4800
Fax: 407-279-3239

OfficeMax
PO Box 228070
Shaker Heights, OH 44122-8070
CEO: Michael Feuer

Specialty stores
http://www.officemax.com
216-921-6900
Fax: 216-491-4040

Ogden
Two Pennsylvania Plaza
New York, NY 10121
CEO: R Richard Ablon

Business services

212-868-6000
Fax: 212-868-5895

Ohio Casualty
136 North Third Street
Hamilton, OH 45025
CEO: Lauren N Patch

Property & casualty ins

513-867-3000
Fax: 513-867-3228

Ohio Edison
76 South Main Street
Akron, OH 44308-1890
CEO: Willard R Holland

Electric util-NC
http://www.ohioedison.com
216-384-5100
Fax: 800-633-4766

Oklahoma Gas & Electric
PO Box 321
Oklahoma City, OK 73101-0321
CEO: James G Harlow Jr

Electric util-SC

405-553-3000
Fax: 405-553-3290

Old Kent Financial
One Vandenberg Center
Grand Rapids, MI 49503
CEO: David J Wagner

Regional bank

616-771-5000
Fax: 616-771-4698

Old National Bancorp
PO Box 718
Evansville, IN 47705-0718
CEO: John N Royse

Regional bank

812-464-1434
Fax: 812-464-1567

Old Republic International
307 North Michigan Avenue
Chicago, IL 60601
CEO: A C Zucaro

Diversified insurance

312-346-8100
Fax: 312-726-0309

Olin
PO Box 4500
Norwalk, CT 06856-4500
CEO: Donald W Griffin

Diversified chemicals

203-750-3000
Fax: 203-750-3065

Olsten
175 Broad Hollow Road
Melville, NY 11747-8905
CEO: Frank N Liguori

Business services
http://www.olsten.com
516-844-7800
Fax: 516-844-7022

Omnicom Group
437 Madison Avenue
New York, NY 10022
CEO: Bruce Crawford

Advertising publishing

212-415-3600
Fax: 212-415-3536

OnBancorp
PO Box 4983
Syracuse, NY 13221-4983
CEO: Robert J Bennett

Regional bank

315-424-4400
Fax: 315-424-5951

One Valley Bancorp of West Virginia
PO Box 1793
Charleston, WV 25326
CEO: J Holmes Morrison

Regional bank

304-348-7000
Fax: 304-348-7250

Oracle
PO Box 659506
Redwood City, CA 94065
CEO: Lawrence J Ellison

Computer software
http://www.oracle.com
415-506-7000
Fax: 415-506-7200

Oryx Energy
PO Box 2880
Dallas, TX 75221-2880
CEO: Robert L Keiser

Miscellaneous energy

214-715-4000
Fax: 214-715-8955

Owens & Minor
PO Box 27626
Richmond, VA 23261-7626
CEO: G Gilmer Minor III

Medical supplies

804-747-9794
Fax: 804-270-7281

Owens Corning
Fiberglas Tower
Toledo, OH 43659
CEO: Glen H Hiner

Building materials
http://www.owens-corning.com
419-248-8000
Fax: 419-248-8445

Owens-Illinois
One SeaGate
Toledo, OH 43666
CEO: Joseph H Lemieux

Packaging

419-247-5000
Fax: 419-247-2839

Oxford Health Plans
800 Connecticut Avenue
Norwalk, CT 06854
CEO: Stephen F Wiggins

Health care services

203-852-1442
Fax: 203-851-2465

Paccar
PO Box 1518
Bellevue, WA 98009
CEO: Charles M Pigott

Autos & trucks

206-455-7400
Fax: 206-455-7464

Pacific Enterprises
555 West 5th Street
Los Angeles, CA 90013-1011
CEO: Willis B Wood Jr

Integrated gas
http://www.pacent.com
213-895-5000
Fax: 213-244-8294

Pacific Gas & Electric
PO Box 770000
San Francisco, CA 94177
CEO: Stanley T Skinner

Electric util-W

415-973-7000
Fax: 415-973-6942

Pacific Telesis Group
130 Kearny Street
San Francisco, CA 94108
CEO: Philip J Quigley

Telecommunications
http://www.pactel.com
415-394-3000
Fax: 415-989-7606

PacifiCare Health Systems
5995 Plaza Drive
Cypress, CA 90630-5028
CEO: Alan R Hoops

Health care services
http://phs.com
714-952-1121
Fax: 714-220-3725

PacifiCorp
700 NE Multnomah Street
Portland, OR 97232-4116
CEO: Frederick W Buckman

Electric util-W

503-731-2000
Fax: 503-731-2136

Paging Network
4965 Preston Park Boulevard
Plano, TX 75093
CEO: Glenn W Marschel

Telecommunications
http://www.pagenet.com
214-985-4100

PaineWebber Group
1285 Avenue of the Americas
New York, NY 10019
CEO: Donald B Marron

Brokerage

212-713-2000
Fax: 212-713-1380

Pall
2200 Northern Boulevard
East Hills, NY 11548
CEO: Eric Krasnoff

Medical supplies

516-484-5400
Fax: 516-484-6164

PanAmSat
One Pickwick Plaza
Greenwich, CT 06830
CEO: Frederick A Landman

Telecommunications

203-622-6664
Fax: 203-622-9163

Panhandle Eastern
PO Box 1642
Houston, TX 77251-1642
CEO: Paul M Anderson

Other gas

713-627-5400
Fax: 713-627-4691

Parametric Technology
128 Technology Drive
Waltham, MA 02154
CEO: Steven C Walske

Computer software
http://www.ptc.com
617-398-5000
Fax: 617-398-6000

Parker Hannifin
17325 Euclid Avenue
Cleveland, OH 44112-1290
CEO: Duane E Collins

Misc industrial equip

216-531-3000
Fax: 216-481-4057

Paychex
911 Panorama Trail South
Rochester, NY 14625-0397
CEO: B Thomas Golisano

Business services

716-385-6666
Fax: 716-383-3423

Payless Cashways
PO Box 419466
Kansas City, MO 64141-0466
CEO: David Stanley

Home improvement stores

816-234-6000
Fax: 816-234-6077

PECO Energy
PO Box 8699
Philadelphia, PA 19101
CEO: Corbin A McNeill Jr

Electric util-NE

215-841-4000
Fax: 215-841-4513

Penn Traffic
PO Box 4737
Syracuse, NY 13221-4737
CEO: John T Dixon

Supermarkets & convenience

315-453-7284
Fax: 315-461-2393

JC Penney
6501 Legacy Drive
Plano, TX 75024-3698
CEO: James E Oesterreicher

Department stores
http://www.jcpenney.com
214-431-1000
Fax: 214-431-4944

Pennzoil
PO Box 2967
Houston, TX 77252-2967
CEO: James L Pate

Miscellaneous energy

713-546-4000
Fax: 713-546-6639

People's Bank
850 Main Street
Bridgeport, CT 06604-4913
CEO: David E A Carson

Thrift
http://www.peoples.com
203-338-7171
Fax: 203-338-3600

PeopleSoft
4440 Rosewood Drive
Pleasanton, CA 94588
CEO: David A Duffield

Computer software
http://www.peoplesoft.com
510-225-3000
Fax: 510-225-3341

PepsiCo
700 Anderson Hill Road
Purchase, NY 10577
CEO: Roger A Enrico

Beverages

914-253-2000
Fax: 914-253-2070

Pfizer
235 East 42nd Street
New York, NY 10017-5755
CEO: William C Steere Jr

Drugs
http://www.pfizer.com
212-573-2323
Fax: 212-573-7851

Pharmacia & Upjohn
7000 Portage Road
Kalamazoo, MI 49001
CEO: John L Zabriskie

Drugs

616-323-4000

Phelps Dodge
2600 North Central Avenue
Phoenix, AZ 85004-3014
CEO: Douglas C Yearley

Nonferrous metals

602-234-8100
Fax: 602-234-8337

PHH
11333 McCormick Road
Hunt Valley, MD 21031
CEO: Robert D Kunisch

Business services

410-771-3600
Fax: 410-771-1123

Philip Morris Cos
120 Park Avenue
New York, NY 10017-5592
CEO: Geoffrey C Bible

Tobacco

212-880-5000
Fax: 212-907-5310

Phillips Petroleum
Phillips Building
Bartlesville, OK 74004
CEO: W Wayne Allen

Miscellaneous energy

918-661-6600
Fax: 918-661-7636

Pinnacle West Capital
PO Box 52132
Phoenix, AZ 85072-2132
CEO: Richard Snell

Electric util-W

602-379-2500
Fax: 602-379-2640

Pioneer Hi-Bred International
400 Locust Street
Des Moines, IA 50309
CEO: Charles S Johnson

Food processor

515-248-4800
Fax: 515-248-4999

Pitney Bowes
1 Elmcroft Road
Stamford, CT 06926-0700
CEO: Michael J Critelli

Business supplies
http://www.pitneybowes.com
203-356-5000
Fax: 203-351-6303

PNC Bank
One PNC Plaza
Pittsburgh, PA 15265
CEO: Thomas H O'Brien

Regional bank

412-762-2000

Portland General
121 Southwest Salmon Street
Portland, OR 97204
CEO: Ken L Harrison

Electric util-W

503-464-8820
Fax: 503-778-5566

Potomac Electric Power
1900 Pennsylvania Avenue NW
Washington, DC 20068
CEO: Edward F Mitchell

Electric util-NE

202-872-2000

PP&L Resources
Two North Ninth Street
Allentown, PA 18101-1179
CEO: William F Hecht

Electric util-NE
http://www.papl.com
610-774-5151
Fax: 610-774-5281

PPG Industries
One PPG Place
Pittsburgh, PA 15272
CEO: Jerry E Dempsey

Diversified chemicals
http://www.ppg.com
412-434-3131

Praxair
39 Old Ridgebury Road
Danbury, CT 06810-5113
CEO: H William Lichtenberger

Specialty chemicals
http://www.praxair.com
203-837-2000
Fax: 203-837-2454

Premark International
1717 Deerfield Road
Deerfield, IL 60015
CEO: Warren L Batts

Home furnishings & recreation

708-405-6000
Fax: 708-405-6013

Premier Industrial
4500 Euclid Avenue
Cleveland, OH 44103
CEO: Morton L Mandel

Electrical equipment

216-391-8300
Fax: 216-391-8327

Price/Costco
999 Lake Drive
Issaquah, WA 98027
CEO: James D Sinegal

Specialty stores
http://www.pricecostco.com
206-313-8100
Fax: 206-313-6593

Procter & Gamble
One Procter & Gamble Plaza
Cincinnati, OH 45202
CEO: John E Pepper

Personal products

513-983-1100
Fax: 513-983-4381

Progressive
6300 Wilson Mills Road
Mayfield Village, OH 44143
CEO: Peter B Lewis

Property & casualty ins
http://www.auto-insurance.com
216-461-5000
Fax: 216-446-7699

Protective Life
PO Box 2606
Birmingham, AL 35202
CEO: Drayton Nabers Jr

Life & health insurance

205-879-9230
Fax: 205-868-3023

Provident Bancorp
One East Fourth Street
Cincinnati, OH 45202
CEO: Allen L Davis

Regional bank

513-579-2000
Fax: 513-345-7185

Provident Cos
One Fountain Square
Chattanooga, TN 37402
CEO: J Harold Chandler

Life & health insurance

423-755-1011
Fax: 423-755-8503

Providian
PO Box 32830
Louisville, KY 40232
CEO: Irving W Bailey II

Life & health insurance

502-560-2000
Fax: 502-584-5960

Prudential Reinsurance Holdings
Three Gateway Center
Newark, NJ 07102-4082
CEO: Joseph V Taranto

Property & casualty ins

201-802-6000

Public Service Co of Colorado
PO Box 840
Denver, CO 80201-0840
CEO: Wayne H Brunetti

Electric util-W
http://www.psco.com
303-571-7511
Fax: 303-294-8815

Public Service Enterprise Group
80 Park Plaza
Newark, NJ 07101
CEO: E James Ferland

Electric util-NE

201-430-7000

Puget Sound Power & Light
PO Box 97034
Bellevue, WA 98009-9734
CEO: Richard R Sonstelie

Electric util-W

206-454-6363
Fax: 206-462-3300

Quaker Oats
PO Box 049001
Chicago, IL 60604-9001
CEO: William D Smithburg

Food processor

312-222-7111
Fax: 312-222-8392

Qualcomm
6455 Lusk Boulevard
San Diego, CA 92121-2779
CEO: Irwin M Jacobs

Telecommunications
http://www.qualcomm.com
619-587-1121

Quantum
500 McCarthy Boulevard
Milpitas, CA 95035
CEO: Michael A Brown

Computer peripherals
http://www.quantum.com
408-894-4000
Fax: 408-894-3218

Quick & Reilly Group
230 South Country Road
Palm Beach, FL 33480
CEO: Leslie C Quick Jr

Brokerage
http://www.quick-reilly.com
407-655-8000

Ralston Purina
Checkerboard Square
St Louis, MO 63164
CEO: William P Stiritz

Food processor

314-982-1000
Fax: 314-982-1211

Raychem
300 Constitution Drive
Menlo Park, CA 94025-1164
CEO: Richard A Kashnow

Computer systems

415-361-3333
Fax: 415-361-7665

Rayonier
1177 Summer Street
Stamford, CT 06905-5529
CEO: Ronald M Gross

Paper & lumber

203-348-7000
Fax: 203-964-4528

Raytheon
141 Spring Street
Lexington, MA 02173
CEO: Dennis J Picard

Aerospace & defense
http://www.raytheon.com
617-862-6600
Fax: 617-860-2172

RCSB Financial
235 East Main Street
Rochester, NY 14604
CEO: Leonard S Simon

Thrift

716-258-3000
Fax: 716-423-7280

Read-Rite
345 Los Coches Street
Milpitas, CA 95035
CEO: Cyril J Yansouni

Computer peripherals

408-262-6700
Fax: 408-956-3205

Reader's Digest Association
Reader's Digest Road
Pleasantville, NY 10570-7000
CEO: James P Schadt

Advertising publishing

914-238-1000
Fax: 914-238-4559

Reebok International
100 Technology Center Drive
Stoughton, MA 02072
CEO: Paul B Fireman

Wearing apparel

617-341-5000
Fax: 617-341-5087

Regions Financial
PO Box 10247
Birmingham, AL 35202-0247
CEO: J Stanley Mackin

Regional bank

205-326-7100
Fax: 205-326-7571

Reliance Group Holdings
55 East 52nd Street
New York, NY 10055
CEO: Saul P Steinberg

Property & casualty ins

212-909-1100
Fax: 212-909-1864

ReliaStar Financial
20 Washington Avenue South
Minneapolis, MN 55401
CEO: John G Turner

Life & health insurance
rscorpcom@aol.com
612-372-5432
Fax: 612-342-3966

Republic New York
452 Fifth Avenue
New York, NY 10018
CEO: Walter H Weiner

Multinational bank
http://www.rnb.com
212-525-6000
Fax: 212-525-5678

Revco DS
1925 Enterprise Parkway
Twinsburg, OH 44087
CEO: D Dwayne Hoven

Drug & discount stores

216-425-9811
Fax: 216-487-1650

Reynolds Metals
PO Box 27003
Richmond, VA 23261-7003
CEO: Richard G Holder

Nonferrous metals
http://www.rme.com
804-281-2000
Fax: 804-281-4160

Rhone-Poulenc Rorer
PO Box 1200
Collegeville, PA 19426
CEO: Michel de Rosen

Drugs
http://www.rpr.rpna.com
610-454-8000

Richfood Holdings
PO Box 26967
Richmond, VA 23261
CEO: Donald D Bennett

Food wholesaler

804-746-6000

Riggs National
1503 Pennsylvania Avenue NW
Washington, DC 20005
CEO: Joe L Allbritton

Regional bank

202-835-6000
Fax: 703-207-8985

Rite Aid
PO Box 3165
Harrisburg, PA 17105-0042
CEO: Martin L Grass

Drug & discount stores
http://www.riteaid.com
717-761-2633
Fax: 717-731-3870

RJR Nabisco
1301 Avenue of the Americas
New York, NY 10019-6013
CEO: Steven F Goldstone

Tobacco

212-258-5600
Fax: 212-969-9173

Roadway Express
PO Box 471
Akron, OH 44309-0471
CEO: Michael W Wickham

Shipping
http://www.roadway.com
216-384-1717
Fax: 216-258-6082

Rockwell International
2201 Seal Beach Boulevard
Seal Beach, CA 90740-8250
CEO: Donald R Beall

Electrical equipment
http://www.rockwell.com
310-797-3311
Fax: 310-797-5049

Rohm & Haas
100 Independence Mall West
Philadelphia, PA 19106-2399
CEO: J Lawrence Wilson

Diversified chemicals
http://www.rohmhaas.com
215-592-3000
Fax: 215-592-3377

Roosevelt Financial Group
900 Roosevelt Parkway
Chesterfield, MO 63017
CEO: Stanley J Bradshaw

Regional bank

314-532-6200
Fax: 314-532-6292

Rubbermaid
1147 Akron Road
Wooster, OH 44691
CEO: Wolfgang R Schmitt

Home furnishings & recreation
http://www.rubbermaid.com
216-264-6464
Fax: 216-287-2982

Ryder System
3600 Northwest 82nd Avenue
Miami, FL 33166
CEO: M Anthony Burns

Shipping
http://www.ryder.com
305-593-3726
Fax: 305-593-4196

Safeco
Safeco Plaza
Seattle, WA 98185
CEO: Roger H Eigsti

Diversified insurance

206-545-5000
Fax: 206-545-5559

Safeway
Fourth & Jackson Streets
Oakland, CA 94660
CEO: Steven A Burd

Supermarkets & convenience

510-891-3000
Fax: 510-891-3126

St Jude Medical
One Lillehei Plaza
St Paul, MN 55117
CEO: Ronald A Matricaria

Medical supplies

612-483-2000
Fax: 612-490-4333

St Paul Bancorp
6700 West North Avenue
Chicago, IL 60635
CEO: Joseph C Scully

Thrift

312-622-5000

St Paul Cos
385 Washington Street
St Paul, MN 55102
CEO: Douglas W Leatherdale

Property & casualty ins

612-221-7911
Fax: 612-310-3378

Sallie Mae
1050 Thomas Jefferson St NW
Washington, DC 20007
CEO: Lawrence A Hough

Lease & finance
http://www.salliemae.com
202-333-8000
Fax: 202-298-3160

Salomon
7 World Trade Center
New York, NY 10048
CEO: Robert E Denham

Brokerage

212-783-6300
Fax: 212-783-2107

Sara Lee
Three First National Plaza
Chicago, IL 60602-4260
CEO: John H Bryan

Food processor

312-726-2600
Fax: 312-558-8653

SBC Communications
PO Box 2933
San Antonio, TX 78299-2933
CEO: Edward E Whitacre Jr

Telecommunications

210-821-4105
Fax: 210-351-3553

Scana
1426 Main Street
Columbia, SC 29201
CEO: Lawrence M Gressette Jr

Electric util-SE
http://www.scana.com/
803-748-3000
Fax: 803-343-2344

Schering-Plough
One Giralda Farms
Madison, NJ 07940-1000
CEO: Richard J Kogan

Drugs

201-822-7000
Fax: 201-822-7048

Charles Schwab
101 Montgomery Street
San Francisco, CA 94104
CEO: Charles R Schwab

Brokerage
http://www.schwab.com
415-627-7000
Fax: 415-627-8538

SCI Systems
2101 Clinton Avenue
Huntsville, AL 35805
CEO: Olin B King

Computer systems
@scismail.sci.com
205-882-4800
Fax: 205-882-4466

EW Scripps
PO Box 5380
Cincinnati, OH 45201-5380
CEO: Lawrence A Leser

Advertising publishing

513-977-3000
Fax: 513-977-3966

Seagate Technology
920 Disc Drive
Scotts Valley, CA 95066
CEO: Alan F Shugart

Computer peripherals
http://www.seagate.com
408-438-6550
Fax: 408-438-4127

Sears, Roebuck
3333 Beverly Road
Hoffman Estates, IL 60179
CEO: Arthur C Martinez

Department stores

847-286-2500
Fax: 847-286-5918

Service Corp International
PO Box 130548
Houston, TX 77219-0548
CEO: Robert L Waltrip

Personal products

713-522-5141
Fax: 713-525-5475

Service Merchandise
PO Box 24600
Nashville, TN 37202-4600
CEO: Raymond Zimmerman

Home shopping

615-660-6000
Fax: 615-660-4810

Shaw Industries
PO Drawer 2128
Dalton, GA 30722-2128
CEO: Robert E Shaw

Home furnishings & recreation

706-278-3812
Fax: 706-278-5029

Sherwin-Williams
101 Prospect Avenue NW
Cleveland, OH 44115-1075
CEO: John G Breen

Specialty chemicals

216-566-2000
Fax: 216-566-3312

Sigma-Aldrich
3050 Spruce Street
St Louis, MO 63103
CEO: Carl T Cori

Specialty chemicals
sig-ald@sial.com
314-771-5765
Fax: 314-652-9115

Signet Banking
PO Box 25970
Richmond, VA 23260
CEO: Robert M Freeman

Regional bank
http://www.signetbank.com
804-747-2000
Fax: 804-771-7311

Silicon Graphics
2011 North Shoreline Boulevard
Mountain View, CA 94043-1389
CEO: Edward R McCracken

Computer systems
http://www.sgi.com
415-933-1980
Fax: 415-969-6289

Smith's Food & Drug Centers
1550 South Redwood Road
Salt Lake City, UT 84104
CEO: Jeffrey P Smith

Supermarkets & convenience

801-974-1400
Fax: 801-974-1662

Solectron
847 Gibraltar Drive
Milpitas, CA 95035
CEO: Koichi Nishimura

Computer peripherals

408-957-8500
Fax: 408-956-6075

Sonat
PO Box 2563
Birmingham, AL 35202-2563
CEO: Ronald L Kuehn Jr

Other gas

205-325-3800
Fax: 205-325-7490

Sonoco Products
PO Box 160
Hartsville, SC 29551-0160
CEO: Charles W Coker

Packaging

803-383-7000
Fax: 803-383-7008

Southern Co
270 Peachtree Street
Atlanta, GA 30303
CEO: Alfred W Dahlberg

Electric util-SE
http://www.southernco.com
770-393-0650
Fax: 770-821-3449

Southern National
PO Box 1250
Winston-Salem, NC 27102-1250
CEO: John A Allison IV

Regional bank

910-671-2000
Fax: 910-607-7092

Southern New England
 Telecommunications
PO Box 1562
New Haven, CT 06510
CEO: Daniel J Miglio

Telecommunications
http://www.snet.com

203-771-5200
Fax: 203-865-5198

Southern Pacific Rail
One Market Plaza
San Francisco, CA 94105
CEO: Jerry R Davis

Railroad

415-541-1000
Fax: 415-541-1881

Southland
PO Box 711
Dallas, TX 75221-0711
CEO: Clark J Matthews II

Supermarkets & convenience

214-828-7011
Fax: 214-828-7090

SouthTrust
PO Box 2554
Birmingham, AL 35290
CEO: Wallace D Malone Jr

Regional bank

205-254-5000
Fax: 205-254-4380

Southwest Airlines
PO Box 36611
Dallas, TX 75235-1611
CEO: Herbert D Kelleher

Airline
http://www.iflyswa.com
214-904-4000
Fax: 214-904-4011

Southwestern Public Service
PO Box 1261
Amarillo, TX 79170
CEO: Bill D Helton

Electric util-SC

806-378-2121
Fax: 806-378-2995

Sovereign Bancorp
PO Box 12646
Reading, PA 19612
CEO: Jay S Sidhu

Thrift

610-320-8400
Fax: 610-320-8448

Spiegel
3500 Lacey Road
Downers Grove, IL 60515
CEO: John J Shea

Home shopping

708-986-8800
Fax: 708-769-2121

Sprint
PO Box 11315
Kansas City, MO 64112
CEO: William T Esrey

Telecommunications
http://www.sprint.com
913-624-3000
Fax: 913-624-3496

Standard Federal Bancorp
2600 West Big Beaver Road
Troy, MI 48084
CEO: Thomas R Ricketts

Thrift

810-643-9600
Fax: 810-637-2782

Stanley Works
1000 Stanley Drive
New Britain, CT 06053
CEO: Richard H Ayers

Misc industrial equip

203-225-5111
Fax: 203-827-3895

Staples
PO Box 9328
Framingham, MA 01701-9328
CEO: Thomas G Stemberg

Specialty stores
http://www.staples.com
508-370-8500
Fax: 508-370-8956

Star Banc
PO Box 1038
Cincinnati, OH 45201-1038
CEO: Jerry A Grundhofer

Regional bank

513-632-4000
Fax: 513-632-5512

State Street Boston
Box 351
Boston, MA 02101
CEO: Marshall N Carter

Regional bank
http://www.statestreet.com
617-786-3000
Fax: 617-654-3386

Sterling Chemicals
1200 Smith Street
Houston, TX 77002-4312
CEO: J Virgil Waggoner

Specialty chemicals

713-650-3700
Fax: 713-654-9551

Stone Container
150 North Michigan Avenue
Chicago, IL 60601-7568
CEO: Roger W Stone

Packaging

312-346-6600
Fax: 312-580-4919

Stop & Shop Cos
PO Box 369
Boston, MA 02101
CEO: Robert G Tobin

Supermarkets & convenience

617-380-8000
Fax: 617-770-6416

StrataCom
1400 Parkmoor Avenue
San Jose, CA 95126
CEO: Richard M Moley

Telecommunications
http://www.stratacom.com
408-294-7600
Fax: 408-999-0836

Stryker
PO Box 4085
Kalamazoo, MI 49003-4085
CEO: John W Brown

Medical supplies

616-385-2600
Fax: 616-385-1062

Sumitomo Bank of California
320 California Street
San Francisco, CA 94104
CEO: Tsuneo Onda

Regional bank

415-445-8000
Fax: 415-445-3952

Summit Bancorp
PO Box 2066
Princeton, NJ 08543-2066
CEO: T Joseph Semrod

Regional bank

609-987-3200
Fax: 609-987-3331

Sun Co
1801 Market Street
Philadelphia, PA 19103-1699
CEO: Robert H Campbell

Miscellaneous energy

215-977-3000
Fax: 215-977-3409

Sun Microsystems
2550 Garcia Avenue
Mountain View, CA 94043-1100
CEO: Scott G McNealy

Computer systems
http://www.sun.com
415-960-1300
Fax: 415-969-9131

SunAmerica
1 SunAmerica Center
Los Angeles, CA 90067-6022
CEO: Eli Broad

Life & health insurance
http://www.sunamerica.com
310-772-6000
Fax: 310-772-6565

Sundstrand
PO Box 7003
Rockford, IL 61125-7003
CEO: Robert H Jenkins

Aerospace & defense

815-226-6000
Fax: 815-226-2699

SunTrust Banks
PO Box 4418
Atlanta, GA 30302
CEO: James B Williams

Regional bank

404-588-7711
Fax: 404-827-6173

Supervalu
PO Box 990
Minneapolis, MN 55440
CEO: Michael W Wright

Food wholesaler

612-828-4000
Fax: 612-828-8998

Synovus Financial
PO Box 120
Columbus, GA 31902-0120
CEO: James H Blanchard

Regional bank

706-649-2387
Fax: 706-649-2342

Sysco
1390 Enclave Parkway
Houston, TX 77077-2099
CEO: Bill M Lindig

Food wholesaler

713-584-1390
Fax: 713-584-1188

Tandem Computers
19333 Vallco Parkway
Cupertino, CA 95014-2599
CEO: Roel Pieper

Computer systems
http://www.tandem.com
408-285-6000
Fax: 408-285-6938

Tandy
PO Box 17180
Fort Worth, TX 76102
CEO: John V Roach

Electronics stores
http://www.tandy.com
817-390-3700
Fax: 817-390-2647

TCF Financial
801 Marquette Avenue
Minneapolis, MN 55402-3475
CEO: William A Cooper

Thrift

612-661-6500
Fax: 612-333-2160

Tech Data
5350 Tech Data Drive
Clearwater, FL 34620
CEO: Steven A Raymund

Computer peripherals
@techdata.com
813-539-7429
Fax: 813-538-5860

TECO Energy
PO Box 111
Tampa, FL 33601
CEO: Timothy L Guzzle

Electric util-SE

813-228-4111
Fax: 813-228-4811

**Tele-Communications-Liberty
 Media Group**
PO Box 5630
Denver, CO 80217
CEO: Peter R Barton

Broadcasting & movies

303-267-5500
Fax: 303-488-3200

Tele-Communications-TCI Group
PO Box 5630
Denver, CO 80217
CEO: Brendan R Clouston

Broadcasting & movies

303-267-5500
Fax: 303-488-3200

Teledyne
2049 Century Park East
Los Angeles, CA 90067-3101
CEO: William P Rutledge

Electrical equipment

310-277-3311
Fax: 310-551-4204

Telephone & Data Systems
30 North LaSalle Street
Chicago, IL 60602
CEO: LeRoy T Carlson Jr

Telecommunications
http://www.teldta.com
312-630-1900
Fax: 312-630-1908

Tellabs
4951 Indiana Avenue
Lisle, IL 60532
CEO: Michael J Birck

Computer peripherals
http://www.tellabs.com
708-969-8800
Fax: 708-852-7346

Temple-Inland
Drawer N
Diboll, TX 75941
CEO: Clifford J Grum

Packaging

409-829-2211
Fax: 409-829-3333

Tenet Healthcare
PO Box 4070
Santa Monica, CA 90411-4070
CEO: Jeffrey C Barbakow

Health care services

310-998-8000
Fax: 310-998-8329

Tenneco
1275 King Street
Greenwich, CT 06831-2946
CEO: Dana G Mead

Heavy equipment

203-863-1000
Fax: 203-863-1130

Teradyne
321 Harrison Avenue
Boston, MA 02118
CEO: Alexander V d'Arbeloff

Computer systems

617-482-2700
Fax: 617-422-2910

Terra Industries
PO Box 6000
Sioux City, IA 51102-6000
CEO: Burton M Joyce

Specialty chemicals

712-277-1340
Fax: 712-233-3648

Texaco
2000 Westchester Avenue
White Plains, NY 10650
CEO: Alfred C DeCrane Jr

International oil
http://www.texaco.com
914-253-4000
Fax: 914-253-7753

Texas Instruments
PO Box 655474
Dallas, TX 75265
CEO: Jerry R Junkins

Computer peripherals

214-995-2011
Fax: 214-995-2632

Texas Utilities
1601 Bryan Street
Dallas, TX 75201-3411
CEO: Erle Nye

Electric util-SC

214-812-4600

Textron
40 Westminster Street
Providence, RI 02903-2525
CEO: James F Hardymon

Aerospace & defense
http://www.textron.com
401-421-2800
Fax: 401-457-2220

Thermo Electron
PO Box 9046
Waltham, MA 02254-9046
CEO: George N Hatsopoulos

Environmental & waste

617-622-1000
Fax: 617-622-1207

3Com
PO Box 58145
Santa Clara, CA 95052-8145
CEO: Eric Benhamou

Computer peripherals
http://www.3com.com
408-764-5000
Fax: 408-764-5001

360° Communications
8725 W Higgins Road
Chicago, IL 60631-2702
CEO: Dennis E Foster

Telecommunications
http://www.360c.com
312-399-2500
Fax: 312-399-3805

TIG Holdings
65 East 55th Street
New York, NY 10022
CEO: Jon W Rotenstreich

Property & casualty ins

212-446-2700
Fax: 212-371-8360

Time Warner
75 Rockefeller Plaza
New York, NY 10019
CEO: Gerald M Levin

Broadcasting & movies
http://pathfinder.com/corp
212-484-8000
Fax: 212-489-6183

Times Mirror
Times Mirror Square
Los Angeles, CA 90053
CEO: Mark H Willes

Advertising publishing

213-237-3700
Fax: 213-237-2998

TJX Cos
770 Cochituate Road
Framingham, MA 01701
CEO: Bernard Cammarata

Apparel stores

508-390-1000
Fax: 508-390-2091

Torchmark
2001 Third Avenue South
Birmingham, AL 35233
CEO: Ronald K Richey

Life & health insurance

205-325-4200
Fax: 205-325-2520

Tosco
72 Cummings Point Road
Stamford, CT 06902
CEO: Thomas D O'Malley

Miscellaneous energy

203-977-1000
Fax: 203-964-3187

Toys 'R' Us
461 From Road
Paramus, NJ 07652
CEO: Michael Goldstein

Specialty stores

201-262-7800
Fax: 201-262-8919

Trans World Airlines
515 North Sixth Street
St Louis, MO 63101
CEO: Jeffrey H Erickson

Airline

314-589-3000

Transamerica
600 Montgomery Street
San Francisco, CA 94111
CEO: Frank C Herringer

Life & health insurance

415-983-4000
Fax: 415-983-4165

Transatlantic Holdings
80 Pine Street
New York, NY 10005
CEO: Robert F Orlich

Property & casualty ins

212-770-2000
Fax: 212-785-7230

Travelers Group
388 Greenwich Street
New York, NY 10013
CEO: Sanford I Weill

Lease & finance

212-816-8000
Fax: 212-816-8915

Tribune
435 North Michigan Avenue
Chicago, IL 60611
CEO: John W Madigan

Advertising publishing
http://www.tribune.com
312-222-9100
Fax: 312-222-9670

Trinity Industries
2525 Stemmons Freeway
Dallas, TX 75207-2401
CEO: W Ray Wallace

Heavy equipment

214-631-4420
Fax: 214-689-0824

Trustmark
PO Box 291
Jackson, MS 39205-0291
CEO: Frank R Day

Regional bank

601-354-5111
Fax: 601-949-6684

TRW
1900 Richmond Road
Cleveland, OH 44124-3760
CEO: Joseph T Gorman

Auto parts
http://www.trw.com
216-291-7000
Fax: 216-291-0620

Turner
375 Hudson Street
New York, NY 10014
CEO: Alfred T McNeill

Builder

212-229-6000

Turner Broadcasting System
One CNN Center
Atlanta, GA 30303
CEO: Robert E Turner

Broadcasting & movies

404-827-1700
Fax: 404-827-4459

Tyco International
One Tyco Park
Exeter, NH 03833-1108
CEO: L Dennis Kozlowski

Misc industrial equip

603-778-9700
Fax: 603-778-7330

Tyson Foods
PO Box 2020
Springdale, AR 72765-2020
CEO: Leland E Tollett

Food processor

501-290-4000
Fax: 501-290-4028

U S West Communications Group
PO Box 6508
Englewood, CO 80155-6508
CEO: Solomon D Trujillo

Telecommunications

303-793-6500

U S West Media Group
PO Box 6508
Englewood, CO 80155-6508
CEO: Charles M Lillis

Broadcasting & movies
http://www.uswest.com
303-793-6500

UAL
PO Box 66919
Chicago, IL 60666
CEO: Gerald Greenwald

Airline
http://www.ual.com
847-952-4000
Fax: 847-952-7347

Ultramar
Two Pickwick Plaza
Greenwich, CT 06830
CEO: Jean Gaulin

Miscellaneous energy

203-622-7000
Fax: 203-622-7006

UMB Financial
PO Box 419226
Kansas City, MO 64141-6226
CEO: R Crosby Kemper

Regional bank
http://www.umb.com
816-860-7000
Fax: 816-860-5675

Unicom
PO Box A-3005
Chicago, IL 60690-3005
CEO: James J O'Connor

Electric util-NC
http://www.ucm.com
312-394-7399
Fax: 312-394-3110

Union Bank
350 California Street
San Francisco, CA 94104-1476
CEO: Kanetaka Yoshida

Regional bank

415-705-7000

Union Camp
1600 Valley Road
Wayne, NJ 07470
CEO: W Craig McClelland

Paper & lumber

201-628-2000
Fax: 201-628-2349

Union Carbide
39 Old Ridgebury Road
Danbury, CT 06817-0001
CEO: William H Joyce

Diversified chemicals

203-794-2000
Fax: 203-794-7031

Union Electric
PO Box 149
St Louis, MO 63166
CEO: Charles W Mueller

Electric util-NC

314-621-3222
Fax: 314-554-2888

Union Pacific
Eighth & Eaton Avenues
Bethlehem, PA 18018
CEO: Drew Lewis

Railroad

610-861-3200
Fax: 610-861-3111

Union Planters
PO Box 387
Memphis, TN 38147
CEO: Benjamin W Rawlins Jr

Regional bank

901-383-6000
Fax: 901-383-2832

Unisys
PO Box 500
Blue Bell, PA 19424-0001
CEO: James A Unruh

Computer systems
http://www.unisys.com
215-986-4011
Fax: 215-986-2312

United Carolina Bancshares
PO Box 632
Whiteville, NC 28472
CEO: E Rhone Sasser

Regional bank

910-642-5131
Fax: 910-642-1276

United HealthCare
9900 Bren Road East
Minnetonka, MN 55343
CEO: William W McGuire

Health care services

612-936-1300
Fax: 612-936-0044

US Bancorp
PO Box 8837
Portland, OR 97208
CEO: Gerry B Cameron

Regional bank
http://www.usbank.com
503-275-6111
Fax: 503-275-3452

US Healthcare
PO Box 1109
Blue Bell, PA 19422
CEO: Leonard Abramson

Health care services
http://www.ushc.com
215-628-4800
Fax: 215-283-6858

US Industries
101 Wood Avenue South
Iselin, NJ 08830
CEO: David H Clarke

Home furnishings & recreation

908-767-0700
Fax: 908-767-2205

US Robotics
8100 North McCormick Boulevard
Skokie, IL 60076
CEO: Casey G Cowell

Computer peripherals
http://www.usr.com
847-982-5010
Fax: 847-933-5551

US Satellite Broadcasting
3415 University Avenue
St Paul, MN 55114
CEO: Stanley E Hubbard

Broadcasting & movies
http://www.ussbtv.com
612-645-4500
Fax: 612-659-7088

United Technologies
One Financial Plaza
Hartford, CT 06101
CEO: George David

Aerospace & defense
http://www.utc.com
203-728-7000
Fax: 203-728-7979

Unitrin
One East Wacker Drive
Chicago, IL 60601
CEO: Richard C Vie

Diversified insurance

312-661-4600
Fax: 312-661-4690

Universal
PO Box 25099
Richmond, VA 23260
CEO: Henry H Harrell

Tobacco

804-359-9311
Fax: 804-254-3594

Unocal
2141 Rosecrans Avenue
El Segundo, CA 90245
CEO: Roger C Beach

Miscellaneous energy

310-726-7600

UNUM
2211 Congress Street
Portland, ME 04122
CEO: James F Orr III

Life & health insurance

207-770-2211
Fax: 207-770-4510

USAir Group
2345 Crystal Drive
Arlington, VA 22227
CEO: Stephen M Wolf

Airline

703-418-7000
Fax: 703-418-5139

USF&G
100 Light Street
Baltimore, MD 21202
CEO: Norman P Blake Jr

Property & casualty ins

410-547-3000
Fax: 410-625-5682

USG
PO Box 6721
Chicago, IL 60680-6721
CEO: William C Foote

Cement & gypsum

312-606-4000
Fax: 312-606-5725

USLife
125 Maiden Lane
New York, NY 10038
CEO: Greer F Henderson

Life & health insurance

212-709-6000
Fax: 212-425-8006

UST Inc
100 West Putnam Avenue
Greenwich, CT 06830
CEO: Vincent A Gierer Jr

Tobacco

203-661-1100
Fax: 203-622-3250

USX-Marathon
600 Grant Street
Pittsburgh, PA 15219-4776
CEO: Thomas J Usher

Miscellaneous energy

412-433-1121
Fax: 412-433-2015

USX-US Steel
600 Grant Street
Pittsburgh, PA 15219-4776
CEO: Thomas J Usher

Steel

412-433-1121
Fax: 412-433-2015

UtiliCorp United
PO Box 13287
Kansas City, MO 64199-3287
CEO: Richard C Green Jr

Miscellaneous energy
http://www.utilicorp.com
816-421-6600
Fax: 816-467-3590

Valero Energy
PO Box 500
San Antonio, TX 78292
CEO: William E Greehey

Miscellaneous energy

210-246-2000
Fax: 210-246-2646

Valley National Bancorp
1455 Valley Road
Wayne, NJ 07470-0558
CEO: Gerald H Lipkin

Regional bank

201-305-8800
Fax: 201-305-8415

Varian Associates
3050 Hansen Way
Palo Alto, CA 94304-1000
CEO: J Tracy O'Rourke

Computer peripherals
http://www.varian.com
415-493-4000
Fax: 415-424-5754

Varity
672 Delaware Avenue
Buffalo, NY 14209
CEO: Victor A Rice

Auto parts

716-888-8000
Fax: 716-888-8010

Vencor
400 West Market Street
Louisville, KY 40202
CEO: W Bruce Lunsford

Health care services

502-569-7300
Fax: 502-569-7499

VF
PO Box 1022
Reading, PA 19603
CEO: Mackey J McDonald

Wearing apparel

610-378-1151
Fax: 610-375-7261

Viacom
1515 Broadway
New York, NY 10036
CEO: Sumner M Redstone

Broadcasting & movies

212-258-6000
Fax: 212-258-6354

Vons Cos
PO Box 3338
Los Angeles, CA 90051-1338
CEO: Lawrence A Del Santo

Supermarkets & convenience
http://vonsshop@aol.com
818-821-7000
Fax: 818-821-7934

Vulcan Materials
PO Box 530187
Birmingham, AL 35253-0187
CEO: Herbert A Sklenar

Cement & gypsum

205-877-3000
Fax: 205-877-3094

Waban
PO Box 9600
Natick, MA 01760
CEO: Herbert J Zarkin

Home improvement stores

508-651-6500
Fax: 508-651-7437

Wachovia
PO Box 3099
Winston-Salem, NC 27150
CEO: Leslie M Baker Jr

Regional bank

910-770-5000
Fax: 910-732-7021

Wal-Mart Stores
702 Southwest 8th Street
Bentonville, AR 72716-8001
CEO: David D Glass

Drug & discount stores

501-273-4000
Fax: 501-273-4053

Walgreen
200 Wilmot Road
Deerfield, IL 60015
CEO: Charles R Walgreen III

Drug & discount stores
http://www.walgreens.com
708-940-2500
Fax: 708-317-3652

Warner-Lambert
201 Tabor Road
Morris Plains, NJ 07950
CEO: Melvin R Goodes

Drugs

201-540-2000
Fax: 201-540-7768

Washington Federal
425 Pike Street
Seattle, WA 98101
CEO: Guy C Pinkerton

Thrift

206-624-7930
Fax: 206-624-2334

Washington Mutual
PO Box 834
Seattle, WA 98111
CEO: Kerry K Killinger

Thrift

206-461-2000
Fax: 206-554-2778

Washington Post
1150 15th Street NW
Washington, DC 20071
CEO: Donald E Graham

Advertising publishing

202-334-6000
Fax: 202-334-1031

WellPoint Health Networks
21555 Oxnard Street
Woodland Hills, CA 91367
CEO: Leonard D Schaeffer

Health care services

818-703-4000
Fax: 818-703-3253

Wells Fargo
420 Montgomery Street
San Francisco, CA 94163
CEO: Paul M Hazen

Regional bank
http://wellsfargo.com
415-477-1000

Western Atlas
360 North Crescent Drive
Beverly Hills, CA 90210-4867
CEO: Alton J Brann

Oilfield services

310-888-2500
Fax: 310-888-2848

Western Digital
8105 Irvine Center Drive
Irvine, CA 92718
CEO: Charles A Haggerty

Computer peripherals
http://www.wdc.com
714-932-5000
Fax: 714-932-6324

Western National
5555 San Felipe Road
Houston, TX 77056
CEO: Michael J Poulos

Life & health insurance

713-888-7800
Fax: 713-888-7893

Western Resources
PO Box 889
Topeka, KS 66601
CEO: John E Hayes Jr

Electric util-NC
http://www.wstnres.com
913-575-6300
Fax: 913-575-8061

Westinghouse Electric
11 Stanwix Street
Pittsburgh, PA 15222-1384
CEO: Michael H Jordan

Electrical equipment

412-244-2000
Fax: 412-642-2466

Westvaco
299 Park Avenue
New York, NY 10171
CEO: John A Luke Jr

Paper & lumber

212-688-5000
Fax: 212-318-5050

Weyerhaeuser
Weyerhaeuser
Tacoma, WA 98477
CEO: John W Creighton Jr

Paper & lumber

206-924-2345
Fax: 206-924-3543

Whirlpool
2000 M-63
Benton Harbor, MI 49022-2692
CEO: David R Whitwam

Appliances

616-923-5000
Fax: 616-923-3978

Whitman
3501 Algonquin Road
Rolling Meadows, IL 60008
CEO: Bruce S Chelberg

Beverages

847-818-5000
Fax: 847-818-5046

Willamette Industries
1300 SW Fifth Avenue
Portland, OR 97201
CEO: Steven R Rogel

Paper & lumber

503-227-5581
Fax: 503-273-5603

Williams Cos
One Williams Center
Tulsa, OK 74172
CEO: Keith E Bailey

Other gas
http://www.twc.com
918-588-2000
Fax: 918-588-2296

Wilmington Trust
1100 North Market Street
Wilmington, DE 19890-0001
CEO: Leonard W Quill

Regional bank

302-651-1000
Fax: 302-651-8010

Winn-Dixie Stores
PO Box B
Jacksonville, FL 32203-0297
CEO: A Dano Davis

Supermarkets & convenience

904-783-5000
Fax: 904-783-5294

Wisconsin Energy
PO Box 2949
Milwaukee, WI 53201
CEO: Richard A Abdoo

Electric util-NC

414-221-2345
Fax: 414-221-2884

WMX Technologies
3003 Butterfield Road
Oak Brook, IL 60521
CEO: Dean L Buntrock

Environmental & waste
http://www.wmx.com
708-572-8800
Fax: 708-572-1340

Woolworth
233 Broadway
New York, NY 10279-0003
CEO: Roger N Farah

Drug & discount stores

212-553-2000
Fax: 212-553-2042

WorldCom
515 East Amite Street
Jackson, MS 39201-2702
CEO: Bernard J Ebbers

Telecommunications
http://www.wcom.com
601-360-8600
Fax: 601-360-8616

Wm Wrigley Jr
410 North Michigan Avenue
Chicago, IL 60611-4287
CEO: William Wrigley

Food processor

312-644-2121
Fax: 312-644-0015

Xerox
PO Box 1600
Stamford, CT 06904
CEO: Paul A Allaire

Business supplies
http://www.xerox.com
203-968-3000
Fax: 203-968-4566

Xilinx
2100 Logic Drive
San Jose, CA 95124-3450
CEO: Willem P Roelandts

Computer software
http://www.xilinx.com
408-559-7778
Fax: 408-559-7114

Yellow
PO Box 7563
Overland Park, KS 66207-0563
CEO: A Maurice Myers

Shipping

913-967-4300
Fax: 913-967-4404

York International
PO Box 1592-364B
York, PA 17405-1592
CEO: Robert N Pokelwaldt

Misc industrial equip
http://www.york.com
717-771-7890
Fax: 717-771-7381

Zions Bancorporation
1380 Kennecott Building
Salt Lake City, UT 84133
CEO: Harris H Simmons

Regional bank

801-524-4787
Fax: 801-524-2136

The Forbes Leading International Companies

ERIC S. HARDY

Edited by Eric S. Hardy and Steve Kichen

Data editors: Ann C. Anderson, John H. Christy, Scott DeCarlo
and Donald E. Popp

Researchers: Ronald Boone Jr., Cecily J. Fluke, Gustavo Lombo, Danielle
Nguyen, Shlomo Z. Reifman, Robert Sherwood, Kieu Vu-Gia and Brian Zajac

Programming: Mitchel Rand and John Chamberlain

Editorial assistants: Ira L. Collings, Eileen Henderson and David Schultz

Data compiled July 1996

If you invest only in U.S. stocks, you ignore 60% of the world's stock market capitalization—worth $9 trillion. These markets and the economies they represent do not all move in the same direction as their U.S. counterparts. Investing in them thus offers worthwhile diversification plus the opportunity to buy into some of the world's fastest-growing economies.

The economies of the 25 nations represented in this survey are marching to very different beats. Their gross domestic product growth ranges from 9% in South Korea to less than 1% in Japan and Switzerland. Two countries (Mexico and Argentina) saw their economies shrink, by 7% and 4%, respectively.

Consumer prices almost doubled last year in Turkey while Japan experienced slight deflation. About one in five employable Spaniards and Finns are unemployed, but tiny Luxembourg has a 2.8% unemployment rate. (Note: Arbed, the only firm from Luxembourg among the 500 largest foreign firms listed here, is shown among the Belgian companies.)

If it's fast growth you want, you will probably opt for South America or Asia. But, as John Horseman of GAM International Fund points out, you pay for this with low yields and a relative lack of liquidity—not to mention high volatility. Horseman prefers Europe, where he has dedicated more than 80% of his $834 million portfolio. One recent pick is Barclays, a British bank with $262 billion in assets. The shares, available in the U.S. via American Depositary Receipts, have another fan: Barclays itself. The company has just started buying back its stock, including a 40-million-share purchase in February.

Another pick is the Netherlands' Fortis AMEV, a financial conglomerate with banking and insurance operations. For details about either of these firms, see the tables that follow in this section.

Why is Horseman buying in Europe, with its high unemployment and interest rates? He believes their economies may have finally hit bottom. Another reason to be optimistic, he says, is the aggressive privatization schedules of nations like Italy and the U.K. Newly privatized European corporations in this year's International 500 ranking include ENI, an Italian oil company ranked 42nd with $35 billion in sales, and Finland's oil company, Neste, which also went public in 1995 and shows up in 247th place.

The recent trend toward stability of European currencies reflects the structural improvements in these economies. "The politicians, in both the majority and opposition parties, realize the government can't just keep spending more money it doesn't have," says Bank Leumi foreign exchange specialist Hillel Waxman.

Japan has a weak economy, but still represents an awesome 207 entries among these 500 stocks. Among them is trading giant Mitsubishi, by sales ($185 billion) the largest company in the world. Japan is also domicile to Tokyu, a trucking and railroad company, which has sales of $4.7 billion and is ranked 500th.

New this year to our International 500 listings is Turkey, whose one entry, Koç Group, is an $11.5 billion (sales) conglomerate with interests in automobiles, large appliances, and foodstuffs.

The World Super Fifty on page 166 shows the largest companies in the world based on a composite score of the best three of four ranks for sales, assets, profits and market value. The top-ranked firm: Royal Dutch/Shell Group, headquartered in both the Netherlands and United Kingdom. This year, U.S. companies account for 22 of the 50 slots on the list.

To get on the International 500 a company must have been publicly traded as of May 31 and be incorporated outside the U.S. and its territories. Seagram, which is incorporated in Canada, is listed as a member of the Forbes International 500 even though it generates far more of its $9 billion in revenues in the U.S. than in Canada.

Sales and net income are converted into U.S. dollars at the average exchange rate prevailing during the company's last fiscal year. For assets, we used the exchange rate as of the end of the company's fiscal year. Stock prices and earnings estimates reflect the May 31, 1996 exchange rate.

Five-year results: The S&P 500 gained 72%; international stocks (in dollar terms), 37%. Time for the overseas markets to catch up?

25 Largest Public Foreign Companies

Company/business	Country	Revenue ($mil)	Employees (thou)
Mitsubishi/trading	Japan	184,510	13.9
Mitsui & Co/trading	Japan	181,661	11.7
Itochu/trading	Japan	169,300	7.2[2]
Sumitomo/trading	Japan	167,662	25.3
Marubeni/trading	Japan	161,184	9.9
Toyota Motor/automobiles	Japan	111,139	142.6
Royal Dutch/Shell Group/energy	Netherlands/UK	109,853	104.0
Nissho Iwai/trading	Japan	97,963	17.0
Hitachi/elec & electron	Japan	84,233	331.9
Nippon Tel & Tel/telecomm	Japan	82,002	231.4
Daimler-Benz Group/automobiles	Germany	72,253	321.2
Matsushita Electric Indl/appliances	Japan	70,454	265.4
Tomen/trading	Japan	67,809	2.9[2]
Nissan Motor/automobiles	Japan	62,618	145.6
Volkswagen Group/automobiles	Germany	61,487	242.3
Siemens Group/elec & electron	Germany	60,673	376.1
British Petroleum/energy	UK	56,992	58.2
Bank of Tokyo-Mitsubishi/banking	Japan	55,243	20.1
Toshiba/elec & electron	Japan	53,089	188.0
Nichimen/trading	Japan	50,882	2.6[2]
Tokyo Electric Power[2]/utilities	Japan	50,343[1]	43.1
Kanematsu/trading	Japan	49,878	2.7
Unilever/food, household	Netherlands	49,638	308.0
Nestlé/food, household	Switzerland	47,767	220.2
Sony/appliances	Japan	47,619	138.0

[1]Figures are latest available. [2]Not fully consolidated.

A fiscal year that ended between June 1995 and May 1996 is designated as fiscal 1995. We used estimated earnings for companies that have not yet reported 1995 and identified those companies with an "E." Earnings estimates come courtesy of IBES International, Inc. Fundamental data are from Morgan Stanley Capital International and *Forbes*. The World Competitiveness Report of the World Economic Forum provided the country-by-country economic data.

The World Super Fifty

This represents a composite of each company's best three out of four rankings for sales, profits, assets and market value.

Rank	Company	Business	Country	Revenue ($mil)	Net income ($mil)	Assets ($mil)	Market value ($mil)	Employees (thou)
1	Royal Dutch/Shell Group	energy	Netherlands	109,853	6,906	117,746	128,665[3]	104.0
2	General Motors	automobiles	United States	168,829	6,933	217,079	73,796	709.0
3	Exxon	energy	United States	107,893	6,470	91,296	105,260	84.0
4	General Electric	elec & electron	United States	70,028	6,573	228,035	137,904	219.0
5	Bank of Tokyo-Mitsubishi	banking	Japan	55,243	980	712,747	110,285	20.1
6	Toyota Motor	automobiles	Japan	111,139	2,665	106,722	85,779	142.6
7	Philip Morris Cos	tobacco	United States	53,139	5,478	53,811	82,457	158.0
8	Ford Motor	automobiles	United States	137,137	4,139	243,283	42,304	347.0
8	International Business Machines	computer systems	United States	71,940	4,178	80,292	58,475	222.6
10	Nippon Telegraph & Telephone	telecommunications	Japan	82,002	2,211	127,938	115,697	231.4
11	Wal-Mart Stores	retailing	United States	93,627	2,740	37,541	59,409	648.5
12	HSBC Group	banking	UK	26,682	3,886	351,569	40,050	101.1
13	Industrial Bank of Japan	banking	Japan	38,694	−659	361,372	60,472	5.3[2]
14	Citicorp	banking	United States	31,690	3,464	256,853	40,844	84.0
15	Mobil	energy	United States	64,767	2,376	42,138	44,536	54.5
16	Sanwa Bank	banking	Japan	34,913	−1,296	501,043	55,829	14.4
17	Fuji Bank	banking	Japan	31,597	−3,374	487,369	62,988	15.8
18	EI du Pont de Nemours	chemicals	United States	36,508	3,293	37,312	44,301	106.0
19	Nestlé	food, household	Switzerland	47,767	2,468	38,471	44,148	220.2
19	Procter & Gamble	personal products	United States	34,923	2,835	28,215	60,319	99.2
21	Chase Manhattan	banking	United States	26,220	2,970	303,989	30,450	75.2
22	Sumitomo Bank	banking	Japan	29,611[1]	2,856[1]	565,971[1]	61,891	17.2
23	British Petroleum	energy	UK	56,992	1,771	50,146	48,244	58.2
24	Dai-Ichi Kangyo Bank	banking	Japan	30,312	817	498,625	56,294	18.1[2]
25	Federal National Mortgage Assn	leasing & finance	United States	22,249	2,156	316,550	33,714	3.4
26	Hewlett-Packard	computer systems	United States	33,503	2,621	25,753	54,308	102.0
27	Unilever	food, household	Netherlands	49,638	2,320	30,036	36,986[4]	308.0
28	American International Group	insurance	United States	25,874	2,510	134,136	44,695	33.5
28	AT&T	telecommunications	United States	79,609	139	88,884	99,720	301.9
30	Deutsche Bank Group	banking	Germany	38,418	1,437	503,429	23,509	74.1
31	ENI	energy	Italy	34,924	2,656	56,005	38,272	86.4
32	BankAmerica	banking	United States	20,386	2,664	232,446	27,555	81.0
33	Allianz Worldwide	insurance	Germany	43,486[1]	592[1]	164,729[1]	37,051	67.8
34	Tokyo Electric Power[2]	utilities	Japan	50,343[1]	871[1]	152,699[1]	33,790	43.1
35	Chrysler	automobiles	United States	53,195	2,121	53,756	25,205	112.5
36	Hitachi	elec & electron	Japan	84,233	1,470	92,242	30,821	331.9
37	Sakura Bank	banking	Japan	25,976	−4,426	478,050	37,909	20.3
38	ING Group	insurance	Netherlands	33,236	1,650	246,986	24,137	52.1
39	ABN-Amro Holding	banking	Netherlands	26,533	1,629	340,642	17,413	63.3
40	PepsiCo	beverages	United States	30,421	1,606	25,432	52,402	475.5
41	Union Bank of Switzerland	banking	Switzerland	18,496	1,415	336,188	24,382	29.1
42	Barclays	banking	UK	23,202	2,153	261,681	18,451	92.4

(Continued)

The World Super Fifty (*Cont.*)

This represents a composite of each company's best three out of four rankings for sales, profits, assets and market value.

Rank	Company	Business	Country	Revenue ($mil)	Net income ($mil)	Assets ($mil)	Market value ($mil)	Employees (thou)
43	NationsBank	banking	United States	16,327	1,950	187,298	22,250	59.3
44	Matsushita Electric Industrial	appliances	Japan	70,454	−590	75,384	36,155	265.4
44	National Westminster Bank Group	banking	UK	23,533	1,916	260,822	17,119	81.8
44	Siemens Group	elec & electron	Germany	60,673	1,268	57,779	30,817	376.1
47	Lloyds TSB Group	banking	UK	18,653	1,517	229,473	25,070	87.0
48	Motorola	telecommunications	United States	27,037	1,781	22,801	39,476	137.0
49	Amoco	energy	United States	27,066	1,862	29,845	35,989	42.9
50	British Telecommunications	telecommunications	UK	22,618	3,109	35,902	34,319	135.2

[1]Figures are latest available. [2]Not fully consolidated. [3]Combined market value for Royal Dutch Petroleum and Shell Transport & Trading. [4]Combined market value for Unilever NV and Unilever Plc.

How do the U.S. Economy and Stock Market Stack up Against Their Overseas Counterparts?

Compare these figures with those for other nations on the following pages. We're behind Japan, for example, in GDP per capita and R&D spending. Data sources: Morgan Stanley Capital International, World Competitiveness Report of the International Institute for Management Development (Lausanne) and the World Economic Forum (Geneva).

United States   P/E 18 • Yield 2.2% • Market Value $6.8 trillion

Country Statistics
Population	261.3 million
Gross domestic product	$6,738.4 billion
GDP per capita	$25.8 thousand
Total national debt/GDP	52.2%
R&D expenditures/GDP	2.8%
Unemployment rate	5.6%
Retail sales per capita	$5.6 thousand

THE FOREIGN 500:
RANKED WITHIN COUNTRY

Data compiled July, 1996.

AUSTRALIA   P/E 16 • Yield 4.0% • Market Value $272 billion

Country Statistics	
Population	18.0 million
Gross domestic product	$323.9 billion
GDP per capita	$18.0 thousand
Total national debt/GDP	13.1%
R&D expenditures/GDP	1.4%
Unemployment rate	8.5%
Retail sales per capita	$3.2 thousand

1995 Rank	Company/business	Revenue ($mil)	Net income ($mil)	Assets ($mil)	Market value ($mil)	Stock price ($)	EPS 1995 ($)	EPS 1996ᴱ ($)	Yield (%)	Employees (thou)
174	•Broken Hill Proprietary/ energy	13,196	905	21,619	29,430	15.10	0.66	0.88	2.7	49.0
188	•Coles Myer/retailing	12,468	314	4,853	3,946	3.66	0.27	0.24	4.8	134.5
256	•Woolworths/retailing	9,500	173	2,072	2,691	2.50	0.17	0.18	4.5	87.0
257	•Natl Australia Bank/banking	9,490	1,463	98,467	13,660	9.39	1.05	1.17	7.1	45.6
275	•News Corp/media	9,043	1,014	21,393	11,218	5.62	0.34	0.36	0.4	26.7
315	•RTZ-CRA/metals-nonfer	7,704	1,286	15,748	21,983³	16.22	0.92	1.16	3.2	51.5
317	•ANZ Banking/banking	7,644	782	75,456	6,744	4.60	0.52	0.58	5.7	39.2
371	•Westpac Banking Group/ banking	6,365	704	71,105	8,877	4.67	0.37	0.49	4.8	31.4
398	•Commonwealth Bank Group/ banking	6,034	730	63,263	8,069	8.15	0.80	0.92	8.0	35.8
450	•Pacific Dunlop/multi-industry	5,427	70	4,930	2,191	2.16	0.17	0.18	8.5	48.2
452	•Qantas Airways/airlines	5,405	134	6,327	1,853	1.79	0.13	0.19	4.5	28.9
489	•Amcor/forest products	4,899	267	5,006	4,243	6.83	0.44	0.53	4.4	24.7

All figures except per-share items are in millions of U.S. dollars. Revenue, net income and 1995 EPS are converted at an average rate of exchange for the fiscal year; assets are converted at fiscal year-end rate. Revenue figures are for group or consolidated operations and exclude excise taxes and duties. For companies with January, February or March fiscal year-ends, 1995 figures are used unless noted. Market value is as of May 31, 1996. •Sponsored ADR. ³Combined market value for RTZ and CRA. Price, EPS and yield are only for CRA.

Sources: Morgan Stanley Capital International and IBES International, Inc. via OneSource Information Services; Bloomberg Financial Markets; Forbes

(Continued)

BELGIUM   P/E 15 • Yield 4.0% • Market Value $104 billion

Country Statistics	
Population	10.5 million
Gross domestic product	$241.0 billion
GDP per capita	$23.0 thousand
Total national debt/GDP	110.8%
R&D expenditures/GDP	1.6%
Unemployment rate	13.0%
Retail sales per capita	$5.5 thousand

1995 Rank	Company/business	Revenue ($mil)	Net income ($mil)	Assets ($mil)	Market value ($mil)	Stock price ($)	EPS 1995 ($)	EPS 1996[E] ($)	Yield (%)	Employees (thou)
83	Fortis Group/insurance	22,619	814	161,121	10,736[4]	135.10	10.55	10.80	2.6	30.4
186	Delhaize Le Lion Group/ retailing	12,499	128	4,006	2,609	50.78	2.49	2.78	2.1	89.5
187	•PetroFina/energy	12,476	394	11,483	6,929	297.99	16.96	19.16	3.8	12.6
226	Tractebel/multi-industry	10,923	384	19,956[1]	6,126	444.75	28.93	27.37	3.5	33.5
230	Générale Bank Group/ banking	10,706	464	161,114	5,218	348.13	31.00	31.84	4.7	20.7
267	•Solvay Group/chemicals	9,272	418	8,300[1]	5,008	600.45	50.10	51.61	3.9	39.9
283	•Arbed/metals-steel	8,721	124	10,507	1,015	114.66	14.04	10.99	1.9	30.0
308	Bank Bruxelles Lambert/ banking	7,824	303	109,638	3,612	185.24	16.03	16.13	4.0	13.3
310	GIB Group/retailing	7,760	−148	2,854[1]	1,498	44.40	−4.43	2.84	1.4	46.5
314	Kredietbank/banking	7,715	392	104,575	4,300	291.92	26.73	26.48	3.4	12.9
340	Cockerill Sambre/metals-steel	7,010	109	5,283[1]	1,679	5.27	0.34	0.42	7.3	27.1
448	Générale de Belgique/ multi-industry	5,448	312	9,527	5,209	73.78	4.43	5.62	5.0	18.4

BRAZIL   P/E 52 • Yield 2.6% • Market Value $176 billion

Country Statistics	
Population	154.9 million
Gross domestic product	$468.3 billion
GDP per capita	$2.9 thousand
Total national debt/GDP	6.2%
R&D expenditures/GDP	NA
Unemployment rate	6.0%
Retail sales per capita	$0.2 thousand

(Continued)

1995 Rank	Company/business	Revenue ($mil)	Net income ($mil)	Assets ($mil)	Market value ($mil)	Stock price* ($)	EPS* 1995 ($)	EPS* 1996ᴱ ($)	Yield* (%)	Employees (thou)
Brazil (*Cont.*)										
125	**Petrobras-Petróleo Brasil/** energy	17,366	677	31,806	9,864	70.94	6.23	6.15	1.3	50.7
127	**Banco do Brasil**/banking	17,221	–4,635	82,071	921	8.92	–6.69	–0.47	0.0	94.7
261	•**Telebrás**/telecomm	9,391	882	36,673	17,460	61.31	2.86	5.30	2.5	95.6
303	**Banco Bradesco Group/** banking	8,092	589	33,774	6,796	6.63	0.63	0.67	4.2	52.9
365	**Banco Itáu Group**/banking	6,480	411	25,193	4,756	398.52	34.14	37.07	2.5	36.6
409	•**Eletrobrás**/utilities	5,889¹	1,856¹	100,187¹	12,994	239.41	NA	NA	0.9	1.4

CANADA   P/E 20 • Yield 2.3% • Market Value $382 billion

Country Statistics

Population	29.2 million
Gross domestic product	$584.4 billion
GDP per capita	$18.8 thousand
Total national debt/GDP	45.5%
R&D expenditures/GDP	1.5%
Unemployment rate	9.5%
Retail sales per capita	$3.4 thousand

1995 Rank	Company/business	Revenue ($mil)	Net income ($mil)	Assets ($mil)	Market value ($mil)	Stock price ($)	EPS 1995 ($)	EPS 1996ᴱ ($)	Yield (%)	Employees (thou)
118	**BCE**/telecomm	17,942	570	27,586¹	12,560	39.85	1.63	2.25	5.0	121.0
221	**Royal Bank of Canada/** banking	11,132	918	132,402	7,505	23.89	2.54	2.90	3.8	49.0
253	**Canadian Imperial Bank/** banking	9,588	738	127,607	6,818	33.17	3.04	3.90	3.3	39.3
259	**George Weston**/retailing	9,447	138	3,799	1,608	34.26	2.93	3.18	1.9	76.2
265	**Alcan Aluminium/** metals-nonfer	9,287	543	9,702	7,399	32.73	2.30	2.89	1.4	39.0
278	**Seagram**/bev & tobacco	8,935	3,406	21,355	12,939	34.59	9.13	1.44	1.7	30.0
279	**Bank of Nova Scotia**/banking	8,795	637	105,730	5,640	24.15	2.46	2.80	4.1	33.7
280	**Bank of Montreal**/banking	8,790	717	110,015	6,235	23.82	2.51	2.85	4.4	33.3

All figures except per-share items are in millions of U.S. dollars. Revenue, net income and 1995 EPS are converted at an average rate of exchange for the fiscal year; assets are converted at fiscal year-end rate. Revenue figures are for group or consolidated operations and exclude excise taxes and duties. For companies with January, February or March fiscal year-ends, 1995 figures are used unless noted. Market value is as of May 31, 1996. •Sponsored ADR. ¹Figures are latest available. NA: Not available. ⁴Combined market value for Fortis AMEV and Fortis AG. Price, EPS and yield are only for Fortis AG. ᴱEstimate. *Figures are per thousand shares.

Sources: Morgan Stanley Capital International and IBES International, Inc. via OneSource Information Services; Bloomberg Financial Markets; Forbes.

(Continued)

1995 Rank	Company/business	Revenue ($mil)	Net income ($mil)	Assets ($mil)	Market value ($mil)	Stock price ($)	EPS 1995 ($)	EPS 1996ᴱ ($)	Yield (%)	Employees (thou)
Canada (Cont.)										
329	**Thomson Corp**/media	7,225	789	9,981	9,745	16.37	1.34	0.88	3.1	44.4
374	**Toronto-Dominion Bank**/ banking	6,333	577	76,528	5,440	18.05	1.83	2.06	4.0	25.4
376	**Imasco**/multi-industry	6,296	161	41,096	4,728	20.35	0.66	1.91	3.9	66.0
393	**Noranda**/metals-nonfer	6,107	380	9,441	5,482	21.63	1.65	1.97	3.4	32.0
405	**Imperial Oil**/energy	5,949	375	8,828	8,128	43.51	1.95	2.37	3.4	7.8
416	**Canadian Pacific**/ multi-industry	5,790	−600	11,748	7,028	20.49	−1.76	1.29	1.3	36.1
469	**Bombardier**/aero & defense	5,188	112	4,683	4,701	14.10	0.33	0.86	1.0	40.0
475	**TransCanada PipeLines**/ utilities	5,105	290	7,614	2,988	14.47	1.28	1.26	5.5	1.9

FRANCE — P/E 72 • Yield 3.0% • Market Value $558 billion

Country Statistics	
Population	57.9 million
Gross domestic product	$1,329.3 billion
GDP per capita	$23.0 thousand
Total national debt/GDP	33.9%
R&D expenditures/GDP	2.41%
Unemployment rate	11.6%
Retail sales per capita	$5.4 thousand

1995 Rank	Company/business	Revenue ($mil)	Net income ($mil)	Assets ($mil)	Market value ($mil)	Stock price ($)	EPS 1995 ($)	EPS 1996ᴱ ($)	Yield (%)	Employees (thou)
30	**UAP-Union des Assurances**/ insurance	43,929	−414	183,768	6,098	19.80	−1.34	1.17	4.4	51.3
32	•**Elf Aquitaine Group**/energy	41,729	1,009	49,428	19,633	72.49	3.79	4.31	5.2	85.5
37	•**Renault Group**/automobiles	36,876	429	45,511	6,542	27.37	1.81	1.86	3.7	140.0
47	•**Peugeot Groupe**/automobiles	32,906	341	29,570	6,990	139.48	6.82	11.31	1.0	139.9
48	•**Générale des Eaux Groupe**/ services	32,530	−738	41,793[1]	12,729	107.13	−6.58	4.46	3.1	215.3
51	•**Alcatel Alsthom**/elec & electron	32,138	−5,125	52,178	13,737	91.24	−34.04	1.32	2.5	196.9
54	**GAN-Assur Nationales**/ insurance	31,213	−358	169,315	1,629	28.48	−6.26	1.03	0.0	35.8
62	**Carrefour Group**/retailing	28,972	708	13,192	14,057	365.49	18.42	16.39	1.7	100.8
63	**Crédit Lyonnais Group**/ banking	28,305	3	339,392	1,440	27.61	0.05	1.78	0.0	59.0
64	**AXA Group**/insurance	28,248	547	192,558	10,769	56.78	3.33	3.40	3.3	35.0
65	•**Total Group**/energy	27,212	450	28,359	17,107	72.39	1.92	3.77	3.5	53.5

(Continued)

1995 Rank	Company/business	Revenue ($mil)	Net income ($mil)	Assets ($mil)	Market value ($mil)	Stock price ($)	EPS 1995 ($)	EPS 1996ᴱ ($)	Yield (%)	Employees (thou)
France (Cont.)										
69	•BNP Group/banking	26,297	357	325,250	7,242	37.54	1.85	2.94	2.8	54.2
71	•Société Générale Group/ banking	25,825	765	326,507	9,315	106.55	9.28	10.05	4.4	45.4
96	Promodès Group/retailing	20,149	205	8,823	4,874	261.72	11.44	12.70	1.3	43.9
97	Groupe Paribas/banking	20,121	−801	272,213	7,312	60.83	−6.79	3.36	5.7	25.8
100	Lyonnaise des Eaux-Dumez/ multi-ind	19,757	182	32,018	5,637	97.06	3.13	4.68	3.4	141.0
101	AGF-Assur Générales de Fr/ insurance	19,499	217	72,757	3,642	26.75	1.59	1.95	4.1	25.6
105	•Suez Group/banking	19,262	−793	128,653	6,168	38.65	−5.32	1.65	6.2	35.0
130	•Rhône-Poulenc Group/ chemicals	16,987	665	27,634	8,033	24.95	1.34	1.63	3.5	82.5
139	•Groupe Danone/food, household	15,917	427	19,027	10,442	146.46	6.20	9.52	3.2	73.8
140	•Groupe Usinor Sacilor/ metals-steel	15,707	888	14,580[1]	3,911	16.08	4.76	2.89	7.2	69.1
141	Pinault-Printemps-Redoute/ retailing	15,586	304	11,064	6,939	309.96	13.57	15.59	2.3	53.8
142	•Péchiney/metals-nonfer	15,434	295	12,921[1]	3,303	42.60	5.83	3.10	6.5	38.0
149	Bouygues Group/construction	14,794	−583	15,088	2,537	108.87	−25.36	4.23	4.5	73.9
158	Saint-Gobain/misc materials	14,086	844	19,692	10,529	127.86	10.40	10.47	3.8	84.5
172	Michelin Group/industrial comp	13,245	560	14,373	5,815	50.47	4.86	5.16	1.6	114.4
181	Casino Groupe/retailing	12,848	127	5,776[1]	3,063	42.04	1.66	1.89	2.8	45.1
200	Schneider/elec & electron	11,904	164	10,704[1]	6,162	46.34	1.23	2.06	2.5	89.8
232	■L'Oréal Group/personal care	10,692	631	9,611	18,729	304.73	10.26	12.02	1.3	39.9
236	•Lagardère Groupe/ multi-industry	10,534	126	12,158	2,345	27.18	1.50	2.05	3.2	43.6
263	Docks de France/retailing	9,363	112	3,738	3,080	227.82	8.58	9.11	1.8	32.8
277	•Groupe Havas/services	8,940	178	6,963	5,486	85.63	2.77	3.56	2.9	20.9
334	•Thomson CSF/aero & defense	7,111	−158	12,651	3,072	26.17	−1.35	1.81	2.9	46.8
338	Saint Louis/forest products	7,066	115	8,642	2,183	271.21	14.26	21.31	4.1	23.0
353	Crédit Commercial/banking	6,690	247	70,177	3,358	48.24	3.56	3.86	3.0	10.7
356	•Lafarge/bldg materials	6,655	471	10,271	6,083	65.94	5.33	5.11	4.4	34.7
360	Eiffage/construction	6,533	41	8,390	978	140.64	5.92	7.43	8.8	46.3
366	■L'Aire Liquide Group/ chemicals	6,449	533	8,639	11,543	174.16	8.04	8.83	2.3	24.6
379	Esso/energy	6,250	−6	1,946	1,466	123.01	−0.47	4.00	5.9	2.9
383	Accor/leisure	6,213	185	11,077	4,173	144.32	6.47	7.02	4.0	146.9

All figures except per-share items are in millions of U.S. dollars. Revenue, net income and 1995 EPS are converted at an average rate of exchange for the fiscal year; assets are converted at fiscal year-end rate. Revenue figures are for group or consolidated operations and exclude excise taxes and duties. For companies with January, February or March fiscal year-ends, 1995 figures are used unless noted. Market value is as of May 31, 1996. •Sponsored ADR. ■Non-sponsored. [1]Figures are latest available. NA: Not available.

Sources: Morgan Stanley Capital International and IBES International, Inc. via OneSource Information Services; Bloomberg Financial Markets; Forbes.

(Continued)

1995 Rank	Company/business	Revenue ($mil)	Net income ($mil)	Assets ($mil)	Market value ($mil)	Stock price ($)	EPS 1995 ($)	EPS 1996^E ($)	Yield (%)	Employees (thou)

France (Cont.)

1995 Rank	Company/business	Revenue ($mil)	Net income ($mil)	Assets ($mil)	Market value ($mil)	Stock price ($)	EPS 1995 ($)	EPS 1996^E ($)	Yield (%)	Employees (thou)
387	Christian Dior/bev & tobacco	6,168	329	18,005[1]	5,939	141.42	7.82	8.17	2.9	19.3
401	•LVMH Group/bev & tobacco	5,965	811	13,027	21,208	242.93	9.34	10.26	2.3	19.5
419	Galeries Lafayette/retailing	5,750	−48	2,922[1]	427	328.36	−36.83	5.41	0.0	29.1
451	Comptoirs Modernes/retailing	5,417	90	2,058	2,318	449.63	17.69	17.86	1.4	19.9
459	Groupe Bull/data processing	5,340	61	3,770	1,056	8.14	0.97	NA	0.0	24.1
479	•Valeo/industrial comp	5,055	202	4,391	3,766	54.34	2.92	3.15	1.4	29.6

GERMANY — P/E 29 • Yield 2.5% • Market Value $578 billion

Country Statistics

Population	81.1 million
Gross domestic product	$2,047.5 billion
GDP per capita	$25.3 thousand
Total national debt/GDP	26.1%
R&D expenditures/GDP	2.5%
Unemployment rate	9.4%
Retail sales per capita	$4.8 thousand

1995 Rank	Company/business	Revenue ($mil)	Net income ($mil)	Assets ($mil)	Market value ($mil)	Stock price ($)	EPS 1995 ($)	EPS 1996^E ($)	Yield (%)	Employees (thou)
11	•Daimler-Benz Group/ automobiles	72,253	−3,959	63,858	28,130	547.60	−77.17	19.30	0.0	321.2
15	•Volkswagen Group/ automobiles	61,487	247	58,648	11,571	353.51	7.00	20.29	1.6	242.3
16	■Siemens Group/elec & electron	60,673	1,268	57,779	30,817	55.04	2.26	3.15	2.2	376.1
27	VEBA Group/utilities	46,278	1,336	47,263	25,595	52.43	3.02	3.09	3.0	123.0
31	Allianz Worldwide/insurance	43,486[1]	592[1]	164,729[1]	37,051	1,662.51	52.12^E	48.39	0.9	67.8
36	•Deutsche Bank Group/ banking	38,418	1,437	503,429	23,509	47.05	2.90	3.28	3.6	74.1
40	■Hoechst Group/chemicals	36,407	1,192	36,754	19,603	33.34	1.68	2.15	3.7	165.9
41	•RWE Group/utilities	35,383	726	52,940	19,552	39.56	1.79	1.84	3.3	136.6
49	■BASF Group/chemicals	32,257	1,724	29,323	16,976	278.40	28.27	25.87	4.7	105.6
50	BMW-Bayerische Motor/ automobiles	32,198	479	28,495	10,886	551.54	24.51	30.53	2.3	106.9
55	•Bayer Group/chemicals	31,107	1,670	30,901	23,621	33.49	2.37	2.50	4.2	144.1
61	VIAG Group/multi-industry	29,259	808	30,067	10,260	389.89	26.31	23.44	2.9	84.5
66	■Thyssen Group/metals-steel	26,742	512	17,670	5,802	185.36	16.36	14.64	5.1	127.0
85	•Mannesmann Group/ machinery & eng	22,394	372	15,835	12,756	347.54	14.65	16.61	1.5	123.1

(Continued)

1995 Rank	Company/business	Revenue ($mil)	Net income ($mil)	Assets ($mil)	Market value ($mil)	Stock price ($)	EPS 1995 ($)	EPS 1996ᴱ ($)	Yield (%)	Employees (thou)
Germany (*Cont.*)										
86	**Münchener Rückversicherun/** insurance	22,086	184	84,809	14,625	1,634.27	22.67	32.31	0.7	16.2
91	•**Dresdner Bank**/banking	21,095	817	332,909	11,179	25.12	1.84	1.84	5.0	47.6
109	•**Commerzbank**/banking	18,893	642	281,385	8,040	208.80	16.67	17.93	6.1	27.2
117	**Preussag Group/** multi-industry	18,013	254	10,612	3,878	254.62	19.14	17.79	3.7	63.6
126	▪**Bayer Vereinsbank**/banking	17,354	419	244,301	7,456	28.23	1.76	1.77	5.0	22.2
132	▪**Karstadt Group**/retailing	16,811ᴱ	76	7,133[1]	3,315	394.62	−14.95	9.78	3.1	105.1
133	**Krupp Hoesch Group/** metals-steel	16,398	352	10,779[1]	3,278	157.58	16.94	14.31	3.0	72.7
134	**ASKO Group**/retailing	16,341	111	5,350	2,862	696.00	7.07	17.20	1.0	83.7
148	•**Kaufhof**/retailing	14,816	96	6,420	3,372	352.92	12.24	13.92	3.2	63.6
151	**Bayerische Hypotheken/** banking	14,646	461	207,995	6,486	25.23	1.79	1.64	5.4	19.0
161	▪**Deutsche Lufthansa**/airlines	13,886	1,023	12,849	5,920	155.29	10.75	10.24	3.0	57.6
170	**Gehe**/personal care	13,367	142	4,325	4,700	644.78	21.07	23.90	1.5	18.8
190	**M A N Group**/machinery & eng	12,439	171	9,063	3,731	258.70	15.18	17.60	3.4	56.1
194	**Metallgesellschaft/** multi-industry	12,060	53	6,258	2,523	18.84	0.77	1.18	0.0	24.1
248	**Henkel Group**/food, household	9,907	302	8,105	6,149	421.21	20.70	23.64	2.6	41.7
258	**Degussa**/misc materials	9,475	191	5,391	2,954	344.39	25.98	26.72	2.4	27.0
284	**SPAR Handels**/retailing	8,664	52	1,881	1,077	417.60	18.72	14.05	1.6	23.0
306	**Philipp Holzmann/** construction	7,867	−323	8,332	1,386	315.82	−70.41	6.04	0.0	47.4
332	•**Continental Group**/industrial comp	7,154	102	4,676	1,622	17.27	1.15	1.25	2.4	48.4
348	**AGIV**/multi-industry	6,842	−27	4,093	798	19.96	−0.67	0.85	0.0	40.2
410	**VEW**/utilities	5,841	158	9,122	6,014	300.72	7.92	11.23	2.8	13.0
418	**Linde**/machinery & eng	5,780	225	5,283	5,408	643.47	27.91	29.02	2.3	29.3
422	**Deutsche Babcock/** machinery & eng	5,686	−6	3,067	433	61.79	−0.85	−5.71	0.0	35.4
453	**AVA**/retailing	5,404	7	1,614[1]	828	269.21	2.38	11.95	0.0	26.2
488	**Bilfinger & Berger/** construction	4,911	73	4,201	1,501	416.94	27.63	25.67	3.0	31.2

All figures except per-share items are in millions of U.S. dollars. Revenue, net income and 1995 EPS are converted at an average rate of exchange for the fiscal year; assets are converted at fiscal year-end rate. Revenue figures are for group or consolidated operations and exclude excise taxes and duties. For companies with January, February or March fiscal year-ends, 1995 figures are used unless noted. Market value is as of May 31, 1996. •Sponsored ADR. ▪Non-sponsored. [1]Figures are latest available. NA: Not available. ᴱEstimate.

Sources: Morgan Stanley Capital International and IBES International, Inc. via OneSource Information Services; Bloomberg Financial Markets; Forbes.

(Continued)

ITALY   P/E 21 • Yield 2.2% • Market Value $239 billion

Country Statistics	
Population	57.2 million
Gross domestic product	$1,017.8 billion
GDP per capita	$17.8 thousand
Total national debt/GDP	83.8%
R&D expenditures/GDP	1.3%
Unemployment rate	12.0%
Retail sales per capita	$5.9 thousand

1995 Rank	Company/business	Revenue ($mil)	Net income ($mil)	Assets ($mil)	Market value ($mil)	Stock price ($)	EPS 1995 ($)	EPS 1996E ($)	Yield (%)	Employees (thou)
26	•Fiat Group/automobiles	46,467	1,318	64,288	14,598	3.51	0.27	0.31	1.8	237.4
42	•ENI/energy	34,924	2,656	56,005	38,272	4.79	0.33	0.38	2.9	86.4
82	•STET/telecomm	22,943	1	44,965[1]	17,853	3.57	0.20	0.21	2.4	133.8
94	Generali Group/insurance	20,487[1]	397[1]	63,406[1]	19,120	23.85	0.55E	0.66	1.0	37.9
145	Sanpaolo Group/banking	14,951	113	156,465[1]	4,961	6.08	0.39	0.48	2.6	24.3
146	•Montedison Group/ multi-industry	14,842	657	6,281[1]	3,680	0.61	0.11	0.06	0.0	32.4
205	Banca di Roma/banking	11,634	53	134,010	3,307	0.99	0.02	0.03	0.0	32.6
243	•Credito Italiano/banking	10,322	121	102,816	2,786	1.24	0.05	0.09	1.8	26.0
246	•Banca Commerciale Italian/ banking	10,119	224	100,386	3,778	2.11	0.13	0.19	4.6	28.0
322	Finmeccanica/machinery & eng	7,515[1]	1[1]	19,596[1]	929	0.55	0.01E	0.04	0.0	59.0
354	■Pirelli Group/industrial comp	6,687	158	6,511	2,536	1.65	0.10	0.11	2.0	38.1
382	Banco di Napoli/banking	6,233	−1,940	53,618	474	0.27	−1.75	NA	0.0	11.8
397	■Olivetti Group/data processing	6,041	−981	7,480[1]	2,276	0.63	−0.27	0.00	0.0	27.9
495	Alitalia Group/airlines	4,811	−53	4,367[1]	374	0.43	−0.05	−0.13	0.0	18.7

JAPAN   P/E 106 • Yield 0.7% • Market Value $3.6 trillion

Country Statistics	
Population	124.9 million
Gross domestic product	$4,590.9 billion
GDP per capita	$36.8 thousand
Total national debt/GDP	56.5%
R&D expenditures/GDP	3.0%
Unemployment rate	3.1%
Retail sales per capita	$8.7 thousand

(Continued)

1995 Rank	Company/business	Revenue ($mil)	Net income ($mil)	Assets ($mil)	Market value ($mil)	Stock price ($)	EPS 1995 ($)	EPS 1996[E] ($)	Yield (%)	Employees (thou)
Japan (*Cont.*)										
1	•Mitsubishi/trading	184,510	346	92,543	21,454	13.69	0.22	0.25	0.5	13.9
2	•Mitsui & Co/trading	181,661	315	69,237	14,295	9.20	0.20	0.24	0.8	11.7
3	▪Itochu/trading	169,300	121	66,146	10,232	7.18	0.09	0.10	0.8	7.2[2]
4	Sumitomo/trading	167,662	211	50,609	11,816	11.10	0.20	0.18	0.7	25.3
5	▪Marubeni/trading	161,184	157	71,923	8,137	5.45	0.11	0.10	1.0	9.9
6	▪Toyota Motor/automobiles	111,139	2,665	106,722	85,779	22.85	0.51	0.72	0.8	142.6
8	Nissho Iwai/trading	97,963	−260	47,071	4,441	5.66	−0.33	0.11	0.8	17.0
9	•Hitachi/elec & electron	84,233	1,470	92,242	30,821	9.25	0.42	0.39	1.1	331.9
10	•Nippon Tel & Tel/telecomm	82,002	2,211	127,938	115,697	7,271.05	138.95	98.46	0.6	231.4
12	•Matsushita Electric Indl/appliances	70,454	−590	75,384	36,155	17.21	−0.28	0.56	0.7	265.4
13	Tomen/trading	67,809	46	22,517	2,571	3.84	0.07	0.08	1.2	2.9[2]
14	•Nissan Motor/automobiles	62,618	−917	66,726	20,665	8.22	−0.37	0.07	0.8	145.6
18	•Bank of Tokyo-Mitsubishi/banking	55,243	980	712,747	110,285	23.68	0.12	0.14	0.3	20.1
19	Toshiba/elec & electron	53,089	937	52,319	22,363	6.95	0.28	0.25	1.3	188.0
20	Nichimen/trading	50,882	44	23,946[1]	1,916	4.52	0.11	0.11	1.2	2.6[2]
21	Tokyo Electric Power2/utilities	50,343[1]	871[1]	152,699[1]	33,790	24.98	0.37	0.42	1.9	43.1
22	Kanematsu/trading	49,878	3	18,887[1]	1,882	6.48	0.01	0.01	0.7	2.7
25	•Sony/appliances	47,619	563	47,476	23,777	63.55	1.39	2.31	0.7	138.0
28	•NEC/elec & electron	45,593	800	44,064	17,023	11.01	0.47	0.44	0.9	152.7
29	•Honda Motor/automobiles	44,090	734	33,083	23,434	24.05	0.75	1.04	0.5	96.8
34	▪Fujitsu/data processing	39,007	654	40,690	16,692	9.07	0.36	0.35	1.0	164.4
35	▪Indl Bank of Japan/banking	38,694	−659	361,372	60,472	25.72	−0.28	0.26	0.3	5.3[2]
38	Mitsubishi Motors/automobiles	36,674	132	28,300	7,724	8.39	0.23	0.25	0.8	28.4[2]
39	▪Mitsubishi Electric/elec & electron	36,408	614	38,486[1]	14,698	6.85	0.27	0.29	1.4	48.5[2]
43	▪Sanwa Bank/banking	34,913	−1,296	501,043	55,829	19.24	−0.45	0.27	0.3	14.4
46	▪Daiei/retailing	33,196	53	20,423	8,715	12.21	0.08	0.07	1.3	16.6[2]
52	▪Fuji Bank/banking	31,597	−3,374	487,369	62,988	21.74	−1.17	0.28	0.3	15.8
53	Mitsubishi Heavy Inds/machinery & eng	31,272	1,076	44,929[1]	28,983	8.59	0.32	0.33	0.9	42.8[2]
56	Nippon Steel/metals-steel	30,638	565	42,598	23,391	3.40	0.08	0.08	0.7	93.9
57	•Ito-Yokado/retailing	30,360	806	16,427	23,548	56.71	1.97	1.84	0.6	35.0
58	▪Dai-Ichi Kangyo Bank/banking	30,312	817	498,625	56,294	18.04	0.26	0.14	0.4	18.1[2]
59	▪Sumitomo Bank/banking	29,611[1]	−2,856[1]	565,971[1]	61,891	19.70	0.12	0.25	0.4	17.2

All figures except per-share items are in millions of U.S. dollars. Revenue, net income and 1995 EPS are converted at an average rate of exchange for the fiscal year; assets are converted at fiscal year-end rate. Revenue figures are for group or consolidated operations and exclude excise taxes and duties. For companies with January, February or March fiscal year-ends, 1995 figures are used unless noted. Market value is as of May 31, 1996. •Sponsored ADR. ▪Non-sponsored. [1]Figures are latest available. [2]Not fully consolidated. NA: Not available. [E]Estimate.

Sources: Morgan Stanley Capital International and IBES International, Inc. via OneSource Information Services; Bloomberg Financial Markets; Forbes.

(Continued)

1995 Rank	Company/business	Revenue ($mil)	Net income ($mil)	Assets ($mil)	Market value ($mil)	Stock price ($)	EPS 1995 ($)	EPS 1996[E] ($)	Yield (%)	Employees (thou)
Japan (Cont.)										
60	**Long-Term Credit Bank**/banking	29,330	−361	298,036	19,347	8.09	−0.15	0.11	0.7	3.8[2]
70	■**Sakura Bank**/banking	25,976	−4,426	478,050	37,909	10.92	−1.29	0.15	0.7	20.3
72	**East Japan Railway**/trucking, RR	25,644	710	69,117	22,017	5,504.16	177.38	135.21	0.8	80.2[2]
73	**Kansai Electric Power**/utilities	25,577[1]	444[1]	73,745[1]	22,361	22.85	0.51	0.45	2.0	26.7
81	•**Canon**/data processing	23,024	585	23,935	16,533	19.61	0.67	0.78	0.6	72.3
87	■**Jusco**/retailing	22,008	327	12,735	9,275	29.60	1.06	0.91	0.6	12.9[2]
88	**Nippon Oil**/energy	21,925[E]	172	26,031	8,135	6.61	0.14	0.10	1.0	11.9
93	**Chubu Electric Power**/utilities	20,806[1]	459[1]	65,647[1]	17,307	23.22	0.61	0.49	2.0	20.9[2]
95	■**Tokai Bank**/banking	20,350	−1,396	347,967[1]	25,964	12.49	−0.69	0.26	0.5	11.6
98	■**Taisei**/construction	20,110[1]	165[1]	35,729[1]	7,688	7.54	−0.02[E]	0.03	0.9	13.4[2]
104	**Japan Energy**/energy	19,348	214	15,636	4,220	3.86	0.20	0.11	1.2	5.4[2]
106	**Mazda Motor**/automobiles	19,108	−123	12,873	5,823	4.76	−0.11	0.07	0.0	26.0[2]
108	**Shimizu**/construction	18,937	76	24,178	9,044	11.47	0.10	0.12	0.7	12.2[2]
110	■**NKK**/metals-steel	18,726	543	25,337	10,300	2.92	0.15	0.10	0.0	43.1
111	■**Isuzu Motors**/machinery & eng	18,664[E]	238[E]	16,173[1]	5,607	5.44	0.20[E]	0.14	0.0	14.9[2]
113	■**Sanyo Electric**/appliances	18,551	166	23,746	11,605	5.95	0.09	0.12	0.8	57.1
116	■**Kajima**/construction	18,286	52	27,116	10,049	10.45	0.05	0.08	0.8	14.5
119	■**Bridgestone**/industrial comp	17,931	576	16,241	13,827	17.39	0.74	0.75	0.6	89.4
120	**Nippon Express**/trucking, RR	17,781	288	10,198	10,733	9.99	0.27	0.25	0.6	62.0
121	**Nichii**/retailing	17,746	11	17,046[1]	4,359	15.82	0.04	0.10	1.2	20.6
124	**Japan Tobacco**/bev & tobacco	17,368[E]	705	18,990	17,095	8,547.64	352.27	301.34	0.6	23.2
128	■**Sharp**/appliances	17,116	480	18,885	18,224	16.28	0.43	0.44	0.7	43.9
129	■**Mitsubishi Chemical**/chemicals	17,088	234	18,678	10,822	4.94	0.11	0.06	0.6	13.6[2]
131	**Toyota Tsusho**/trading	16,942	24	6,982	1,757	6.94	0.09	0.15	1.0	2.0[2]
135	**Nippon Credit Bank**/banking	16,339	−793	156,145	6,486	3.74	−0.46	0.28	1.4	2.6
138	**Cosmo Oil**/energy	16,135	68	12,100	4,108	6.50	0.11	0.13	1.1	3.7[2]
143	•**Kobe Steel**/metals-steel	15,314	936	22,312	7,816	2.76	0.33	0.15	0.0	16.6[2]
144	•**Tokio Marine & Fire Ins**/insurance	15,020	293	47,215	20,070	12.95	0.19	0.20	0.6	15.0
147	•**Sumitomo Metal Inds**/metals-steel	14,842	223	23,070	9,689	3.08	0.07	0.11	0.9	18.4[2]
150	■**Nippondenso**/industrial comp	14,751	517	14,838	18,757	21.55	0.59	0.47	0.6	55.9
153	**Tohoku Electric Power**/utilities	14,495[1]	536[1]	39,538[1]	11,444	22.76	0.73	0.66	2.0	14.5
155	**Suzuki Motor**/automobiles	14,321	276	8,963	5,686	12.67	0.62	0.48	0.5	14.1[2]
156	**Obayashi**/construction	14,310[1]	74[1]	26,041[1]	6,852	9.20	0.17[E]	0.16	0.8	12.4[2]
159	**Kyushu Electric Power**/utilities	13,962[1]	469[1]	46,089[1]	11,405	24.05	0.92	0.74	1.9	14.7[2]
162	■**Sekisui House**/construction	13,853	433	16,603[1]	8,282	11.75	0.62	0.57	1.4	14.0
166	■**Japan Air Lines**/airlines	13,570[1]	−147[1]	24,127[1]	14,333	8.06	−0.05[E]	0.00	0.0	20.4[2]
167	**Seiyu**/retailing	13,552	−66	14,565	2,898	12.95	−0.30	0.18	1.1	8.9[2]
168	**Kawasho**[2]/trading	13,424	3	6,402	602	5.00	0.02	0.03	0.0	2.0
171	■**Asahi Glass**/misc materials	13,259	258	15,861	14,133	12.03	0.22	0.24	0.7	9.1[2]
178	■**Dai Nippon Printing**/services	12,912	549	12,577	13,897	18.50	0.73	0.63	0.8	31.8
180	**Takashimaya**/retailing	12,889	209	8,276	4,597	16.28	0.74	0.09	0.4	8.7[2]
183	■**Asahi Chemical Ind**/chemicals	12,548	96	11,621	10,463	7.25	0.07	0.13	0.8	16.3[2]
185	**Mitsui Fudosan**/real estate	12,500[1]	91[1]	40,846[1]	10,296	12.67	0.12[E]	0.10	0.7	1.5[2]

(Continued)

1995 Rank	Company/business	Revenue ($mil)	Net income ($mil)	Assets ($mil)	Market value ($mil)	Stock price ($)	EPS 1995 ($)	EPS 1996[E] ($)	Yield (%)	Employees (thou)
Japan (*Cont.*)										
191	▪Asahi Bank/banking	12,346	−1,449	297,722[1]	27,934	12.03	−0.62	0.13	0.5	14.4
193	•Kawasaki Steel/metals-steel	12,073	246	20,856	12,031	3.70	0.08	0.09	0.8	15.4[2]
196	▪Sumitomo Electric Inds/ industrial comp	12,035	291	11,735	9,667	13.60	0.41	0.42	0.7	54.6
197	Snow Brand Milk Prods/food, household	11,994	59	5,008	2,219	6.85	0.18	0.22	0.9	16.0
198	▪Matsushita Electric Works/ bldg matl	11,940	268	12,363	8,034	10.64	0.36	0.35	1.2	34.2
202	Sumitomo Trust & Banking/ banking	11,757[1]	40[1]	168,589[1]	17,265	13.88	−1.33[E]	0.38	0.5	7.1
203	▪Mitsubishi Trust & Bank/ banking	11,748	−1,567	154,532	21,685	16.65	−1.20	0.36	0.4	6.3
204	Mitsubishi Materials/ metals-nonfer	11,693	118	14,653	6,610	5.83	0.10	0.11	0.8	9.2
206	Mitsubishi Oil/energy	11,622	103	9,582	3,907	8.71	0.23	0.20	1.1	2.5
207	•Ricoh/data processing	11,541	227	14,194	6,593	10.08	0.35	0.38	0.9	59.7
210	▪Toppan Printing/services	11,377[1]	160[1]	11,965[1]	9,962	14.25	0.53	0.47	0.8	33.0
211	Daiwa Bank/banking	11,346	−1,138	152,753	11,612	7.35	−0.76	0.14	0.6	9.2[2]
216	Kawasaki Heavy Inds/ machinery & eng	11,263	171	11,784	7,060	5.23	0.13	0.12	1.0	16.8[2]
217	▪Fuji Photo Film/leisure goods	11,250	756	17,378	15,996	31.08	1.47	1.26	0.6	29.9
219	▪Fuji Heavy Inds/automobiles	11,170	201	6,579	2,680	4.58	0.34	0.18	1.0	15.5[2]
220	Sekisui Chemical/bldg materials	11,146	271	8,542	6,535	11.84	0.49	0.57	0.9	6.0[2]
222	•Kubota/machinery & eng	11,112	267	12,575	9,415	6.68	0.19	0.17	0.8	16.1[2]
225	Nippon Paper Inds/forest products	11,051	250	11,741	6,362	6.71	0.26	0.27	1.1	7.9[2]
227	▪Daiwa House Industry[2]/ construction	10,884	375	11,532	7,635	15.26	0.75	0.77	1.0	12.1[2]
228	Sumikin Bussan/trading	10,862	11	5,175	540	5.13	0.11	0.11	0.9	1.8
231	▪Mitsukoshi/retailing	10,694	−27	5,684[1]	5,295	11.01	−0.06	0.02	0.5	11.7[2]
233	Yasuda Fire & Marine Ins[2]/ insurance	10,653	109	34,319	6,605	7.44	0.12	0.12	0.9	12.9
235	Mitsui Trust & Banking/banking	10,570[1]	74[1]	151,319[1]	13,191	11.01	−2.20	0.22	0.6	6.0[2]
237	Nittetsu Shoji/trading	10,468[1]	−7[1]	9,588[1]	336	3.56	−0.18	0.10	0.0	0.8[2]
238	Chugoku Electric Power[2]/utilities	10,450[1]	288[1]	29,292[1]	8,375	22.57	0.62	0.64	2.0	11.2
241	•Komatsu/machinery & eng	10,362	148	14,989	9,566	9.53	0.15	0.19	0.8	28.0
242	▪Yasuda Trust & Banking/ financial svcs	10,337	−998	79,608	6,675	6.05	−0.91	0.12	0.8	5.1[2]

All figures except per-share items are in millions of U.S. dollars. Revenue, net income and 1995 EPS are converted at an average rate of exchange for the fiscal year; assets are converted at fiscal year-end rate. Revenue figures are for group or consolidated operations and exclude excise taxes and duties. For companies with January, February or March fiscal year-ends, 1995 figures are used unless noted. Market value is as of May 31, 1996. •Sponsored ADR. ▪Non-sponsored. [1]Figures are latest available. [2]Not fully consolidated. [E]Estimate.

Sources: Morgan Stanley Capital International and IBES International, Inc. via OneSource Information Services; Bloomberg Financial Markets; Forbes.

(Continued)

1995 Rank	Company/business	Revenue ($mil)	Net income ($mil)	Assets ($mil)	Market value ($mil)	Stock price ($)	EPS 1995 ($)	EPS 1996E ($)	Yield (%)	Employees (thou)
Japan (Cont.)										
245	**Ishikawajima-Harima**/machinery & eng	10,297[1]	144[1]	15,190[1]	5,958	4.59	0.16	0.13	1.2	27.3
249	**Sumitomo Chemical**/chemicals	9,870	192	12,548	8,101	5.00	0.12	0.12	0.6	17.4
250	**Maruha**/food, household	9,850	14	4,194	1,096	3.65	0.05	0.07	0.0	13.7
252	■**Toray Industries**/chemicals	9,761	189	12,341	9,464	6.75	0.14	0.13	1.0	32.9
254	**UNY**/retailing	9,573	130	5,381	3,993	21.09	0.69	0.52	0.7	9.5
260	■**Kirin Brewery**/bev & tobacco	9,429E	426	14,345	13,046	12.40	0.41	0.37	0.9	8.4[2]
264	■**Kumagai Gumi**/construction	9,328[1]	–94[1]	20,676[1]	2,865	4.21	–0.12E	–0.07	0.7	8.6[2]
266	**Kinki Nippon Railway**/trucking, RR	9,283[1]	21[1]	16,146[1]	11,975	7.39	0.02E	0.03	0.6	12.4[2]
268	■**Nippon Yusen**/shipping	9,246	35	13,204	6,890	5.87	0.03	0.07	0.6	2.5
269	**Fuji Electric**/elec & electron	9,232	61	8,280	3,936	5.50	0.09	0.12	1.3	13.6[2]
270	**Tokyo Gas**/utilities	9,217[1]	111[1]	17,999[1]	10,632	3.78	0.05E	0.05	1.2	12.9[2]
271	•**All Nippon Airways**/airlines	9,201[1]	–75[1]	15,278[1]	15,482	10.73	–0.05E	0.01	0.3	14.4[2]
276	**Dainippon Ink & Chems**/chemicals	9,004	72	9,753	3,873	4.88	0.09	0.10	1.1	25.6
285	■**Kao**/food, household	8,664	254	7,938[1]	8,006	13.32	0.42	0.40	0.8	7.1[2]
286	**Toshoku**/trading	8,656	14	7,885	1,422	6.57	0.07	0.09	0.8	1.9
288	**Aisin Seiki**/industrial comp	8,590	156	6,059	4,255	15.36	0.56	0.47	0.7	11.3[2]
289	■**New Oji Paper**/forest products	8,552	167	9,620	6,482	8.72	0.23	0.30	1.0	9.0
292	■**Nomura Securities**/financial svcs	8,461	508	131,423	37,044	18.87	0.26	0.31	0.5	15.7
293	**Nippon Meat Packers**/food, household	8,454	128	5,453	3,330	14.62	0.56	0.51	1.0	20.0
295	**Daimaru**/retailing	8,339	70	3,631	1,974	7.29	0.19	0.13	0.5	6.6[2]
297	**Takeda Chemical Inds**/personal care	8,309	621	11,039	14,501	16.56	0.71	0.63	0.8	17.6
299	**Daihatsu Motor**/automobiles	8,228	76	6,067[1]	2,627	6.15	0.18	0.15	0.5	11.7[2]
307	**Toyo Seikan Kaisha**/misc materials	7,841[1]	315[1]	7,697[1]	7,203	35.71	1.19E	1.04	0.2	6.7[2]
309	■**Ajinomoto**/food, household	7,785	109	7,316	7,804	12.03	0.17	0.18	0.8	13.3
320	**Yamaha Motor**/leisure goods	7,599	38	6,021	2,323	10.08	0.17	0.26	0.6	11.1
323	**Nishimatsu Construction**[2]/construction	7,486	149	8,009	2,939	10.64	0.56	0.49	1.0	5.8
326	■**Mitsui Marine & Fire Ins**/insurance	7,365	91	24,936	5,610	7.72	0.13	0.13	0.8	9.5
328	**Sumitomo Forestry**/bldg materials	7,242	113	3,737	2,741	15.54	0.64	0.56	0.5	3.9[2]
331	**Osaka Gas**/utilities	7,161[1]	–92[1]	12,770[1]	9,846	3.90	0.05E	0.06	1.2	9.1[2]
336	■**Fujita**/construction	7,094[1]	45[1]	16,917[1]	2,598	5.25	0.08	0.05	1.1	5.9[2]
342	**Asahi Breweries**/bev & tobacco	6,952	70	16,803	5,030	11.84	0.17	0.15	0.7	11.1
343	**DDI**/telecomm	6,943	44	6,273[1]	18,798	8,658.65	142.53	106.52	0.1	2.8[2]
346	■**Yamazaki Baking**/food, household	6,870	144	3,990	4,361	19.80	0.66	0.61	0.6	17.6[2]
347	**Mitsui O.S.K. Lines**/shipping	6,865	49	9,958	3,799	3.43	0.04	0.03	0.0	1.5
350	**Yamato Transport**/trucking, RR	6,797	131	4,915	4,408	12.03	0.36	0.31	1.0	67.5
351	■**Furukawa Electric**/industrial comp	6,752[1]	32[1]	9,163[1]	3,861	5.88	0.10	0.07	0.9	9.8
352	•**Kyocera**/electronic comp	6,710	856	9,086	12,798	68.46	4.55	3.25	0.8	29.0
357	**Oki Electric Industry**/elec & electron	6,612[1]	325[1]	8,271[1]	4,242	6.93	0.42	0.28	0.7	23.6

(Continued)

1995 Rank	Company/business	Revenue ($mil)	Net income ($mil)	Assets ($mil)	Market value ($mil)	Stock price ($)	EPS 1995 ($)	EPS 1996[E] ($)	Yield (%)	Employees (thou)
Japan (*Cont.*)										
358	**Sumitomo Marine & Fire**[2]/ insurance	6,590	105	24,588	6,021	8.97	0.16	0.17	0.7	7.5
364	**Toda**/construction	6,486	70	7,798	2,654	8.25	0.22	0.22	1.0	6.0
367	■**Teijin**/chemicals	6,415	88	8,150	5,039	5.17	0.09	0.08	1.1	16.2
369	**Tokyu Construction**/ construction	6,392[1]	−5[1]	9,097[1]	1,149	4.95	−0.02[E]	0.04	1.4	5.0[2]
378	**Chori**/trading	6,262	−8	3,209	476	4.86	−0.09	0.28	0.0	1.3[2]
380	**Tonen**/energy	6,240	214	6,787	9,570	14.80	0.33	0.21	2.5	2.3[2]
384	**Sato Kogyo**/construction	6,187[1]	−39[1]	12,199[1]	1,761	6.74	0.05	0.06	0.8	5.5[2]
386	**UBE Industries**/misc materials	6,175[1]	−32[1]	10,159[1]	3,162	3.77	0.06	0.07	0.7	6.8[2]
388	■**Kanebo**/textile, apparel	6,166	−285	6,996	1,585	3.09	−0.56	−0.18	0.0	7.0[2]
389	**Yuasa Trading**/trading	6,151[1]	−7[1]	4,846[1]	629	5.64	0.05	0.08	1.0	1.7[2]
390	■**Bank of Yokohama**/banking	6,132	−677	106,659	9,736	8.56	−0.60	0.12	0.5	6.3
392	**Nippon Light Metal**/ metals-nonfer	6,111[1]	−51[1]	7,210[1]	3,104	5.78	0.00	0.06	0.3	4.9[2]
394	**Hanwa**/retailing	6,099	12	5,710	1,482	3.78	0.03	0.04	0.0	1.4
395	■**Hino Motors**[2]/machinery & eng	6,083	77	3,496	3,262	9.00	0.21	0.16	0.6	9.3
402	**Shin-Etsu Chemical**/chemicals	5,964	392	6,668	6,794	19.89	1.21	0.92	0.3	16.1
408	**Isetan**/retailing	5,891	−329	4,658	2,996	13.60	−1.49	0.14	0.7	5.6[2]
413	**Kinden**[2]/construction	5,827	210	5,706	4,256	16.00	0.87	0.66	0.6	9.5
414	**Nichirei**/food, household	5,822	2	3,594	2,206	7.10	0.01	0.11	0.9	8.1
415	•**Shiseido**/personal care	5,815	182	5,461	4,961	12.40	0.45	0.32	0.9	24.0
417	**Penta-Ocean Construction**[2]/ construction	5,789	45	5,669	2,402	6.74	0.13	0.11	1.2	5.3
420	**Showa Denko**/chemicals	5,744	−2	7,458	3,342	3.22	0.00	0.02	0.0	5.1[2]
421	**Hazama**/construction	5,718[1]	35[1]	10,933[1]	1,470	4.58	0.07	0.05	1.0	5.2
424	**Odakyu Electric Railway**/ trucking, RR	5,670[1]	31[1]	11,605[1]	4,892	6.68	0.05[E]	0.04	0.7	4.2[2]
425	■**Mitsubishi Estate**/real estate	5,670[1]	152[1]	27,904[1]	18,148	13.97	−0.75[E]	NA	0.5	2.1[2]
426	**Sumitomo Rubber Inds**/ industrial comp	5,670	5	5,781	1,793	8.74	0.02	0.16	1.0	24.0
431	•**TDK**/electronic comp	5,614	287	5,875	7,485	56.89	2.16	2.16	0.8	27.0
432	**Iwatani International**/utilities	5,608[1]	4[1]	4,681[1]	1,435	5.71	0.04[E]	0.03	1.0	1.7[2]
433	**Tostem Corp**/bldg materials	5,593[1]	257[1]	6,507[1]	6,396	29.23	1.13[E]	1.08	0.6	12.4
434	**Shikoku Electric Power**/utilities	5,567[1]	155[1]	16,311[1]	6,401	22.85	0.61	0.57	2.0	6.0[2]
435	**Sankyo**/personal care	5,566[1]	394[1]	7,494[1]	10,615	23.68	0.99[E]	0.91	0.8	7.0[2]
436	■**Marui**/retailing	5,549	195	6,506	7,564	20.54	0.53	0.48	1.0	8.2[2]
437	**Seibu Railway**/trucking, RR	5,546[1]	−23[1]	13,797[1]	22,888	52.82	−0.01[E]	NA	0.1	5.4[2]

All figures except per-share items are in millions of U.S. dollars. Revenue, net income and 1995 EPS are converted at an average rate of exchange for the fiscal year; assets are converted at fiscal year-end rate. Revenue figures are for group or consolidated operations and exclude excise taxes and duties. For companies with January, February or March fiscal year-ends, 1995 figures are used unless noted. Market value is as of May 31, 1996. •Sponsored ADR. ■Non-sponsored. [1]Figures are latest available. [2]Not fully consolidated. NA: Not available. [E]Estimate.

Sources: Morgan Stanley Capital International and IBES International, Inc. via OneSource Information Services; Bloomberg Financial Markets; Forbes.

(Continued)

Japan (*Cont.*)

1995 Rank	Company/business	Revenue ($mil)	Net income ($mil)	Assets ($mil)	Market value ($mil)	Stock price ($)	EPS 1995 ($)	EPS 1996[E] ($)	Yield (%)	Employees (thou)
439	**Toyota Auto Body**/automobiles	5,523	35	2,296[1]	953	11.10	0.41	0.30	0.8	8.6[2]
440	**Hitachi Zosen**/machinery & eng	5,510[1]	68[1]	7,470[1]	5,553	5.54	0.09	0.12	1.0	4.5[2]
441	**Yamaha**/leisure goods	5,508	98	4,835	3,124	16.10	0.50	0.72	0.3	10.8[2]
443	**Nagase & Co**/trading	5,501[1]	61[1]	3,256[1]	1,499	9.90	0.41[E]	0.40	0.7	1.2[2]
444	**Hokkaido Electric Power**/utilities	5,473[1]	236[1]	14,954[1]	4,993	22.66	0.78	0.68	2.0	6.6
445	**Daiwa Securities**/financial svcs	5,468	488	66,591	18,033	13.41	0.36	0.36	0.6	10.2
446	**Maeda**[2]/construction	5,462	31	6,410	1,876	10.27	0.17	0.18	0.8	4.4
447	**Matsuzakaya**/retailing	5,454	0	2,706[1]	2,134	12.49	0.00	0.04	0.6	7.1[2]
449	■**Omron**/elec & electron	5,447	151	6,370[1]	5,310	20.26	0.57	0.73	0.6	23.0
454	**Tokyu Dept Store**/retailing	5,401	−18	4,194	1,957	7.09	−0.07	−0.01	0.8	4.5[2]
455	**General Sekiyu Group**/energy	5,391	136	3,668	3,341	8.78	0.36	0.23	2.6	1.3[2]
457	**Mitsui Toatsu Chemicals**/ chemicals	5,369	48	7,323	3,246	4.15	0.06	0.10	0.7	5.1[2]
458	**Kandenko**[2]/construction	5,352	80	4,124	2,583	12.58	0.43	0.29	0.7	10.6[2]
461	■**Chichibu Onoda Cement**/ bldg materials	5,315[1]	−61[1]	9,455[1]	3,464	6.00	−0.01[E]	0.01	0.8	2.6[2]
462	**Sumitomo Metal Mining**/ metals-nonfer	5,308	111	5,875	5,298	9.34	0.20	0.22	0.5	3.7[2]
463	**Meiji Milk Products**/food, household	5,280[1]	38[1]	2,962[1]	1,850	6.24	0.08	0.08	0.9	6.0[2]
464	**Daikyo**/real estate	5,257[1]	−20[1]	17,458[1]	1,462	7.89	0.40	0.21	1.2	2.4[2]
465	•**Pioneer Electronic**/appliances	5,253	−104	5,004	3,987	22.20	−0.58	−0.08	0.4	18.8
468	■**Konica**/leisure goods	5,209[1]	39[1]	6,097[1]	2,571	7.19	0.06	0.14	1.3	5.1[2]
470	**Sumitomo Heavy Inds**/ machinery & eng	5,184	62	6,573	2,391	4.06	0.11	0.08	0.0	6.0[2]
471	**Nippon Fire & Marine Ins**[2]/ insurance	5,183	73	18,443	3,835	6.61	0.13	0.13	1.0	6.5
472	**Shinsho**[2]/trading	5,147	5	2,633	385	4.90	0.06	0.05	0.9	0.9
474	**Haseko**/construction	5,133	−2,223	10,307	1,918	4.47	−5.18	−0.18	0.0	2.4[2]
476	■**Ebara**/machinery & eng	5,091	83	5,034	4,359	15.17	0.29	0.34	0.6	11.5
481	**Dai-Tokyo Fire & Marine**[2]/ insurance	5,043	67	14,564	2,957	7.26	0.17	0.17	0.9	7.2
482	**Mitsui Construction**[2]/ construction	5,019	3	5,859	866	4.16	0.02	0.01	0.7	4.7
484	**Toyo Trust & Banking**/banking	4,984[1]	60[1]	88,654[1]	7,489	9.53	−1.06[E]	0.23	0.7	5.2
486	**Itoham Foods**/food, household	4,953	32	2,176	1,788	7.83	0.14	0.14	1.2	4.4[2]
487	**Misawa Homes**/construction	4,920[1]	25[1]	6,988[1]	1,206	9.44	0.34	0.31	1.2	2.0[2]
492	■**Nippon Suisan Kaisha**/food, household	4,860	−45	2,556	1,295	4.36	−0.15	0.04	0.0	2.5[2]
494	**Toyoda Auto Loom**/machinery & eng	4,821[1]	107[1]	4,781[1]	5,689	20.17	0.50	0.43	0.6	9.7
496	■**Toyobo**/textile, apparel	4,782	36	5,415	2,531	3.66	0.05	0.05	1.3	6.9[2]
497	**Hokuriku Electric Power**/utilities	4,744[1]	153[1]	16,191[1]	5,055	22.94	0.59	0.51	2.0	5.8
499	**Honshu Paper**/forest products	4,732[1]	27[1]	6,290[1]	2,446	7.08	0.12[E]	0.17	0.8	5.6[2]
500	**Tokyu**/trucking, RR	4,726[1]	19[1]	17,570[1]	8,220	7.48	0.03[E]	0.04	0.6	5.1[2]

NETHERLANDS P/E 16 • Yield 3.1% • Market Value $337 billion

Country Statistics	
Population	15.4 million
Gross domestic product	$330.3 billion
GDP per capita	$21.5 thousand
Total national debt/GDP	64.6%
R&D expenditures/GDP	1.9%
Unemployment rate	8.4%
Retail sales per capita	$4.5 thousand

1995 Rank	Company/business	Revenue ($mil)	Net income ($mil)	Assets ($mil)	Market value ($mil)	Stock price ($)	EPS 1995 ($)	EPS 1996[E] ($)	Yield (%)	Employees (thou)
7	•Royal Dutch/Shell Group/ energy	109,853	6,906	117,746	128,665[5]	152.01	8.16	8.39	3.7	104.0
23	•Unilever/food, household	49,638	2,320	30,036	36,986[6]	136.35	8.26	8.65	2.7	308.0
33	•Philips Group/appliances	40,146	1,568	32,562	12,268	35.55	4.62	4.22	2.6	263.6
45	•ING Group/insurance	33,236	1,650	246,986	24,137	82.49	5.98	2.42	3.0	52.1
68	•ABN-Amro Holding/banking	26,533	1,629	340,642	17,413	55.27	4.79	4.82	3.8	63.3
83	•Fortis Group/insurance	22,619	814	161,121	10,736[7]	78.09	5.98	6.12	3.2	30.4
115	•Ahold/retailing	18,445	285	5,762	6,696	53.74	2.33	2.40	1.0	84.4
169	•Akzo Nobel Group/chemicals	13,383	818	11,583	8,620	121.27	11.52	10.94	3.4	70.1
176	•Aegon Insurance Group/ insurance	13,066	824	93,868	12,595	47.99	3.14	3.22	2.9	19.8
199	•Royal PTT Nederlands/ telecomm	11,929	1,406	18,014	16,787	36.26	3.05	3.15	4.2	90.3
262	•KNP-BT/forest products	9,364	293	5,493	2,535	24.99	2.68	2.98	4.1	28.6
318	Schlumberger/energy equip	7,622	649	8,910	20,259	83.37	2.69	3.26	1.8	51.0
339	•Vendex Intl Group/retailing	7,041	260	2,783[1]	2,537	32.09	3.09	2.96	2.7	46.7
391	•DSM/chemicals	6,117	667	6,263	2,978	102.90	18.44	15.45	4.6	17.8
403	•KLM/airlines	5,954	342	9,982	3,252	35.79	3.66	3.77	3.3	31.3
429	■Heineken/bev & tobacco	5,640	414	6,009	11,400	227.22	8.25	8.71	0.9	22.6
477	•Reed Elsevier/media	5,059	874	8,523	37,010[8]	15.55	0.62	0.66	2.2	25.6
480	■Royal Hoogovens/metals-steel	5,045	316	5,163	1,226	37.78	9.79	5.98	4.7	19.0

All figures except per-share items are in millions of U.S. dollars. Revenue, net income and 1995 EPS are converted at an average rate of exchange for the fiscal year; assets are converted at fiscal year-end rate. Revenue figures are for group or consolidated operations and exclude excise taxes and duties. For companies with January, February or March fiscal year-ends, 1995 figures are used unless noted. Market value is as of May 31, 1996. •Sponsored ADR. ■Non-sponsored. [1]Figures are latest available. [2]Not fully consolidated. [5]Combined market value for Royal Dutch Petroleum and Shell Transport & Trading. Price, EPS and yield are only for Royal Dutch Petroleum. [6]Combined market value for Unilever NV and Unilever Plc. Price, EPS and yield are only for Unilever NV. [7]Combined market value for Fortis AMEV and Fortis AG. Price, EPS and yield are only for Fortis AMEV. [8]Combined market value for Reed and Elsevier. Price, EPS and yield are only for Elsevier. [E]Estimate.

Sources: Morgan Stanley Capital International and IBES International, Inc. via OneSource Information Services; Bloomberg Financial Markets; Forbes.

(Continued)

SOUTH KOREA · P/E 14 · Yield 1.6% · Market Value $172 billion

Country Statistics

Population	44.5 million
Gross domestic product	$379.6 billion
GDP per capita	$8.5 thousand
Total national debt/GDP	6.7%
R&D expenditures/GDP	2.1%
Unemployment rate	2.4%
Retail sales per capita	$1.7 thousand

1995 Rank	Company/business	Revenue ($mil)	Net income ($mil)	Assets ($mil)	Market value ($mil)	Stock price ($)	EPS 1995 ($)	EPS 1996[E] ($)	Yield (%)	Employees (thou)
74	•Samsung/trading	24,964	27	6,825	1,634	25.64	1.03	0.74	2.5	9.7
79	Hyundai/trading	23,274	7	1,389	207	27.92	1.09	2.28	2.0	0.7
92	•Samsung Electronics/ electronic comp	20,991	3,248	17,506	10,173	87.58	36.46	26.26	1.1	71.4
102	Daewoo/trading	19,480	78	11,285	1,278	11.30	0.69	0.72	4.5	12.9
164	•Hyundai Motor/automobiles	13,757	193	10,225	2,592	42.27	4.42	4.92	1.8	45.1
173	LG International/trading	13,218	18	1,613	376	14.09	0.83	0.81	3.6	3.7
177	•Korea Electric Power/utilities	12,984	1,180	35,065	23,948	38.33	1.91	2.50	1.7	30.8
201	•Yukong/energy	11,805	131	12,140	1,962	31.10	2.26	2.05	2.4	6.0[2]
218	•Pohang Iron and Steel/ metals-steel	11,206	1,230	18,995	6,460	68.80	13.41	8.40	1.8	20.2
290	LG Electronics[2]/electronic comp	8,547	103	7,759	2,947	27.54	1.15	1.73	1.4	35.1
301	Hyundai Eng & Const/ construction	8,183	257	11,618	2,613	50.52	5.58	0.92	0.2	18.9
325	•Kia Motors/automobiles	7,375	15	8,134	1,555	20.56	0.20	0.26	0.0	29.6
345	Hyundai Motor Service/ automobiles	6,873	42	4,287	622	41.38	3.24	3.50	1.8	14.5
349	Ssangyong/multi-industry	6,800	6	533	95	11.68	0.74	1.06	5.4	1.0
467	Sunkyong/trading	5,246	12	1,230	503	23.48	0.72	0.74	0.5	1.2

Spain · P/E 14 · Yield 3.5% · Market Value $156 billion

Country Statistics

Population	39.1 million
Gross domestic product	$482.8 billion
GDP per capita	$12.4 thousand
Total national debt/GDP	40.3%
R&D expenditures/GDP	0.9%
Unemployment rate	22.9%
Retail sales per capita	$2.5 thousand

(Continued)

1995 Rank	Company/business	Revenue ($mil)	Net income ($mil)	Assets ($mil)	Market value ($mil)	Stock price ($)	EPS 1995 ($)	EPS 1996[E] ($)	Yield (%)	Employees (thou)
Spain *(Cont.)*										
152	•Repsol/energy	14,586	944	13,742	10,291	34.30	3.15	3.44	3.9	18.9
160	•Telefónica/telecomm	13,959	1,068	39,686	16,919	18.01	1.14	1.26	3.3	99.2
175	•Banco Santander/banking	13,084	605	135,614	7,309	45.76	3.79	4.13	4.8	39.9
212	•Banco Bilbao Vizcaya/banking	11,327	674	116,426	8,524	37.93	3.00	3.31	4.1	34.2
281	•Banco Central Hispanoamer/ banking	8,770	100	92,389	3,301	20.15	0.61	1.61	2.9	30.5
291	**Argentaria**/banking	8,538	595	109,474	5,274	42.02	4.74	4.94	5.0	16.7
337	•**Endesa Group**/utilities	7,089	1,202	15,707[1]	16,115	61.98	4.62	5.07	2.3	16.3
363	**Iberdrola**/utilities	6,490	682	23,894[1]	9,447	10.17	0.73	0.82	5.0	14.7
375	**Cepsa-Cia Española de Pet**/ energy	6,332	175	4,164	2,722	30.52	1.97	2.27	3.1	8.8

SWEDEN   P/E 13 • Yield 2.0% • Market Value $190 billion

Country Statistics	
Population	8.7 million
Gross domestic product	$196.6 billion
GDP per capita	$22.5 thousand
Total national debt/GDP	57.2%
R&D expenditures/GDP	3.1%
Unemployment rate	7.5%
Retail sales per capita	$3.3 thousand

All figures except per-share items are in millions of U.S. dollars. Revenue, net income and 1995 EPS are converted at an average rate of exchange for the fiscal year; assets are converted at fiscal year-end rate. Revenue figures are for group or consolidated operations and exclude excise taxes and duties. For companies with January, February or March fiscal year-ends, 1995 figures are used unless noted. Market value is as of May 31, 1996. •Sponsored ADR. ■Non-sponsored. [1]Figures are latest available. [2]Not fully consolidated. [E]Estimate.

Sources: Morgan Stanley Capital International and IBES International, Inc. via OneSource Information Services; Bloomberg Financial Markets; Forbes.

(Continued)

1995 Rank	Company/business	Revenue ($mil)	Net income ($mil)	Assets ($mil)	Market value ($mil)	Stock price ($)	EPS 1995 ($)	EPS 1996[E] ($)	Yield (%)	Employees (thou)
Sweden *(Cont.)*										
44	•ABB Group/elec & electron	33,667	1,312	32,062	20,531[9]	101.49	7.00	7.46	2.3	209.6
76	•Volvo Group/automobiles	24,044	1,298	20,831	8,609	18.55	2.83	1.83	3.2	80.4
136	•Electrolux Group/appliances	16,234	385	12,489	3,727	50.89	5.26	5.61	3.6	112.3
163	•LM Ericsson/elec & electron	13,848	762	13,642	21,383	22.33	0.83	1.04	1.2	84.5
272	•SCA-Svenska Cellulosa/ forest products	9,157	486	10,232	3,851	19.51	2.46	2.17	3.6	34.9
304	Stora Group/forest products	8,006	752	9,252	4,260	13.28	2.34	1.56	4.2	25.6
312	Skandia Insurance/insurance	7,733	71	26,567	2,604	25.45	0.69	2.03	1.2	10.0
411	Svenska Handelsbanken/ banking	5,834	593	71,538	4,112	19.83	2.50	2.46	2.8	7.4
428	Skandinaviska Enskilda Bk/ banking	5,658	355	65,900	4,144	7.86	0.67	0.89	2.8	9.7
456	Skanska/construction	5,383	242	6,264	4,092	32.49	1.93	2.02	2.3	32.7
473	•SKF Group/industrial comp	5,145	284	4,956	2,502	22.40	2.52	2.55	3.5	42.6
483	•Astra/personal care	5,019	1,229	6,566	28,046	45.03	1.99	2.37	1.0	17.0

SWITZERLAND P/E 20 • Yield 1.6% • Market Value $368 billion

Country Statistics	
Population	7.0 million
Gross domestic product	$260.5 billion
GDP per capita	$37.2 thousand
Total national debt/GDP	20.2%
R&D expenditures/GDP	2.7%
Unemployment rate	4.2%
Retail sales per capita	$7.7 thousand

1995 Rank	Company/business	Revenue ($mil)	Net income ($mil)	Assets ($mil)	Market value ($mil)	Stock price ($)	EPS 1995 ($)	EPS 1996[E] ($)	Yield (%)	Employees (thou)
24	•Nestlé/food, household	47,767	2,468	38,471	44,148	1,128.45	62.92	66.43	1.9	220.2
44	•ABB Group/elec & electron	33,667	1,312	32,062	20,531[10]	1,197.28	76.28	76.19	2.0	209.6
75	•CS Holding Group/banking	24,788	1,185	358,734	16,304	86.44	6.43	6.96	3.7	34.2
77	Zurich Insurance Group/ insurance	23,994	739	83,317	12,018	264.11	16.24	17.05	1.8	36.5
90	Winterthur Group/insurance	21,224	355	70,610	5,187	589.84	40.31	42.58	2.6	26.7
114	•Union Bank of Switzerland/ banking	18,496	1,415	336,188	24,382	937.98	55.17	58.42	2.7	29.1
123	•Ciba-Geigy Group/chemicals	17,505	1,823	26,484	31,932	1,098.84	63.76	65.63	1.5	84.1
154	•Swiss Bank/banking	14,400	891	250,565	14,117	178.07	11.72	13.05	3.6	25.2
179	•Sandoz Group/personal care	12,892	1,742	17,747	39,348	1,042.02	46.01	49.30	1.2	49.9

(Continued)

1995 Rank	Company/business	Revenue ($mil)	Net income ($mil)	Assets ($mil)	Market value ($mil)	Stock price ($)	EPS 1995 ($)	EPS 1996[E] ($)	Yield (%)	Employees (thou)
Switzerland (*Cont.*)										
189	•**Roche Group**/personal care	12,450	2,852	30,912	73,477	12,184.87	330.60	370.79	0.4	50.5
239	**Swiss Re Group**/insurance	10,418[1]	681[1]	32,405[1]	13,595	966.79	65.85	68.19	1.2	7.4
335	**Bâloise Group**/insurance	7,098	136	30,550	2,353	2,168.87	132.77	132.69	1.7	9.1
341	•**Holderbank**/bldg materials	6,994	392	12,559	5,471	768.31	63.17	60.10	1.8	43.9
373	**Alusuisse-Lonza Holding**/ multi-industry	6,334	324	5,344	4,805	782.71	53.22	58.34	1.9	25.8
399	•**Cie Financière Richemont**/ multi-industry	5,991[1]	435[1]	8,513[1]	8,525	1,484.59	0.80[E]	0.92	0.7	24.9
406	**Swissair Group**/airlines	5,931	−124	8,701	2,276	988.40	−53.98	35.13	0.0	32.7
493	**Sulzer Group**/machinery & eng	4,854	78	5,728	2,148	636.26	22.50	40.98	1.5	27.6

UNITED KINGDOM   P/E 14 • Yield 4.1% • Market Value $1.4 trillion

Country Statistics	
Population	58.4 million
Gross domestic product	$1,024.7 billion
GDP per capita	$17.6 thousand
Total national debt/GDP	34.1%
R&D expenditures/GDP	2.1%
Unemployment rate	8.2%
Retail sales per capita	$5.2 thousand

1995 Rank	Company/business	Revenue ($mil)	Net income ($mil)	Assets ($mil)	Market value ($mil)	Stock price ($)	EPS 1995 ($)	EPS 1996[E] ($)	Yield (%)	Employees (thou)
7	•**Royal Dutch/Shell Group**/ energy	109,853	6,906	117,746	128,665[11]	14.23	0.76	0.82	4.6	104.0
17	•**British Petroleum**/energy	56,992	1,771	50,146	48,244	8.61	0.32	0.62	3.4	58.2
23	•**Unilever**/food, household	49,638	2,320	30,036	36,986[12]	18.61	1.25	1.36	3.1	308.0
67	•**HSBC Group**/banking	26,682	3,886	351,569	40,050	15.24	1.48	1.54	4.1	101.1
78	•**National Westminster Bank**/ banking	23,533	1,916	260,822	17,119	9.66	1.07	1.05	5.1	81.8

All figures except per-share items are in millions of U.S. dollars. Revenue, net income and 1995 EPS are converted at an average rate of exchange for the fiscal year; assets are converted at fiscal year-end rate. Revenue figures are for group or consolidated operations and exclude excise taxes and duties. For companies with January, February or March fiscal year-ends, 1995 figures are used unless noted. Market value is as of May 31, 1996. •Sponsored ADR. [1]Figures are latest available. [9]Combined market value for ABB AB and ABB AG. Price, EPS and yield are only for ABB AB. [10]Combined market value for ABB AB and ABB AG. Price, EPS and yield are only for ABB AG. [11]Combined market value for Royal Dutch Petroleum and Shell Transport & Trading. Price, EPS and yield are only for Shell Transport & Trading. [12]Combined market value for Unilever NV and Unilever Plc. Price, EPS and yield are only for Unilever Plc. [E]Estimate.

Sources: Morgan Stanley Capital International and IBES International, Inc. via OneSource Information Services; Bloomberg Financial Markets; Forbes.

(Continued)

1995 Rank	Company/business	Revenue ($mil)	Net income ($mil)	Assets ($mil)	Market value ($mil)	Stock price ($)	EPS 1995 ($)	EPS 1996E ($)	Yield (%)	Employees (thou)
United Kingdom (Cont.)										
80	•Barclays/banking	23,202	2,153	261,681	18,451	11.64	1.32	1.30	4.4	92.4
84	•British Telecom/telecomm	22,618	3,109	35,902	34,319	5.50	0.50	0.51	6.2	135.2
89	•Prudential/insurance	21,407	1,196	107,478[1]	12,667	6.65	0.63	0.42	4.7	22.9
99	•J Sainsbury/retailing	19,770	764	10,302	11,261	6.14	0.42	0.45	3.8	95.5
103	•B. A. T Industries/ multi-industry	19,450	2,323	70,096	24,790	8.03	0.75	0.79	5.3	84.0
107	•Tesco/retailing	19,009	732	9,529	10,055	4.67	0.35	0.37	4.0	84.9
112	Lloyds TSB Group/banking	18,653	1,517	229,473	25,070	4.85	0.30	0.45	4.8	87.0
122	Commercial Union/insurance	17,672	701	87,273	6,311	9.38	1.02	0.74	5.8	25.3
137	•Imperial Chemical Inds/ chemicals	16,209	844	14,682	9,577	13.21	1.17	1.23	4.5	64.8
157	•BTR/multi-industry	14,222	1,515	15,322	17,294	4.36	0.41	0.38	6.4	125.1
165	•British Gas/utilities	13,576	803	26,981	12,923	2.95	0.18	0.35	9.5	55.4
192	•British Airways/airlines	12,150	741	15,316	8,341	8.68	0.77	0.74	2.9	55.3
195	•Glaxo Wellcome/ personal care	12,056	2,687	13,239	45,713	13.04	0.79	0.88	5.2	52.4
209	•Hanson/multi-industry	11,382	1,608	37,340	14,957	2.88	0.31	0.30	8.1	65.0
213	General Accident/insurance	11,302	636	30,599	4,947	10.31	1.05	0.86	5.9	25.0
214	•Marks & Spencer/retailing	11,287	1,022	9,204[1]	20,067	7.16	0.38	0.42	2.8	45.5
215	•Grand Metropolitan/food, household	11,287	952	17,606	14,224	6.75	0.46	0.49	4.4	66.0
223	•Abbey National/banking	11,074	1,078	159,844	11,302	8.56	0.82	0.88	4.9	19.7
224	•SmithKline Beecham/ personal care	11,067	1,531	12,637	28,040	10.19	0.57	0.59	2.6	52.4
240	•Peninsular & Oriental/ shipping	10,372	373	11,248	4,906	8.11	0.60	0.60	7.3	66.9
244	Sun Alliance Group/insurance	10,318	635	46,180	5,020	6.16	0.76	0.50	5.5	24.2
251	Inchcape/trading	9,825	−69	5,905	2,505	4.75	−0.13	0.28	4.2	36.8
255	Argyll Group/retailing	9,503	471	5,385	6,237	5.49	0.41	0.42	4.5	48.0
273	■General Electric/elec & electron	9,088[1]	877[1]	10,183[1]	15,866	5.77	0.35E	0.38	3.8	82.3
274	British Aerospace/aero & defense	9,062	218	11,850	5,859	13.77	0.77	0.97	1.8	45.2
282	•Legal & General Group/ insurance	8,741	308	58,982	5,400	10.95	0.63	0.58	4.4	8.0
287	•Cable & Wireless/telecomm	8,638	950	13,759	15,135	6.87	0.43	0.45	2.5	39.6
296	•Kingfisher/retailing	8,316	363	4,947	6,323	9.44	0.54	0.54	3.3	43.6
298	ASDA Group/retailing	8,276	280	4,583	5,272	1.81	0.11E	0.13	2.6	36.2
302	Royal Insurance Holdings/ insurance	8,173	619	35,884	4,332	6.56	0.95	0.65	4.7	21.0
305	•Thorn Emi/leisure goods	7,915	352	5,242[1]	11,950	27.82	0.82	1.26	2.6	33.5
311	■Associated British Food/food, household	7,755	396	5,340	5,287	5.88	0.44	0.46	2.1	43.7
313	•Zeneca Group/personal care	7,731	530	7,894	20,123	21.26	0.56	1.08	2.8	31.4
315	Guardian Royal Exchange/ insurance	7,704	1,072	28,612	3,719	4.14	1.22	0.31	4.1	13.8

(Continued)

1995 Rank	Company/business	Revenue ($mil)	Net income ($mil)	Assets ($mil)	Market value ($mil)	Stock price ($)	EPS 1995 ($)	EPS 1996[E] ($)	Yield (%)	Employees (thou)
United Kingdom (*Cont.*)										
315	•RTZ-CRA/metals-nonfer	7,704	1,286	15,748	21,983[13]	15.58	0.92	1.11	3.4	51.5
319	Dalgety/food, household	7,608	81	2,393	1,664	5.78	0.32	0.34	7.5	17.9
321	•Cadbury Schweppes/food, household	7,539	488	7,122	7,435	7.49	0.49	0.54	4.1	41.8
324	•British Steel/metals-steel	7,441[1]	728[1]	10,055[1]	5,320	2.64	0.55[E]	0.43	5.3	40.0
327	•Allied Domecq/bev & tobacco	7,341	371	9,948	7,763	7.50	0.36	0.55	6.1	71.8
330	•Royal Bank of Scotland/ banking	7,189	631	80,650	6,515	8.09	0.70	0.73	3.8	25.9
333	•Tate & Lyle Group/food, household	7,146	314	4,712	2,804	7.06	0.79	0.65	4.4	17.7
355	•Booker/multi-industry	6,666	81	2,012	1,368	6.06	0.36	0.49	7.4	21.6
359	•Cordiant/services	6,586	−59	1,539	852	1.89	−0.20	0.07	0.0	10.6
362	RMC Group/bldg materials	6,497	274	5,546	3,873	15.60	1.29	1.23	3.1	30.0
368	BICC Group/industrial comp	6,413	−183	3,844[1]	1,784	5.04	−0.59	0.26	4.9	34.1
372	•Bass/leisure	6,335	602	10,385	11,087	12.62	0.69	0.73	3.4	76.9
377	■Boots/retailing	6,279	533	5,323	8,979	9.44	0.56	0.59	3.4	80.9
385	•National Power/utilities	6,181	952	7,492[1]	9,122	8.08	0.81	0.76	3.6	5.1
400	Wolseley/bldg materials	5,990	260	3,008	3,967	7.13	0.48	0.44	2.6	21.5
407	■Ladbroke Group/leisure	5,922	95	5,371	3,418	2.93	0.08	0.15	4.2	43.1
412	•Tomkins/multi-industry	5,834	326	3,546	4,682	3.95	0.29[E]	0.32	4.3	46.1
423	•Rolls-Royce/aero & defense	5,678	224	5,665	5,077	3.47	0.16	0.19	2.7	43.2
430	■BOC Group/chemicals	5,616	395	6,892	6,938	14.42	0.82	0.90	3.6	39.7
438	Standard Chartered Group/ banking	5,525	713	60,348	9,676	9.94	0.73	0.81	2.2	27.0
442	•Guinness/bev & tobacco	5,503	939	12,777	13,879	7.21	0.46	0.52	4.0	22.5
477	•Reed Elsevier/media	5,059	874	8,523	37,010[14]	17.29	0.82	0.88	2.8	25.6
478	De Beers Centenary/misc materials	5,057	983	10,221	12,374	32.55	2.58	2.73	0.7	9.0
498	Kwik Save Group/retailing	4,743	127	1,354	1,087	6.99	0.82	0.67	5.5	15.9

All figures except per-share items are in millions of U.S. dollars. Revenue, net income and 1995 EPS are converted at an average rate of exchange for the fiscal year; assets are converted at fiscal year-end rate. Revenue figures are for group or consolidated operations and exclude excise taxes and duties. For companies with January, February or March fiscal year-ends, 1995 figures are used unless noted. Market value is as of May 31, 1996. •Sponsored ADR. ■Non-sponsored. [1]Figures are latest available. [13]Combined market value for RTZ and CRA. Price, EPS and yield are only for RTZ. [14]Combined market value for Fletcher Challenge Forests, Building, Energy, and Paper Shares. Price, EPS and yield are only for Fletcher Challenge Forests. [E]Estimate.

Sources: Morgan Stanley Capital International and IBES International, Inc. via OneSource Information Services; Bloomberg Financial Markets; Forbes.

(Continued)

THE REST OF THE WORLD

1995 Rank	Company/business	Revenue ($mil)	Net income ($mil)	Assets ($mil)	Market value ($mil)	Stock price ($)	EPS 1995 ($)	EPS 1996[E] ($)	Yield (%)	Employees (thou)
ARGENTINA										
485	•YPF/energy	4,955	822	9,137	7,775	22.03	2.25	1.89	3.6	9.3
AUSTRIA										
404	•ÖMV Group/energy	5,950[1]	54[1]	5,722[1]	2,785	103.13	6.35	6.30	1.8	10.4
490	Creditanstalt/banking	4,898	207	63,921	2,874	70.33	5.16	5.12	1.3	9.7
FINLAND										
184	UPM-Kymmene/forest products	12,535	431	15,282	5,152	19.27	4.60	2.91	5.0	45.7
247	Neste/energy	9,924	151	7,668	1,977	20.07	1.74	1.91	2.5	8.8
294	•Nokia/multi-industry	8,430	400	7,517	13,040	43.53	1.41	2.73	1.5	31.9
396	Kesko Group/trading	6,054	148	3,042	1,149	12.74	1.20	1.19	3.2	5.8
HONG KONG										
234	•Jardine Matheson Holdings/ multi-ind	10,636	420	11,583	5,635	7.70	0.72	0.73	3.2	80.0
344	•Swire Pacific/multi-industry	6,937	834	17,895	14,087	8.89	0.53	0.58	2.3	37.0
381	•Dairy Farm International/ retailing	6,236	149	2,935	1,450	0.84	0.08	0.10	7.1	51.6
466	•First Pacific/multi-industry	5,250	257	7,191	3,180	1.38	0.13	0.09	0.2	35.7
MEXICO										
229	•Grupo Financiero Bancomer/ banking	10,743	84	23,174	2,249	0.32	0.02	0.02	0.0	27.8
361	■Teléfonos de México/ telecomm	6,511	1,450	13,346	17,489	1.65	0.15	0.20	2.4	48.8[2]
NEW ZEALAND										
460	•Fletcher Challenge/forest products	5,319	294	8,877	3,889[15]	1.28	0.11	0.04	3.2	23.0
NORWAY										
182	•Norsk Hydro/energy	12,586	1,129	14,063	10,904	47.60	4.93	4.80	1.9	32.4
SINGAPORE										
491	Singapore Airlines/airlines	4,885	855	9,371	10,240	10.29	0.57	0.63	1.6	26.3
SOUTH AFRICA										
300	•So African Breweries/ bev & tobacco	8,189	452	5,283	9,033	30.48	1.54	1.54	1.9	106.9
370	•Smith (CG)/food, household	6,386	168	3,627	2,707	5.74	0.38	0.38	2.0	74.1
427	AMIC-Anglo American Inds/ multi-ind	5,659	445	4,765[1]	2,961	43.39	4.33	4.54	2.9	NA
TURKEY										
208	Koç Group/multi-industry	11,504	425	4,253	1,285	0.21	0.01	0.01	0.0	36.3

All figures except per-share items are in millions of U.S. dollars. Revenue, net income and 1995 EPS are converted at an average rate of exchange for the fiscal year; assets are converted at fiscal year-end rate. Revenue figures are for group or consolidated operations and exclude excise taxes and duties. For companies with January, February or March fiscal year-ends, 1995 figures are used unless noted. Market value is as of May 31, 1996. •Sponsored ADR. ■Non-sponsored. [1]Figures are latest available. [2]Not fully consolidated. [15]Combined market value for Fletcher Challenge Forests, Building, Energy, and Paper Shares. Price, EPS and yield are only for Fletcher Challenge Forests. NA: Not available. [E]Estimated.

Sources: Morgan Stanley Capital International and IBES International, Inc. via OneSource Information Services; Bloomberg Financial Markets; Forbes.

THE FOREIGN 500:
ALPHABETICAL LIST

Company/country	Rank	Company/country	Rank
ABB Group/Switzerland, Sweden	44	**Argentaria**/Spain	291
Abbey National/UK	223	**Argyll Group**/UK	255
ABN-Amro Holding/Netherlands	68	**Asahi Bank**/Japan	191
Accor/France	383	**Asahi Breweries**/Japan	342
Aegon Insurance Group/Netherlands	176	**Asahi Chemical Ind**/Japan	183
AGF-Assur Générales de Fr/France	101	**Asahi Glass**/Japan	171
AGIV/Germany	348	**ASDA Group**/UK	298
Ahold/Netherlands	115	**ASKO Group**/Germany	134
Aisin Seiki/Japan	288	**Associated British Foods**/UK	311
Ajinomoto/Japan	309	**Astra**/Sweden	483
Akzo Nobel Group/Netherlands	169	**ANZ Banking**/Australia	317
Alcan Aluminium/Canada	265	**AVA**/Germany	453
Alcatel Alsthom/France	51	**AXA Group**/France	64
Alitalia Group/Italy	495	**B. A. T Industries**/UK	103
All Nippon Airways/Japan	271	**Bâloise Group**/Switzerland	335
Allianz Worldwide/Germany	31	**Banca Commerciale Italian**/Italy	246
Allied Domecq/UK	327	**Banca di Roma**/Italy	205
Alusuisse-Lonza Holding/Switzerland	373	**Banco Bilbao Vizcaya**/Spain	212
Amcor/Australia	489	**Banco Bradesco Group**/Brazil	303
AMIC-Anglo American Inds/South Africa	427	**Banco Central Hispanoamer**/Spain	281
Arbed/Belgium	283	*(Continued)*	

The Forbes Foreign 500 (*Cont.*)

Company/country	Rank	Company/country	Rank
Banco di Napoli/Italy	382	Chichibu Onoda Cement/Japan	461
Banco do Brasil/Brazil	127	Chori/Japan	378
Banco Itáu Group/Brazil	365	Chubu Electric Power/Japan	93
Banco Santander/Spain	175	Chugoku Electric Power/Japan	238
Bank Bruxelles Lambert/Belgium	308	Ciba-Geigy Group/Switzerland	123
Bank of Montreal/Canada	280	Cockerill Sambre/Belgium	340
Bank of Nova Scotia/Canada	279	Coles Myer/Australia	188
Bank of Tokyo-Mitsubishi/Japan	18	Commercial Union/UK	122
Bank of Yokohama/Japan	390	Commerzbank/Germany	109
BNP Group/France	69	Commonwealth Bank Group/Australia	398
Barclays/UK	80	Comptoirs Modernes/France	451
BASF Group/Germany	49	Continental Group/Germany	332
Bass/UK	372	Cordiant/UK	359
Bayer Group/Germany	55	Cosmo Oil/Japan	138
Bayerische Hypotheken/Germany	151	Crédit Commercial/France	353
Bayer Vereinsbank/Germany	126	Crédit Lyonnais Group/France	63
BCE/Canada	118	Creditanstalt/Austria	490
BICC Group/UK	368	Credito Italiano/Italy	243
Bilfinger & Berger/Germany	488	CS Holding Group/Switzerland	75
BMW-Bayerische Motor/Germany	50	Daewoo/South Korea	102
BOC Group/UK	430	Dai Nippon Printing/Japan	178
Bombardier/Canada	469	Dai-Ichi Kangyo Bank/Japan	58
Booker/UK	355	Dai-Tokyo Fire & Marine/Japan	481
Boots/UK	377	Daiei/Japan	46
Bouygues Group/France	149	Daihatsu Motor/Japan	299
Bridgestone/Japan	119	Daikyo/Japan	464
British Aerospace/UK	274	Daimaru/Japan	295
British Airways/UK	192	Daimler-Benz Group/Germany	11
British Gas/UK	165	Dainippon Ink & Chems/Japan	276
British Petroleum/UK	17	Dairy Farm International/Hong Kong	381
British Steel/UK	324	Daiwa Bank/Japan	211
British Telecom/UK	84	Daiwa House Industry/Japan	227
Broken Hill Proprietary/Australia	174	Daiwa Securities/Japan	445
BTR/UK	157	Dalgety/UK	319
Groupe Bull/France	459	Groupe Danone/France	139
Cable & Wireless/UK	287	DDI/Japan	343
Cadbury Schweppes/UK	321	De Beers Centenary/UK	478
Canadian Imperial Bank/Canada	253	Degussa/Germany	258
Canadian Pacific/Canada	416	Delhaize Le Lion Group/Belgium	186
Canon/Japan	81	Deutsche Babcock Group/Germany	422
Carrefour Group/France	62	Deutsche Bank Group/Germany	36
Casino Groupe/France	181	Deutsche Lufthansa/Germany	161
Cepsa-Cia Española de Pet/Spain	375	Christian Dior/France	387

The Forbes Foreign 500 (*Cont.*)

Company/country	Rank	Company/country	Rank
Docks de France/France	263	Haseko/Japan	474
Dresdner Bank/Germany	91	Groupe Havas/France	277
DSM/Netherlands	391	Hazama/Japan	421
East Japan Railway/Japan	72	Heineken/Netherlands	429
Ebara/Japan	476	Henkel Group/Germany	248
Eiffage/France	360	Hino Motors/Japan	395
Electrolux Group/Sweden	136	Hitachi/Japan	9
Eletrobrás/Brazil	409	Hitachi Zosen/Japan	440
Elf Aquitaine Group/France	32	Hoechst Group/Germany	40
Endesa Group/Spain	337	Hokkaido Electric Power/Japan	444
ENI/Italy	42	Hokuriku Electric Power/Japan	497
LM Ericsson/Sweden	163	Holderbank/Switzerland	341
Esso/France	379	Philipp Holzmann/Germany	306
Fiat Group/Italy	26	Honda Motor/Japan	29
Finmeccanica/Italy	322	Honshu Paper/Japan	499
First Pacific/Hong Kong	466	HSBC Group/UK	67
Fletcher Challenge/New Zealand	460	Hyundai/South Korea	79
Fortis Group/Netherlands, Belgium	83	Hyundai Eng & Const/South Korea	301
Fuji Bank/Japan	52	Hyundai Motor/South Korea	164
Fuji Electric/Japan	269	Hyundai Motor Service/South Korea	345
Fuji Heavy Inds/Japan	219	Iberdrola/Spain	363
Fuji Photo Film/Japan	217	Imasco/Canada	376
Fujita/Japan	336	Imperial Chemical Inds/UK	137
Fujitsu/Japan	34	Imperial Oil/Canada	405
Furukawa Electric/Japan	351	Inchcape/UK	251
Galeries Lafayette/France	419	Indl Bank of Japan/Japan	35
GAN-Assur Nationales/France	54	ING Group/Netherlands	45
Gehe/Germany	170	Isetan/Japan	408
General Accident/UK	213	Ishikawajima-Harima/Japan	245
General Electric/UK	273	Isuzu Motors/Japan	111
General Sekiyu Group/Japan	455	Ito-Yokado/Japan	57
Générale Bank Group/Belgium	230	Itochu/Japan	3
Générale de Belgique/Belgium	448	Itoham Foods/Japan	486
Générale des Eaux/France	48	Iwatani International/Japan	432
Generali Group/Italy	94	Japan Air Lines/Japan	166
GIB Group/Belgium	310	Japan Energy/Japan	104
Glaxo Wellcome/UK	195	Japan Tobacco/Japan	124
Grand Metropolitan/UK	215	Jardine Matheson Holdings/Hong Kong	234
Grupo Financiero Bancomer/Mexico	229	Jusco/Japan	87
Guardian Royal Exchange/UK	315	Kajima/Japan	116
Guinness/UK	442	Kandenko/Japan	458
Hanson/UK	209	Kanebo/Japan	388
Hanwa/Japan	394	*(Continued)*	

The Forbes Foreign 500 (*Cont.*)

Company/country	Rank	Company/country	Rank
Kanematsu/Japan	22	Mannesmann Group/Germany	85
Kansai Electric Power/Japan	73	Marks & Spencer/UK	214
Kao/Japan	285	Marubeni/Japan	5
Karstadt Group/Germany	132	Maruha/Japan	250
Kaufhof/Germany	148	Marui/Japan	436
Kawasaki Heavy Inds/Japan	216	Matsushita Electric Indl/Japan	12
Kawasaki Steel/Japan	193	Matsushita Electric Works/Japan	198
Kawasho/Japan	168	Matsuzakaya/Japan	447
Kesko Group/Finland	396	Mazda Motor/Japan	106
Kia Motors/South Korea	325	Meiji Milk Products/Japan	463
Kinden/Japan	413	Metallgesellschaft/Germany	194
Kingfisher/UK	296	Michelin Group/France	172
Kinki Nippon Railway/Japan	266	Misawa Homes/Japan	487
Kirin Brewery/Japan	260	Mitsubishi Chemical/Japan	129
KLM/Netherlands	403	Mitsubishi/Japan	1
KNP-BT/Netherlands	262	Mitsubishi Electric/Japan	39
Kobe Steel/Japan	143	Mitsubishi Estate/Japan	425
Koç Group/Turkey	208	Mitsubishi Heavy Inds/Japan	53
Komatsu/Japan	241	Mitsubishi Materials/Japan	204
Konica/Japan	468	Mitsubishi Motors/Japan	38
Korea Electric Power/South Korea	177	Mitsubishi Oil/Japan	206
Kredietbank/Belgium	314	Mitsubishi Trust & Bank/Japan	203
Krupp Hoesch Group/Germany	133	Mitsui & Co/Japan	2
Kubota/Japan	222	Mitsui Construction/Japan	482
Kumagai Gumi/Japan	264	Mitsui Fudosan/Japan	185
Kwik Save Group/UK	498	Mitsui Marine & Fire Ins/Japan	326
Kyocera/Japan	352	Mitsui O.S.K. Lines/Japan	347
Kyushu Electric Power/Japan	159	Mitsui Toatsu Chemicals/Japan	457
L'Aire Liquide Group/France	366	Mitsui Trust & Banking/Japan	235
L'Oréal Group/France	232	Mitsukoshi/Japan	231
Ladbroke Group/UK	407	Montedison Group/Italy	146
Lafarge/France	356	Münchener Rückversicherun/Germany	86
Lagardère Groupe/France	236	Nagase & Co/Japan	443
Legal & General Group/UK	282	Natl Australia Bank/Australia	257
LG Electronics/South Korea	290	National Power/UK	385
LG International/South Korea	173	National Westminster Bank/UK	78
Linde/Germany	418	NEC/Japan	28
Lloyds TSB Group/UK	112	Neste/Finland	247
Long-Term Credit Bank/Japan	60	Nestlé/Switzerland	24
LVMH Group/France	401	New Oji Paper/Japan	289
Lyonnaise des Eaux-Dumez/France	100	News Corp/Australia	275
M A N Group/Germany	190	Nichii/Japan	121
Maeda/Japan	446	Nichimen/Japan	20

The Forbes Foreign 500 (*Cont.*)

Company/country	Rank	Company/country	Rank
Nichirei/Japan	414	Promodès Group/France	96
Nippon Credit Bank/Japan	135	Prudential/UK	89
Nippon Express/Japan	120	Qantas Airways/Australia	452
Nippon Fire & Marine Ins/Japan	471	Reed Elsevier/UK, Netherlands	477
Nippon Light Metal/Japan	392	Renault Group/France	37
Nippon Meat Packers/Japan	293	Repsol/Spain	152
Nippon Oil/Japan	88	Rhône-Poulenc Group/France	130
Nippon Paper Inds/Japan	225	Cie Financière Richemont/Switzerland	399
Nippon Steel/Japan	56	Ricoh/Japan	207
Nippon Suisan Kaisha/Japan	492	RMC Group/UK	362
Nippon Tel & Tel/Japan	10	Roche Group/Switzerland	189
Nippon Yusen/Japan	268	Rolls-Royce/UK	423
Nippondenso/Japan	150	Royal Bank of Canada/Canada	221
Nishimatsu Construction/Japan	323	Royal Bank of Scotland/UK	330
Nissan Motor/Japan	14	Royal Dutch/Shell/Netherlands, UK	7
Nissho Iwai/Japan	8	Royal Hoogovens/Netherlands	480
Nittetsu Shoji/Japan	237	Royal Insurance Holdings/UK	302
NKK/Japan	110	Royal PTT Nederlands/Netherlands	199
Nokia/Finland	294	RTZ-CRA/UK, Australia	315
Nomura Securities/Japan	292	RWE Group/Germany	41
Noranda/Canada	393	J Sainsbury/UK	99
Norsk Hydro/Norway	182	Saint-Gobain/France	158
Obayashi/Japan	156	Saint Louis/France	338
Odakyu Electric Railway/Japan	424	Sakura Bank/Japan	70
Oki Electric Industry/Japan	357	Samsung/South Korea	74
Olivetti Group/Italy	397	Samsung Electronics/South Korea	92
Omron/Japan	449	Sandoz Group/Switzerland	179
ÖMV Group/Austria	404	Sankyo/Japan	435
Osaka Gas/Japan	331	Sanpaolo Group/Italy	145
Pacific Dunlop/Australia	450	Sanwa Bank/Japan	43
Groupe Paribas/France	97	Sanyo Electric/Japan	113
Péchiney/France	142	Sato Kogyo/Japan	384
Peninsular & Oriental/UK	240	SCA-Svenska Cellulosa/Sweden	272
Penta-Ocean Construction/Japan	417	Schlumberger/Netherlands	318
Petrobras-Petróleo Brasil/Brazil	125	Schneider/France	200
PetroFina/Belgium	187	Seagram/Canada	278
Peugeot Groupe/France	47	Seibu Railway/Japan	437
Philips Group/Netherlands	33	Seiyu/Japan	167
Pinault-Printemps-Redoute/France	141	Sekisui Chemical/Japan	220
Pioneer Electronic/Japan	465	Sekisui House/Japan	162
Pirelli Group/Italy	354	Sharp/Japan	128
Pohang Iron and Steel/South Korea	218	Shikoku Electric Power/Japan	434
Preussag Group/Germany	117		*(Continued)*

The Forbes Foreign 500 (*Cont.*)

Company/country	Rank	Company/country	Rank
Shimizu/Japan	108	Swiss Re Group/Switzerland	239
Shin-Etsu Chemical/Japan	402	Swissair Group/Switzerland	406
Shinsho/Japan	472	Taisei/Japan	98
Shiseido/Japan	415	Takashimaya/Japan	180
Showa Denko/Japan	420	Takeda Chemical Inds/Japan	297
Siemens Group/Germany	16	Tate & Lyle Group/UK	333
Singapore Airlines/Singapore	491	TDK/Japan	431
Skandia Insurance/Sweden	312	Teijin/Japan	367
Skandinaviska Enskilda Bk/Sweden	428	Telebrás/Brazil	261
Skanska/Sweden	456	Telefónica/Spain	160
SKF Group/Sweden	473	Teléfonos de México/Mexico	361
Smith (CG)/South Africa	370	Tesco/UK	107
SmithKline Beecham/UK	224	Thomson Corp/Canada	329
Snow Brand Milk Prods/Japan	197	Thomson CSF/France	334
Société Générale Group/France	71	Thorn Emi/UK	305
Solvay Group/Belgium	267	Thyssen Group/Germany	66
Sony/Japan	25	Toda/Japan	364
So African Breweries/South Africa	300	Tohoku Electric Power/Japan	153
SPAR Handels/Germany	284	Tokai Bank/Japan	95
Ssangyong/South Korea	349	Tokio Marine & Fire Ins/Japan	144
Standard Chartered Group/UK	438	Tokyo Electric Power/Japan	21
STET/Italy	82	Tokyo Gas/Japan	270
Stora Group/Sweden	304	Tokyu/Japan	500
Suez Group/France	105	Tokyu Construction/Japan	369
Sulzer Group/Switzerland	493	Tokyu Dept Store/Japan	454
Sumikin Bussan/Japan	228	Tomen/Japan	13
Sumitomo Bank/Japan	59	Tomkins/UK	412
Sumitomo Chemical/Japan	249	Tonen/Japan	380
Sumitomo/Japan	4	Toppan Printing/Japan	210
Sumitomo Electric Inds/Japan	196	Toray Industries/Japan	252
Sumitomo Forestry/Japan	328	Toronto-Dominion Bank/Canada	374
Sumitomo Heavy Inds/Japan	470	Toshiba/Japan	19
Sumitomo Marine & Fire/Japan	358	Toshoku/Japan	286
Sumitomo Metal Inds/Japan	147	Tostem Corp/Japan	433
Sumitomo Metal Mining/Japan	462	Total Group/France	65
Sumitomo Rubber Inds/Japan	426	Toyo Seikan Kaisha/Japan	307
Sumitomo Trust & Banking/Japan	202	Toyo Trust & Banking/Japan	484
Sun Alliance Group/UK	244	Toyobo/Japan	496
Sunkyong/South Korea	467	Toyoda Automatic Loom/Japan	494
Suzuki Motor/Japan	155	Toyota Auto Body/Japan	439
Svenska Handelsbanken/Sweden	411	Toyota Motor/Japan	6
Swire Pacific/Hong Kong	344	Toyota Tsusho/Japan	131
Swiss Bank/Switzerland	154	Tractebel/Belgium	226

The Forbes Foreign 500 (*Cont.*)

Company/country	Rank	Company/country	Rank
TransCanada PipeLines/Canada	475	Westpac Banking Group/Australia	371
UAP-Union des Assurances/France	30	Winterthur Group/Switzerland	90
UBE Industries/Japan	386	Wolseley/UK	400
Unilever/Netherlands, UK	23	Woolworths/Australia	256
Union Bank of Switzerland/Switzerland	114	Yamaha/Japan	441
UNY/Japan	254	Yamaha Motor/Japan	320
UPM-Kymmene/Finland	184	Yamato Transport/Japan	350
Groupe Usinor Sacilor/France	140	Yamazaki Baking/Japan	346
Valeo/France	479	Yasuda Fire & Marine Ins/Japan	233
VEBA Group/Germany	27	Yasuda Trust & Banking/Japan	242
Vendex Intl Group/Netherlands	339	YPF/Argentina	485
VEW/Germany	410	Yuasa Trading/Japan	389
VIAG Group/Germany	61	Yukong/South Korea	201
Volkswagen Group/Germany	15	Zeneca Group/UK	313
Volvo Group/Sweden	76	Zurich Insurance Group/Switzerland	77
George Weston/Canada	259		

THE 100 LARGEST
U.S. MULTINATIONALS

BRIAN ZAJAC

Those who want the U.S. to put up new trade barriers should consider what would happen to U.S. firms if other countries put up barriers. In 1995, foreign operations of America's 100 largest multinational corporations accounted for 40% of the total sales of these firms. These 100 U.S.-based multinational companies generated $850 billion in sales outside of America's borders, a 14% increase over 1994. As for profits, these companies earned $57 billion overseas, a 9% increase over the previous year.

How are foreign-generated revenues important to the U.S. balance of trade? For starters, these foreign operations create economies of scale, which helps the parent companies compete in world markets. U.S. corporations often establish a manufacturing presence in a foreign country in order to do business in that nation. These beachheads also create export opportunities for the U.S. operations.

The largest U.S.-based multinational is Exxon. In 1995, $84 billion of Exxon's total revenue of $108 billion came from foreign operations. Second place went to General Motors, which had $49 billion in foreign sales. Our figures for all firms show only sales originating overseas. In the case of GM, for example, we didn't count GM's estimated $5 billion in automobile and technology exports from the U.S.

The Largest U.S. Multinationals

1995 Rank	Company	REVENUE foreign ($mil)	REVENUE total ($mil)	REVENUE foreign as % of total	NET PROFIT[1] foreign ($mil)	NET PROFIT[1] total ($mil)	NET PROFIT[1] foreign as % of total	ASSETS foreign ($mil)	ASSETS total ($mil)	ASSETS foreign as % of total
1	Exxon	83,907	107,893	77.8	4,949	6,470	76.5	53,841	91,296	59.0
2	General Motors	49,015	168,829	29.0	3,738	6,933	53.9	58,307	217,079	26.9
3	IBM	45,151	71,940	62.8	3,567	4,178	85.4	44,385	80,292	55.3
4	Mobil	44,287[2]	66,724[2]	66.4	1,855[3]	2,682[3]	69.2	26,010	42,138	61.7
5	Ford Motor	41,884	137,137	30.5	578	4,139	14.0	69,209	243,283	28.4
6	Texaco[4]	26,992	48,118	56.1	755[3]	1,091[3]	69.2	13,695	29,446	46.5
7	Citicorp	18,802	31,690	59.3	2,005	3,464	57.9	155,000[5]	269,000[5]	57.6
8	Philip Morris Cos	18,186	53,139	34.2	1,333	5,478	24.3	19,505	53,811	36.2
9	Chevron[4]	17,967	39,363	45.6	1,153	930	124.0	16,628	37,347	44.5
10	General Electric	17,832	70,028	25.5	879	6,573	13.4	59,331	228,035	26.0
11	Hewlett-Packard	17,556	31,519	55.7	1,490	2,433	61.2	13,022	24,427	53.3
12	Procter & Gamble	16,822[6]	33,434	50.3	861	2,645	32.6	12,062[6]	28,125	42.9
13	EI du Pont de Nemours	16,034	36,508	43.9	1,272	3,293	38.6	14,367	37,312	38.5
14	American Intl Group	13,777	25,874	53.2	1,380	2,510	55.0	49,680	134,136	37.0
15	Coca-Cola	12,702	18,018	70.5	2,051	2,986	68.7	7,482	15,041	49.7
16	Motorola	12,700 E	27,037	47.0	1,901[7]	3,201[7]	59.4	8,260	22,801	36.2
17	Xerox[4]	11,882	19,950	59.6	756	1,174	64.4	13,878	27,341	50.8
18	Dow Chemical	11,165	20,200	55.3	1,353[8]	2,087[8]	64.8	13,455	23,582	57.1
19	Johnson & Johnson	9,652	18,842	51.2	1,261	2,403	52.5	8,188	17,873	45.8
20	United Technologies	9,348[2]	22,802[2]	41.0	633[8]	880[8]	71.9	5,975	15,958	37.4
21	Digital Equipment	8,997	13,813	65.1	285	57	500.0	5,657	9,947	56.9
22	PepsiCo	8,747	30,421	28.8	504	1,606	31.4	7,737	25,432	30.4
23	AT&T	8,713	79,609	10.9	−928	139	D-P	12,085	88,884	13.6
24	Intel	8,280	16,202	51.1	1,818	3,566	51.0	4,404	17,504	25.2
25	Eastman Kodak	8,002	14,980	53.4	434	1,252	34.7	6,058	14,477	41.8
26	Compaq Computer	7,500[6]	14,755	50.8	564	789	71.5	3,385[6]	7,818	43.3
27	Minn Mining & Mfg	7,253	13,460	53.9	536[8]	1,383[8]	38.8	5,438	14,183	38.3
28	Chase Manhattan	7,187	26,368	27.3	851	2,970	28.7	98,923[5]	307,385[5]	32.2
29	Sara Lee	7,083	17,719	40.0	374	804	46.5	6,396	12,431	51.5
30	JP Morgan & Co	7,045	13,838	50.9	984	1,296	75.9	94,336	184,879	51.0
31	Amoco	6,719[2]	27,665[2]	24.3	517	1,862	27.8	9,059	29,845	30.4
32	Texas Instruments	6,371	13,128	48.5	NA	1,088	NA	3,508	9,215	38.1
33	Aflac	6,116	7,191	85.1	330[3]	349	94.6	22,837	25,338	90.1
34	Kimberly-Clark[4]	6,100 E	14,727	41.4	NA	33	NA	5,163	11,926	43.3
35	Bristol-Myers Squibb	6,082	13,767	44.2	883	1,812	48.7	4,651	13,929	33.4
36	Goodyear Tire & Rubber	5,916	13,166	44.9	402	611	65.8	3,495	9,790	35.7
37	Chrysler	5,906	53,195	11.1	159	2,121	7.5	6,962	53,756	13.0
38	Colgate-Palmolive	5,884[6]	8,358	70.4	311	172	180.8	4,446[6]	7,642	58.2
39	Merrill Lynch	5,775 E	21,513	26.8	341	1,114	30.6	78,859	176,857	44.6
40	CPC International	5,547	8,432	65.8	345[8]	539[8]	64.0	4,624	7,502	61.6

The Largest U.S. Multinationals (*Cont.*)

1995 Rank	Company	REVENUE			NET PROFIT[1]			ASSETS		
		foreign ($mil)	total ($mil)	foreign as % of total	foreign ($mil)	total ($mil)	foreign as % of total	foreign ($mil)	total ($mil)	foreign as % of total
41	Alcoa	5,457	12,500	43.7	675[8]	1,024[8]	65.9	5,660	13,643	41.5
42	International Paper	5,450 E	19,797	27.5	347[8]	1,309[8]	26.5	10,069	23,977	42.0
43	American Home Products	5,447	13,376	40.7	1,345	1,680	80.1	6,617	21,363	31.0
44	Merck	5,361	16,681	32.1	1,231[7]	4,673[7]	26.3	3,942[6]	23,832	16.5
45	McDonald's	5,321	9,795	54.3	804	1,427	56.3	8,206	15,415	53.2
46	UAL	5,309	14,943	35.5	NA	378	NA	NA	11,641	NA
47	RJR Nabisco	5,200 E	16,008	32.5	484[9]	1,266[9]	38.2	5,834	31,518	18.5
48	American Express	4,975 E	16,445	30.3	502	1,564	32.1	20,095	107,405	18.7
49	Apple Computer	4,932	11,062	44.6	477	424	112.5	2,194	6,231	35.2
50	Pfizer	4,908	10,021	49.0	880[8]	1,561[8]	56.4	5,695	12,729	44.7
51	AMR	4,748	16,910	28.1	NA	196	NA	NA	19,556	NA
52	Pharmacia & Upjohn	4,744	7,095	66.9	442	739	59.8	7,169	11,461	62.6
53	Gillette	4,730	6,795	69.6	583	824	70.8	4,286	6,340	67.6
54	ITT Industries	4,387	8,884	49.4	91	21	433.3	2,670	5,879	45.4
55	BankAmerica	4,281	20,386	21.0	344	2,664	12.9	50,044	232,446	21.5
56	Salomon	4,234	8,933	47.4	369	457	80.7	80,560	188,428	42.8
57	Warner-Lambert	4,017	7,040	57.1	444[8]	870[8]	51.0	3,050	6,101	50.0
58	Manpower	3,933	5,484	71.7	159[7]	235[7]	67.7	1,114	1,518	73.4
59	Abbott Laboratories	3,891	10,012	38.9	439	1,689	26.0	2,774	9,413	29.5
60	Rhone-Poulenc Rorer	3,828	5,142	74.4	190	357	53.2	3,857	8,987	42.9
61	Unisys	3,797	6,202	61.2	–374	–627	D-D	1,324	7,113	18.6
62	Morgan Stanley[6]	3,725 E	10,797	34.5	NA	609	NA	60,850 E	143,753	42.3
63	Caterpillar	3,707	16,072	23.1	323[7]	1,681[7]	19.2	3,582	16,830	21.3
64	Emerson Electric	3,618	10,013	36.1	245	929	26.4	3,936	9,399	41.9
65	AlliedSignal	3,612	14,346	25.2	141[3]	875	16.1	3,771	12,465	30.3
66	Archer Daniels Midland	3,495	12,672	27.6	124[7]	1,213[7]	10.2	1,181	9,757	12.1
66	Safeway	3,495	16,398	21.3	75	328	22.9	933	5,194	18.0
68	Fluor	3,487	9,301	37.5	74	232	31.9	465	3,229	14.4
69	Whirlpool	3,475 E	8,347	41.6	71[8]	214[8]	33.2	4,137	7,800	53.0
70	HJ Heinz	3,458	8,087	42.8	284	591	48.1	3,435	8,247	41.7
71	Sears, Roebuck	3,367	34,925	9.6	–30	1,025	D-P	2,611	33,130	7.9
72	TRW	3,356	10,172	33.0	126	446	28.3	2,002	5,890	34.0
73	Atlantic Richfield	3,354	15,819	21.2	114	1,376	8.3	6,186	23,999	25.8
74	Rockwell International	3,350 E	12,981	25.8	179	742	24.1	3,073	12,505	24.6
75	Monsanto	3,331	8,962	37.2	215	739	29.1	3,162	10,611	29.8

[1]From continuing operations. [2]Includes other income. [3]Net income before corporate expense. [4]Includes proportionate interest in unconsolidated subsidiaries or affiliates. [5]Average assets. [6]Excludes Canadian operations. [7]Operating profit. [8]Net income before minority interest. [9]Pretax income. D-D: Deficit to deficit. D-P: Deficit to profit. E: Estimate. NA: Not available.

(Continued)

The Largest U.S. Multinationals (*Cont.*)

1995 Rank	Company	Revenue foreign ($mil)	Revenue total ($mil)	Revenue foreign as % of total	Net profit[1] foreign ($mil)	Net profit[1] total ($mil)	Net profit[1] foreign as % of total	Assets foreign ($mil)	Assets total ($mil)	Assets foreign as % of total
76	Price/Costco	3,280	18,247	18.0	76[7]	433[7]	17.6	929	4,437	20.9
77	Cigna	3,240	18,955	17.1	15	211	7.1	9,589	95,903	10.0
78	Northwest Airlines	3,170	9,085	34.9	NA	342	NA	NA	8,412	NA
79	American Brands	3,158	5,905	53.5	455	543	83.8	3,306	8,021	41.2
80	Bankers Trust New York	3,100 E	8,309	37.3	67	215	31.2	62,621	104,002	60.2
81	General Re	3,060	7,210	42.4	166[8]	870[8]	19.1	12,107	35,946	33.7
82	Woolworth	3,034	8,224	36.9	−135	−164	D-D	1,621	3,506	46.2
83	AMP	2,989	5,227	57.2	170	427	39.8	2,280	4,505	50.6
84	ITT	2,953	6,346	46.5	123[8]	168[8]	73.2	2,518	8,692	29.0
85	Eli Lilly	2,951	6,764	43.6	647	1,307	49.5	3,705	14,413	25.7
86	Kellogg	2,923	7,004	41.7	175	490	35.7	2,108	4,415	47.7
87	Deere & Co	2,914	10,291	28.3	158	706	22.4	2,354	13,847	17.0
88	Avon Products	2,907	4,492	64.7	171[8]	289[8]	59.2	1,214	2,053	59.1
89	Ralston Purina	2,856	5,622	50.8	NA	263	NA	1,694	4,567	37.1
90	Sun Microsystems	2,766	5,902	46.9	227	356	63.8	1,896	3,545	53.5
91	Honeywell	2,644	6,731	39.3	143	334	42.8	1,836	5,060	36.3
92	Toys 'R' Us	2,635	9,427	28.0	−74[7]	359[7]	D-P	2,483	6,738	36.9
93	Dresser Industries	2,625 E	5,629	46.6	105[8]	233[8]	45.1	1,637	4,707	34.8
94	Time Warner	2,620	8,067	32.5	−18	−124	D-D	2,831	22,132	12.8
95	Walt Disney[4]	2,609	12,468	20.9	25	1,380	1.8	2,933	15,838	18.5
96	Delta Air Lines	2,600	12,194	21.3	NA	494	NA	NA	12,143	NA
97	Halliburton	2,589[2]	5,699[2]	45.4	37[8]	235[8]	15.7	1,424	3,647	39.0
98	GTE	2,583	19,957	12.9	220	2,538	8.7	6,210	37,019	16.8
99	Johnson Controls	2,457	8,330	29.5	50[8]	225[8]	22.2	1,485	4,321	34.4
100	Baxter International	2,414	5,048	47.8	400	371	107.8	1,980	9,437	21.0

[1]From continuing operations. [2]Includes other income. [3]Net income before corporate expense. [4]Includes proportionate interest in unconsolidated subsidiaries or affiliates. [5]Average assets. [6]Excludes Canadian operations. [7]Operating profit. [8]Net income before minority interest. [9]Pretax income. D-D: Deficit to deficit. D-P: Deficit to profit. E: Estimate. NA: Not available.

The 200 Best Small Companies in America

A funny thing happened to a lot of the companies on last year's 200 Best list. They lost momentum.

STEVE KICHEN AND MICHELLE CONLIN

Of last year's 200 Best Small Companies in America, only 89 firms are on the 1996 list. That's attrition of 56%. How could companies be so good one year and not make the grade the next?

A few, 17, were going so strong they shot right off the list, growing beyond our definition of a small company—less than $350 million in sales. Maxim Integrated Products, Parametric Technology and Applebees International were among those that moved onward and upward.

Twelve others were gobbled up by larger competitors. CUC International, a Stamford, Conn.-based membership shopping service bought two from last year's list—Davidson & Associates, a maker of software for kids, and Advance Ross, which makes cash advances on tax refunds. Waterhouse Investor Services, a New York-based discount securities brokerage, was acquired by Toronto-Dominion Bank.

But graduation and acquisition account for only 26% of the drop-offs. Not all of the drop-offs are duds. The majority, 76, simply lost momentum. It takes exceptional skill and luck to deliver 49% annual earnings growth, and no company can keep up the pace for more than a few years.

Consider medical software maker Cerner Corp., a member of our list for four of the past six years. Cerner, based in Kansas City, Mo., developed a sophisticated hospital software system that could link hospitals, doctors' offices and clinics. Cerner ran rings around competitor HBO & Co. But you can't count on your competition remaining asleep. HBO began acquiring other software companies, broadening its product line to

203

THE GRADUATES AND THE DROPOUTS

Few companies stay on our 200 Best Small Companies list for long. Over half of the last year's list members aren't on our this year's list. This sampling includes companies that outgrew the list and those that stumbled.

GRADUATES	DROPOUTS
Company/business	**Company**/business
Altera/logic chips & software	**Cerner**/software for healthcare industries
Applebees International/restaurants	**Digi International**/computer hardware & software
Brightpoint/telecommunications equipment	**Falcon Products**/office furniture
Linear Technology/integrated circuits	**First Team Sports**/in-line roller skates
Maxim Integrated Products/integrated circuits	**Franklin Quest**/time-management books
Parametric Technology/engineering software	**Gainsco**/property & casualty insurance
Paychex/payroll accounting services	**Hilite Industries**/auto parts
Sierra Health Services/HMO	**Jean Philippe Fragrances**/cosmetics & fragrances
VeriFone/electronic transaction systems	**Norstan**/telecommunications systems
Vivra/kidney dialysis services	**Ryan, Beck & Co**/investment banking

include software like home health programs that Cerner didn't yet have. Cerner began losing market share.

Our requirements for the 200 Best Small Companies list are stringent (*see box on page 205*). The slightest sign of stumbling—like Cerner's 82% drop in third-quarter earnings per share—is grounds for disqualification.

First Team Sports, a list member in 1995, rode the in-line skates craze for years. But crazes fade and the Anoka, Minn.-based company rolled right off our list this year. In 1996 industry sales of in-line skates are off about 20%. First Team is facing tough competition from K2 Corp.'s soft-boot skates and Rollerblade's lower-priced skates.

And what about Franklin Quest, peddler of time-management seminars, planning aids and software? It was a 200 Best Small Company for the past three years, but was disqualified when its latest quarterly earnings dropped 71% and the company took a writeoff for excess inventory. Salt Lake City, Utah-based Franklin depends on a faithful core of customers willing to pay premium prices for its seminars and organizers. A standard Franklin planner sells for $64, compared with prices as low as $29 for a standard Day Runner planner sold by Irvine, Calif.-based Day Runner, number 141 on our list. Franklin still has its faithful followers but it has had trouble expanding its market beyond them.

Some companies continued to flourish but were pushed aside by others that simply did better. Last year the 200th-ranked company, Veri-Fone, had a five-year average return on equity of 12.4%. Had the company

HOW WE DETERMINE THE RESULTS

Who's eligible

FORBE's annual list of the 200 Best Small Companies in America is restricted to publicly traded, U.S.-based corporations with latest 12-month sales of at least $5 million but no more than $350 million. Equity must be in the form of common shares; we don't consider publicly traded limited partnership units, real estate investment trusts or closed-end mutual funds. Companies of all industries are considered except banks and S&Ls, which were dropped in the late 1980s because their low capital bases produced unsustainably high returns on equity.

We require average daily trading volume of at least 1,000 shares. Any shares selling for under $5 are not considered. Companies whose stock price has performed in the lowest tenth percentile among all public companies are eliminated.

We also require that firms file an annual proxy statement on ownership and executive compensation with the Securities & Exchange Commission.

Profitability

Companies are ranked by their five-year average return on equity. This year's minimum is 14.5%. We also require five-year average sales and earnings growth per share of at least 15% and 9%, respectively.

Highly leveraged companies need not apply. Firms are dropped if their debt exceeds their stockholders' equity or if their equity is negative.

Growth

All companies must have had net income in excess of $1 million for the past 12 months and cannot have posted losses during any of the four latest fiscal years. Because many of these firms have not been public for a full five years, we consider data from the period that the company was private—including information provided in stock offering prospectuses.

ERIC S. HARDY

not outgrown the list this year, it would have been cut. Why? This year the lowest qualifying return was Viewlogic Systems' 14.5%. Outfits such as Falcon Products and Norstan missed the higher hurdle by just a whisker.

We dropped five other companies whose stocks performed in the lowest tenth percentile of all companies.

So remember this about the Forbes 200 Best Small Companies: It's a fast-stepping crowd. Before investing in any of them, ask this question: Does this company have an edge that is sustainable, or is it simply riding a temporary wave, a fad, a bubble? Both sorts will eventually drop off the list. The former because they become too big, the latter because their brief moment of glory has passed.

CEOs

Eric S. Hardy

It's in to be an entrepreneur. It's also tough as hell: Just 38% of all new companies survive beyond their sixth birthday; less than 20% make it past their eighth year. Of these survivors, only a tiny fraction ever make it to the 200 Best list. The chief executives of those that do are nicely compensated. This year the average 200 Best chief executive earned a total compensation of $910,000, up 10% from the prior year.

Of that, $473,000 is basic salary and bonus. Most of the rest is stock options. Other benefits—such as automobile allowances, company-paid life insurance premiums, vested stock grants and company contributions to 401(k) plans—added $71,000.

Of the 54 chief executives who exercised options, the median gain was $527,000—a figure that reflects last year's 38% gain in the S&P 500.

For all the splash that the youngsters are making in Silicon Valley, most successful entrepreneurs aren't kids. Our average chief executive is 52 years old and has been boss for 11 years.

Why, legend to the contrary, does it take so long to be a successful entrepreneur? An obvious reason is this: Few hit it big on their first try. The history of many successful entrepreneurs can be summed up by the cliché: try, try and try again.

Note that in calculating share ownership we include only those shares that the most recent proxy designates as being beneficially owned by the executive, his (or her) minor children and spouse—provided the spouse is not an officer of the company. Excluded are options to purchase shares in the company and shares that are pledged to foundations or other charities.

CEOs of the Best Small Companies

Chief executive (age) Company	Birthplace	YEARS with company	as CEO	COLLEGE undergraduate/ graduate	degrees	COMPENSATION ($THOU) salary + bonus	other	stock gains	total	STOCK OWNED %	mkt val* ($thou)
Gary K Judis (58) Aames Financial	US	17	4			4,860.0	40.0	942.5	5,842.5	7.76	72,493
James E MacDougald (53) ABR Information Services	US	14	14	U of Maryland	BA	300.9	3.8	—	304.7	4.44	44,447
Mark C Smith (56) Adtran	US	10	10	Georgia Tech	BSEE	216.4	4.6	—	221.0	32.31	581,194
Gaylen D Miller (47) Ag Services of America	US	11	1	U of Northern Iowa	BS	235.3	4.7	—	240.0	6.09	3,619
Larry I Kane (56) Alternative Resources	US	8	8	Illinois Tech U of Chicago	BS MBA	375.0	1.4	—	376.4	10.34	48,267
Finis F Teeter (52) American Homestar	US	25	25			412.5	35.8	—	448.3	17.48	35,017
Robert H Lutz Jr (47) Amresco	US	2	2	Furman U Georgia State U	BA MBA	1,350.0	119.1	—	1,469.1	0.18	1,118
Mark S Crossen (47) Amrion	US	8	5	U of Colorado	BA	367.8	9.0	—	376.8	17.89	21,063
Sidney V Corder (54) Analytical Surveys	US	6	3			211.1	6.9	534.7	752.7	0.17	95
Theodore G Schwartz (43) APAC TeleServices	US	23	23			312.0	2.2	—	314.2	48.17	1,154,543
John G Sperling (75) Apollo Group	US	23	23	Reed C Cambridge	BA PhD	496.0	—	—	496.0	25.07	352,152
James R Carreker (49) Aspect Telecommunications	US	11	11	Georgia Tech Stanford U	BEE MSEE	418.1	4.6	—	422.7	2.98	38,509
Lawrence B Evans (62) Aspen Technology	US	15	15	U of Oklahoma U of Michigan	BS MSE, PhD	372.0	0.3	—	372.3	4.19	29,060
John C Kennedy (38) Autocam	US	8	8	U of Detroit	BS	355.0	88.2	—	443.2	59.63	29,932
Herbert D Weiss (66) Balchem	US	29	23	CUNY Queens U of Texas Austin	BS PhD	184.0	19.7	27.2	230.9	2.17	545
Dale H Ballard (73) Ballard Medical Products		18	18	U of Utah	BS	235.5	—	—	235.5	7.28	38,754
Andrew Rudd (46) Barra	UK	21	12	Sussex U U of Cal Berkeley	BS MBA, PhD	600.0	—	—	600.0	23.50	45,609

Stock prices as of Oct. 4, 1996. *Includes all share classes. †Less than 0.01%.

(Continued)

CEOs of the Best Small Companies

Chief executive (age) / Company	Birthplace	Years with company	as CEO	College undergraduate/ graduate	degrees	salary + bonus	other	stock gains	total	%	mkt val* ($thou)
William W Sherertz (50) / Barrett Business Services	US	25	16	Oregon State U	BS	144.0	—	—	144.0	26.27	8,514
Joel A Schwartz (54) / Benihana	US	16	13	Seton Hall U	BS, BA	256.4	—	—	256.4	0.26	195
Robert L Johnson (50) / BET Holdings	US	17	17	U of Illinois Princeton	BA MA	869.9	179.6	—	1,049.5	48.49	36,583
William T Spane (59) / BHC Financial	US	12	10	US Naval Acad	BS	425.3	107.0	—	532.3	0.46	417
Edgar W Blanch Jr (60) / EW Blanch Holdings	US	38	20			895.0	80.4	—	975.4	13.04	33,696
Anthony P Conza (56) / Blimpie International	US	32	32			253.2	3.3	—	256.5	32.56	38,200
Robert J Therrien (62) / Brooks Automation	US	7	7			346.6	1.8	—	348.4	18.25	17,726
Daniel J Hirschfield (55) / Buckle	US	34	28			72.0	4.3	—	76.3	72.21	156,870
Paul S Bush (60) / Bush Industries	US	35	23	Rensselaer	BS	987.3	310.1	—	1,297.4	32.76	72,438
Warren J Hayford (67) / BWAY	US	7	7	US Military Acad	BS	333.0	0.4	—	333.4	20.51	23,652
Matthew W Chapman (46) / CFI ProServices	US	9	9	U of Portland U of Oregon	BA JD	198.4	10.5	3,352.0	3,560.9	8.27	7,503
J Phillip London (59) / CACI International	US	24	12	US Naval Acad George Washington U	BS PhD	573.4	83.9	—	657.3	7.17	13,300
James K Sims (50) / Cambridge Tech Partners	US	5	5			730.0	155.5	150.0	1,035.5	2.79	3,336
George A Fait (70) / Capitol Transamerica	US	36	36	U of Wis Madison	BBA	581.1	15.4	—	596.5	17.89	30,716
George W Off (49) / Catalina Marketing	US	13	2	Colo Sch Mines	BS	393.6	50.7	412.5	856.8	0.72	7,440
Jerry F Wilson (57) / Cavalier Homes	US	12	12	U of Alabama	BS	1,217.3	7.7	—	1,225.0	1.75	3,273
Emanuel Pinez (58) / Centennial Technologies	Israel	9	9	Hebrew U (Israel)	BS	75.0	2.4	—	77.4	26.52	103,400
Monroe J Carell Jr (65) / Central Parking	US	28	28	Vanderbilt U	BSEE	1,296.9	14.8	—	1,311.7	64.28	360,587
Charles R Adams (69) / Chad Therapeutics	US	14	14	Baylor U	BS	334.1	14.9	—	349.0	4.57	9,064
Marshall T Reynolds (59) / Champion Industries	US	32	4			150.0	0.1	—	150.1	60.90	71,813

Stock prices as of Oct. 4, 1996. *Includes all share classes. †Less than 0.01%.

(Continued)

CEOs of the Best Small Companies

Chief executive (age) Company	Birthplace	Years with company	as CEO	College undergraduate/ graduate	degrees	Compensation ($thou) salary + bonus	other	stock gains	total	Stock owned %	mkt val* ($thou)
Bobby G Stevenson (54) Ciber	US	22	22	Texas Tech U	BA	349.1	5.0	—	354.1	37.57	239,178
Robert J Shillman (50) Cognex	US	15	15	Northeastern U MIT	BSEE MSEE, PhD	432.7	0.9	2,482.4	2,916.0	17.13	109,347
Daniel L McGinnis (57) Coherent Com Sys	US	8	2	U of Notre Dame Lehigh U	BA MBA	340.0	16.5	2,861.3	3,217.8	4.63	13,186
Charles A Schwan (57) Cohu	US	25	0	Duquesne U	BS	392.3	13.0	322.2	727.5[1]	1.17	1,992
Ronald G Canada (41) Computational Systems	US	12	12	U of Tenn Knoxville	BS	262.6	—	—	262.6	22.34	16,465
Peter A Bracken (55) Computer Data Systems	US	0	0	William & Mary U of Maryland	BS MA	28.8	22.1	—	50.9[2]	0.02	24
Dan M Palmer (53) Concord EFS	US	14	7	U of Memphis	BA	443.7	—	4,601.2	5,044.9	0.54	7,253
S Duane Southerland Jr (47) Conso Products	US	1	1	Duke U Duke U	BSE MS, MBA	222.5	25.7	219.5	467.7	0.75	763
Joe R Davis (53) Consolidated Graphics	US	11	11	U of Arkansas	BBA	228.0	—	—	228.0	22.05	31,189
James E Moore (50) ContiFinancial	US	13	1	Georgetown U Harvard	BSFS MBA	2,643.3	1,608.6	—	4,251.9	0.68	9,160
John R Harding (41) Cooper & Chyan Tech	US	1	1	Drew U	BA	258.4	—	195.0	453.4	—	—[3]
V Gordon Clemons (53) CorVel	US	8	8	Oregon State U U of Oregon	BS MBA	239.6	0.5	10,105.0	10,345.1	7.20	10,167
Donald A Foss (52) Credit Acceptance	US	24	4			400.0	5.6	—	405.6	52.51	637,695
John B Scheumann (47) Crossmann Communities	US	19	4	Ball State U	BS	315.0	19.2	—	334.2	31.00	30,288
Ignatius J Panzica (53) Custom Chrome	US	26	5			952.4	0.5	298.6	1,251.5	2.87	2,651
Charles V Prothro (54) Dallas Semiconductor	US	12	7	Stanford U Harvard	BS MBA	1,556.9	89.3	57.8	1,704.0	2.36	11,161
Michael J Mellinger (47) Data Research Associates	US	21	21			466.3	1.5	—	467.8	34.14	25,755
Larry G Blackwell (55) Datastream Systems	US	10	10	U of Mississippi Georgia Tech	BS MS	192.0	5.5	—	197.5	19.42	46,301

Stock prices as of Oct. 4, 1996. *Includes all share classes. ‡Less than 0.01%. [1]Became chief executive March 1996. Compensation is for position of executive vice president and chief operating officer. [2]Became chief executive May 1996. [3]Holdings are in the form of options.

(Continued)

CEOs of the Best Small Companies

Chief executive (age) Company	Birthplace	Years with company	as CEO	College undergraduate/ graduate	degrees	Compensation ($thou) salary + bonus	other	stock gains	total	Stock Owned %	mkt val* ($thou)
Mark A Vidovich (46) Day Runner	US	10	10	Cal St Long Beach	BA	585.5	3.0	978.1	1,566.6	2.83	5,322
William A Bassett (59) Decorator Industries	US	17	3	Rutgers	BS	283.1	35.0	105.0	423.1	4.38	1,155
Edward R Bazinet (52) Department 56	US	12	3			746.2	21.8	—	768.0	4.37	23,873
William H Gibbs (52) DH Technology	US	11	11	U of Arkansas	BSEE	430.0	1.5	—	431.5	0.25	505
Howard G Bubb (42) Dialogic	US	5	3	Cal Tech	BS	220.3	7.1	620.0	847.4	—	21
David O'Brien (56) Elantec Semiconductor	UK	9	9	U of Wales U of Wales	BS MSEE, PhD	229.5	1.4	435.0	665.9	2.35	1,383
Curtis S Wozniak (41) Electroglas	US	0	0	GMI Institute Stanford U	BS MBA	—	—	—	—[4]	—[‡]	—
Dan J Avida (33) Electronics for Imaging	Israel	7	1	Technion-Israel Tech	BS	435.8	—	2,985.6	3,421.4	0.09	1,630
Marvin D Brody (52) Employee Solutions	US	5	2	U of Illinois John Marshall Law	BS JD	166.0	25.7	—	191.7	9.54	53,818
David A Purcell (58) Encad		15	15			297.7	3.8	—	301.5	7.82	39,872
Stephen P Robeck (48) Equity Marketing	US	11	5	Lake Forest C	BA	475.0	82.0	—	557.0	28.34	36,031[5]
Fred S L Chan (49) ESS Technology	Hong Kong	11	2	U of Hawaii U of Hawaii	BS MS	489.4	—	1,740.8	2,230.2	17.81	117,002
Thomas B Waldin (54) Essef	Estonia	6	6	MIT York U	BS MBA	218.5	4.5	—	223.0	0.40	359
Larry E Rosenberger (50) Fair, Isaac & Co	US	22	5	MIT U of Cal Berkeley	BS MS, ME	327.5	333.5	1,215.7	1,876.7	2.44	11,708
Robert A Kierlin (57) Fastenal	US	29	29	U of Minnesota U of Minnesota	BS MBA	122.5	—	—	122.5	11.96	216,675
Christopher C Multhauf (42) First Commonwealth	US	10	10	U of Texas Austin Cornell	BA MBA	178.3	11.2	—	189.5	10.42	8,595
Eric C Cooper (37) FORE Systems	US	6	6	Harvard U of Cal Berkeley	BS PhD	256.2	6.6	—	262.8	4.00	143,969

Stock prices as of Oct. 4, 1996. *Includes all share classes. [‡]Less than 0.01%. [4]Became chief executive April 1996. Compensation data not available. [5]Donald A Kurz is president and co-chief executive.

(Continued)

CEOs of the Best Small Companies

Chief executive (age) Company	Birthplace	YEARS with company	as CEO	COLLEGE undergraduate/ graduate	degrees	COMPENSATION ($THOU) salary + bonus	other	stock gains	total	STOCK OWNED %	mkt val* ($thou)
Gerald R Szczepanski (48) Gadzooks	US	12	12	Marquette U	MBA	526.2	9.4	—	535.6	2.46	7,469
Gary A Dachis (52) Game Financial	US	6	6	U of Minnesota	BA	180.0	30.0	—	210.0	8.06	3,692
Fred T Bauer (53) Gentex	US	17	11	Michigan State U	BS	327.9	3.4	—	331.3	6.95	60,955
William J Dore (54) Global Industries	US	23	23	McNeese State U McNeese State U	BA MEd	275.0	30.2	—	305.2	40.64	259,437
Andrew E Lietz (58) Hadco	US	12	1	Wayne State U	BA	392.7	1.5	234.5	628.7[6]	0.30	980
Bjorn E Olsson (50) Harmon Industries	Sweden	6	1	U of London	MBA	264.7	44.3	—	309.0	0.48	548
James C Smith (55) HealthCare Compare	US	12	12	Northeastern U	BA	1,017.7	18.9	1,837.5	2,874.1	1.44	24,110
Russell A Gerdin (55) Heartland Express	US	18	18	Moorhead State U	BA	300.0	—	—	300.0	48.40	273,455
Robert J Lepofsky (51) Helix Technology	US	23	7	Drexel U	BS	425.0	5.9	4,870.0	5,300.9	1.56	4,326
Michael E Henry (35) Jack Henry & Associates	US	17	2			175.7	—	470.0	645.7	18.83	71,793
Henry Arnberg (53) Hirsch International	US	26	16	U of Bridgeport Adelphi U	BS MBA	1,045.8	20.8	—	1,066.6	24.89	36,398
Mark S Vaughn (49) Home State Holdings	US	2	0	West Washington U	BA	175.2	5.4	—	180.6[7]	—	—[8]
Thomas W Haley (60) Innovex	US	24	24	U of Minnesota	BA	328.5	4.5	—	333.0	11.33	14,835
Gary D Owens (49) Input/Output	US	19	3	U of Texas Arlington	BSEE	606.5	67.2	3,583.1	4,256.8	0.23	3,014
Steven R Vana-Paxhia (49) INSO	US	5	2	SUNY Cortland Rochester Tech	BA MBA	296.7	4.6	—	301.3	0.16	1,182
Dennis M Jones (58) Jones Medical Industries	US	15	15			375.0	17.4	—	392.4	16.67	184,646
Marshall T Leeds (41) JW Charles Financial Services	US	13	13			1,314.4	13.0	—	1,327.4	12.26	2,760
Kenneth D Cole (42) Kenneth Cole Productions	US	14	14	Emory U	BA	500.0	—	—	500.0	44.19	114,985

Stock prices as of Oct. 4, 1996. *Includes all share classes. [†]Less than 0.01%. [6]Became chief executive October 1995. Compensation is for position of vice president and chief operating officer. [7]Became chief executive June 1996. Compensation is for position of senior vice president. [8]Became chief executive June 1996. Holdings are in the form of options.

(Continued)

CEOs of the Best Small Companies

Chief executive (age) Company	Birthplace	YEARS with company	YEARS as CEO	COLLEGE undergraduate/ graduate	degrees	COMPENSATION ($THOU) salary + bonus	other	stock gains	total	STOCK OWNED %	mkt val* ($thou)
Francis D John (42) **Key Energy Group**	US	8	7	Seton Hall U Fairleigh Dickinson	BS MBA	325.0	—	—	325.0	0.68	703
Kevin P Knight (40) **Knight Transportation**	US	6	6			253.0	1.9	—	254.9	15.22	32,401
Mark A Betker (46) **Koala**	US	1	1	U of Wis Milwaukee Regis C	BBA MBA	22.9	—	—	22.9[9]	—	—[10]
Mark S Ain (53) **Kronos**	US	19	19	MIT U of Rochester	BS MBA	337.5	0.8	—	338.3	6.28	15,773
Tilman J Fertitta (39) **Landry's Seafood Rest**	US	9	9	U of Houston	BBA	461.5	—	—	461.5	19.84	114,425
Cyrus Y Tsui (51) **Lattice Semiconductor**	China	8	8	USC Stanford U	BS MS	1,485.5	32.6	5,345.0	6,863.1	1.22	8,213
Arnold J Scheine (57) **LCS Industries**	US	26	26	Hofstra U	BS	687.3	15.4	63.0	765.7	10.99	6,887
Robert S Pepper (61) **Level One Com**	US	10	10	U of Cal Berkeley U of Cal Berkeley	BS MS, PhD	317.2	4.3	—	321.5	0.81	3,277
Robert W MacDonald (53) **Life USA Holdings**	US	9	9	Western State U Col	BSL	1,000.0	100.0	—	1,100.0	9.48	17,985
James T Kelly (50) **Lincare Holdings**	US	10	10			843.0	7.5	2,731.3	3,581.8	0.52	5,877
Richard E Rivera (49) **Longhorn Steaks**	US	2	2	Washington & Lee U	BA	525.0	9.6	—	534.6	—	—[11]
Richard B Mazess (57) **Lunar**	US	16	16	Penn State U U of Wis Madison	BA PhD	36.4	1.6	226.9	264.9	34.51	85,507
Leonard R Jaskol (59) **Lydall**	US	23	8	American U CUNY City	BA MBA	700.0	95.5	1,649.7	2,445.2	3.16	11,566
William L Larson (40) **McAfee Associates**	US	3	3	U of Pennsylvania Stanford U	BA JD	449.7	—	3,751.7	4,201.4	—	—[12]
William B Summers Jr (46) **McDonald & Co Investments**	US	25	2	Baldwin-Wallace C	BA	1,020.0	7.0	—	1,027.0	1.84	4,485
John P McConnell (46) **Medic Computer Systems**	US	14	14	Virginia Polytech	BS	537.0	19.5	1,573.6	2,130.1	8.08	56,209

Stock prices as of Oct. 4, 1996. *Includes all share classes. ‡Less than 0.01%. [9]Not annualized. Became chief executive November 1995. [10]Holdings are in the form of options. [11]Holdings are in the form of options. [12]Holdings are in the form of options.

(Continued)

CEOs of the Best Small Companies

Chief executive (age) Company	Birthplace	Years with company	as CEO	College undergraduate/ graduate	degrees	salary + bonus	other	stock gains	total	%	mkt val* ($thou)
Robert S Evans (52)	US	10	10	U of Pennsylvania	BA	389.5	680.8	190.2	1,260.5	4.04	20,850
Medusa				Columbia	MBA						
Christopher J Conway (57)	UK	27	27	U of Minnesota	BA	679.2	5.0	—	684.2	2.16	14,515
Mentor											
William J Motto (55)	US	20	20			343.8	8.7	—	352.5	32.23	60,391
Meridian Diagnostics											
John W Castro (48)	US	18	12			550.0	32.2	—	582.2	13.26	25,104
Merrill											
Luke R Schmieder (53)	US	14	14			96.1	—	—	96.1	11.51	3,289
Mesa Laboratories											
William J McGinley (73)	US	50	50	Amherst C	BA	1,053.3	767.5	—	1,820.8	3.90	26,530
Methode Electronics											
D Michael Walden (46)	US	14	14	Auburn U	BS	273.8	5.1	—	278.9	20.25	10,934
Metrotrans											
Steve Sanghi (41)	India	6	5	Punjab U	BS	339.2	168.7	4,254.7	4,762.6	1.83	23,631
Microchip Technology				U of Massachusetts	MS						
William G Miller (49)	US	6	6	U of Michigan	BSE	191.7	—	—	191.7	27.48	143,588
Miller Industries				U of Michigan	MBA						
Gregory L Wilson (49)	US	9	9	Brigham Young U	BA	135.7	1.9	—	137.6	29.68	8,868
Mity-Lite				Indiana U	MBA						
Allen B Morgan Jr (54)	US	27	27	U of North Carolina	BA	920.3	1.6	—	921.9	12.05	37,067
Morgan Keegan											
Mel Marks (69)	US	28	28			427.0	—	—	427.0	14.31	9,255
Motorcar Parts & Accessories											
James J Truchard (53)	US	20	20	U of Texas Austin	BS	225.1	4.6	—	229.7	28.30	161,934
National Instruments				U of Texas Austin	MS, PhD						
William F Coyro Jr (53)	US	14	14	U of Michigan	BS	183.8	4.6	366.0	554.4	4.93	13,718
National TechTeam				U of Detroit	DDS						
Robert P Schechter (48)	US	1	1	Rensselaer	BS	160.0	1.0	—	161.0[13]	0.02	48
Natural MicroSystems				U of Penn-Wharton	MBA						
Kristine F Hughes (58)	US	24	0			—	—	—	—[14]	17.21	62,090
Nature's Sunshine Prods											

Stock prices as of Oct. 4, 1996. *Includes all share classes. ‡Less than 0.01%. [13]Annualized salary. [14]Became chief executive September 1996. Compensation data not available.

(Continued)

CEOs of the Best Small Companies

Chief executive (age) Company	Birthplace	Years with company	as CEO	College undergraduate/ graduate	degrees	salary + bonus	other	stock gains	total	%	mkt val* ($thou)
Harvey L Sanders (46) Nautica Enterprises	US	23	19	U of Maryland	BA	1,493.0	2.5	—	1,495.5	10.10	133,201
Johnie Schulte Jr (61) NCI Building Systems	US	12	12			372.8	—	—	372.8	5.78	15,393
Leslie G Denend (55) Network General	US	3	3	Air Force Stanford U	BS MBA, PhD	552.9	7.3	830.0	1,390.2	—‡	76
William E Lipner (49) NFO Research	US	22	14	U of Toledo	BS	664.2	11.0	—	675.2	4.56	10,116
Richard D Ennen (68) NN Ball & Roller	US	16	16	John Carroll U	BS	212.9	53.8	—	266.7	21.92	46,797
Terry E Trexler (57) Nobility Homes	US	29	29	Butler U	BA	145.5	37.1	—	182.6	39.18	20,850
Quentin E Finkelson (60) Nortech Systems	US	8	8	Hamline U U of Minnesota	BA MBA	122.5	—	—	122.5	4.74	630
David E O'Reilly (47) O'Reilly Automotive	US	24	3	Drury C	BA	466.0	7.0	—	473.0	10.81	38,951
Mike Parnell (44) Oakley		11	10			1,699.7	—	—	1,699.7	6.78	109,205
H Tom Buelter (55) On Assignment	Germany	7	7	U of Maryland	BA	281.3	—	366.9	648.2	2.45	4,261
James W Bagley (57) OnTrak Systems	US	0	0	Mississippi State Mississippi State	BS MS	100.0	—	—	100.0¹⁵ —		—¹⁶
Rafi Yizhar (48) Opal	Israel	8	5	Hebrew U (Israel)	BS	171.9	51.6	—	223.5	2.91	2,597
John H Schnatter (34) Papa John's International	US	10	6	Ball State U	BS	134.5	407.8	—	542.3	32.90	342,832
Arthur Hershaft (59) Paxar	US	35	9	Carnegie-Mellon	BS	859.7	—	189.9	1,049.6	14.69	67,625
Kenneth A Swanstrom (56) Penn Engineering & Mfg	US	36	3			399.4	17.7	—	417.1	14.33	17,492
David A Duffield (56) PeopleSoft	US	9	9	Cornell Cornell	BSEE MBA	326.8	7.7	—	334.5	30.93	1,358,322
Charles E Maginness (63) Performance Tech	US	12	1	Rochester Tech	BSME	249.3	8.4	—	257.7	8.08	4,685
Richardson M Roberts (38) PMT Services	US	12	12	U of Alabama	BA	244.5	—	—	244.5	6.55	41,327

Stock prices as of Oct. 4, 1996. *Includes all share classes. ‡Less than 0.01%. ¹⁵Became chief executive June 1996. Salary is annualized. ¹⁶Holdings are in the form of options.

(Continued)

CEOs of the Best Small Companies

Chief executive (age) Company	Birthplace	Years with company	as CEO	College undergraduate/ graduate	degrees	Compensation ($thou) salary + bonus	other	stock gains	total	Stock Owned %	mkt val* ($thou)
J Hyatt Brown (59) **Poe & Brown**	US	37	35	U of Florida	BS	505.9	6.0	—	511.9	22.02	46,444
David B Pomeroy II (47) **Pomeroy Comp Resources**	US	15	4			679.8	—	—	679.8	31.03	41,088
Jack Mildren (47) **Pre-Paid Legal Services**		1	0	U of Oklahoma	BBA	144.1	—	—	144.1	—	—[17]
Richard H Lewis (47) **Prima Energy**	US	16	16	U of Colorado	BS	228.8	7.5	—	236.3	14.13	9,734
— **Project Software & Dev**[18]	—	—	—	—	—	—	—	—	—	—	—
Michael L Campbell (42) **Regal Cinemas**	US	7	7			620.5	—	952.9	1,573.4	1.66	14,348
James L Packard (54) **Regal-Beloit**	US	17	12			576.4	9.2	155.6	741.2	1.50	5,107
James M Usdan (47) **RehabCare Group**	US	6	5	Harvard	AB	502.4	4.7	—	507.1	0.53	499
Lawrence L Garlick (47) **Remedy**	US	5	5	Stanford U Stanford U	BSEE MSEE	322.7	—	—	322.7	12.76	158,766
Phil Simpson (61) **Republic Group**	US	35	29	Rice U U of Penn- Wharton	BA MBA	420.7	24.5	15.3	460.5	19.26	30,635
Ronald G Geary (49) **Res-Care**	US	6	3	U of Kentucky U of Louisville	BS JD	313.4	11.9	—	325.3	5.08	7,974
Dennis S Meteny (42) **Respironics**	US	12	2	Penn State U U of Pittsburgh	BS MBA	265.9	130.5	—	396.4[19]	1.40	6,224
Carl DeSantis (57) **Rexall Sundown**	US	20	20			331.2	10.0	—	341.2	41.66	422,481
Richard J Pinola (50) **Right Mngmnt Consult**	US	4	4	King's C	BS	897.5	48.3	76.9	1,022.7	0.82	1,043
David L Dunkel (42) **Romac International**	US	16	16	Babson C Babson C	BS MBA	200.0	—	—	200.0	20.10	68,283
Derrick N Key (48) **Roper Industries**	UK	14	4	Reading Tech UK	BS	539.9	45.4	—	585.3	2.62	19,042
David C Prosser (72) **RTW**	US	13	13	U of Minnesota	BS	622.9	91.8	—	714.7	3.54	11,192
Warren S Rustand (53) **Rural-Metro**	US	1	1	U of Arizona U of Arizona	BA MS	435.3	—	—	435.3[20]	0.25	1,043
Richard B Jaffe (43) **Safeskin**	US	8	3	Cornell	BS	400.0	—	—	400.0	5.65	27,742

Stock prices as of Oct. 4, 1996. *Includes all share classes. [‡]Less than 0.01%. [17]Became chief executive March 1996. Holdings are in the form of options. [18]Office of chief executive is vacant. [19]Compensation data for fiscal year ended June 1995. [20]Became chief executive August 1996. Figure includes an annualized salary of $275,000 and a bonus.

(Continued)

CEOs of the Best Small Companies

Chief executive (age) Company	Birthplace	YEARS with company	as CEO	COLLEGE undergraduate/ graduate	degrees	COMPENSATION ($THOU) salary + bonus	other	stock gains	total	STOCK OWNED %	mkt val* ($thou)
Robert E Gray (71) St John Knits	US	34	34	USC	BA	1,263.3	1.9	—	1,265.2	5.21	43,107
Ben C Bryant Jr (49) SCB Computer Tech	US	20	20	U of Memphis U of Memphis	BBA MS	1,882.4	—	—	1,882.4	24.98	37,679
Richard C Osborne (52) Scotsman Industries	US	17	7	SUNY Buffalo Sangamon State	BS MA	543.8	16.3	18.4	578.5	0.66	1,408
Gary R Christophersen (50) Seattle FilmWorks	US	14	8	Whitman C U of Washing- ton	BA MBA	233.4	10.6	333.8	577.8	5.60	12,188
Charles R Stuckey Jr (54) Security Dynamics Tech	US	9	9	Ohio U	BSME	473.4	5.0	47.3	525.7	0.94	11,227
Shahrokh Sedaghat (31) Seda Specialty Packaging	Iran	11	1			360.2	17.8	—	378.0	20.87	20,085
Harold J Tenoso (58) Serologicals	US	3	3	UCLA UCLA	BA PhD	288.0	65.3	—	353.3	0.05	170
Thomas J Fitzmyers (55) Simpson Manufacturing	US	18	2	Cal St Fullerton	BS	718.8	25.0	—	743.8	6.78	16,288
Joseph W Carreras (43) Sinter Metals	Uruguay	4	2	Cleveland State U	BBA	375.0	—	—	375.0	6.43	10,549
William W Smith Jr (48) Smith Micro Software	US	13	13	Grove City C	BA	450.5	2,999.2	—	3,449.7	69.68	61,188
Michael G Wordeman (47) Sodak Gaming	US	7	7			439.8	12.4	—	452.2	15.92	88,690
E R Pickard (48) Sofamor Danek Group	US	6	5			311.1	45.9	—	357.0	1.50	10,987
J Clifford Hudson (41) Sonic	US	12	1	U of Oklahoma Georgetown U	BA JD	281.7	6.0	—	287.7	2.65	9,058
Richard D Reinhold (58) SOS Staffing Services	US	23	23	U of Kansas	BS	185.1	47.6	—	232.7	60.50	43,084
Wendell L Batchelor (54) Southern Energy Homes	US	13	13	U of North Alabama	BS	484.5	—	—	484.5	6.33	16,742
O Bruton Smith (70) Speedway Motorsports	US	37	21			1,090.0	96.3	—	1,186.3	70.29	779,375
Frank F Ferola (53) Stephan	US	15	9			493.1	—	—	493.1	13.11	6,485
Bill R Sanford (52) Steris	US	9	9	Kansas State U	BS	500.9	—	3,596.9	4,097.8	—	—[21]
Ronald S Spolane (42) Sterling Electronics	US	19	2	U of Texas Austin	BBA	541.7	—	—	541.7	1.06	875

Stock prices as of Oct. 4, 1996. *Includes all share classes. ‡Less than 0.01%. [21]Holdings are in the form of options.

(Continued)

CEOs of the Best Small Companies

Chief executive (age) Company	Birthplace	Years with company	as CEO	College undergraduate/ graduate	degrees	salary + bonus	other	stock gains	total	%	mkt val* ($thou)
Aart J de Geus (42) Synopsys	Netherlands	9	2	Swiss Fed Polytech SMU	MSEE PhD	330.3	1.5	1,316.8	1,648.6	1.06	20,294
M Sreenivasan (47) Synthetech	India	9	1	Indian Tech Bucknell U	BS MS	192.0	3.2	518.2	713.4	3.12	3,271
Thomas E Oland (55) Techne	US	12	10	U of Minnesota	BA	175.0	17.7	—	192.7	3.14	7,727
Van M Hubbard (56) Tecnol Medical Products	US	20	18	Texas Tech U U of Texas Austin	BBA MBA	463.2	0.5	—	463.7	14.08	39,516
Robert B Barnhill Jr (52) Tessco Technologies	US	27	27	Cornell U of Penn-Wharton	BS MBA	240.0	13.9	—	253.9	21.26	37,017
Li-San Hwang (61) Tetra Tech	China	29	8	National Taiwan U Cal Tech	BS PhD	265.0	24.5	—	289.5	9.76	32,881
John Gorman (62) Timberline Software	US	28	25	U of Oregon	BS	151.5	11.4	—	162.9	13.95	6,244
Richard W Ussery (49) Total System Services	US	31	13	Auburn U	BA	536.2	102.4	—	638.6	0.43	16,089
Joseph M Ahearn (42) Toy Biz	US	6	3	Fordham U Northwestern U	BS MA	350.0	—	—	350.0	—‡	2
George K Broady (58) Ultrak	US	9	5	Iowa State	BS	268.0	2.2	—	270.2	15.83	47,812
Jorn I Budde (52) UniMark Group	Denmark	4	4			120.0	—	—	120.0	7.24	7,361
William H Wilcox (44) United Dental Care	US	0	0	Vanderbilt U Tulane U	BA MA	—	—	—	—[22]	—	—
Lawrence Flinn Jr (61) United Video Satellite	US	20	20	Yale Columbia	BA MBA	919.8	50.0	—	969.8	34.41	241,279
Richard A Hayne (49) Urban Outfitters	US	26	26	Lehigh U	BA	225.3	15.0	284.4	524.7	45.65	158,449
Uri M Evan (60) USA Detergents	Israel	7	4	Technion-Israel Tech Technion-Israel Tech	BS MS	118.3	21.5	—	139.8	7.17	40,365
Jeffrey G Webb (47) Varsity Spirit	US	22	22	U of Oklahoma	BS	135.9	0.3	—	136.2	12.36	8,814

Stock prices as of Oct. 4, 1996. *Includes all share classes. ‡Less than 0.01%. [22]Became chief executive May 1996.

(Continued)

CEOs of the Best Small Companies

Chief executive (age) Company	Birthplace	YEARS with company	as CEO	COLLEGE undergraduate/ graduate	degrees	COMPENSATION ($THOU) salary + bonus	other	stock gains	total	STOCK OWNED %	mkt val* ($thou)
E. David Willette (61) **Vaughn Communications**	US	25	25	U of Notre Dame	BSME	256.8	—	—	256.8	18.42	6,103
Alain J Hanover (48) **Viewlogic Systems**	France	12	12	MIT Harvard	BS, BSEE MS	284.0	12.8	14.0	310.8	0.68	1,020
Donald C Tomasso (51) **Vitalink Pharmacy Services**	US	5	1	Drexel U Drexel U	BS MBA, MS	545.6	5.8	—	551.4[23]	—[†]	28[24]
George C Zoley (46) **Wackenhut Corrections**	Greece	8	2	Florida Atlantic U Nova U	BA PhD	319.0	—	1,178.5	1,497.5	—	—[25]
Allen Y Chao (51) **Watson Pharmaceuticals**	China	13	13	Taipei Medical C Purdue U	BS PhD	450.0	2.1	—	452.1	4.46	53,219
Dale Sydnor (40) **Wireless Telecom Group**	US	8	0	U of Delaware	BSEE	293.4	7.4	506.9	807.7[26]	1.24	1,989

Stock prices as of Oct. 4, 1996. *Includes all share classes. [†]Less than 0.01%. [23]Chief executive is compensated by Manor Care, which owns 82.3% of Vitalink. [24]Shares owned indirectly through chief executive's holdings in Manor Care. [25]Holdings are in the form of options. [26]Became chief executive May 1996. Compensation is for position of president and chief operating officer.

RANKINGS

Data compiled November, 1996.

Ranking the Best Small Companies in America

WHERE THEY RANK							5-year			Market*
5-year average ROE	sales	profits	market value	Company	Exchange	Ticker symbol	average return on equity	Sales ($mil)	Profits ($mil)	value ($mil)
71	99	29	33	Aames Financial	n	AAM	24.3%	$128	$31.1	$934
119	182	146	32	ABR Information Services	o	ABRX	19.4	31	5.7	1,001
59	43	24	8	Adtran	o	ADTN	26.0	216	35.3	1,799
196	83	177	182	Ag Services of America	o	AGSV	14.6	142	3.8	59
10	66	92	71	Alternative Resources	o	ALRC	45.5	179	12.1	467
104	35	105	121	American Homestar	o	HSTR	20.3	238	10.6	200
31	76	42	51	Amresco	o	AMMB	31.2	151	23.6	609
132	172	175	152	Amrion	o	AMRI	18.6	45	3.9	118
188	194	197	185	Analytical Surveys	o	ANLT	15.0	19	1.7	55
12	69	70	4	APAC TeleServices	o	APAC	42.7	174	16.0	2,397
3	51	58	13	Apollo Group	o	APOL	77.7	201	19.3	1,405
144	32	28	19	Aspect Telecommunications	o	ASPT	17.7	247	31.3	1,291
173	116	113	42	Aspen Technology	o	AZPN	15.5	104	9.2	694
86	156	150	188	Autocam	o	ACAM	22.4	58	5.6	50
193	186	195	198	Balchem	a	BCP	14.8	26	1.8	25
97	125	40	61	Ballard Medical Products	n	BMP	20.7	96	24.1	532
140	149	124	124	Barra	o	BARZ	17.9	65	8.5	194
39	59	157	157	Barrett Business Services	o	BBSI	29.6	191	4.9	109

(Continued)

*Includes all share classes. a: American Stock Exchange. n: New York Stock Exchange. o: Nasdaq.

Ranking the Best Small Companies in America (*Cont.*)

| WHERE THEY RANK | | | | | | | | 5-year | | | |
5-year average ROE	sales	profits	market value	Company	Exchange	Ticker symbol	average return on equity	Sales ($mil)	Profits ($mil)	Market* value ($mil)
133	135	164	174	Benihana	o	BNHN	18.6	84	4.6	76
98	100	50	67	BET Holdings	n	BTV	20.6	128	21.7	488
126	131	61	167	BHC Financial	o	BHCF	18.8	92	17.5	92
23	124	62	103	EW Blanch Holdings	n	EWB	34.5	96	17.5	259
35	181	174	153	Blimpie International	o	BMPE	30.4	35	4.0	117
68	139	133	163	Brooks Automation	o	BRKS	24.5	78	7.9	97
156	61	101	116	Buckle	o	BKLE	16.8	190	11.3	217
135	33	65	114	Bush Industries	n	BSH	18.5	245	17.2	221
157	28	97	155	BWAY	o	BWAY	16.8	256	11.7	115
101	170	169	168	CFI ProServices	o	PROI	20.5	47	4.3	91
194	34	107	130	CACI International	o	CACI	14.8	245	9.9	185
24	72	69	12	Cambridge Technology Partners	o	CATP	34.2	161	16.1	1,556
170	148	72	134	Capitol Transamerica	o	CATA	15.6	65	15.8	172
37	84	46	29	Catalina Marketing	n	POS	29.7	142	23.2	1,038
152	9	99	129	Cavalier Homes	n	CAV	17.1	312	11.5	187
117	175	158	76	Centennial Technologies	a	CTN	19.5	38	4.9	390
65	86	94	57	Central Parking	n	PK	25.0	139	12.0	561
14	190	156	122	Chad Therapeutics	a	CTU	41.9	23	5.0	198
51	160	183	151	Champion Industries	o	CHMP	27.3	55	3.2	118
87	74	111	49	Ciber	o	CIBR	22.3	157	9.4	637
116	96	15	48	Cognex	o	CGNX	19.6	131	41.1	638
58	169	125	95	Coherent Communications Sys	o	CCSC	26.2	47	8.5	285
81	56	31	135	Cohu	o	COHU	23.1	198	30.7	172
177	173	179	176	Computational Systems	o	CSIN	15.3	45	3.5	74
160	29	108	145	Computer Data Systems	o	CDSI	16.3	251	9.8	136
94	81	51	14	Concord EFS	o	CEFT	21.1	147	21.7	1,353
75	140	141	160	Conso Products	o	CNSO	24.1	71	6.4	102
161	127	151	143	Consolidated Graphics	o	COGI	16.3	94	5.5	142
42	105	1	15	ContiFinancial	n	CFN	29.0	122	84.8	1,343
150	188	185	91	Cooper & Chyan Technology	o	CCTI	17.3	24	3.1	312
178	111	134	144	CorVel	o	CRVL	15.3	112	7.7	141
95	119	23	21	Credit Acceptance	o	CACC	20.9	103	35.7	1,214
54	54	93	162	Crossmann Communities	o	CROS	26.8	198	12.1	98
166	115	126	166	Custom Chrome	o	CSTM	15.9	104	8.5	93
184	25	17	70	Dallas Semiconductor	n	DS	15.1	260	39.8	473
158	178	170	175	Data Research Associates	o	DRAI	16.5	37	4.3	75
34	184	144	111	Datastream Systems	o	DSTM	30.5	27	5.9	238
141	103	95	127	Day Runner	o	DAYR	17.9	125	11.8	188
83	176	189	197	Decorator Industries	a	DII	22.6	37	2.6	26
20	26	5	60	Department 56	n	DFS	37.4	259	53.2	547
198	114	96	123	DH Technology	o	DHTK	14.5	109	11.8	198
66	60	57	59	Dialogic	o	DLGC	25.0	191	19.6	553
123	180	165	183	Elantec Semiconductor	o	ELNT	19.1	36	4.6	59
43	57	14	106	Electroglas	o	EGLS	28.8	197	41.7	248
134	36	6	9	Electronics for Imaging	o	EFII	18.6	238	48.5	1,782
4	23	128	55	Employee Solutions	o	ESOL	59.6	271	8.3	564
50	138	127	65	Encad	o	ENCD	27.6	78	8.5	510

(Continued)

*Includes all share classes. a: American Stock Exchange. n: New York Stock Exchange. o: Nasdaq.

Ranking the Best Small Companies in America (*Cont.*)

5-year average ROE	sales	profits	market value	Company	Exchange	Ticker symbol	5-year average return on equity	Sales ($mil)	Profits ($mil)	Market* value ($mil)
8	109	137	148	Equity Marketing	o	EMAK	50.3	113	7.1	127
27	73	12	46	ESS Technology	o	ESST	32.4	158	42.3	657
142	58	129	170	Essef	o	ESSF	17.9	194	8.3	89
110	88	71	69	Fair, Isaac & Co	n	FIC	19.9	138	16.0	480
55	31	33	7	Fastenal	o	FAST	26.3	250	30.5	1,812
22	177	191	172	First Commonwealth	o	FCWI	35.5	37	2.3	83
136	22	18	3	FORE Systems	o	FORE	18.5	275	39.3	3,600
121	121	152	93	Gadzooks	o	GADZ	19.3	102	5.5	303
17	197	199	190	Game Financial	o	GFIN	40.0	13	1.3	46
124	93	43	34	Gentex	o	GNTX	19.1	134	23.6	878
155	70	45	47	Global Industries	o	GLBL	16.9	167	23.5	638
174	5	34	87	Hadco	o	HDCO	15.5	326	30.1	334
105	75	118	156	Harmon Industries	o	HRMN	20.2	152	8.9	115
79	39	2	10	HealthCare Compare	o	HCCC	23.6	232	74.0	1,679
118	46	47	54	Heartland Express	o	HTLD	19.5	211	22.9	565
45	80	36	98	Helix Technology	o	HELX	28.5	147	26.6	277
49	144	91	77	Jack Henry & Associates	o	JKHY	27.8	68	12.3	381
62	118	136	142	Hirsch International	o	HRSH	25.5	103	7.6	146
89	122	145	192	Home State Holdings	o	HOMS	22.1	99	5.9	41
145	152	90	147	Innovex	o	INVX	17.5	62	12.6	131
179	15	13	16	Input/Output	n	IO	15.3	297	41.9	1,321
25	164	79	39	INSO	o	INSO	33.1	53	14.5	726
169	142	87	27	Jones Medical Industries	o	JMED	15.8	70	13.3	1,108
38	130	159	199	JW Charles Financial Services	o	KORP	29.7	92	4.9	23
21	95	104	102	Kenneth Cole Productions	n	KCP	36.5	133	10.7	260
197	147	180	159	Key Energy Group	a	KEG	14.6	66	3.5	103
28	146	140	118	Knight Transportation	o	KNGT	32.0	66	6.6	213
114	200	196	193	Koala	o	KARE	19.8	8	1.8	39
176	91	102	104	Kronos	o	KRON	15.4	135	10.9	251
63	89	88	52	Landry's Seafood Restaurants	o	LDRY	25.5	137	12.9	577
162	49	11	44	Lattice Semiconductor	o	LSCC	16.1	201	43.4	673
164	126	130	181	LCS Industries	o	LCSI	16.0	94	8.1	63
128	128	89	75	Level One Communications	o	LEVL	18.7	92	12.8	404
189	17	54	125	Life USA Holdings	o	LUSA	15.0	294	20.7	190
84	10	4	24	Lincare Holdings	o	LNCR	22.6	311	59.9	1,121
111	97	147	131	Longhorn Steaks	o	LOHO	19.9	130	5.7	179
185	145	114	105	Lunar	o	LUNR	15.1	67	9.2	248
109	27	41	80	Lydall	n	LDL	20.0	257	24.1	366
19	98	22	5	McAfee Associates	o	MCAF	38.7	130	36.6	2,368
163	37	49	109	McDonald & Co Investments	n	MDD	16.1	238	22.5	244
102	71	59	41	Medic Computer Systems	o	MCSY	20.5	162	18.2	696
15	13	7	64	Medusa	n	MSA	40.8	299	47.8	516
99	64	38	45	Mentor	o	MNTR	20.6	185	25.4	671
153	183	162	128	Meridian Diagnostics	o	KITS	17.1	27	4.7	187
129	19	78	126	Merrill	o	MRLL	18.7	284	14.8	189
107	199	198	196	Mesa Laboratories	o	MLAB	20.1	8	1.7	29

(Continued)

*Includes all share classes. a: American Stock Exchange. n: New York Stock Exchange. o: Nasdaq.

Ranking the Best Small Companies in America (*Cont.*)

| WHERE THEY RANK | | | | | | | | 5-year average | | | Market* |
5-year average ROE	sales	profits	market value	Company	Exchange	Ticker symbol	return on equity	Sales ($mil)	Profits ($mil)	value ($mil)
127	7	27	43	Methode Electronics	o	METHA	18.8	318	33.7	680
2	141	181	186	Metrotrans	o	MTRN	100.0+	70	3.4	54
137	16	10	18	Microchip Technology	o	MCHP	18.4	296	44.4	1,294
9	90	119	62	Miller Industries	n	MLR	46.6	135	8.9	523
46	196	194	195	Mity-Lite	o	MITY	28.5	16	2.0	30
78	12	26	92	Morgan Keegan	n	MOR	23.7	301	33.9	308
190	165	172	180	Motorcar Parts & Accessories	o	MPAA	15.0	52	4.2	65
53	65	53	53	National Instruments	o	NATI	27.2	181	20.8	572
147	162	188	97	National TechTeam	o	TEAM	17.4	54	3.0	278
76	174	171	112	Natural MicroSystems	o	NMSS	24.0	41	4.3	234
56	40	80	79	Nature's Sunshine Products	o	NATR	26.3	232	14.5	368
154	2	20	17	Nautica Enterprises	o	NAUT	17.1	340	37.0	1,318
61	14	52	100	NCI Building Systems	o	BLDG	25.7	299	21.6	266
199	50	21	31	Network General	o	NETG	14.5	201	36.9	1,010
180	134	135	113	NFO Research	o	NFOR	15.3	89	7.7	222
13	133	84	117	NN Ball & Roller	o	NNBR	42.5	90	13.6	214
139	179	182	187	Nobility Homes	o	NOBH	18.1	36	3.3	53
67	191	200	200	Nortech Systems	o	NSYS	24.7	23	1.3	13
191	38	67	81	O'Reilly Automotive	o	ORLY	15.0	232	16.8	360
7	48	9	11	Oakley	n	OO	53.2	202	46.2	1,611
72	143	163	132	On Assignment	o	ASGN	24.3	69	4.7	174
5	158	161	154	OnTrak Systems	o	ONTK	57.5	56	4.8	117
60	155	98	169	Opal	o	OPAL	25.8	58	11.6	89
41	11	82	28	Papa John's International	o	PZZA	29.4	308	14.3	1,042
175	47	64	72	Paxar	n	PXR	15.5	208	17.3	460
195	78	83	150	Penn Engineering & Mfg	n	PNN	14.8	150	13.8	122
165	8	16	1	PeopleSoft	o	PSFT	16.0	317	40.2	4,391
40	192	184	184	Performance Technologies	o	PTIX	29.6	22	3.2	58
90	77	122	50	PMT Services	o	PMTS	21.5	150	8.6	631
47	110	73	120	Poe & Brown	o	POBR	28.5	113	15.5	211
112	24	153	146	Pomeroy Computer Resources	o	PMRY	19.9	265	5.5	132
73	168	109	99	Pre-Paid Legal Services	a	PPD	24.2	48	9.8	274
125	193	155	179	Prima Energy	o	PENG	19.0	22	5.2	69
74	153	117	78	Project Software & Development	o	PSDI	24.2	62	9.0	372
182	42	48	35	Regal Cinemas	o	REGL	15.2	218	22.9	862
130	18	25	84	Regal-Beloit	a	RBC	18.7	292	34.5	340
69	123	142	165	RehabCare Group	o	RHBC	24.5	98	6.1	94
18	159	103	20	Remedy	o	RMDY	39.0	55	10.8	1,244
183	107	76	138	Republic Group	n	RGC	15.2	118	14.9	159
122	52	132	139	Res-Care	o	RSCR	19.2	200	8.0	157
159	102	74	73	Respironics	o	RESP	16.5	126	15.3	445
106	67	66	30	Rexall Sundown	o	RXSD	20.2	177	16.9	1,014
103	104	115	149	Right Management Consultants	o	RMCI	20.4	123	9.2	127
57	151	176	85	Romac International	o	ROMC	26.3	64	3.9	340
32	44	32	38	Roper Industries	o	ROPR	30.7	214	30.6	727
11	157	116	90	RTW	o	RTWI	44.6	57	9.1	316
70	30	100	74	Rural Metro	o	RURL	24.5	250	11.5	423

(Continued)

*Includes all share classes. a: American Stock Exchange. n: New York Stock Exchange. o: Nasdaq.

Ranking the Best Small Companies in America (*Cont.*)

5-year average ROE	WHERE THEY RANK			Company	Exchange	Ticker symbol	5-year average return on equity	Sales ($mil)	Profits ($mil)	Market* value ($mil)
	sales	profits	market value							
1	92	55	66	Safeskin	o	SFSK	100.0+	134	20.3	507
44	62	39	36	St John Knits	n	SJK	28.6	190	24.7	827
131	166	193	140	SCB Computer Technology	o	SCBI	18.7	51	2.1	151
181	1	63	119	Scotsman Industries	n	SCT	15.3	348	17.5	213
26	137	138	115	Seattle FilmWorks	o	FOTO	32.8	79	6.9	218
192	171	120	22	Security Dynamics Technologies	o	SDTI	15.0	46	8.7	1,197
91	163	148	164	Seda Specialty Packaging	o	SSPC	21.4	54	5.7	96
77	154	139	89	Serologicals	o	SERO	24.0	59	6.9	320
151	63	68	110	Simpson Manufacturing	o	SMCO	17.2	186	16.3	240
186	117	121	136	Sinter Metals	n	SNM	15.1	103	8.7	164
30	189	160	171	Smith Micro Software	o	SMSI	31.6	23	4.9	88
171	112	75	58	Sodak Gaming	o	SODK	15.6	112	15.3	557
48	45	19	37	Sofamor Danek Group	n	SDG	28.1	212	39.3	733
148	85	77	83	Sonic	o	SONC	17.4	142	14.9	342
88	120	186	178	SOS Staffing Services	o	SOSS	22.3	102	3.1	71
6	21	85	101	Southern Energy Homes	o	SEHI	54.2	280	13.5	264
16	132	44	26	Speedway Motorsports	n	TRK	40.7	90	23.6	1,109
100	187	166	189	Stephan	a	TSC	20.6	25	4.6	50
113	53	56	25	Steris	o	STRL	19.9	199	20.0	1,110
138	4	106	173	Sterling Electronics	n	SEC	18.2	334	10.5	82
172	6	8	6	Synopsys	o	SNPS	15.6	323	46.3	1,906
82	198	187	158	Synthetech	o	NZYM	22.9	10	3.1	105
85	161	123	107	Techne	o	TECH	22.5	55	8.6	246
167	87	60	96	Tecnol Medical Products	o	TCNL	15.9	139	17.7	281
187	113	167	133	Tessco Technologies	o	TESS	15.1	110	4.6	174
93	55	112	86	Tetra Tech	o	WATR	21.3	198	9.4	337
96	185	192	191	Timberline Software	o	TMBS	20.8	26	2.2	45
120	20	30	2	Total System Services	n	TSS	19.4	283	30.8	3,717
33	41	35	68	Toy Biz	n	TBZ	30.7	222	29.0	482
92	106	173	94	Ultrak	o	ULTK	21.4	119	4.2	302
64	167	178	161	UniMark Group	o	UNMG	25.3	49	3.7	102
146	129	154	108	United Dental Care	o	UDCI	17.5	92	5.5	246
29	3	37	40	United Video Satellite Group	o	UVSGA	31.9	336	26.5	701
80	82	86	82	Urban Outfitters	o	URBN	23.5	145	13.5	347
36	94	131	56	USA Detergents	o	USAD	30.1	133	8.1	563
115	136	168	177	Varsity Spirit	o	VARS	19.7	80	4.5	71
143	150	190	194	Vaughn Communications	o	VGHN	17.9	65	2.6	33
200	101	110	141	Viewlogic Systems	o	VIEW	14.5	127	9.7	150
168	79	81	88	Vitalink Pharmacy Services	o	VTLK	15.9	149	14.4	330
149	108	149	63	Wackenhut Corrections	n	WHC	17.4	116	5.7	522
108	68	3	23	Watson Pharmaceuticals	o	WATS	20.1	175	66.3	1,195
52	195	143	137	Wireless Telecom Group	a	WTT	27.3	19	6.1	161

*Includes all share classes. a: American Stock Exchange. n: New York Stock Exchange. o: Nasdaq.

ADDRESSES

Aames Financial
3731 Wilshire Boulevard
Los Angeles, CA 90010
213-351-6100 Gary K Judis

ABR Information Services
34125 US Highway 19 North
Palm Harbor, FL 34684
813-785-2819 James E MacDougald

Adtran
901 Explorer Boulevard
Huntsville, AL 35806
205-971-8000 Mark C Smith

Ag Services of America
PO Box 668
Cedar Falls, IA 50613
319-277-0261 Gaylen D Miller

Alternative Resources
75 Tri-State International, Suite 100
Lincolnshire, IL 60069
847-317-1000 Larry I Kane

American Homestar
2450 South Shore Boulevard, Suite 300
League City, TX 77573
713-334-9700 Finis F Teeter

Amresco
700 North Pearl Street, Suite 2400
Dallas, TX 75201
214-953-7700 Robert H Lutz Jr

Amrion
6565 Odell Place
Boulder, CO 80301
303-530-2525 Mark S Crossen

Analytical Surveys
1935 Jamboree Drive
Colorado Springs, CO 80920
719-593-0093 Sidney V Corder

APAC TeleServices
One Parkway North Center, Suite 510
Deerfield, IL 60015
847-945-0055 Theordore G Schwartz

Apollo Group
4615 East Elwood Street
Phoenix, AZ 85040
602-966-5394 John G Sperling

Aspect Telecommunications
1730 Fox Drive
San Jose, CA 95131
408-325-2200 James R Carreker

Aspen Technology
Ten Canal Park
Cambridge, MA 02141
617-577-0100 Lawrence B Evans

Autocam
4070 East Paris Avenue
Kentwood, MI 49512
616-698-0707 John C Kennedy

Balchem
PO Box 175
Slate Hill, NY 10973
914-355-5300 Herbert D Weiss

Ballard Medical Products
12050 South Lone Peak Parkway
Draper, UT 84020
801-572-6800 Dale H Ballard

Barra
1995 University Avenue, Suite 400
Berkeley, CA 94704
510-548-5442 Andrew Rudd

Barrett Business Services
4724 SW Macadam Avenue
Portland, OR 97201
503-220-0988 William W Sherertz

Benihana
8685 Northwest 53rd Terrace
Miami, FL 33102
305-593-0770 Joel A Schwartz

BET Holdings
1900 W Place NE
Washington, DC 20018
202-608-2000 Robert L Johnson

BHC Financial
One Commerce Square, 2005 Market Street
Philadelphia, PA 19103
215-636-3000 William T Spane

EW Blanch Holdings
3500 West 80th Street
Minneapolis, MN 55431
612-835-3310 Edgar W Blanch, Jr

Blimpie International
740 Broadway
New York, NY 10003
212-673-5900 Anthony P Conza

Brooks Automation
15 Elizabeth Drive
Chelmsford, MA 01824
508-262-2400 Robert J Therrien

Buckle
2407 West 24th Street
Kearney, NE 68847
308-236-8491 Daniel J Hirschfield

Bush Industries
One Mason Drive
Jamestown, NY 14701
716-665-2000 Paul S Bush

BWAY
8607 Roberts Drive, Suite 250
Atlanta, GA 30350
770-587-0888 Warren J Hayford

CFI ProServices
400 SW Sixth Avenue
Portland, OR 97204
503-274-7280 Matthew W Chapman

CACI International
1100 North Glebe Road
Arlington, VA 22201
703-841-7800 J Phillip London

Cambridge Technology Partners
304 Vassar Street
Cambridge, MA 02139
617-374-9800 James K Sims

Capitol Transamerica
4610 University Avenue
Madison, WI 53705
608-231-4450 George A Fait

Catalina Marketing
11300 Ninth Street North
St Petersburg, FL 33716
813-579-5000 George W Off

Cavalier Homes
US Highway 41 North and Cavalier Road
Addison, AL 35540
205-747-1575 Jerry F Wilson

Centennial Technologies
37 Manning Road
Billerica, MA 01821
508-670-0646 Emanuel Pinez

Central Parking
2401 21st Avenue South, Suite 200
Nashville, TN 37212
615-297-4255 Monroe J Carell Jr

Chad Therapeutics
21622 Plummer Street
Chatsworth, CA 91311
818-882-0883 Charles R Adams

Champion Industries
2450-90 First Avenue
Huntington, WV 25703
304-528-2791 Marshall T Reynolds

Ciber
5251 DTC Parkway, Suite 1400
Englewood, CO 80111
303-220-0100 Bobby G Stevenson

Cognex
One Vision Drive
Natick, MA 01760
508-650-3000 Robert J Shillman

Coherent Communications Sys
44084 Riverside Parkway
Leesburg, VA 20176
703-729-6400 Daniel L McGinnis

Cohu
5755 Kearny Villa Road
San Diego, CA 92123
619-277-6700 Charles A Schwan

Computational Systems
835 Innovation Drive
Knoxville, TN 37932
423-675-2110 Ronald G Canada

Computer Data Systems
One Curie Court
Rockville, MD 20850
301-921-7000 Peter A Bracken

Concord EFS
2525 Horizon Lake Drive, Suite 120
Memphis, TN 38133
901-371-8000 Dan M Palmer

Conso Products
513 North Duncan Bypass
Union, SC 29379
864-427-9004 S Duane Southerland Jr

Consolidated Graphics
2210 West Dallas Street
Houston, TX 77019
713-529-4200 Joe R Davis

ContiFinancial
277 Park Avenue
New York, NY 10172
212-207-2800 James E Moore

Cooper & Chyan Technology
1601 Saratoga-Sunnyvale Road, Suite 255
Cupertino, CA 95014
408-366-6966 John R Harding

CorVel
1920 Main Street, Suite 1090
Irvine, CA 92614
714-851-1473 V Gordon Clemons

Credit Acceptance
25505 West Twelve Mile Road
Southfield, MI 48034
810-353-2700 Donald A Foss

Crossmann Communities
9202 North Meridian, Suite 300
Indianapolis, IN 46260
317-843-9514 John B Scheumann

Custom Chrome
16100 Jacqueline Court
Morgan Hill, CA 95037
408-778-0500 Ignatius J Panzica

Dallas Semiconductor
4401 South Beltwood Parkway
Dallas, TX 75244
972-371-4000 Charles V Prothro

Data Research Associates
1276 North Warson Road
St Louis, MO 63132
314-432-1100 Michael J Mellinger

Datastream Systems
50 Datastream Plaza
Greenville, SC 29605
864-422-5001 Larry G Blackwell

Day Runner
15295 Alton Parkway
Irvine, CA 92618
714-680-3500 Mark A Vidovich

Decorator Industries
10011 Pines Boulevard
Pembroke Pines, FL 33024
954-436-8909 William A Bassett

Department 56
6436 City West Parkway
Eden Prairie, MN 55344
612-944-5600 Edward R Bazinet

DH Technology
15070 Avenue of Science
San Diego, CA 92128
619-451-3485 William H Gibbs

Dialogic
1515 Route 10
Parsippany, NJ 07054
201-993-3000 Howard G Bubb

Elantec Semiconductor
1996 Tarob Court
Milpitas, CA 95035
408-945-1323 David O'Brien

Electroglas
2901 Coronado Drive
Santa Clara, CA 95054
408-727-6500 Curtis S Wozniak

Electronics for Imaging
2855 Campus Drive
San Mateo, CA 94403
415-286-8600 Dan J Avida

Employee Solutions
2929 East Camelback Road, Suite 220
Phoenix, AZ 85016
602-955-5556 Marvin D Brody

Encad
6059 Cornerstone Court, West
San Diego, CA 92121
619-452-0882 David A Purcell

Equity Marketing
131 South Rodeo Drive
Beverly Hills, CA 90212
310-887-4300 Stephen P Robeck

ESS Technology
48401 Fremont Boulevard
Fremont, CA 94538
510-226-1088 Fred S L Chan

Essef
220 Park Drive
Chardon, OH 44024
216-286-2200 Thomas B Waldin

Fair, Isaac & Co
120 North Redwood Drive
San Rafael, CA 94903
415-472-2211 Larry E Rosenberger

Fastenal
2001 Theurer Boulevard
Winona, MN 55987
507-454-5374 Robert A Kierlin

First Commonwealth
444 North Wells Street, Suite 600
Chicago, IL 60610
312-644-1800 Christopher C Multhauf

FORE Systems
174 Thorn Hill Road
Warrendale, PA 15086
412-772-6600 Eric C Cooper

Gadzooks
4801 Spring Valley Road Suite 108B
Dallas, TX 75244
214-991-5500 Gerald R Szczepanski

Game Financial Corp
10911 West Highway 55, Suite 205
Minneapolis, MN 55441
612-544-0062 Gary A Dachis

Gentex
600 North Centennial Street
Zeeland, MI 49464
616-772-1800 Fred T Bauer

Global Industries
107 Global Circle
Lafayette, LA 70503
318-989-0000 William J Dore

Hadco
12A Manor Parkway
Salem, NH 03079
603-898-8000 Andrew E Lietz

Harmon Industries
1300 Jefferson Court
Blue Springs, MO 64015
816-229-3345 Bjorn E Olsson

HealthCare Compare
3200 Highland Avenue
Downers Grove, IL 60515
708-241-7900 James C Smith

Heartland Express
2777 Heartland Drive
Coralville, IA 52241
319-645-2728 Russell A Gerdin

Helix Technology
Nine Hampshire Street
Mansfield, MA 02048
508-337-5111 Robert J Lepofsky

Jack Henry & Associates
PO Box 807
Monett, MO 65708
417-235-6652 Michael E Henry

Hirsch International
200 Wireless Boulevard
Hauppauge, NY 11788
516-436-7100 Henry Arnberg

Home State Holdings
Three South Revmont Drive
Shrewsbury, NJ 07702
908-935-2600 Mark S Vaughn

Innovex
1313 Fifth Street South
Hopkins, MN 55343
612-938-4155 Thomas W Haley

Input/Output
11104 West Airport Boulevard
Stafford, TX 77477
713-933-3339 Gary D Owens

INSO
31 St James Avenue
Boston, MA 02116
617-753-6500 Steven R Vana-Paxhia

Jones Medical Industries
1945 Craig Road
St Louis, MO 63146
314-576-6100 Dennis M Jones

JW Charles Financial Services
980 North Federal Highway, Suite 210
Boca Raton, FL 33432
407-338-2600 Marshall T Leeds

Kenneth Cole Productions
152 West 57th Street
New York, NY 10019
212-265-1500 Kenneth D Cole

Key Energy Group
Two Tower Center
East Brunswick, NJ 08816
908-247-4822 Francis D John

Knight Transportation
5601 West Buckeye Road
Phoenix, AZ 85043
602-269-2000 Kevin P Knight

Koala
11600 East 53rd Avenue
Denver, CO 80239
303-574-1000 Mark A Betker

Kronos
400 Fifth Avenue
Waltham, MA 02154
617-890-3232 Mark S Ain

Landry's Seafood Restaurants
1400 Post Oak Boulevard, Suite 1010
Houston, TX 77056
713-850-1010 Tilman J Fertitta

Lattice Semiconductor
5555 NE Moore Court
Hillsboro, OR 97124
503-681-0118 Cyrus Y Tsui

LCS Industries
120 Brighton Road
Clifton, NJ 07012
201-778-5588 Arnold J Scheine

Level One Communications
9750 Goethe Road
Sacramento, CA 95827
916-855-5000 Robert S Pepper

Life USA Holdings
300 South Highway 169
Minneapolis, MN 55426
612-546-7386 Robert W MacDonald

Lincare Holdings
19337 US 19 North, Suite 500
Clearwater, FL 34624
813-530-7700 James T Kelly

Longhorn Steaks
8215 Roswell Road
Atlanta, GA 30350
770-399-9595 Richard E Rivera

Lunar
313 West Beltline Highway
Madison, WI 53713
608-274-2663 Richard B Mazess

Lydall
One Colonial Road
Manchester, CT 06045
860-646-1233 Leonard R Jaskol

McAfee Associates
2710 Walsh Avenue
Santa Clara, CA 95051
408-988-3832 William L Larson

McDonald & Co Investments
800 Superior Avenue
Cleveland, OH 44114
216-443-2300 William B Summers Jr

Medic Computer Systems
8601 Six Forks Road, Suite 300
Raleigh, NC 27615
919-847-8102 John P McConnell

Medusa
3008 Monticello Boulevard
Cleveland Heights, OH 44118
216-371-4000 Robert S Evans

Mentor
5425 Hollister Avenue
Santa Barbara, CA 93111
805-681-6000 Christopher J Conway

Meridian Diagnostics
3471 River Hills Drive
Cincinnati, OH 45244
513-271-3700 William J Motto

Merrill
One Merrill Circle
St Paul, MN 55108
612-646-4501 John W Castro

Mesa Laboratories
12100 West Sixth Avenue
Lakewood, CO 80228
303-987-8000 Luke R Schmieder

Methode Electronics
7444 West Wilson Avenue
Chicago, IL 60656
708-867-9600 William J McGinley

Metrotrans
777 Greenbelt Parkway
Griffin, GA 30223
770-229-5995 D Michael Walden

Microchip Technology
2355 West Chandler Boulevard
Chandler, AZ 85224
602-786-7200 Steve Sanghi

Miller Industries
900 Circle 75 Parkway
Atlanta, GA 30339
770-988-0797 William G Miller

Mity-Lite
1301 West 400 North
Orem, UT 84057
801-224-0589 Gregory L Wilson

Morgan Keegan
50 North Front Street
Memphis, TN 38103
901-524-4100 Allen B Morgan Jr

Motorcar Parts & Accessories
2727 Maricopa Street
Torrance, CA 90503
310-212-7910 Mel Marks

National Instruments
6504 Bridge Point Parkway
Austin, TX 78730
512-794-0100 James J Truchard

National TechTeam
22000 Garrison Avenue
Dearborn, MI 48124
313-277-2277 William F Coyro Jr

Natural MicroSystems
8 Erie Drive
Natick, MA 01760
508-650-1300 Robert P Schechter

Nature's Sunshine Products
75 East 1700 South
Provo, UT 84606
801-342-4300 Kristine F Hughes

Nautica Enterprises
40 West 57th Street
New York, NY 10019
212-541-5990 Harvey L Sanders

NCI Building Systems
PO Box 40220
Houston, TX 77240
713-466-7788 Johnie Schulte Jr

Network General
4200 Bohannon Drive
Menlo Park, CA 94025
415-473-2000 Leslie G Denend

NFO Research
2 Pickwick Plaza
Greenwich, CT 06830
203-629-8888 William E Lipner

NN Ball & Roller
800 Tennessee Road
Erwin, TN 37650
423-743-9151 Richard D Ennen

Nobility Homes
3741 Southwest 7th Street
Ocala, FL 34474
352-732-5157 Terry E Trexler

Nortech Systems
641 East Lake Street, Suite 244
Wayzata, MN 55391
612-473-0833 Quentin E Finkelson

O'Reilly Automotive
233 South Patterson
Springfield, MO 65802
417-862-6708 David E O'Reilly

Oakley
10 Holland
Irvine, CA 92718
714-951-0991 Mike Parnell

On Assignment
26651 West Agoura Road
Calabasas, CA 91302
818-878-7900 H Tom Buelter

OnTrak Systems
1010 Rincon Circle
San Jose, CA 95131
408-577-1010 James W Bagley

Opal
3203 Scott Boulevard
Santa Clara, CA 95054
408-727-6060 Rafi Yizhar

Papa John's International
11492 Bluegrass Parkway, Suite 175
Louisville, KY 40299
502-266-5200 John H Schnatter

Paxar
105 Corporate Park Drive
White Plains, NY 10604
914-697-6800 Arthur Hershaft

Penn Engineering & Mfg
5190 Old Easton Road
Danboro, PA 18916
215-766-8853 Kenneth A Swanstrom

PeopleSoft
4440 Rosewood Drive
Pleasanton, CA 94588
510-225-3000 David A Duffield

Performance Technologies
315 Science Parkway
Rochester, NY 14620
716-256-0200 Charles E Maginness

PMT Services
Two Maryland Farms, Suite 200
Brentwood, TN 37027
615-254-1539 Richardson M Roberts

Poe & Brown
220 South Ridgewood Avenue
Daytona Beach, FL 32114
904-252-9601 J Hyatt Brown

Pomeroy Computer Resources
1020 Petersburg Road
Hebron, KY 41048
606-282-7111 David B Pomeroy II

Pre-Paid Legal Services
321 East Main Street
Ada, OK 74820
405-436-1234 Jack Mildren

Prima Energy
1801 Broadway, Suite 500
Denver, CO 80202
303-297-2100 Richard H Lewis

Project Software & Development
20 University Road
Cambridge, MA 02138
617-661-1444

Regal Cinemas
7132 Commercial Park Drive
Knoxville, TN 37918
423-922-1123 Michael L Campbell

Regal-Beloit
200 State Street
Beloit, WI 53511
608-364-8800 James L Packard

RehabCare Group
7733 Forsyth Boulevard, Suite 1700
St Louis, MO 63105
314-863-7422 James M Usdan

Remedy
1505 Salado Drive
Mountain View, CA 94043
415-903-5200 Lawrence L Garlick

Republic Group
PO Box 1307
Hutchinson, KS 67504
316-727-2700 Phil Simpson

Res-Care
10140 Linn Station Road
Louisville, KY 40223
502-394-2100 Ronald G Geary

Respironics
1001 Murry Ridge Drive
Murrysville, PA 15668
412-733-0200 Dennis S Meteny

Rexall Sundown
851 Broken Sound Parkway Northwest
Boca Raton, FL 33487
561-241-9400 Carl DeSantis

Right Management Consultants
1818 Market Street
Philadelphia, PA 19103
215-988-1588 Richard J Pinola

Romac International
120 West Hyde Park Place
Tampa, FL 33606
813-258-8855 David L Dunkel

Roper Industries
160 Ben Burton Road
Bogart, GA 30622
706-369-7170 Derrick N Key

RTW
8500 Normandale Lake Boulevard #1400
Minneapolis, MN 55437
612-893-0403 David C Prosser

Rural Metro
8401 East Indian School Road
Scottsdale, AZ 85251
602-994-3886 Warren S Rustand

Safeskin
12671 High Bluff Drive
San Diego, CA 92130
619-794-8111 Richard B Jaffe

St John Knits
17422 Derian Avenue
Irvine, CA 92714
714-863-1171 Robert E Gray

SCB Computer Technology
1365 West Brierbrook Road
Memphis, TN 38138
901-754-6577 Ben C Bryant Jr

Scotsman Industries
775 Corporate Woods Parkway
Vernon Hills, IL 60061
847-215-4500 Richard C Osborne

Seattle FilmWorks
1260 16th Avenue West
Seattle, WA 98119
206-281-1390 Gary R Christophersen

Security Dynamics Technologies
20 Crosby Drive
Bedford, MA 01730
617-687-7000 Charles R Stuckey Jr

Seda Specialty Packaging
2501 West Rosecrans Boulevard
Los Angeles, CA 90059
310-635-4444 Shahrokh Sedaghat

Serologicals
780 Park North Boulevard, Suite 110
Clarkston, GA 30021
404-296-5595 Harold J Tenoso

Simpson Manufacturing
4637 Chabot Drive, Suite 200
Pleasanton, CA 94588
510-460-9912 Thomas J Fitzmyers

Sinter Metals
50 Public Square, Suite 3200
Cleveland, OH 44113
216-771-6700 Joseph W Carreras

Smith Micro Software
51 Columbia
Aliso Viejo, CA 92656
714-362-5800 William W Smith Jr

Sodak Gaming
5301 South Highway 16
Rapid City, SD 57701
605-341-5400 Michael G Wordeman

Sofamor Danek Group
1800 Pyramid Place
Memphis, TN 38132
901-396-3133 E R Pickard

Sonic
101 Park Avenue
Oklahoma City, OK 73102
405-280-7654 J Clifford Hudson

SOS Staffing Services
1415 South Main Street
Salt Lake City, UT 84115
801-484-4400 Richard D Reinhold

Southern Energy Homes
US Highway 41 North
Addison, AL 35540
205-747-8589 Wendell L Batchelor

Speedway Motorsports
US Highway 29 North
Concord, NC 28026
704-455-3239 O Bruton Smith

Stephan
1850 West McNab Road
Fort Lauderdale, FL 33309
954-971-0600 Frank F Ferola

Steris
5960 Heisley Road
Mentor, OH 44060
216-354-2600 Bill R Sanford

Sterling Electronics
4201 Southwest Freeway
Houston, TX 77027
713-627-9800 Ronald S Spolane

Synopsys
700 East Middlefield Road
Mountain View, CA 94043
415-962-5000 Aart J de Geus

Synthetech
1290 Industrial Way
Albany, OR 97321
541-967-6575 M Sreenivasan

Techne
614 McKinley Place Northeast
Minneapolis, MN 55413
612-379-8854 Thomas E Oland

Tecnol Medical Products
7201 Industrial Park Boulevard
Fort Worth, TX 76180
817-581-6424 Van M Hubbard

Tessco Technologies
34 Loveton Circle
Sparks, MD 21152
410-472-7000 Robert B Barnhill Jr

Tetra Tech
670 North Rosemead Boulevard
Pasadena, CA 91107
818-449-6400 Li-San Hwang

Timberline Software
9600 SW Nimbus Avenue
Beaverton, OR 97008
503-626-6775 John Gorman

Total System Services
PO Box 1755
Columbus, GA 31902
706-649-2300 Richard W Ussery

Toy Biz
333 East 38th Street
New York, NY 10016
212-682-4700 Joseph M Ahearn

Ultrak
1220 Champion Circle, Suite 100
Carrollton, TX 75006
214-280-9675 George K Broady

UniMark Group
124 McMakin Road
Lewisville, TX 75067
817-491-2992 Jorn I Budde

United Dental Care
14755 Preston Road, Suite 300
Dallas, TX 75240
214-458-7474 William H Wilcox

United Video Satellite Group
7140 South Lewis Avenue
Tulsa, OK 74136
918-488-4000 Lawrence Flinn Jr

Urban Outfitters
1809 Walnut Street
Philadelphia, PA 19103
215-564-2313 Richard A Hayne

USA Detergents
1735 Jersey Avenue
North Brunswick, NJ 08902
908-828-1800 Uri M Evan

Varsity Spirit
2525 Horizon Lake Drive
Memphis, TN 38133
901-387-4370 Jeffrey G Webb

Vaughn Communications
5050 West 78th Street
Minneapolis, MN 55435
612-832-3200 E. David Willette

Viewlogic Systems
293 Boston Post Road West
Marlboro, MA 01752
508-480-0881 Alain J Hanover

Vitalink Pharmacy Services
1250 East Diehl Road, Suite 208
Naperville, IL 60563
630-245-4800 Donald C Tomasso

Wackenhut Corrections
4200 Wackenhut Drive #100
Palm Beach Gardens, FL 33410
561-622-5656 George C Zoley

Watson Pharmaceuticals
311 Bonnie Circle
Corona, CA 91720
909-270-1400 Allen Y Chao

Wireless Telecom Group
East 49 Midland Avenue
Paramus, NJ 07652
201-261-8797 Dale Sydnor

The 500 Largest Private Companies in America

With the Dow at 6200, all manner of once very private companies are coming out of the woodwork with stock offerings. These 500 outfits either don't need the capital or can't stand the public scrutiny.

Edited by Steve Kichen, Tina Russo McCarthy and Peter Newcomb

Researchers: Ronald Boone Jr., John H. Christy, Cecily J. Fluke, Anita Khosla, Shlomo Z. Reifman, David Schultz, Robert J. Sherwood and Saira Stewart

Illustrations by Elsa Warnick

Data compiled December, 1996.

With the market for new issues as effervescent as it is, it's a wonder that any large company at all is left that hasn't gone public. In the past year Estée Lauder Cos., the cosmetics giant; Dominick's Finer Foods, a $2.5 billion grocery and drug chain; Lexmark, the former IBM typewriter and printer division; and Guess, the stylish jeans company, all trooped to Wall Street in search of public capital.

It's hard to resist the temptation. If you can go public at 20 times earnings, you are, in a sense, buying capital at a cost of 5%. These days your eager new shareholders usually don't even expect a cash dividend. It beats borrowing money from a bank.

But plenty of giant firms are determined to stay private. Either they don't need the capital or they will go to great lengths to avoid public scrutiny. This list of the 500 largest privately held companies in the U.S. accounts for 4 million employees and for combined sales of $752 billion.

Among the private giants: the world's largest brandname apparel maker (Levi Strauss), the largest package delivery service outside of the U.S. Postal Service (United Parcel Service), the largest mutual fund distributor (Fidelity Investments), and one of the largest candy makers (Mars) and grain traders (Cargill).

One of the fastest-growing members of the Forbes Private 500 is a chemical company (Huntsman) that makes a business of buying plants

	The most net income . . .			... the most operating income			
	PROFITS				**PROFITS**		
Company	operating ($mil)	net ($mil)	Revenues ($mil)	Company	operating ($mil)	net ($mil)	Revenues ($mil)
Goldman Sachs Group	$1,554	$1,348	$14,324	United Parcel Service	$3,032	$1,043	$21,045
United Parcel Service	3,032	1,043	21,045	Goldman Sachs Group	1,554	1,348	14,324
Cargill	3,080e	902	56,000	Levi Strauss & Co	1,103	735	6,708
Levi Strauss & Co	1,103	735	6,708	MacAndrews & Forbes Holdings	832	44	6,196
Fidelity Investments	1,540e	431	4,277	Continental Cablevision	605	–112	1,442
Marmon Group	850e	307	6,083	Huntsman	545	—	4,170
Peter Kiewit Sons'	314	244	2,902	Alamo Rent-A-Car	513	–50	1,398
Publix Super Markets	449	242	9,393	Aramark	475	110	6,120
Baker & McKenzie	255	228	646	Publix Super Markets	449	242	9,393
International Data Group	240	145	1,550	Peter Kiewit Sons'	314	244	2,902

e: Estimate.

Cargill's revenues of $56 billion make it the biggest privately held company in sales. If operating income (net before depreciation, interest and taxes) is the yardstick, United Parcel Service leads. Goldman Sachs Group is tops in net income. Note: The rankings above omit those companies for which we have only estimated results.

and lines of business from public companies. A public chemical company may have to apologize to its shareholders for hanging on to an out-of-favor commodity product line. The family that owns Huntsman does not have any apologies to make and, to judge from its apparent wealth (see The Forbes Four Hundred) seems to be getting the better end of these bargains.

The bustle of activity in the market for new issues, coupled with a brisk level of business in mergers and acquisitions among both public and private firms, has caused a considerable reshuffling in the Private 500 list over the past year. Hotel franchisor HFS bought Avis, the car rental company; Toronto-based Thomson bought West Publishing, the case-law publisher; Ziff-Davis, of computer magazine fame, sold out to the Japanese outfit Softbank; and privately held Stroh Brewery (ranked 113 this year) acquired G. Heileman Brewing (ranked 301 last year).

We lost Kingston Technology, a manufacturer and marketer of computer memory, to another Softbank buyout offer. But we gained another firm that has grown rapidly by selling computer memory modules: PNY Electronics of Moonachie, N.J. With $500 million in 1995 revenues, PNY is ranked 411.

Another interesting newcomer is West Chester, Pa-based Amkor Electronics. The firm was founded in 1968 by James Kim, a Korean immigrant. Amkor gets raw chips and components from giants like Intel and Motorola and mounts and assembles them into plastic and ceramic packages.

Spalding & Evenflo, a maker of baby and athletic equipment, is back on the Private 500 list after a three-year hiatus. Spalding was disqualified in

1993 when we discovered that the Cisneros brothers of Venezuela controlled the firm. In 1996, investment firm Kohlberg Kravis Roberts bought out the company, so foreign ownership is no longer an issue.

Packard Bell is now Packard Bell NEC. Combined with NEC's non-Japanese computer operations, Packard Bell has pro forma revenues of $8 billion. Even though NEC is foreign, it owns only 20% of Packard Bell, so Packard Bell remains on our list.

FORBES published its first ranking of the largest private companies in 1985. A lot has changed since then, but a few things remain constant. One is that wholesale and retail distribution (supermarkets, car dealerships) is overrepresented among private companies as compared with its contribution to our list of public companies that appears in the spring. Another is that manufacturing and technology are underrepresented. Among the exceptions in the latter category, besides the PC-related firms already mentioned: SAS Institute, a software developer ranked 366, and Science Applications International, a high-tech consulting and defense contracting firm that appears in slot 56.

What's a private company? It's one that either has too few shareholders to have to file financial reports with the Securities & Exchange Commission (Mars, for example) or has enough shareholders but restricts ownership to a narrow group (United Parcel Service is the classic case—it limits stock ownership to employees and their families). All told, 1 in 8 of these 500 files with the SEC, often on account of a public bond offering.

We exclude certain categories of companies from this list: mutually owned firms like Prudential Insurance; cooperatives like Affiliated Foods; trading firms with fewer than 100 employees; foreign-owned firms; and firms that are 50% or more owned by another corporation.

Our sources, besides the Securities & Exchange Commission, include the companies themselves, which are sometimes willing to share copies of audited financial reports with us; industry analysts; trade publications; and competitors.

We show profit figures where we either know them precisely or can get reasonably accurate estimates from outside sources. The net income figure is aftertax (caution: a handful of partnerships on this list do not pay corporate taxes); the operating income is net before depreciation, interest and taxes. This year employee counts reflect total employees rather than full-time or full-time equivalents.

ACKNOWLEDGMENTS

Advertising Age, NYC; Agnomics Research, St. Paul, Minn.; *American Lawyer,* NYC; Association of Management Consulting Firms, NYC; *Atlanta Business Chronicle,* Atlanta; *Automotive News,* Detroit; Kurt Barnard, *Barnard's Retail Report,* Berkley Heights, N.J.; *Beverage World,* Great Neck,

N.Y.; *BIA* Publications, Chantilly, Va.; *Birmingham Business Journal,* Birmingham, Ala.; *Boston Business Journal,* Boston; Arthur Bowman, *Bowman's Accounting Report,* Atlanta; *Broiler Industry,* Cullman, Ala; *Building Design & Construction,* Des Plaines, Ill.; *Business Journal,* Milwaukee; *Business North Carolina,* Charlotte; *Carpet & Rug Industry,* Ramsey, N.J.; Steve Kay, *Cattle Buyer's Weekly,* Petaluma, Calif.; *Chain Store Age Executive,* NYC; *Chain Store Guide Directory of Supermarket Chains 1996,* Tampa, Fla.; Matt Weinstock, Chemical Manufacturers Association, Arlington, Va.; Hassan Fattah, *Chemical Week,* NYC; *Convenience Store News,* NYC; *Corporate Report Minnesota,* Minneapolis; *Crain's Publications,* NYC; *Dallas Business Journal,* Dallas; *Dallas Morning News,* Dallas; *Datamation,* Newton, Mass.; *Dayton Daily News,* Dayton, Ohio; *Dealer Business,* Van Nuys, Calif.; *Denver Business Journal,* Denver; Dillon, Read & Co., Inc., NYC; *Directory of Corporate Affiliations 1996; Electrical Wholesaling,* Overland Park, Kans.; Energy Information Administration, Washington, D.C.; *ENR,* NYC; Matt Wooldridge, Federal Filings, Washington, D.C.; *Florida Trend,* St. Petersburg; Food Marketing Institute, Washington, D.C.; FORBES library; Shelly Snyder, General Aviation Manufacturers, Washington, D.C.; *Georgia Trend,* Atlanta; *HFD,* NYC; *Hispanic Business,* Santa Barbara, Calif.; IMS, America, Blue Bell, Pa.; *Inc.,* NYC; Indepth Data, NYC; *Indianapolis Business Journal,* Indianapolis; Ray Wisbrock, Information Resources, Chicago; *Institutional Distribution,* NYC; Julien J. Studley, Inc., Chicago; James Kennedy, Kennedy Publications, Fitzwilliam, N.H.; *Milwaukee Sentinel,* Milwaukee; Minnesota Department of Commerce, St. Paul; *National Home Center News,* NYC; National Multi Housing Council, Washington, D.C.; *New Jersey Beverage Journal,* Union, N.J.; Jay Gallagher, Petroconsultants, Houston; Petroleum Information Corp., Houston; PKF Consulting, Houston; Kathy Ruber, Polk Company, Detroit; *Professional Builder & Remodeler,* Denver, *Progressive Grocer,* Stamford, Conn.; *Progressive Grocer's Marketing Guidebook* 1997, Stamford, Conn.; *Puget Sound Business Journal,* Seattle; Real Estate Board, NYC; *Restaurants & Institutions,* Des Plaines, Ill.; *Sacramento Business Journal,* Sacramento, Calif.; *St. Louis Business Journal,* St. Louis; Chip Dillon, Salomon Brothers, NYC; Frank C. Walters, M. Shanken Communications, NYC; Simba Information, Stamford, Conn.; Smith Travel Research, Hendersonville, Tenn.; *Supermarket News,* NYC; Chris Urban, Techomic, Chicago; Tony Munoz, T.M. Marketing, Larkspur, Calif.; *TWICE,* NYC; U.S. Department of Agriculture, Washington, D.C.; *U.S. Distribution Journal,* NYC; Mark Stanley, *Walden's Fiber & Board Report,* Washington, D.C.; *Washington CEO Magazine,* Seattle; *Washington Post,* Washington, D.C.; *Working Woman,* Harlan, Iowa.

RANKING THE PRIVATE 500

1996 Ranking of the 500 Largest Private Companies

RANK '96	'95	Company business	Chief executive	Revenues ($mil)	PROFITS operating ($mil)	net ($mil)	Employees	Fiscal year-end
1	1	**Cargill** intl marketer & processor of agricultural & industrial commodities	Ernest S Micek	$56,000	$3,080e	$902	76,500	May
2	2	**Koch Industries** oil & gas, chemicals, agriculture, minerals, real estate, finance	Charles Koch	25,200e	3,270e	850e	13,000	June
3	3	**United Parcel Service** package delivery	Kent C Nelson	21,045	3,032	1,043	332,000	Dec
4	4	**Continental Grain** markets commods, processes poultry, runs cattle feed lots; finl svcs; aquaculture	Donald L Staheli	15,000	830e	240e	15,300	Mar
5	6	**Goldman Sachs Group** securities brokerage, investment banking	Jon S Corzine	14,324	1,554	1,348	8,159	Nov
6	5	**Mars** makes candy, ice cream & pet food; rice; beverages; electronics	Forrest E Mars Jr	14,000	1,770e	800e	28,000	Dec
7	9	**Ingram Industries** distributes computer products, books & videos; operates barges; insurance	Martha R Ingram	11,150	500e	190e	14,309	Dec
8	8	**Andersen Worldwide** accounting, auditing, tax & consulting services	Lawrence A Weinbach	9,499	2,380e	1,710e	91,572	Aug
9	7	**Publix Super Markets** 525 supermarkets in Alabama, Florida, Georgia & South Carolina	Howard M Jenkins	9,393	449	242	95,000	Dec
10	10	**Bechtel Group** engineering, construction & management	Riley P Bechtel	8,504	450e	210e	28,000	Dec

e: Estimate.

(Continued)

243

1996 Ranking of the 500 Largest Private Companies (*Cont.*)

RANK '96 '95	Company business	Chief executive	Revenues ($mil)	PROFITS operating ($mil)	net ($mil)	Employees	Fiscal year-end

> Ernest Micek of number-one-ranked Cargill is only the third nonfamily member in 131 years to head this agribusiness giant.

RANK '96 '95	Company business	Chief executive	Revenues ($mil)	operating ($mil)	net ($mil)	Employees	Fiscal year-end
11 13	**KPMG Peat Marwick** accounting, auditing, tax & consulting services	Stephen G Butler	8,100	2,030e	1,540e	82,000	Sept
12 38	**Packard Bell NEC** sells computer products through department & discount stores	Beny Alagem	8,000*	320e*	—	8,000	Dec
13 12	**Ernst & Young** accounting, assurance, tax & consulting services	Philip A Laskawy	7,550e	1,890e	1,360e	66,000	Sept
14 11	**Montgomery Ward & Co** department stores, Home Ideas & Lechmere stores, catalog sales	Bernard F Brennan	7,085	220	11	55,000	Dec
15 15	**Coopers & Lybrand** accounting, auditing, tax & consulting services	Nicholas G Moore	6,755e	1,350e	1,020e	71,000	Sept
16 14	**Levi Strauss & Co** Levis & Dockers jeans & related products	Robert D Haas	6,708	1,103	735	37,700	Nov
17 17	**Deloitte Touche Tohmatsu International** accounting, auditing, tax & consulting services	J Michael Cook	6,500	1,630e	1,200e	63,440	June
18 30	**MacAndrews & Forbes Holdings** Revlon, Marvel Entertainment, Coleman, Consolidated Cigar	Ronald O Perelman	6,196	832	44	30,563	June
19 19	**Aramark** distributes food to hospitals & schools; health care & other services	Joseph Neubauer	6,120	475	110	150,000	Oct
20 20	**Marmon Group** 60 manufacturing & service companies	Robert A Pritzker	6,083	850e	307	30,000	Dec
21 16	**Meijer** general merchandise & grocery stores in the Midwest	Fred Meijer	6,000e	240e	170e	60,000	June
22 18	**∗Borden** Cracker Jack, soups & other food & dairy products; industrial products	C Robert Kidder	5,944	155	–366	27,500	Dec
23 21	**HE Butt Grocery** H-E-B & H-E-B Pantry Food stores; milk plant & bread bakery in Texas	Charles C Butt	5,800[1]	285[1]	99[1]	42,000	Oct
24 22	**Amway** direct sales of household & personal care products	Steve Van Andel[2]	5,352e	650e	290e	13,000	Aug
25 23	**Advance Publications** newspaper chain, Random House, Condé Nast, New Yorker	SI Newhouse Jr	5,349e	1,070e	200e	24,000	Dec

1996 Ranking of the 500 Largest Private Companies (*Cont.*)

Rank '96	'95	Company business	Chief executive	Revenues ($mil)	Profits operating ($mil)	net ($mil)	Employees	Fiscal year-end
26	25	**Price Waterhouse** accounting, auditing, tax & consulting services	James J Schiro	5,020	1,350e	1,050e	53,000	June
27	28	**JM Family Enterprises** independent distributor of Toyotas; auto dealerships	Pat Moran	4,500	140e	60e	2,000	Dec
28	26	**Ralphs Grocery** supermarkets in California & the Midwest	George G Golleher	4,335	175	–260	30,101	Jan
29	35	**Fidelity Investments** mutual funds, discount brokerage, pension management	Edward C Johnson 3d	4,277	1,540e	431	18,000	Dec
30	27	**∗Alliant Foodservice** distributes food to restaurants, hospitals & other nonretail outlets	James A Miller	4,226	100e	50e	8,500	Dec
31	29	**Pathmark Stores** supermarkets & drugstores in eastern US	James Donald	4,182	265	33	31,000	Jan
32	31	**Huntsman** chemicals, polymers, packaging	Jon M Huntsman	4,170	545	—	8,250	June
33	37	**Cox Enterprises** newspapers, broadcasting, broadbrand communications, auto auctions	James C Kennedy	3,806	1,180e	300e	38,000	Dec
34	32	**SC Johnson & Son** specialty products for home, personal care & insect control	William D George Jr	3,800e	570e	230e	12,500	June

Forbes Four Hundred members and their families own 92 of the largest private companies, including Bechtel, Meijer and Parsons & Whittemore.

Rank '96	'95	Company business	Chief executive	Revenues ($mil)	Profits operating ($mil)	net ($mil)	Employees	Fiscal year-end
35	33	**Hallmark Cards** greeting cards & related products; television programming; art materials	Irvine O Hockaday Jr	3,400	450e	170e	36,100	Dec
36	43	**C&S Wholesale Grocers** wholesales food to supermarkets, retail stores & military bases	Richard B Cohen	3,348	120e	40e	2,850	Sept
37	46	**Enterprise Rent-A-Car** auto rental, leasing, car sales	Andrew C Taylor	3,127	470e	160e	28,806	July
38	39	**Peter Kiewit Sons'** heavy construction, coal mining, telecomm, private toll road in California	Walter Scott Jr	2,902	314	244	14,300	Dec
39	42	**Hy-Vee** Hy-Vee Food stores, Drug Town drugstores & Heartland Pantry convenience stores	Ronald D Pearson	2,800[3]	70e	30e	36,000	Sept

*Pro forma figures.   ∗ Went private via leveraged buyout since 1991.   e: Estimate.   [1]Company provided estimate for October 1996.   [2]Dick DeVos is co-chief executive.   [3]Company provided estimate for September 1996.

(Continued)

1996 Ranking of the 500 Largest Private Companies (*Cont.*)

RANK '96 '95	Company business	Chief executive	Revenues ($mil)	PROFITS operating ($mil)	PROFITS net ($mil)	Employees	Fiscal year-end
40 41	**Milliken & Co** textiles & chemical products	Roger Milliken	2,800e	290e	80e	14,000	Nov
41 173	**Trace International Holdings** home furnishings; auto dealerships	Marshall Cogan	2,772e	135e	−42e	7,800	Dec
42 47	**Graybar Electric** wholesales & distributes electrical & communications equipment	Carl Hall	2,765	117	37	6,000	Dec
43 48	**Hearst** newspapers, magazines, cable TV, books, broadcasting, syndicates comic strips	Frank A Bennack Jr	2,718e	518e	150e	14,000	Dec
44 51	**Menards** home improvement centers in the Midwest	John Menard	2,700e	149e	81e	6,534	Dec
45 55	**JR Simplot** processes potatoes, vegetables, cheese & other foods; fertilizer; livestock	Stephen A Beebe	2,700	270e	122e	13,000	Aug
46 44	**Steelcase** manufactures & distributes office furniture & systems	James P Hackett	2,600	205e	148e	19,000	Dec
47 34	**Penske** leases trucks; auto dealerships; motorsports	Roger S Penske	2,570e	540e	97e	21,800	Dec
48 50	**Transammonia** trades & ships fertilizers, liquefied petroleum gas & petrochemicals	Ronald P Stanton	2,478	20e	8e	235	Apr
49 49	**Randall's Food Markets** Tom Thumb Food & Pharmacy, Randall's Food & Pharmacy stores	R Randall Onstead Jr	2,400	67e	34e	22,000	June
50 53	**Global Petroleum** distributes petroleum	Alfred A Slifka	2,386e	23e	14e	175	Dec
51 54	**Schwan's Sales Enterprises** delivers frozen pizzas & other frozen foods to homes, hospitals & schools	Alfred Schwan	2,338e	232e	111e	6,000	Dec
52 64	**Jordan Group** auto dealerships & fleet sales	Jordan Kapson	2,322	38e	24e	200	Dec
53 57	**Hendrick Automotive Group** auto dealerships in 9 states	JR Hendrick III	2,315	63e	32e	4,500	Dec
54 83	**✳Wesco Distribution** distributes electrical supplies, components & related products	Roy W Haley	2,258*	83*	30*	4,471	Dec
55 56	**Giant Eagle** supermarkets in Pennsylvania, Ohio & West Virginia; wholesales food	David S Shapira	2,160e	61e	28e	12,000	June
56 65	**Science Applications International** technology research & development & systems integration	JR Beyster	2,156	142	57	21,100	Jan
57 52	**Red Apple Group** supermarket chain in New York City; refines oil; real estate	John Catsimatidis	2,150	83	37	4,300	May

1996 Ranking of the 500 Largest Private Companies (*Cont.*)

RANK '96 '95	Company business	Chief executive	Revenues ($mil)	PROFITS operating ($mil)	PROFITS net ($mil)	Employees	Fiscal year-end
58 99	*Entex Information Services	John McKenna	2,144	64e	21e	5,200	June
	PC & network support services for large corporations & government agencies						
59 60	Wegmans Food Markets	Robert B Wegman	2,130	70e	23e	24,446	Dec
	Wegmans Food Markets stores, Chase-Pitkin home & garden centers						
60 61	Southern Wine & Spirits	Harvey Chaplin	2,125e	85e	43e	4,000	Dec
	distributes wine & spirits						
61 66	Core-Mark International	Gary L Walsh	2,100e	69e	21e	2,063	Dec
	distributes tobacco products, candy, health & beauty aids						
62 81	Perdue Farms	James A Perdue	2,100	215e	58e	18,000	Mar
	processes poultry						
63 68	TLC Beatrice International Holdings	Loida Nicolas Lewis	2,073	116	15	4,600	Dec
	wholesales & retails food in Europe; makes ice cream & other desserts						
64 92	*American Axle & Manufacturing	Richard E Dauch	2,000	210e	90e	8,550	Dec
	makes gears, axles & forged prods for General Motors & other automakers						
65 74	Mid-Atlantic Cars	Frank Cuteri	2,000e	54e	28e	3,600	Dec
	auto dealerships						
66 62	*Specialty Foods	Paul Liska	1,975	178	–270	14,000	Dec
	breads, cookies, specialty cheeses, premium snacks & other food products						
67 134	Scoular	Marshall E Faith	1,955	29e	6e	285	May
	trades & stores grain & feed ingredients						
68 76	Dunavant Enterprises	William B Dunavant Jr	1,927	105e	30e	920	June
	gins & trades cotton; real estate						
69 69	Raley's	Charles L Collings	1,912	54e	25e	11,000	June
	Raley's Food & Drug stores, Bel Air Markets						
70 89	Southwire	Roy Richards Jr	1,900	190e	96e	5,000	Dec
	copper & aluminum rods, electrical power cables & specialty wires						
71 70	Gulf Oil	John Kaneb	1,890[1]	10e	6e	200	Sept
	wholesales & distributes oil & petroleum products						
72 72	Kohler	Herbert V Kohler Jr	1,835e	180e	55e	15,000	Dec
	plumbing products, engines, generators, furniture, hotels						
73 77	Metromedia	John W Kluge	1,821e	309e	63e	65,000	Dec
	Ponderosa steakhouses & Bennigan's restaurants; telecomm; Empire Hotels						

* Went private via leveraged buyout since 1991.   e: Estimate.   *Pro forma figures.   [1]Company provided estimate for September 1996.

(*Continued*)

1996 Ranking of the 500 Largest Private Companies (*Cont.*)

RANK '96 '95	Company business	Chief executive	Revenues ($mil)	PROFITS operating ($mil)	PROFITS net ($mil)	Employees	Fiscal year-end
74 100	**McKinsey & Co** international business consulting firm	Rajat Gupta	1,800	540e	400e	7,000	Dec
75 82	**Renco Group** makes steel, fabricates metal; builds HumVee & Hummer all-terrain vehicles	Ira L Rennert	1,800[1]	150e	60e	7,150	Oct
76 78	**Helmsley Enterprises** real estate, Helmsley & Harley hotels	Harry B Helmsley	1,770e	225e	46e	13,000	Dec

Founded as Andersen Lumber Co. by Danish immigrant Hans Andersen in 1903, Andersen Corp. is now the largest U.S. maker of wooden-framed windows and patio doors.

RANK '96 '95	Company business	Chief executive	Revenues ($mil)	PROFITS operating ($mil)	PROFITS net ($mil)	Employees	Fiscal year-end
77 79	**VT** auto & boat dealerships	Larry Van Tuyl[2]	1,755	47e	25e	3,950	Dec
78 110	**Guardian Industries** flat glass, fiberglass insulation, plastics, auto glass	William Davidson	1,750e	263e	114e	10,500	Dec
79 ■	**Keystone Foods** processes & distributes beef & poultry for fast-food & other restaurants	Herbert Lotman	1,736	87e	26e	3,800	Dec
80 90	**Stater Bros Markets** 110 Stater Bros supermarkets in California	Jack H Brown	1,721	60	16	10,000	Sept
81 93	**Lennox International** climate-control systems & equipment	John W Norris Jr	1,710e	222e	103e	8,000	Dec
82 105	**Schneider National** truckload carrier	Donald J Schneider	1,710	214e	43e	15,800	Dec
83 73	**Belk Stores Services** Belk & Leggett department stores	John M Belk	1,700e	85e	34e	29,000	Jan
84 88	**MBM** distributes food & related products to restaurant chains	Jerry L Wordsworth	1,700	48	18	1,500	Dec
85 59	**Simpson Investment** lumber, logging, plywood, doors, paper	Colin Moseley	1,700e	371e	134e	6,600	Dec
86 127	**Parsons & Whittemore** manufactures pulp & paper	George F Landegger	1,667e	379e	126e	2,000	Mar
87 85	**Carlson Cos** TGI Friday's & Country Kitchen rests, Radisson hotels, Carlson Wagonlit Travel	Curtis L Carlson	1,665e	142e	39e	130,000	Dec
88 67	**Ed Morse Automotive Group** auto dealerships	Edward J Morse	1,662	34	10	2,188	Dec

1996 Ranking of the 500 Largest Private Companies (*Cont.*)

Rank '96 '95	Company business	Chief executive	Revenues ($mil)	Profits operating ($mil)	Profits net ($mil)	Employees	Fiscal year-end
89 94	**Gulf States Toyota** independent distributor of Toyotas	Jerry Pyle	1,660e	33e	17e	1,500	Dec
90 103	**DeMoulas Super Markets** DeMoulas & Market Basket supermarkets in Massachusetts & New Hampshire	Telemachus A Demoulas	1,650	99e	25e	11,700	Dec
91 86	**Consolidated Electrical Distributors** wholesales & distributes electrical equipment	Keith W Colburn	1,600e	136e	32e	4,000	Dec
92 107	**Holman Enterprises** auto dealerships, fleet sales & leasing; remanufactures auto parts	John W Kolb	1,590e	34e	19e	3,200	Dec
93 106	**CH Robinson** transportation & financial services; distributes produce	Sid Verdoorn	1,580	79e	17e	1,550	Dec
94 63	**Schnuck Markets** 91 Schnucks supermarkets in the Midwest	Craig D Schnuck	1,570e	38e	20e	15,500	Oct
95 97	**Del Monte Foods** processes canned vegetables & fruits	Paul H Mullan[3]	1,553e	93e	28e	12,500	June
96 95	**Eby-Brown** distributes candy, tobacco, food & merchandise	Richard W Wake[4]	1,550	16e	4e	1,403	Dec
97 115	**International Data Group** computer publications & market research; computer trade shows	Patrick J McGovern	1,550	240	145	8,800	Sept
98 84	**Lefrak Organization** real estate development & management; entertainment; oil & gas	Samuel J LeFrak	1,535e	192e	35e	17,500	Dec

Ronald Perelman's MacAndrews & Forbes, ranked 18, has a controlling interest in nine public companies, including Revlon, Marvel, Toy Biz and Coleman.

Rank '96 '95	Company business	Chief executive	Revenues ($mil)	Profits operating ($mil)	Profits net ($mil)	Employees	Fiscal year-end
99 101	**Clark Enterprises** contractor & builder of hotels, office bldgs, sports & convention facilities	A James Clark	1,500e	38e	15e	3,000	Dec
100 91	**Parsons Corp** international engineering & construction company	James F McNulty	1,500	53e	26e	10,000	Dec
101 137	**General Medical** supplies medical equipment to hospitals, clinics & nursing homes	Steven B Nielsen	1,492	35	–14	3,151	Dec

■ Not on last year's list.   e: Estimate.   [1] Company provided estimate for October 1996.   [2] Cecil Van Tuyl is co-chief executive.
[3] Brian E. Haycox is co-chief executive.   [4] Thomas G. Wake is co-chief executive.

(*Continued*)

1996 Ranking of the 500 Largest Private Companies (*Cont.*)

RANK '96 '95	Company business	Chief executive	Revenues ($mil)	PROFITS operating ($mil)	net ($mil)	Employees	Fiscal year-end
102 125	**Continental Cablevision**[1] cable television service to 7 million homes; broadband communication services	Amos B Hostetter Jr	1,442	605	–112	9,200	Dec
103 126	**QuikTrip** gasoline & convenience stores in 7 southern & midwestern states	Chester Cadieux	1,423	49	12	4,075	Apr
104 167	**UniGroup** United Van Lines & Mayflower Transit moving services	Maurice Greenblatt	1,406	51	19	1,050	Dec
105 117	**Gordon Food Service** distributes food to restaurants, schools & health care facilities	Paul Gordon	1,400[2]	52e	29e	3,000	Oct
106 112	**Alamo Rent-A-Car**[3] auto rental	D Keith Cobb	1,398	513	–50	8,100	Dec
107 121	**Sinclair Oil** oil refineries, ski resorts, hotels, gas stations	RE Holding	1,390e	184e	39e	5,600	Dec
108 124	**Golub** Price Chopper supermarkets & Mini Chopper convenience stores	Lewis Golub	1,375e	44e	19e	15,500	Apr
109 108	**JM Huber** chemicals; natural resources; explores for oil & gas; makes electronic equip	Peter T Francis	1,371e	87e	31e	5,000	Dec
110 118	**Gilbane Building** constructs water treatment plants, airports, educational & govt facilities	Paul J Choquette Jr	1,371	37e	15e	856	Dec

Among the private giants are 60 that are at least a century old. Among them: Menasha, Gilbane Building and Moyer Packing.

RANK '96 '95	Company business	Chief executive	Revenues ($mil)	PROFITS operating ($mil)	net ($mil)	Employees	Fiscal year-end
111 120	**Golden State Foods** processes & distributes food & supplies to McDonald's outlets	James E Williams	1,370e	52e	15e	1,700	Dec
112 109	**Schreiber Foods** makes cheese for schools, fast-food restaurants & private-label brands	Jack Meng	1,370e	77e	45e	2,300	Sept
113 180	**Stroh Brewery** Stroh's, Schaefer, Schlitz & other malt beverage products; Chaos iced tea	William L Henry	1,355e[4]	35e[4]	—	4,500	Mar
114 ■	**∗Riverwood International** coated kraft paperboard for packaging; paper mills; packaging machinery	Thomas H Johnson	1,342	156	46	6,400	Dec
115 132	**GAF** specialty chemicals; distributes roofing & other building materials	Samuel J Heyman	1,339	243	33	5,209	Dec
116 179	**Sammons Enterprises** insurance; industrial equipment	Robert W Korba	1,315e	214e	82e	2,400	Dec

1996 Ranking of the 500 Largest Private Companies (*Cont.*)

Rank '96 '95	Company business	Chief executive	Revenues ($mil)	Profits operating ($mil)	Profits net ($mil)	Employees	Fiscal year-end
117 114	**Alex Lee** distributes food; supermarkets	Boyd L George	1,300	43e	14e	5,400	Sept
118 185	**Tang Industries** fabricates & distributes metal; pharmaceuticals; office furniture	Cyrus Tang	1,300	126e	43e	4,000	Dec
119 141	**Great Dane Holdings** manufactures truck trailers; stamps auto parts; operates taxis; insurance	David R Markin	1,293	113	35	5,750	Dec
120 133	**Potamkin Cos** auto dealerships in New York, New Jersey, Florida & Pennsylvania	Alan Potamkin[5]	1,290	28e	13e	2,500	Dec
121 ■	**Grant Thornton** accounting & consulting	Robert Kleckner	1,285	257e	193e	18,300	Dec
122 152	**Flying J** truck & travel plaza stops; oil refining, production & exploration	J Phillip Adams	1,282	58e	10e	7,600	Jan
123 111	**Roll International** grows almonds, olives, oranges, pistachios; Teleflora; Franklin Mint	Stewart Resnick	1,280e	125e	59e	7,500	Dec
124 129	**Brookshire Grocery** Brookshire & Super 1 supermarkets	James Hardin	1,270e	29e	10e	9,500	Oct
125 149	**Neuman Distributors** distributes pharmaceuticals & medical equipment to hospitals & drugstores	Samuel Toscano Jr	1,262	12	1	710	Apr
126 136	**Duchossois Industries** railroad equip; military ordnance; Arlington Racetrack; garage door openers	Richard L Duchossois	1,260e	55e	7e	8,000	Dec
127 113	**84 Lumber** 388 discount building materials stores	Joseph A Hardy Sr	1,260	65e	20e	3,500	Dec
128 87	**Holiday Cos** Holiday Station & Holiday Plus stores; wholesales food; sporting goods stores	Ronald A Erickson	1,260e	81e	23e	6,000	Dec
129 116	**Schottenstein Stores** off-price & liquidation department stores	Jay L Schottenstein	1,260e	65e	19e	11,948	July
130 131	**Connell Limited Partnership** recycles & manufactures metal products; industrial equipment	William F Connell	1,257	143e	50e	2,900	Dec
131 157	**Pilot** 52 convenience stores in Tennessee, Virginia & West Virginia; 89 travel plazas	James A Haslam III	1,257	58	44	4,407	Dec
132 139	**Hughes Family Markets** Hughes Markets in California; Santee Dairies	Roger K Hughes	1,220e	31e	12e	5,100	Feb

■ Not on last year's list.   ✶ Went private via leveraged buyout since 1991.   e: Estimate.   [1]Announced plans to be acquired by U S West.   [2]Company provided estimates for October 1996.   [3]Announced plans to be acquired by Republic Industries.   [4]Reflects acquisition of G Heileman Brewing.   [5]Robert Potamkin is co-chief executive.

(Continued)

1996 Ranking of the 500 Largest Private Companies (*Cont.*)

RANK '96 '95	Company business	Chief executive	Revenues ($mil)	PROFITS operating ($mil)	net ($mil)	Employees	Fiscal year-end
133 156	**Essex Group** manufactures wire, cable & electrical insulation	Steven R Abbott	1,202	109	23	4,102	Dec
134 140	**Andersen Corp** manufactures windows	Jerold W Wulf	1,200e	240e	144e	3,700	Dec
135 148	**Connell** leases heavy equipment; trades rice & sugar	Grover Connell	1,200	66e	19e	200	Dec

Family-owned Huntsman Corp. is the fourteenth-largest chemical manufacturer in the U.S., behind publicly held Lyondell Petrochemical and Union Carbide.

RANK '96 '95	Company business	Chief executive	Revenues ($mil)	operating ($mil)	net ($mil)	Employees	Fiscal year-end
136 150	**Frank Consolidated Enterprises** auto dealerships, fleet leasing	James S Frank	1,200	18e	12	675	Aug
137 98	**Grocers Supply Co** distributes food to convenience stores & supermarkets	Max Levit[1]	1,200	36e	12e	1,200	Dec
138 151	**National Car Rental** auto rental	William E Lobeck	1,200e	185e	20e	7,000	Dec
139 166	**Nobody Beats the Wiz** electronics stores in the New York metropolitan area	Lawrence Jemal	1,200e	62e	30e	4,700	Dec
140 153	**Services Group of America** distributes food; insurance; real estate	Thomas J Stewart	1,200	42e	20e	3,000	Dec
141 230	**TAD Resources International** temporary employment agency for technical, clerical & telecomm workers	James S Davis	1,200e	72e	36e	35,000	Dec
142 147	**Young & Rubicam** advertising, marketing, communications	Peter A Georgescu	1,198	198e	80e	11,100	Dec
143 128	**Jitney Jungle Stores of America** Jitney Jungle & Sack & Save supermarkets; Pump & Save gas stations	WH Holman Jr	1,179	65	16	10,000	Apr
144 160	**Haworth** designs & manufactures office furniture & seating	Richard G Haworth	1,150	115e	40e	9,000	Dec
145 130	**Amsted Industries** railroad & industrial equipment, building materials	Gordon Lohman	1,143	144	77	8,700	Sept
146 135	**Save Mart Supermarkets** supermarkets in northern & central California	Robert Piccinini	1,135	47	13	6,010	Mar

1996 Ranking of the 500 Largest Private Companies (*Cont.*)

Rank '96 '95	Company business	Chief executive	Revenues ($mil)	Profits operating ($mil)	net ($mil)	Employees	Fiscal year-end
147 146	**Maritz** marketing, research, motivation programs, travel	William E Maritz	1,117	66	25	6,800	Mar
148 144	**Lincoln Property** real estate development & management	A Mack Pogue	1,115	46	3	4,025	June
149 145	**Budget Rent a Car**[2] international auto & truck rental	William N Plamondon[3]	1,113	405e	—	24,000	Dec
150 ■	**Prospect Motors** fleet dealer of General Motors vehicles	William Halvorson	1,106	17e	11e	103	May
151 171	**McCombs Enterprises** auto dealerships	Gary V Woods	1,103	30e	15e	3,000	Dec
152 169	**Black & Veatch** engineering, construction & technical consulting services	PJ Adam	1,102	25	20	6,100	Dec
153 202	**Silgan** manufactures aluminum, steel & plastic containers	R Philip Silver	1,102	135	10	5,110	Dec
154 143	**BeefAmerica** runs slaughterhouses	Robert R Norton Jr	1,100[3]	28e	8e	1,600	Oct
155 168	**Booz, Allen & Hamilton** management & technology consulting	William F Stasior	1,100	220e	110e	6,900	Mar
156 142	**Crowley Maritime** marine transport & harbor services, barge & containerized services	Thomas B Crowley Jr	1,100	44	22	5,000	Dec
157 ■	**Jasper** building supplies	Walter F Johnsey	1,100e	75e	20e	3,300	Dec
158 ■	**Leprino Foods** makes mozzarella cheese	James Leprino	1,100e	55e	33e	2,200	Oct
159 159	**Rich Products** Coffee Rich, Rich's Whip Topping & other frozen foods; broadcasting; pro sports	Robert E Rich Jr	1,100	156e	61e	6,500	Dec
160 122	**Cumberland Farms** convenience stores, gas stations, VSH Realty	Lily H Bentas	1,091	75	35	7,210	Sept
161 158	**Johnson & Higgins** insurance brokerage, risk management	David A Olsen	1,083	—	—	8,400	Dec
162 170	**LL Bean** outdoor sporting goods sold by mail order & some retail stores	Leon A Gorman	1,078	65e	31e	3,800	Feb

■ Not on last year's list.   e: Estimate.   [1]Milton Levit is co-chief executive.   [2]Announced plans to be acquired by Ford Motor. [3]Jack Frazee is co-chief executive.

(Continued)

1996 Ranking of the 500 Largest Private Companies (*Cont.*)

RANK '96 '95	Company business	Chief executive	Revenues ($mil)	PROFITS operating ($mil)	net ($mil)	Employees	Fiscal year-end
163 228	**GSC Enterprises** wholesales food	Michael K McKenzie	1,066	16e	5e	1,939	Dec
164 218	**Dillingham Construction** general contracting; commercial, industrial & marine construction mgmt svcs	William L Higgins	1,065[1]	16[1]	3[1]	1,200	Oct
165 175	**WL Gore & Associates** manufactures Gore-Tex, electronics, industrial & medical products	Robert W Gore	1,064	213e	106e	6,100	Mar
166 195	**ICC Industries** manufactures chemicals, plastics & pharmaceuticals	John J Farber	1,062	141e	54e	2,550	Dec
167 282	**Enterprise Products** processes, stores & distributes liquefied petroleum gas	Dan L Duncan	1,057	144	66	1,020	Dec
168 189	**RaceTrac Petroleum** RaceTrac & Raceway convenience stores & gasoline stations in 13 states	Carl Bolch Jr	1,056	68e	19	2,800	Dec
169 360	**Avondale** manufactures cotton & cotton blend yarns, denim & other fabrics	G Stephen Felker	1,040*	112*	26*	7,500	Feb
170 ■	**＊Purina Mills** supplies animal feed	David L Abbott	1,036	90	–3	2,500	Dec
171 191	**Little Caesar Enterprises** pizza restaurants	Michael Ilitch	1,035e	64e	21e	8,230	Dec
172 154	**Earle M Jorgensen** distributes metal products in the US, Canada, Mexico & UK	Neven Hulsey	1,026	27	–29	2,600	Apr
173 182	**DiGiorgio** wholesales & distributes White Rose food products	Arthur M Goldberg	1,020	23	—	1,135	Dec
174 181	**North Pacific Lumber** trades & distributes forest, agricultural, steel & other products	TJ Tomjack	1,012	18	8	715	Dec
175 162	**A-Mark Financial** wholesales precious metals & bullion coins; real estate	Steven C Markoff	1,000	—	—	118	July
176 163	**Crawford Fitting** valves, pipe fittings	FJ Callahan	1,000e	180e	90e	2,500	Dec
177 215	**Dart Container** manufactures polystyrene cups & other food containers	Kenneth Dart	1,000e	230e	90e	4,300	Dec
178 184	**GS Industries** steel wire rods, high carbon steel balls for mineral processing	Roger R Regelbrugge	1,000e	70e	11e	3,800	Dec
179 213	**Bill Heard Enterprises** auto dealerships; leasing	William T Heard	1,000	34	12	1,600	Dec
180 470	**IMG** talent management services; special events; produces television programs; advertising	Mark H McCormack	1,000e	—	—	1,500	Dec

1996 Ranking of the 500 Largest Private Companies (*Cont.*)

RANK '96 '95	Company business	Chief executive	Revenues ($mil)	PROFITS operating ($mil)	net ($mil)	Employees	Fiscal year-end

> Deseret Management Corp., ranked 278 with an estimated $700 million in sales, has interests in insurance, broadcasting and real estate. The Mormon Church has a controlling interest in this for-profit private company.

RANK '96 '95	Company business	Chief executive	Revenues ($mil)	operating ($mil)	net ($mil)	Employees	Fiscal year-end
181 468	**Nesco** industrial equipment, engineering services	Robert J Tomsich	1,000e	84e	—	6,000	Dec
182 222	**Quad/Graphics** full-service printer of magazines, catalogs, books & other commercial products	Harry V Quadracci	1,000	110e	50e	8,500	Dec
183 ■	**TRT Holdings** produces & markets oil & gas; Omni & other hotels	Robert B Rowling	1,000e	135e	38e	2,200	Dec
184 188	**Young's Market** distributes wine & spirits	Vernon O Underwood	1,000	30e	10e	1,600	Feb
185 ■	**Hoffman Construction** construction	Cecil W Drinkward	990e	27e	12e	850	Sept
186 178	**MTS** Tower Records stores	Russell Solomon	990e	50e	15e	7,600	July
187 253	**PMC/SLIC** manufactures specialty chemicals, foam, films & plastics; plastic molding equip	Philip Kamins	981e*	157e*	59e*	5,130	Dec
188 164	**E&J Gallo Winery** generic & premium wines & wine products	Ernest Gallo	980e	92e	44e	4,000	Dec
189 ■	**Honickman Affiliates** bottles soft drinks	Jeffrey Honickman	980e	117e	20e	5,200	Dec
190 174	**Battelle Memorial Institute** technology development & commercialization	Douglas E Olesen	974	21	17	7,429	Dec
191 187	**Moorman Manufacturing** makes livestock feed; processes & refines soybeans	Thomas M McKenna	973e	29e	10e	2,800	Mar
192 165	**Lykes Bros** processes citrus fruits; insurance; fertilizer & crop protection prods; trucking	Thompson L Rankin	960e	67e	29e	3,000	Dec
193 197	**Ormet** smelts aluminum; makes semifinished aluminum products & sheet aluminum	R Emmett Boyle	960	136e	24e	3,300	Dec

■ Not on last year's list. * Went private via leveraged buyout since 1991. e: Estimate. *Pro forma figures. ¹Company provided estimate for October 1996.

(Continued)

1996 Ranking of the 500 Largest Private Companies (*Cont.*)

RANK '96 '95	Company business	Chief executive	Revenues ($mil)	PROFITS operating ($mil)	net ($mil)	Employees	Fiscal year-end
194 206	**DHL Airways** international air freight package delivery	Patrick Foley	959	54	19	8,500	Dec
195 198	**Quality King Distributors** distributes pharmaceuticals & health & beauty aids	Glenn Nussdorf	950[1]	27e	12e	900	Oct
196 238	**Sierra Pacific Industries** lumber & millwork products; windows	Red Emmerson	950e	129e	47e	3,000	Dec
197 270	**Larry H Miller Group** auto dealerships; Utah Jazz basketball team	Larry H Miller	926	40e	15e	2,121	Dec
198 ■	**Oppenheimer Group** brokerage, investment banking, money management	Stephen Robert[2]	925	88e	66e	3,222	Apr
199 192	**Sutherland Lumber** home improvement centers	Donna Sutherland Pearson	920e	37e	9e	3,000	Dec
200 220	**Dobbs Brothers Management** auto dealerships; distributes beer & wine	James K Dobbs III	919	25e	12e	1,580	Dec
201 214	**Mary Kay Cosmetics** sells cosmetics & toiletries in 23 countries through direct marketing	John P Rochon	918e	88e	23e	2,400	Dec
202 234	**Menasha** packaging, plastics, commercial printing, forest products, promotion graphics	RD Bero	916	124e	64e	5,200	Dec
203 ■	**Ebsco Industries** subscription services, printing	James T Stephens	909e	91e	46e	4,000	June
204 155	**DynCorp** aircraft services, technical services & consulting, information technology	Dan R Bannister	909	20	5	16,900	Dec
205 208	**Wawa** convenience stores in 5 mid-Atlantic states	Richard D Wood Jr	901	25	14	10,000	Dec
206 58	**Polo Ralph Lauren** designer apparel, home furnishings & accessories	Ralph Lauren	900e	110e	90e	3,500	Apr
207 194	**Sweetheart Holdings** paper & plastic food containers & cups; packaging products	William F McLaughlin	900e	84e	—	7,500	Sept
208 183	**WWF Paper** distributes fine paper in North America & Western Europe	Edward V Furlong Jr	900	36e	18e	395	June
209 205	**Restaurant Co** Friendly's & Perkins Family Restaurants	Donald N Smith	895e	110e	—	36,600	Dec
210 ■	**Howmet** makes components for gas turbine engines	David L Squier	890	110	58	8,500	Dec
211 196	**Farm Fresh** Farm Fresh, Rack & Sack & other warehouse stores in Virginia & North Carolina	Michael E Julian Jr	885	46	−26	7,000	Dec
212 204	**National Distributing** distributes alcoholic & nonalcoholic beverages	Michael C Carlos	880e	28e	9e	1,500	Dec
213 225	**Minyard Food Stores** Minyard Food, Sack 'n Save & Carnival stores	Liz Minyard[3]	875	17	3	7,200	June

1996 Ranking of the 500 Largest Private Companies (*Cont.*)

RANK '96 '95	Company business	Chief executive	Revenues ($mil)	PROFITS operating ($mil)	PROFITS net ($mil)	Employees	Fiscal year-end
214 217	**Coca-Cola Bottling Co of Chicago** soft drinks	Marvin J Herb	872e	129e	19e	4,200	Dec
215 302	**Flint Ink** printing ink, color pigments, printing blankets	H Howard Flint II	871*	35e*	24e*	2,868	Dec
216 211	**UIS** original & replacement automotive parts; confectionery prods; millwork prods	Andrew G Pietrini	$871	$101	$47	8,000	Dec
217 186	**Wilbur-Ellis** distributes agricultural chems & fertilizers in US; distributes ind chems in Asia	Brayton Wilbur Jr	870	31e	9e	2,000	Dec
218 119	**H Group Holding** Hyatt hotels; tobacco	Jay Pritzker	869e	194e	90e	70,000	Dec
219 203	**Asplundh Tree Expert** vegetation mgmt for electric utils, railroads & pipelines; maintains utility poles	Christopher B Asplundh	868	104e	26e	18,500	Dec
220 239	**Towers Perrin** management & compensation consulting, risk management, reinsurance	John T Lynch	868	87e	43e	5,500	Dec
221 201	**Beaulieu of America** manufactures carpet & rugs	Carl Bouckaert	864	81e	16e	6,500	Mar
222 219	**Westfield Cos** property, casualty & life insurance	Cary Blair	856	100	96	2,238	Dec
223 292	**Bloomberg Financial Markets** on-line financial data, business news service	Michael Bloomberg	850	170e	43e	2,500	Dec
224 243	**Chemcentral** distributes industrial chemicals	H Daniel Wenstrup	850	24	8	850	Dec
225 241	**Jeld-Wen** manufactures windows & doors; building materials; develops resorts	Richard L Wendt	850e	47e	17e	9,000	Dec
226 244	**Roseburg Forest Products** plywood, particleboard & other forest products	Kenneth Ford	850e	115e	42e	3,050	Mar
227 161	**Wickland** stores & trades petroleum; real estate	J Al Wickland Jr	850e	—	—	200	Dec

Andrew and Peter Kiewit founded $2.9 billion Peter Kiewit Sons' in 1884 as a construction company. Now it also mines coal and sells communication services.

■ Not on last year's list.   e: Estimate.   *Pro forma figures.   [1]Company provided estimate for October 1996.   [2]Nathan Gantcher is co-chief executive.   [3]Gretchen Minyard Williams is co-chief executive.

(*Continued*)

1996 Ranking of the 500 Largest Private Companies (*Cont.*)

RANK '96 '95	Company business	Chief executive	Revenues ($mil)	PROFITS operating ($mil)	net ($mil)	Employees	Fiscal year-end
228 233	**Rosenthal Cos** auto dealerships	Robert M Rosenthal	846	21	13	1,600	Dec
229 229	**Domino's Pizza** pizza delivery & carryout	Thomas S Monaghan	834e	52e	18e	3,500	Dec
230 266	**Bartlett and Co** sells & stores grain; mills flour; runs cattle feed lots	Paul D Bartlett Jr	825e	12e	4e	525	Dec
231 223	**Foster Farms** processes poultry	Robert A Fox	825	34e	12e	6,800	Dec
232 254	**Shamrock Foods** distributes food, processes dairy products	Norman McClelland	818	25e	11e	2,064	Sept
233 240	**Day & Zimmermann** engineering, consulting, business services, defense prods & services, software	Harold L Yoh Jr	812	28	5	14,000	Dec
234 212	**BE&K** engineers, constructs & maintains paper & pulp plants & other ind facilities	T Michael Goodrich	807	40e	25e	7,600	Mar
235 275	**Leo Burnett** advertising agency	William T Lynch	806	129e	52e	7,500	Dec
236 209	**Gould Paper** distributes paper	Harry E Gould Jr	805	14	8e	425	Dec
237 276	**CH2M Hill Companies** designs, develops, constructs & operates water, env & transportation infrastructure	Ralph R Peterson	805	205e	62e	7,400	Dec
238 249	**Follett** operates college bookstores; wholesales educational prods & svcs to schools	P Richard Litzsinger	800	36	14	7,500	Mar
239 210	**RB Pamplin** textiles, concrete & asphalt	Robert B Pamplin Sr	800	98	18	6,500	May
240 177	**McCarthy** general contracting, construction management	Michael M McCarthy	795	8e	4e	1,000	Mar
241 255	**Big Y Foods** 42 supermarkets in Connecticut & Massachusetts	Donald H D'Amour	789	22e	10e	6,253	June
242 256	**Warren Equities** trades & wholesales petroleum; convenience stores; distributes merchandise	Warren Alpert	786	20	550		May
243 343	**Boscov's Department Stores** 28 department stores	Albert Boscov	783	39e	16e	8,500	Jan
244 236	**MA Mortenson** general contractor & construction manager of health & correctional facilities	MA Mortenson	780e	12e	7e	1,500	Dec
245 308	**Charlie Thomas Dealerships** auto dealerships	Charlie Thomas	780	18	9	3,000	Dec
246 267	**HB Zachry** general contractor for power plants & other industrial processing facilities	H Bartell Zachry Jr	780	22e	8e	10,200	Dec
247 264	**Don Massey Cadillac** auto dealerships	Donald E Massey	774	22	16	1,227	Dec

1996 Ranking of the 500 Largest Private Companies (*Cont.*)

RANK '96 '95	Company business	Chief executive	Revenues ($mil)	PROFITS operating ($mil)	PROFITS net ($mil)	Employees	Fiscal year-end
248 242	**Big V Supermarkets** 32 ShopRite & PriceRite Club supermarkets in Conn, NY, NJ & Pa	Joseph V Fisher	769	39	–5	4,600	Dec
249 ■	**Amkor Electronics** subcontract manufacturer of integrated circuits	James J Kim	763e	195e	92e	325	Dec
250 295	**ABC Supply** wholesale distributor of roofing, siding & windows	Kenneth Hendricks	762	56	12	2,100	Apr
251 245	**Lanoga** Lumbermen's Building Centers & other building materials stores in 15 states	Daryl D Nagel	761	34	18	3,600	Dec
252 200	**Schwegmann Giant Super Markets** supermarkets in Louisiana	John F Schwegmann	758e	—	—	4,625	June
253 268	**Sheetz** convenience stores & gas stations in Pa, Maryland, Virginia & West Virginia	Stanton R Sheetz	756	38e	15e	4,900	Sept
254 232	✳**Baker & Taylor** distributes books, prerecorded video & audio cassettes	Craig M Richards	751	23e	8e	2,000	June
255 288	**M Fabrikant & Sons** wholesales jewelry	Charles Fortgang	751	54e	26e	875	July
256 123	**Delaware North Cos** greyhound tracks; park, airport & stadium concessions; FleetCenter in Boston	Jeremy M Jacobs	750e	—	—	20,000	Dec
257 297	**Sherwood Food Distributors** distributes food	J Lawrence Tushman[1]	750	23e	8e	500	Oct
258 324	**Taylor** printing, direct mail marketing, office supplies	Glen Taylor	750	150	45	8,000	Dec
259 363	**Icon Health & Fitness** treadmills, exercise bikes, cross country skis & other home fitness equipment	Scott R Watterson	748	62	7	4,300	May
260 265	**Carpenter** manufactures polyurethane foam	Stanley F Pauley	745	73e	18e	6,574	Dec
261 269	**Fiesta Mart** Fiesta supermarkets in Texas	Louis Kaptopodis	745e	19e	9e	6,500	May
262 247	**J Crew** sells apparel by mail order & retail stores	Arthur Cinader	742	18	9	6,000	Feb
263 274	**McKee Foods** Little Debbie & Sunbelt snack foods	Ellsworth McKee	735	63e	22e	4,675	June
264 237	**Club Corporation International** manages resorts, country, city & athletic clubs	Robert H Dedman Sr	733	63	–27	19,800	Dec

■ Not on last year's list.   ✳ Went private via leveraged buyout since 1991.   e: Estimate.   [1]Earl Ishbia is co-chief executive.

(*Continued*)

1996 Ranking of the 500 Largest Private Companies (*Cont.*)

RANK '96 '95	Company business	Chief executive	Revenues ($mil)	PROFITS operating ($mil)	PROFITS net ($mil)	Employees	Fiscal year-end

Baker & Taylor (number 254) dates to 1828. But at least 62 of the private giants aren't even 20 years old.

RANK '96 '95	Company business	Chief executive	Revenues ($mil)	operating ($mil)	net ($mil)	Employees	Fiscal year-end
265 337	**Whiting-Turner Contracting** mall renovations, hospitals, light rail systems & other commercial projects	Willard Hackerman	730e	29e	11e	1,500	Dec
266 248	**Hensel Phelps Construction** commercial construction	Jerry L Morgensen	726	13	8	1,540	May
267 252	**Coulter** medical diagnostic systems	Wallace H Coulter	725e	100e	50e	5,500	Mar
268 271	**Drummond** mines coal	Garry N Drummond	725	65e	22e	3,350	Dec
269 277	**Queen Carpet** manufactures residential & commercial carpets & rugs	Julian Saul	720e	73e	16e	4,600	Dec
270 286	**Edward D Jones & Co** securities brokerage	John W Bachmann	720	104	58	10,998	Dec
271 289	**Island Lincoln-Mercury Group** auto dealerships & fleet sales	R Bruce Deardoff	719	7	4	210	Dec
272 290	**Berwind** industrial equipment, specialty chemicals, financial svcs, pharmaceutical svcs	C Graham Berwind Jr	719	94	32	3,800	Dec
273 287	**Klaussner Furniture Group** manufactures upholstered home & office furniture	JB Davis	717	57e	29e	6,736	Dec
274 262	**Hale-Halsell** retails & wholesales food	Robert D Hawk	715	1	2	5,163	Dec
275 257	**Irvine Co** real estate investment & development in Calif; Irvine Apartment Communities	Donald Bren	710	89e	16e	190	June
276 423	**Crown Equipment** manufactures heavy-duty electric lift trucks & television antenna rotators	James F Dicke	707	75	30	5,800	Mar
277 319	**Bose** music systems, loudspeakers, auto sound systems & aviation headsets	Amar G Bose	700	82e	50e	3,500	Apr
278 304	**Deseret Management** insurance; TV & radio stations; real estate management	Rodney H Brady	700e	—	—	3,000	Dec
279 258	**King Kullen Grocery** 46 supermarkets in the New York metropolitan area	John B Cullen	700	15e	6e	4,500	Sept
280 ■	**Micro Electronics** Micro Center computer stores; WinBook laptop computers	John F Baker	700e	43e	15e	1,200	Dec
281 259	**Newark Group** recycles paperboard into new paper products	Fred G von Zuben	700	80	34	3,000	Apr

1996 Ranking of the 500 Largest Private Companies (*Cont.*)

RANK '96 '95	Company business	Chief executive	Revenues ($mil)	PROFITS operating ($mil)	net ($mil)	Employees	Fiscal year-end
282 294	**Purity Wholesale Grocers** distributes groceries	Jeff Levitetz	700	22	10	300	June
283 379	**Stevedoring Services of America** loads & unloads ships & provides port services	Ricky Smith	700e	84e	35e	5,000	Jan
284 246	**Lupient Automotive Group** auto dealerships	James Lupient	695	19e	10e	1,000	Dec
285 ■	**✳Spalding & Evenflo** manufactures golf balls, basketballs & other sporting goods; consumer products	Paul L Whiting	694*	—	—	3,000	Sept
286 376	**DeBruce Grain** runs grain elevators, merchandises grain, trades fertilizer	Paul DeBruce	688	10e	2e	150	Mar
287 291	**Bashas'** Bashas', AJ Fine Foods & other supermarkets in Arizona	Edward N Basha Jr	684e	18e	8e	5,500	Dec
288 336	**Specialty Retailers** Bealls, Palais Royal & Stage apparel stores	Carl E Tooker	683	60	20	9,946	Jan
289 311	**General Parts** Carquest auto parts stores; distributes auto parts	O Temple Sloan Jr	680	68e	32e	5,008	Dec
290 419	**Perry H Koplik & Sons** international sales representative of pulp, paper & forest products	Michael R Koplik	674	9e	3e	110	Dec
291 300	**Inductotherm Industries** manufactures induction melting systems for foundries	Henry M Rowan	674	80e	46	4,974	Apr
292 303	**Barton Malow** sports stadiums, health facilities, industrial & other heavy construction svcs	Ben Maibach III	669	9e	2e	776	Mar
293 305	**McJunkin** distributes pipes, valve fittings & electrical equipment	HB Wehrle III	667	29e	9e	1,312	Dec
294 284	**Sunbelt Beverage** wholesales wine & spirits	Charles Andrews	665e	20e	5e	1,485	Mar
295 347	**Waremart** Cub Foods & Waremart Food Center stores	William D Long	665	19e	10e	3,850	Mar
296 313	**Parisian** department stores specializing in apparel, cosmetics & gifts	Donald E Hess	664	49	9	7,700	Jan

Six generations after its founding by the Fribourg family, Continental Grain is still owned and run by the Fribourg family.

■ Not on last year's list.   ✳ Went private via leveraged buyout since 1991.   e: Estimate.   *Pro forma figures.

(Continued)

1996 Ranking of the 500 Largest Private Companies (*Cont.*)

Rank '96 '95	Company business	Chief executive	Revenues ($mil)	Profits operating ($mil)	net ($mil)	Employees	Fiscal year-end
297 384	**Walbridge, Aldinger** construction	John Rakolta Jr	660	26e	13e	600	Dec
298 314	**Topa Equities** insurance, financial services, auto dealerships; distributes beverages	John E Anderson	656	3	–5	1,289	Dec
299 296	**Georgia Crown Distributing** wholesales & distributes alcoholic beverages & bottled water	Donald M Leebern Jr	656	23e	8e	1,600	July
300 261	**Sealy** Sealy, Posturepedic, Stearns & Foster bedding	Ronald Jones	654	85	20	4,520	Nov
301 ■	**Charles Pankow Builders** designs & builds shopping malls, hotels, condominiums & office buildings	Charles Pankow	648	19e	8e	115	Dec
302 328	**Baker & McKenzie** law firm	John C Klotsche	646	255	228	5,680	June
303 312	**D'Arcy Masius Benton & Bowles** advertising agency	Roy Bostock	646e	65e	16e	6,591	Dec
304 362	**Green Bay Packaging** paperboard, shipping containers, pressure-sensitive roll stock	William F Kress	645e	105e	45e	2,800	Dec
305 341	**MTD Products** lawn mowers & other outdoor power equip; tools, dies, metal stampings	Curtis E Moll	645e	63e	31e	5,500	July
306 315	**Charmer Industries** distributes wine & spirits	Herman Merinoff	640e	21e	6e	1,260	Dec
307 260	＊**Packerland Packing** runs slaughterhouses	Richard V Vesta	640	17	4	1,920	Dec
308 329	**K-VA-T Food Stores** Food City supermarkets in Kentucky, Virginia & Tennessee	Jack C Smith	636	17e	10e	6,000	Dec
309 334	**Peerless Importers** distributes wine & spirits	John Magliocco	635e	20e	6e	1,250	Dec
310 335	**Skadden, Arps, Slate, Meagher & Flom** law firm	Robert C Sheehan	635e	255e	210e	3,000	Dec
311 298	**Long John Silver's** fast-food seafood restaurants	Rolf H Towe	634	50	–41	18,500	June
312 138	**Family Restaurants** Chi-Chi's, Casa Gallardo, El Torito, Charley Brown's & other restaurants	Kevin S Relyea	632*	—	–82*	25,400	Dec
313 ■	**Discount Tire Co** operates over 300 tire stores in 14 states	Bruce T Halle	632	40	22	4,714	Dec
314 231	**Homeland Stores** supermarkets in Oklahoma, Kansas & Texas Panhandle	James Demme	630	–2	–30	4,384	Dec
315 ■	**Six Flags** Six Flags Great Adventure & other theme parks	Larry D Bouts	630	150	5	25,000	Dec

1996 Ranking of the 500 Largest Private Companies (*Cont.*)

RANK '96 '95	Company business	Chief executive	Revenues ($mil)	PROFITS operating ($mil)	PROFITS net ($mil)	Employees	Fiscal year-end
316 317	**Washington Cos** Montana rail services, mines copper, machinery & construction	Dennis Washington	628e	176e	38e	3,000	Dec
317 332	**Boler** manufactures axle suspensions, truck bumpers, leaf springs	John Boler	625e	63e	30e	3,000	Dec
318 320	**Feld Entertainment** Ringling Brothers and Barnum & Bailey Circus & other live entertainment acts	Kenneth Feld	625e	88e	31e	2,500	Dec
319 283	**Huber Hunt & Nichols** general contractor & construction manager of office buildings & sports arenas	Robert C Hunt	625	15	4	500	June
320 316	**Mark III Industries** converts vans & pickups	Larry W Lincoln	625e	31e	9e	900	June
321 279	**Sverdrup** engineering, architecture, construction, technical svcs; real estate development	Richard E Beumer	625	22e	9e	5,000	Dec
322 353	**Faulkner Organization** auto dealerships	Henry Faulkner III	623	17e	9e	1,100	Dec
323 321	**Olan Mills** portrait photography studios	Robert McDowell	620e	87e	25e	14,000	Sept
324 331	**County Seat Stores** specialty apparel stores	Gil Osnos	619	35	–97	7,714	Jan
325 348	**CMI International** manufactures automotive engine & suspension components	Ray H Witt	618	62e	29e	4,330	May
326 ■	**Conair** hair dryers & other consumer appliances; personal care products	Leandro P Rizzuto	614	50	23	3,431	Dec
327 406	**Kinray** distributes pharmaceuticals, health & beauty aids & medical equipment	Stewart Rahr	610	9	4	250	June
328 429	**Austin Industries** heavy, commercial & industrial construction; construction management	William T Solomon	608	27e	7e	5,000	Dec

Internet firms go public, biotech firms go public, but iron and steel firms just don't have the sex appeal. Our list includes 14 metal companies, including Grede Foundries in Wisconsin and Metallurg in New York.

RANK '96 '95	Company business	Chief executive	Revenues ($mil)	PROFITS operating ($mil)	PROFITS net ($mil)	Employees	Fiscal year-end
329 342	**TTC Illinois** temporary employment agency for financial & technical workers	Michael McCafferty	606	9	1	23,720	Dec

■ Not on last year's list.   ✳ Went private via leveraged buyout since 1991.   e: Estimate.   ✳Pro forma figures.

(Continued)

1996 Ranking of the 500 Largest Private Companies (*Cont.*)

RANK '96 '95	Company business	Chief executive	Revenues ($mil)	PROFITS operating ($mil)	net ($mil)	Employees	Fiscal year-end
330 322	**Rayovac** disposable & rechargeable batteries, battery-operated products; flashlights	David Jones	605	76e	30e	2,400	June
331 352	**Genuardi Family Markets** supermarkets in Pennsylvania	Charles A Genuardi	605	22e	9e	4,200	Mar
332 207	**McCrory** variety & discount stores	Meshulam Riklis	604	–55	–80	8,900	Jan
333 415	**Metallurg**[1] mines, manufactures & trades ferrous & nonferrous metals & alloys	Michael A Standen	602	31	16	1,259	Dec
334 338	**Brylane** mail order catalogs for Lane Bryant, Roaman's & Lerner	Bob Pulciani	601	59	28	2,300	Jan
335 293	**＊Delco-Remy America** makes starters, generators & other auto & truck parts; remanufactures auto parts	Harold Sperlich	600	—	—	2,000	Aug
336 235	**Hunt Consolidated/Hunt Oil** develops, refines & explores for oil & gas	Ray L Hunt	600e	282e	34e	1,300	Dec
337 ■	**Russ Darrow Group** auto dealerships	Russell Darrow	598e	16e	8e	650	Dec
338 372	**Journal Communications** Milwaukee Journal Sentinel; broadcasting, printing, telecommunications	Robert A Kahlor	592	99	44	6,550	Dec
339 391	**Sheehy Automotive** auto dealerships	Vincent Sheehy	591	19	12	1,700	Dec
340 371	**Glazer's Wholesale Distributors** distributes wine & distilled beverages	Robert S Glazer	590e	21e	7e	1,050	Aug
341 344	**K&B** 185 drugstores in 6 southern states	Sydney J Besthoff III	585	20	11	4,500	Sept
342 226	**Wirtz** distributes liquor; real estate; Chicago Blackhawks & United Center in Chicago	William Wirtz	585e	53e	17e	1,800	June
343 383	**Ricart Automotive** auto dealerships	Rhett Ricart	582	16e	8e	1,100	Dec
344 345	**Tuttle-Click Automotive Group** auto dealerships, bank, insurance	James H Click[2]	582	18	11	1,500	Dec
345 368	**Greenwood Mills** fabrics, denim, textiles	William Mathews Self	580e	41e	15e	7,025	Dec
346 224	**Hartz Group** pet food & supplies; Village Voice newspaper; real estate	Leonard N Stern	580e	40e	—	2,600	Dec
347 340	**Steiner** makes linens & uniforms; cans food	Richard Steiner	580e	60e	$18e	9,100	June
348 356	**Tishman Realty & Construction** construction; real estate management	John Tishman	580	23e	6e	600	June

1996 Ranking of the 500 Largest Private Companies (*Cont.*)

RANK '96 '95	Company business	Chief executive	Revenues ($mil)	Profits operating ($mil)	Profits net ($mil)	Employees	Fiscal year-end
349 359	**Ben E Keith** distributes Anheuser-Busch beer; distributes food to hospitals, schools & restaurants	Robert Hallam	580	18e	6e	1,600	June
350 457	**Burt Automotive Network** auto dealerships & fleet sales	Lloyd G Chavez	576	12e	7e	790	Dec
351 351	**American Foods Group** runs slaughterhouses	Carl W Kuehne	575	20e	6e	1,800	June
352 378	**Intrepid** manufactures Trek bicycles; distributes flooring & electric products	Richard A Burke	575	70e	29e	2,300	Sept
353 403	**Santa Monica Ford** fleet sales & auto dealership	Robert Karlin[3]	572	17e	11e	100	Dec
354 485	**Inland Group** real estate brokerage, management & financing	Daniel L Goodwin	570	71e	13e	756	June
355 333	**Printpack** manufactures candy wrappers, snack food bags & other flexible packaging	Dennis M Love	570	46e	19e	2,330	June
356 250	**Transnational Motors** distributes Mazda automobiles & parts	Robert L Hooker	570e	9e	—	130	Feb
357 ■	**Hewitt Associates** employee benefits, compensation & human resources consulting firm	Dale Gifford	568	57e	28e	5,500	Sept
358 326	**LDI** distributes videocassettes, motorcycle & mountain bike parts & accessories	Andre Lacy	568	20e	—	1,300	Dec
359 382	**Mullinax Management** auto dealerships	Ed Mullinax	568e	15e	8e	500	Dec
360 ■	**Watkins Associated Industries** trucking; wholesales fresh seafood; real estate	William W Watkins	567e	46e	12e	6,179	Dec
361 502	**Technical Aid** temporary employment agency	Salvatore Balsamo	566	34e	17e	1,060	Sept
362 350	**Jim Koons Management** auto dealerships	James E Koons	564	—	—	1,070	Dec
363 358	**Benjamin Moore & Co** paints, stains, chemicals	Richard Roob	564	63	31	1,968	Dec
364 411	**Medline Industries** manufactures & distributes medical-surgical products & textiles	James S Mills	564	54	49	2,400	Dec
365 475	**Comark** distribs computers, software & peripherals under Comark & PC Wholesale banners	Chuck Wolande[4]	563	11	8	570	Dec
366 402	**SAS Institute** computer software & services	James H Goodnight	562	281e	84e	4,138	Dec

■ Not on last year's list.   ＊ Went private via leveraged buyout since 1991.   e: Estimate.   [1]In Chapter 11.   [2]Robert H. Tuttle is co-chief executive.   [3]L. Wayne Harding is co-chief executive.   [4]Philip E. Corcoran is co-chief executive.

(Continued)

1996 Ranking of the 500 Largest Private Companies (*Cont.*)

RANK '96 '95	Company business	Chief executive	Revenues ($mil)	PROFITS operating ($mil)	PROFITS net ($mil)	Employees	Fiscal year-end
367 346	**All-Phase Electric Supply** wholesales electrical equipment	Ken Renwick	560e	48e	11e	1,733	Feb
368 365	**Goya Foods** Hispanic foods	Joseph A Unanue	560e	82e	30e	2,000	Dec
369 437	**Walsh Group** construction manager, general contractor	Matthew M Walsh	560	15	9	1,500	Dec
370 370	**Fletcher Jones Management Group** auto dealerships	Fletcher Jones Jr	554	75	14	1,032	June
371 392	**Genmar Holdings** manufactures Hatteras & other brands of recreational boats	Irwin Jacobs	553	13	–9	5,200	Dec
372 354	**Horsehead Industries** processes zinc, calcined & petroleum coke products; environmental svcs	William E Flaherty	550	30	—	2,000	Dec
373 396	**OmniSource** processes & wholesales smelting products, ferrous & nonferrous scrap metal	Leonard Rifkin	550e	63e	22e	800	Sept
374 323	**S&P Co** Pabst, Falstaff & Pearl beers; real estate	Lutz Isslieb	550	38e	—	1,300	June
375 380	**Sansone Auto Network** auto dealerships	Paul Sansone	550e	15e	8e	545	Dec
376 417	**Townsend's** processes poultry; refines soybean oil	P Coleman Townsend Jr	550	17e	4e	4,500	May
377 309	**Builder Marts of America** wholesales building materials & lumber products	Brian S Mackenzie	547	19e	—	142	Dec
378 393	**MediaNews Group** newspapers	W Dean Singleton	545	80e	11e	7,000	Sept
379 361	**Moyer Packing** runs slaughterhouses	R Lee Delp	545	19e	6e	1,500	June
380 ■	**Shorenstein** real estate	Walter H Shorenstein	545	51e	9e	1,400	Dec
381 299	**Rickel Home Centers**[1] home improvement centers	Joseph Nusim	541	–8	–76	3,500	Dec
382 386	**Beverage America** bottles & distributes 7-Up, RC Cola, Canada Dry, Dr Pepper & other soft drinks	James WF Brooks	540e	48e	12e	2,800	Dec
383 449	**ACF Industries** manufactures, sells & leases railroad freight & tank cars; investments	Carl C Icahn	540e	222e	84e	2,400	Dec
384 327	**Elder-Beerman Stores**[1] El-Bee shoe stores & Elder-Beerman stores	Max Gutmann	540	4	–40	8,000	Jan
385 408	**Parsons Brinckerhoff** engineering & construction management	Thomas J O'Neill	538[2]	19[2]	12[2]	5,200	Oct
386 464	**Sullivan Communications** prints advertising inserts, comic books, Sunday comics	James T Sullivan	536	52	–29	2,893	Mar

1996 Ranking of the 500 Largest Private Companies (*Cont.*)

Rank '96 '95	Company business	Chief executive	Revenues ($mil)	Profits operating ($mil)	net ($mil)	Employees	Fiscal year-end
387 401	**Tasha** auto dealerships	Henry Torian	535	13	4	800	Dec
388 428	**Gilman Investment** manufactures multiwall paper bags; operates paper & pulp mills & linehaul railroad	Howard Gilman	529e	106e	37e	2,600	Dec
389 385	**Freedom Communications** owns 27 daily & 31 weekly newspapers; TV stations	James N Rosse	527e	137e	47e	6,800	Dec
390 325	**Pacific Holding** real estate, building materials, natural resources, textiles	David H Murdock	523e	—	—	2,400	Dec
391 416	**Fareway Stores** Fareway & Fastco Food Stores	F William Beckwith	520e	14e	6e	3,500	Mar

In the last 12 months 12 of last year's largest private companies had initial public offerings. Among them: Dominick's Finer Foods, Gulfstream Aerospace, Donna Karan International and Dal-Tile International.

Rank '96 '95	Company business	Chief executive	Revenues ($mil)	Profits operating ($mil)	net ($mil)	Employees	Fiscal year-end
392 ■	**Keywell** scrap metal	Jay Mark Lozier	520e	—	—	341	Dec
393 375	**NW Transport Service** motor carrier	Jerry McMorris	520e	—	—	6,560	Dec
394 395	**Ourisman Automotive Enterprises** auto dealerships, insurance	Mandell J Ourisman	520	17	14	926	Dec
395 398	**Les Schwab Tire Centers** tire stores	Philip Wick	520e	38e	14e	4,225	Dec
396 409	**Blue Bird** manufactures school buses	Paul E Glaske	517	55	17	2,428	Oct
397 448	**Arthur D Little** management consulting	Charles R LaMantia	514	77e	51e	3,039	Dec
398 427	**✱Reltec** telecommunications systems, equipment & services	Dudley Sheffler	514*	56*	–11*	3,800	Dec
399 373	**El Camino Resources** wholesales, retails & leases mainframe & midrange computer equip; tech support	David Harmon	510	13	7	473	Apr
400 425	**Harris Chemical Group** produces salt, soda products, boron chemicals & specialty fertilizers	D George Harris	509	110	–29	2,500	Mar

■ Not on last year's list.   e: Estimate.   *Pro forma figures.   [1]In Chapter 11.   [2]Company provided estimate for October 1996.

(Continued)

1996 Ranking of the 500 Largest Private Companies (*Cont.*)

RANK '96 '95	Company business	Chief executive	Revenues ($mil)	PROFITS operating ($mil)	net ($mil)	Employees	Fiscal year-end
401 418	**Jordan Industries** consumer & industrial products	John W Jordan II	507	61	–8	6,103	Dec
402 394	**Drug Guild Distributors** wholesales & distributes drugs & sundries	Joseph Churchman	505e	3e	–2e	310	July
403 330	**Lewis Homes Management** residential construction; develops real estate in California & Nevada	John M Goodman	503	37e	14e	850	Dec
404 467	**David McDavid Auto Dealerships** auto dealerships	David McDavid Sr	500	14e	7e	928	Dec
405 434	**Goodman Manufacturing** manufactures air-conditioning & heating equipment	Frank Murray	500e	58e	22e	1,700	Dec
406 ■	**GoodTimes Entertainment** produces, distributes & licenses videocassettes & software	Joe Cayre	500e	70e	35e	600	Dec
407 388	**Inserra Supermarkets** Shop Rite supermarkets in New Jersey & New York	Lawrence R Inserra	500e	13e	6e	2,300	Dec
408 399	**Johnson Brothers Wholesale Liquor** wholesales liquor	Lynn Johnson	500e	18e	6e	1,050	Dec
409 ■	**Landmark Communciations** publishing, programming, broadcasting, cable TV, Weather Channel, magazines	John O Wynne	500	108e	28e	4,500	Dec
410 413	**McWane** cast iron pipe, valves & fittings; water treatment equipment; coal production	John J McMahon Jr	500e	44e	17e	8,000	Dec
411 ■	**PNY Electronics** memory upgrades, semiconductors & related products	Gadi Cohen	500	45e	30e	230	Dec
412 407	**Rocco** Shady Brook Farms, Marval & Valley Chef poultry products	George W Pace	500	23e	5e	4,100	Dec
413 ■	**Rooney Brothers** construction, electronics, real estate, building materials	LF Rooney III	500	13	5	1,800	Sept
414 389	**Rosen's Diversified** runs slaughterhouses; distributes agrochemicals; develops agricultural software	Thomas J Rosen	500	15e	5e	900	Sept
415 ■	**Tube City** processes & brokers scrap metal & slag	Michael Coslov	500	57e	20e	375	Dec
416 ■	**Quill** distributes office supplies & computer products	Jack Miller	497e	34e	19e	1,063	Dec
417 453	**Darcars** auto dealerships	John Darvish	494	13e	7e	1,363	Dec
418 438	**Cowles Media** Star Tribune in Minneapolis; magazines, videos & other information services	David C Cox	493	70	24	3,411	Mar
419 ■	**Watson Wyatt Worldwide** human resources, pension & employee benefit consulting	Peter Smith	493[1]	47[1]	9[1]	4,980	June

1996 Ranking of the 500 Largest Private Companies (*Cont.*)

RANK '96 '95	Company business	Chief executive	Revenues ($mil)	PROFITS operating ($mil)	PROFITS net ($mil)	Employees	Fiscal year-end
420 ■	**Ris Paper** distributes paper & paper products	Mark Griffin	490	20e	13e	640	Dec
421 444	**Simmons** Beautyrest, Maxipedic, Beautysleep, BackCare & other mattresses & waterbeds	Zenon S Nie	490	40	9	2,600	Dec
422 491	**Turner Industries** maintains & constructs oil refineries, chemical & petrochemical plants	Bert Turner	486	24e	11e	10,000	Oct
423 490	**Maroone Automotive Group** auto dealerships	Michael E Maroone	485	12e	7e	700	Dec
424 405	**Williamson-Dickie Manufacturing** manufactures uniforms & work clothing	Philip Williamson	485	58e	22e	5,500	Dec
425 374	**Home Interiors & Gifts** wholesales decorative accessories	Donald J Carter	483	85	50	1,500	Dec
426 410	**Ukrop's Super Markets** 25 supermarkets in Virginia	James E Ukrop	483e	14e	5e	5,100	July
427 439	**Hitchcock Automotive Resources** auto dealerships	Fritz Hitchcock	478	7	4	550	Dec

John Richard Simplot made one fortune in potatoes (J.R. Simplot Co., a private company) and another smaller fortune in Micron Technology (public since 1984).

RANK '96 '95	Company business	Chief executive	Revenues ($mil)	PROFITS operating ($mil)	PROFITS net ($mil)	Employees	Fiscal year-end
428 ■	**Southern California Auto Group** auto dealerships	William J Adkins	477	13e	7e	743	Dec
429 404	**Bugle Boy Industries** casual pants, jeans, sportswear & related apparel for men, boys & women	William Mow	475	63e	21e	2,200	Apr
430 445	**Rand McNally** publishes maps; prints books, tickets & labels; produces & packages software	Andrew McNally IV	475e	35e	16e	3,800	Dec
431 ■	**Great Lakes Cheese** manufactures, processes & packages cheese	Hans Epprecht	473	20e	13e	830	Dec
432 318	**JPS Textile Group** carpet, elastics, apparel, industrial fabrics, building materials	Steven Friedman	473	42	–51	4,500	Oct
433 451	**CB Commercial Real Estate Group** commercial real estate, brokerage, property mgmt & mortgage banking svcs	James J Didion	470	43	7	4,000	Dec
434 450	**Copps** distributes & wholesales food	Michael W Copps	470e	14e	5e	3,058	Jan

■ Not on last year's list.   e: Estimate.   ¹U.S. Operations only.

(*Continued*)

1996 Ranking of the 500 Largest Private Companies (*Cont.*)

RANK '96 '95	Company business	Chief executive	Revenues ($mil)	PROFITS operating ($mil)	net ($mil)	Employees	Fiscal year-end
435 447	**Mason** disassembles weapons; nuclear weapons; researches & develops warheads	Richard M Loghry	470	56e	24e	5,000	Dec
436 414	**Progressive Tool & Industries** designs & installs robot-assisted welding & assembly tools	Anthony Wisne	470e	64e	29e	3,000	Nov
437 ■	**Montgomery Securities** investment banking, institutional brokerage	Thomas Weisel	467	110e	26e	982	Dec
438 441	**Sauder Woodworking** ready-to-assemble furniture; church furniture	Maynard Sauder	467	46e	20e	3,200	Dec
439 452	**Darby Group Cos** dental, medical, veterinary & vitamin products	Michael Ashkin	465e	69e	35e	2,000	Dec
440 435	**Kraus-Anderson** general contracting, real estate, commercial insurance, entertainment centers	Lloyd Engelsma	465	6e	2e	900	Dec
441 ■	**Herb Chambers Cos** auto dealerships	Herbert G Chambers	461	13e	7e	703	Dec
442 ■	**Grede Foundries** iron & steel castings for automotive, farm & construction equipment	Bruce Jacobs	461	62e	18e	433	Dec
443 ■	**Brown & Brown Automotive Group** auto dealerships	Henry E Brown	460	11	9	860	Dec
444 426	**Copper & Brass Sales** distributes nonferrous metals	William Howenstein	460e	23e	—	940	Dec
445 488	**Earnhardt's Motor Cos** auto dealerships	Hal J Earnhardt III	460	12	7	995	Dec
446 ■	**Merit Behavioral Care** managed behavioral health care	Albert S Waxman	457	45	—	3,275	Sept
447 ■	**TIC** general contractor for power & petrochemical plants & other industrial facilities	Ron McKenzie	456	—	—	5,000	Dec
448 469	**Chronicle Publishing** publishes newspapers & books; broadcasting	John B Sias	455e	130e	40e	2,700	Dec
449 443	**Texas Petrochemicals** manufactures industrial organic chemicals	Bill Waycaster	454*	74*	−10*	350	May
450 472	**Coggin Automotive Group** auto dealerships, hotels, finance, real estate	Luther Coggin	453	75	14	935	Dec
451 498	**IPC** paper & plastic packaging for food & other products	George Bayly	452	63	−13	2,405	Dec
452 285	**Alberici** general contractor & construction manager for the auto, commercial & env inds	Robert F McCoole	451	18e	6e	1,500	Dec
453 481	**Phil Long Dealerships** auto dealerships	Jay Cimino	451	11	8	1,134	Dec

1996 Ranking of the 500 Largest Private Companies (*Cont.*)

Rank '96 '95	Company business	Chief executive	Revenues ($mil)	Profits operating ($mil)	net ($mil)	Employees	Fiscal year-end
454 ■	**Apcoa** manages & develops parking lots	G Walter Stuelpe Jr	450	49e	25e	4,000	Dec
455 484	**Chief Auto Parts** retails & wholesales auto parts	David H Eisenberg	450	35	—	5,200	Dec
456 387	**Dick Corp** general, commercial & ind contracting; constructs airports, bridges & prisons	DE Dick	450	15	—	5,000	Dec
457 432	**Field Container** manufactures folding cartons; recycled paperboard; ink & specialty packaging	Larry Field	450*	72e*	27e*	2,200	Apr
458 433	**GFI America** runs slaughterhouses	Robert D Goldberger	450e	17e	7e	1,125	July
459 462	**Iams** premium dog & cat food	Clay Mathile	450e	90e	36e	1,100	Dec
460 458	**Krasdale Foods** wholesales food	Charles A Krasne	450	13e	4e	600	Dec
461 460	**Pacific Coast Building Products** roofing materials, wallboard, clay pipe, concrete prods; distribs bldg materials	David J Lucchetti	450	23e	9e	2,500	Apr
462 ■	**PC Richard & Son** appliance, home office & electronics stores	Gary H Richard	450	24e	11e	1,500	Jan
463 424	**Randall Stores** Randall Foods, Cub Foods, Super Valu & other supermarkets in the Midwest	Ronald F Randall	450e	15e	5e	3,449	Oct
464 463	**LaRoche Industries** organic & inorganic chemicals	Grant Reed	449	61	19	884	Feb
465 421	**American Restaurant Group** Black Angus, Grandy's & other restaurants	Anwar S Soliman	446	11	–40	14,400	Dec
466 436	**PrimeSource** fabricates metal; distributes building materials	Paul Hylbert[1]	446	25e	11e	865	Dec
467 442	**Webb Automotive Group** auto dealerships	Lewis M Webb	446	12	6	716	Dec
468 455	**National Wine & Spirits** distributes wine & spirits in the Midwest	James LaCrosse	443	15	4e	1,200	Mar
469 ■	**McCoy's Building Supply Centers** building supply stores in Texas & nearby states	Michael McCoy[2]	441	29e	12e	1,700	Dec
470 446	**Jockey International** manufactures underwear & loungewear	Donna W Steigerwaldt	440e	44e	11e	4,500	Dec
471 466	**Marathon Cheese** packages cheese for Kraft & other food companies	Ray Goldbach	440e	24e	7e	1,000	June

■ Not on last year's list.   e: Estimate.   *Pro forma figures.   [1]Marvin Miller is co-chief executive.   [2]Brian McCoy is co-chief executive.

(Continued)

1996 Ranking of the 500 Largest Private Companies (*Cont.*)

RANK '96 '95	Company business	Chief executive	Revenues ($mil)	PROFITS operating ($mil)	net ($mil)	Employees	Fiscal year-end
472 492	**United Co** coal mining, oil drilling, real estate, financial services	James W McGlothlin	437	95	45	1,059	Dec
473 473	**Nibco** plumbing valves, copper & plastic fittings, thermoplastic fluid-control prods	Rex Martin	434	41	24	3,257	Dec

Big money in candy wrappers and snack food bags? Sure. Atlanta, Ga.-based Printpack, controlled by the Love family, does $570 million a year in this obscure specialty.

RANK '96 '95	Company business	Chief executive	Revenues ($mil)	PROFITS operating ($mil)	net ($mil)	Employees	Fiscal year-end
474 495	**Galpin Motors** auto dealerships	Herbert F Boeckmann II	434	15	12	671	Dec
475 412	**Furman Lumber** distributes lumber & building materials	Barry Kronick	434	5	—	327	Feb
476 390	**Wherehouse Entertainment**[1] audio, video & multimedia software stores in 6 western states	Jerry Goldress	433	36	–44	7,100	Jan
477 ■	**Montgomery Watson** environmental engineering, site design, construction & maintenance	Murli Tolaney	433	20	6	3,500	Sept
478 456	**Morris Communications** newspapers, magazines, outdoor advertising	William S Morris III	432e	95e	19e	5,100	Dec
479 471	**Toresco Enterprises** Autoland of New Jersey & other auto dealerships	Donald Toresco	430	12e	6e	782	Dec
480 461	**Titan Industrial** markets steel	Michael S Levin	428	24e	9e	175	Dec
481 454	**David Weekley Homes** builds semicustom homes in Texas, Colorado, Florida & North Carolina	David Weekley	427	26e	15e	600	Dec
482 422	**Pepper Cos** general contractor & construction manager in over 40 states	J Stanley Pepper	426	5	6	1,260	Sept
483 ■	**Coca-Cola Bottling Co United** bottles Coca-Cola	Claude B Nielsen	425	38	9	2,500	Dec
484 ■	**Sterling McCall Group** auto dealerships	Sterling B McCall	425e	12e	6e	385	Dec
485 493	**Southern Foods Group** processes milk & manufactures other dairy products	Peter Schenkel	425e	25e	10e	2,200	Mar
486 430	**Fred W Albrecht Grocery** Acme Stores, Acme Super Centers, Y-Mart stores	F Steven Albrecht	424e	6e	1e	2,419	Dec
487 496	**Braman Enterprises** auto dealerships	Norman Braman	423	11e	6e	750	Dec

1996 Ranking of the 500 Largest Private Companies (*Cont.*)

Rank '96 '95	Company business	Chief executive	Revenues ($mil)	Profits operating ($mil)	Profits net ($mil)	Employees	Fiscal year-end
488 480	**Bissell** carpet sweepers, vacuum cleaners, floor & rug shampooers	Mark Bissell	420e	31e	14e	2,450	Dec
489 500	**Haggen** Haggen Foods & Top Food & Drug stores in Washington	Donald Haggen	420	8e	—	2,600	Dec
490 251	**Oxbow** composite pipes, fossil fuels, geothermal energy, real estate	William I Koch	420e	100e	41e	900	Dec
491 ■	**Sundt** construction & construction management services	H Wilson Sundt	417	14e	6e	4,000	Sept

When Charles Kettering was running Dayton Engineering Laboratories, it was private. General Motors bought the business in 1918. Now it's private again, under the name Delco Remy America.

Rank '96 '95	Company business	Chief executive	Revenues ($mil)	Profits operating ($mil)	Profits net ($mil)	Employees	Fiscal year-end
492 ■	**Swope Automotive Group** auto dealerships	Samuel G Swope	416	11e	3	967	Dec
493 ■	**Fortunoff** department stores specializing in fine jewelry & home furnishings	Alan Fortunoff	415e	35e	15e	2,500	July
494 476	**General Automotive** manufactures buses	Cruse W Moss	415e	—	—	2,200	June
495 ■	**Swinerton** construction	David H Grubb	412	11e	5e	1,000	Dec
496 ■	**Pacifico Group** auto dealerships, fleet sales	Kerry T Pacifico	411	11e	6e	370	Dec
497 ■	**Longaberger** handcrafted baskets, pottery & other home decor products	Dave Longaberger	410	44e	24e	5,026	Dec
498 ■	**Maidenform Worldwide** manufactures & markets women's intimate apparel	Elizabeth J Coleman	410	39e	13e	9,000	Dec
499 ■	**Houchens Industries** Houchens & Save-A-Lot supermarkets	Jim Gipson	409e	5e	–1e	3,100	Sept
500 501	**Shapell Industries** develops land & builds luxury homes in California	Nathan Shapell	408e	25e	8e	300	Dec

■ Not on last year's list.   e: Estimate.   ¹In Chapter 11.

ADDRESSES

Company	Rank
A-Mark Financial	175
100 Wilshire Boulevard, 3rd Floor	
Santa Monica, CA 90401	
310-319-0200	
ABC Supply	250
One ABC Parkway	
Beloit, WI 53511	
608-362-7777	
ACF Industries	383
620 North Second Street	
St Charles, MO 63301	
314-940-5000	
Advance Publications	25
950 Fingerboard Road	
Staten Island, NY 10305	
718-981-1234	
Alamo Rent-A-Car	106
110 South East Sixth Street	
Fort Lauderdale, FL 33301	
954-522-0000	

Company	Rank
Alberici	452
2150 Kienlen Avenue	
St Louis, MO 63121	
314-261-2611	
Fred W Albrecht Grocery	486
2700 Gilchrist Road	
Akron, OH 44305	
330-733-2861	
Alex Lee	117
PO Box 800	
Hickory, NC 28603	
704-323-4424	
All-Phase Electric Supply	367
3401 South Lakeshore Drive	
St Joseph, MI 49085	
616-926-6194	
Alliant Foodservice (1995)	30
PO Box 324	
Deerfield, IL 60015	
847-405-8500	

Company	Rank
American Axle & Manufacturing (1994) 1840 Holbrook Avenue Detroit, MI 48212 313-974-2000	64
American Foods Group 544 Acme Street Green Bay, WI 54302 414-437-6330	351
American Restaurant Group 450 Newport Center Drive, Suite 600 Newport Beach, CA 92660 714-721-8000	465
Amkor Electronics 1345 Enterprise Drive West Chester, PA 19380 610-431-9600	249
Amsted Industries 205 N Michigan Avenue, Blvd Towers South Chicago, IL 60601 312-645-1700	145
Amway 7575 Fulton Street East Ada, MI 49355 616-787-6000	24
Anderson Corp 100 Fourth Avenue North Bayport, MN 55003 612-439-5150	134
Andersen Worldwide 1345 Avenue of the Americas New York, NY 10105 212-708-4000	8

Company	Rank
Apcoa 800 Superior Avenue Cleveland, OH 44124 216-522-0700	454
Aramark Aramark Tower, 1101 Market Street Philadelphia, PA 19107 215-238-3000	19
Asplundh Tree Expert 708 Blair Mill Road Willow Grove, PA 19090 215-784-4200	219
Austin Industries PO Box 1590 Dallas, TX 75221 214-443-5500	328
Avondale PO Box 1109 Monroe, GA 30655 770-267-2226	169
Baker & McKenzie 130 East Randolph Street Chicago, IL 60601 312-861-8800	302
Baker & Taylor (1992) 2709 Water Ridge Parkway, Suite 500 Charlotte, NC 28217 704-357-3500	254
Bartlett and Co 4800 Main Street, Suite 600 Kansas City, MO 64112 816-753-6300	230

Company	Rank
Barton Malow	292
27777 Franklin Road, Suite 800	
Southfield, MI 48034	
810-351-4500	
Bashas'	287
PO Box 488	
Chandler, AZ 85244	
602-895-9350	
Battelle Memorial Institute	190
505 King Avenue	
Columbus, OH 43201	
800-201-2011	
BE&K	234
2000 International Park Drive	
Birmingham, AL 35243	
205-969-3600	
LL Bean	162
Casco Street	
Freeport, ME 04033	
207-865-4761	
Beaulieu of America	221
PO Box 1248	
Dalton, GA 30722	
706-278-6666	
Bechtel Group	10
PO Box 193965	
San Francisco, CA 94119	
415-768-1234	
BeefAmerica	154
14748 West Center Road, Suite 201	
Omaha, NE 68144	
402-330-1899	

Company	Rank
Belk Stores Services	83
2801 West Tyvola Road	
Charlotte, NC 28217	
704-357-1836	
Berwind	272
3000 Centre Square West	
1500 Market Street	
Philadelphia, PA 19102	
215-563-2800	
Beverage America	382
545 East 32nd Street	
Holland, MI 49423	
616-396-1281	
Big V Supermarkets	248
176 North Main Street	
Florida, NY 10921	
914-651-4411	
Big Y Foods	241
280 Chestnut Street, PO Box 7840	
Springfield, MA 01102	
413-784-0600	
Bissell	488
2345 Walker Road, NW	
Grand Rapids, MI 49504	
616-453-4451	
Black & Veatch	152
8400 Ward Parkway	
Kansas City, MO 64114	
913-339-2000	
Bloomberg Financial Markets	223
499 Park Avenue	
New York, NY 10022	
212-318-2000	

Company	Rank
Blue Bird	396

3920 Arkwright Road
Macon, GA 31210
912-757-7100

Boler	317

500 Park Boulevard
Itasca, IL 60143
708-773-9111

Booz, Allen & Hamilton	155

8283 Greensboro Drive
McLean, VA 22102
703-902-5000

Borden (1995)	22

180 East Broad Street
Columbus, OH 43215
614-225-4000

Boscov's Department Stores	243

4500 Perkiomen Avenue
Reading, PA 19606
610-779-2000

Bose	277

The Mountain
Framingham, MA 01701
508-879-7330

Braman Enterprises	487

One South East Third Avenue, Suite 2130
Miami, FL 33131
305-358-1889

Brookshire Grocery	124

PO Box 1411
Tyler, TX 75710
903-534-3000

Company	Rank
Brown & Brown Automotive Group	443

PO Box 1059
Mesa, AZ 85211
602-833-3456

Brylane	334

463 Seventh Avenue
New York, NY 10018
212-613-9500

Budget Rent a Car	149

4225 Naperville Road
Lisle, IL 60532
708-955-1900

Bugle Boy Industries	429

2900 Madera Road
Simi Valley, CA 93065
805-582-1010

Builder Marts of America	377

PO Box 47
Greenville, SC 29602
864-297-6101

Leo Burnett	235

35 West Wacker Drive
Chicago, IL 60601
312-220-5959

Burt Automotive Network	350

5200 South Broadway
Englewood, CO 80110
303-761-0333

C&S Wholesale Grocers	36

Old Ferry Road
Brattleboro, VT 05301
802-257-4371

Company	Rank
Cargill	1
PO Box 9300	
Minneapolis, MN 55440	
612-742-6000	
Carlson Cos	87
Carlson Parkway, PO Box 59159	
Minneapolis, MN 55459	
612-540-5000	
Carpenter	260
PO Box 27205	
Richmond, VA 23261	
804-359-0800	
CB Commercial Real Estate Group	433
533 South Fremont Avenue	
Los Angeles, CA 90071	
213-613-3501	
CH2M Hill Companies Ltd	237
6060 South Willow Drive	
Greenwood Village, CO 80111	
303-771-0900	
Herb Chambers Cos	441
259 McGrath Highway	
Somerville, MA 02145	
617-666-8333	
Charmer Industries	306
1950 48th Street	
Long Island City, NY 11105	
718-726-2500	
Chemcentral	224
7050 West 71st Street	
Bedford Park, IL 60638	
708-594-7000	

Company	Rank
Chief Auto Parts	455
5400 LBJ Freeway, Suite 200	
Dallas, TX 75240	
972-404-1114	
Chronicle Publishing	448
901 Mission Street	
San Francisco, CA 94103	
415-777-1111	
Clark Enterprises	99
7500 Old Georgetown Road	
Bethesda, MD 20814	
301-657-7100	
Club Corporation International	264
3030 LBJ Freeway, Suite 700	
Dallas, TX 75234	
214-243-6191	
CMI International	325
30333 Southfield Road	
Southfield, MI 48076	
810-642-9450	
Coca-Cola Bottling Co of Chicago	214
7400 North Oak Park Avenue	
Niles, IL 60714	
312-775-0900	
Coca-Cola Bottling Co United	483
4600 East Lake Boulevard	
Birmingham, AL 35217	
205-841-2653	
Coggin Automotive Group	450
PO Box 16469	
Jacksonville, FL 32245	
904-730-2464	

Company	Rank
Comark	365
444 Scott Drive	
Bloomingdale, IL 60108	
708-924-6700	
Conair	326
150 Milford Road	
East Windsor, NJ 08520	
609-426-1300	
Connell	135
45 Cardinal Drive	
Westfield, NJ 07090	
908-233-0700	
Connell Limited Partnership	130
One International Place, Fort Hill Square	
Boston, MA 02110	
617-737-2700	
Consolidated Electrical Distributors	91
31356 Via Colinas	
Westlake Village, CA 91362	
818-991-9000	
Continental Cablevision	102
The Pilot House, Lewis Wharf	
Boston, MA 02110	
617-742-9500	
Continental Grain	4
277 Park Avenue	
New York, NY 10172	
212-207-5100	
Coopers & Lybrand	15
1251 Avenue of the Americas	
New York, NY 10020	
212-536-2000	

Company	Rank
Copper & Brass Sales	444
17401 Ten Mile Road	
Eastpointe, MI 48021	
810-775-7710	
Copps	434
2828 Wayne Street	
Stevens Point, WI 54481	
715-344-5900	
Core-Mark International	61
395 Oyster Point Boulevard, Suite 415	
South San Francisco, CA 94080	
415-589-9445	
Coulter	267
PO Box 169015	
Miami, FL 33116	
305-380-3800	
County Seat Stores	324
17950 Preston Road, Suite 1000	
Dallas, TX 75252	
214-248-5100	
Cowles Media	418
329 Portland Avenue	
Minneapolis, MN 55415	
612-673-7100	
Cox Enterprises	33
PO Box 105357	
Atlanta, GA 30348	
404-843-5123	
Crawford Fitting	176
29500 Solon Road	
Solon, OH 44139	
216-248-4600	

Company	Rank
Crowley Maritime	156
155 Grand Avenue	
Oakland, CA 94612	
510-251-7500	
Crown Equipment	276
40 South Washington Street	
New Bremen, OH 45869	
419-629-2311	
Cumberland Farms	160
777 Dedham Street	
Canton, MA 02021	
617-828-4900	
D'Arcy Masius Benton & Bowles	303
1675 Broadway	
New York, NY 10019	
212-468-3622	
Darby Group Cos	439
865 Merrick Avenue	
Westbury, NY 11590	
516-683-1800	
Darcars	417
PO Box 9126	
Silent Spring, MD 20916	
301-622-0300	
Russ Darrow Group	337
4524 Dollar Drive	
West Bend, WI 53095	
414-629-5531	
Dart Container	177
500 Hogsback Road	
Mason, MI 48854	
517-676-3800	
David Weekley Homes	481
1300 Post Oak Boulevard, Suite 1000	
Houston, TX 77056	
713-963-0500	

Company	Rank
Day & Zimmermann	233
1818 Market Street	
Philadelphia, PA 19103	
215-299-8000	
DeBruce Grain	286
2702 Rock Creek Parkway, Suite 400	
Kansas City, MO 64117	
816-421-8182	
Del Monte Foods	95
PO Box 193575	
San Francisco, CA 94119	
415-247-3000	
Delaware North Cos	256
1 Delaware North Place, 438 Main Street	
Buffalo, NY 14202	
716-858-5000	
Delco-Remy America (1994)	335
2902 Enterprise Drive	
Anderson, IN 46013	
317-778-6499	
Deloitte Touche Tohmatsu International	17
Ten Westport Road	
Wilton, CT 06897	
203-761-3000	
DeMoulas Super Markets	90
875 East Street	
Tewksbury, MA 01876	
508-851-8000	
Deseret Management	278
60 East South Temple, Suite 575	
Salt Lake City, UT 84111	
801-538-0651	

Company	Rank
DHL Airways	194
333 Twin Dolphin Drive	
Redwood City, CA 94065	
415-593-7474	
Dick Corp	456
PO Box 10896	
Pittsburgh, PA 15236	
412-384-1000	
DiGiorgio	173
380 Middlesex Avenue	
Carteret, NJ 07008	
908-541-5555	
Dillingham Construction	164
5960 Inglewood Drive	
Pleasanton, CA 94588	
510-463-3300	
Discount Tire	313
1463 North Scottsdale Road	
Scottsdale, AZ 85254	
602-951-1938	
Dobbs Brothers Management	200
5170 Sanderlin Avenue, Suite 102	
Memphis, TN 38117	
901-685-8881	
Domino's Pizza	229
PO Box 997	
Ann Arbor, MI 48106	
313-930-3030	
Drug Guild Distributors	402
350 Meadowlands Parkway	
Secaucus, NJ 07096	
201-348-3700	
Drummond	268
PO Box 10246	
Birmingham, AL 35202	
205-387-0501	

Company	Rank
Duchossois Industries	126
845 Larch Avenue	
Elmhurst, IL 60126	
708-279-3600	
Dunavant Enterprises	68
PO Box 443	
Memphis, TN 38101	
901-369-1500	
DynCorp	204
2000 Edmund Halley Drive	
Reston, VA 22091	
703-264-0330	
Earnhardt's Motor Cos	445
1301 North Arizona Avenue	
Gilbert, AZ 85233	
602-926-4000	
Ebsco Industries	203
PO Box 1943	
Birmingham, AL 35201	
205-991-6600	
Eby-Brown	96
280 Shuman Boulevard, Suite 280	
Naperville, IL 60563	
708-778-2800	
84 Lumber	127
PO Box 8484	
Eighty Four, PA 15384	
412-228-8820	
El Camino Resources	399
21051 Warner Center Lane	
Woodland Hills, CA 91364	
818-226-6600	
Elder-Beerman Stores	384
3155 El-Bee Road	
Dayton, OH 45439	
513-296-2700	

Company	Rank
Enterprise Products	167
PO Box 4324	
Houston, TX 77210	
713-880-6500	
Enterprise Rent-A-Car	37
600 Corporate Park Drive	
St Louis, MO 63105	
314-512-5000	
Entex Information Services	58
(1993)	
Six International Drive	
Rye Brook, NY 10573	
914-935-3600	
Ernst & Young	13
787 Seventh Avenue	
New York, NY 10019	
212-773-3000	
Essex Group	133
PO Box 1601	
Fort Wayne, IN 46801	
219-461-4000	
M Fabrikant & Sons	255
One Rockefeller Plaza	
New York, NY 10020	
212-757-0790	
Family Restaurants	312
18831 Von Karman Avenue	
Irvine, CA 92612	
714-757-7900	
Fareway Stores	391
PO Box 70	
Boone, IA 50036	
515-432-2623	

Company	Rank
Farm Fresh	211
7530 Tidewater Drive	
Norfolk, VA 23505	
804-480-6700	
Faulkner Organization	322
4437 Street Road	
Trevose, PA 19053	
215-364-3980	
Feld Entertainment	318
8607 Westwood Center Drive	
Vienna, VA 22182	
703-448-4000	
Fidelity Investments	29
82 Devonshire Street	
Boston, MA 02109	
617-570-7000	
Field Container	457
1500 Nicholas Boulevard	
Elk Grove Village, IL 60007	
708-437-1700	
Fiesta Mart	261
5235 Katy Freeway	
Houston, TX 77007	
713-869-5060	
Flint Ink	215
25111 Glendale Avenue	
Detroit, MI 48239	
313-538-6800	
Flying J	122
PO Box 678	
Brigham City, UT 84302	
801-734-6400	

Company	Rank
Follett	**238**
2233 West Street	
River Grove, IL 60171	
708-583-2000	
Fortunoff	**493**
70 Charles Lindburgh Boulevard	
Uniondale, NY 11553	
516-832-9000	
Foster Farms	**231**
PO Box 457	
Livingston, CA 95334	
209-394-7901	
Frank Consolidated Enterprises	**136**
666 Garland Place	
Des Plaines, IL 60016	
847-699-7000	
Freedom Communications	**389**
PO Box 19549	
Irvine, CA 92623	
714-553-9292	
Furman Lumber	**475**
PO Box 130	
Nutting Lake, MA 01865	
508-670-3800	
GAF	**115**
1361 Alps Road	
Wayne, NJ 07470	
201-628-3000	
E&J Gallo Winery	**188**
PO Box 1130	
Modesto, CA 95353	
209-579-3111	
Galpin Motors	**474**
15505 Roscoe Boulevard	
North Hills, CA 91343	
818-787-3800	

Company	Rank
General Automotive	**494**
2015 Washtenaw Avenue	
Ann Arbor, MI 48104	
313-994-8000	
General Medical	**101**
8741 Landmark Road	
Richmond, VA 23228	
804-264-7500	
General Parts	**289**
PO Box 26006	
Raleigh, NC 27611	
919-876-6171	
Genmar Holdings	**371**
100 South Fifth Street, Suite 2400	
Minneapolis, MN 55402	
612-339-7900	
Genuardi Family Markets	**331**
805 East Germantown Pike	
Norristown, PA 19401	
610-277-6000	
Georgia Crown Distributing	**299**
PO Box 7908	
Columbus, GA 31908	
706-568-4580	
GFI America	**458**
2815 Blaisdell Avenue, South	
Minneapolis, MN 55408	
612-872-6262	
Giant Eagle	**55**
101 Kappa Drive	
Pittsburgh, PA 15238	
412-963-6200	
Gilbane Building	**110**
Seven Jackson Walkway	
Providence, RI 02940	
401-456-5800	

Company	Rank
Gilman Investment	**388**
111 West 50th Street	
New York, NY 10020	
212-246-3300	
Glazer's Wholesale Distributors	**340**
14860 Landmark Boulevard	
Dallas, TX 75240	
214-702-0900	
Global Petroleum	**50**
800 South Street	
Waltham, MA 02254	
617-894-8800	
Golden State Foods	**111**
18301 Von Karman Avenue, Suite 1100	
Irvine, CA 92612	
714-252-2000	
Goldman Sachs Group	**5**
85 Broad Street	
New York, NY 10004	
212-902-1000	
Golub	**108**
501 Duanesburg Road	
Schenectady, NY 12306	
518-355-5000	
Goodman Manufacturing	**405**
1501 Seamist Drive	
Houston, TX 77008	
713-861-2500	
GoodTimes Entertainment	**406**
16 East 40th Street	
New York, NY 10016	
212-951-3000	
Gordon Food Service	**105**
PO Box 1787	
Grand Rapids, MI 49501	
616-530-7000	

Company	Rank
WL Gore & Associates	**165**
555 Paper Mill Road	
Newark, DE 19711	
302-738-4880	
Gould Paper	**236**
315 Park Avenue South, 19th Floor	
New York, NY 10010	
212-505-1000	
Goya Foods	**368**
100 Seaview Drive	
Secaucus, NJ 07096	
201-348-4900	
Grant Thornton	**121**
801 Prudential Plaza, Suite 800	
Chicago, IL 60601	
312-856-0200	
Graybar Electric	**42**
PO Box 7231	
St Louis, MO 63177	
314-727-3900	
Great Dane Holdings	**119**
2016 North Pitcher Street	
Kalamazoo, MI 49007	
616-343-6121	
Great Lakes Cheese	**431**
PO Box 335	
Newbury, OH 44065	
216-564-7181	
Grede Foundries	**442**
9898 West Bluemond Road	
Milwaukee, WI 53226	
414-257-3600	
Green Bay Packaging	**304**
1700 North Webster Court	
Green Bay, WI 54302	
414-433-5111	

Company	Rank
Greenwood Mills	345
PO Box 1017	
Greenwood, SC 29648	
864-229-2571	
Grocers Supply Co	137
PO Box 14200	
Houston, TX 77221	
713-747-5000	
GS Industries (1993)	178
1901 Roxborough Road, Suite 200	
Charlotte, NC 28211	
704-366-6901	
GSC Enterprises	163
PO Box 638	
Sulphur Springs, TX 75483	
903-885-7621	
Guardian Industries	78
2300 Harmon Road	
Auburn Hills, MI 48326	
810-340-1800	
Gulf Oil	71
90 Everett Avenue	
Chelsea, MA 02150	
617-889-9000	
Gulf States Toyota	89
PO Box 40306	
Houston, TX 77240	
713-744-3300	
H Group Holding	218
200 West Madison Street, 39th Floor	
Chicago, IL 60606	
312-750-1234	
Haggen	489
PO Box 9704	
Bellingham, WA 98227	
360-733-8720	

Company	Rank
Hale-Halsell	274
PO Box 582898	
Tulsa, OK 74158	
918-835-4484	
Hallmark Cards	35
2501 McGee, PO Box 419580	
Kansas City, MO 64141	
816-274-5111	
Harris Chemical Group	400
399 Park Avenue, 32nd Floor	
New York, NY 10022	
212-207-6400	
Hartz Group	346
667 Madison Avenue	
New York, NY 10021	
212-308-3336	
Haworth	144
One Haworth Center	
Holland, MI 49423	
616-393-3000	
HE Butt Grocery	23
646 South Main Avenue	
San Antonio, TX 78204	
210-246-8000	
Bill Heard Enterprises	179
PO Box 6749	
Columbus, GA 31907	
706-323-1111	
Hearst	43
959 Eighth Avenue	
New York, NY 10019	
212-649-2000	
Helmsley Enterprises	76
230 Park Avenue	
New York, NY 10169	
212-679-3600	

Company	Rank
Hendrick Automotive Group PO Box 18649 Charlotte, NC 28218 704-568-5550	53
Hensel Phelps Construction 420 Sixth Avenue Greeley, CO 80631 970-352-6565	266
Hewitt Associates 100 Half Day Road Lincolnshire, IL 60069 847-295-5000	357
Hitchcock Automotive Resources PO Box 8610 City of Industry, CA 91748 818-839-8400	427
Hoffman Construction PO Box 1300 Portland, OR 97207 503-221-8811	185
Holiday Cos PO Box 1224 Minneapolis, MN 55440 612-830-8700	128
Holman Enterprises 7411 Maple Avenue Pennsauken, NJ 08109 609-663-5200	92
Home Interiors & Gifts 4550 Spring Valley Road Dallas, TX 75244 972-386-1000	425
Homeland Stores 2601 Northwest Expressway Oklahoma City, OK 73112 405-879-6600	314

Company	Rank
Honickman Affiliates 8275 Route 130 Pennsauken, NJ 08110 609-665-6200	189
Horsehead Industries 110 East 59th Street New York, NY 10022 212-527-3000	372
Houchens Industries PO Box 90009 Bowling Green, KY 42102 502-843-3252	499
Howmet 475 Steamboat Road Greenwich, CT 06830 203-661-4600	210
JM Huber 333 Thornall Street Edison, NJ 08818 908-549-8600	109
Huber Hunt & Nichols PO Box 128 Indianapolis, IN 46206 317-241-6301	319
Hughes Family Markets 14005 Live Oak Avenue Irwindale, CA 91706 818-856-6580	132
Hunt Consolidated/Hunt Oil 1445 Ross at Field, Fountain Place Dallas, TX 75202 214-978-8000	336
Huntsman 500 Huntsman Way Salt Lake City, UT 84108 801-532-5200	32

Company	Rank
Hy-Vee 5820 Westown Parkway West Des Moines, IA 50266 515-267-2800	39
Iams 7250 Poe Avenue Dayton, OH 45414 513-898-7387	459
ICC Industries 460 Park Avenue New York, NY 10022 212-521-1700	166
Icon Health & Fitness 1500 South 1000 West Logan, UT 84321 801-750-5000	259
IMG One Erieview Plaza, Suite 1300 Cleveland, OH 44114 216-522-1200	180
Inductotherm Industries Ten Indel Avenue Rancocas, NJ 08073 609-267-9000	291
Ingram Industries 4400 Harding Road Nashville, TN 37205 615-298-8200	7
Inland Group 2901 Butterfield Road Oak Brook, IL 60521 630-218-8000	354
Inserra Supermarkets 20 Ridge Road Mahwah, NJ 07430 201-529-5900	407

Company	Rank
International Data Group One Exeter Plaza, 15th Floor Boston, MA 02116 617-534-1200	97
Intrepid N14 W23833 Stone Ridge Drive Suite 250 Waukesha, WI 53188 414-523-3000	352
IPC 100 TriState Drive, Suite 200 Lincolnshire, IL 60069 847-945-9100	451
Irvine PO Box 6370 Newport Beach, CA 92658 714-720-2000	275
Island Lincoln-Mercury Group 1850 East Merritt Island Causeway Merritt Island, FL 32952 407-452-9220	271
J Crew 625 Avenue of the Americas New York, NY 10011 212-886-2500	262
Jasper PO Box 12404 Birmingham, AL 35202 205-942-9100	157
Jeld-Wen 3250 Lakeport Boulevard Klamath Falls, OR 97601 541-882-3451	225

Company	Rank
Jitney Jungle Stores of America	143
PO Box 3409	
Jackson, MS 39207	
601-965-8600	
JM Family Enterprises	27
100 Northwest 12th Avenue	
Deerfield Beach, FL 33442	
954-429-2000	
Jockey International	470
2300 60th Street	
Kenosha, WI 53140	
414-658-8111	
Johnson & Higgins	161
125 Broad Street	
New York, NY 10004	
212-574-7000	
Johnson Brothers Wholesale Liquor	408
2285 University Avenue West	
St Paul, MN 55114	
612-646-5977	
SC Johnson & Son	34
1525 Howe Street	
Racine, WI 53403	
414-260-2000	
Fletcher Jones Management Group	370
175 East Reno, Suite C-6	
Las Vegas, NV 89119	
702-739-9800	
Edward D. Jones & Co	270
201 Progress Parkway	
Maryland Heights, MO 63043	
314-515-2000	

Company	Rank
Jordan Group	52
609 East Jefferson Boulevard	
Mishawaka, IN 46545	
219-259-1981	
Jordan Industries	401
1751 Lake Cook Road, Suite 550	
Deerfield, IL 60015	
847-945-5591	
Earle M Jorgensen	172
3050 East Birch Street	
Brea, CA 92821	
714-579-8823	
Journal Communications	338
PO Box 661	
Milwaukee, WI 53201	
414-224-2000	
JPS Textile Group	432
555 North Pleasantburg Drive	
Suite 202	
Greenville, SC 29607	
864-239-3900	
K&B	341
K&B Plaza, Lee Circle	
New Orleans, LA 70130	
504-586-1234	
K-VA-T Food Stores	308
PO Box 769	
Grundy, VA 24614	
540-935-4587	
Ben E Keith	349
1805 Record Crossing	
Dallas, TX 75235	
214-634-1500	

Company	Rank
Keystone Foods	**79**
401 City Avenue, Suite 800	
Bala Cynwyd, PA 19004	
610-667-6700	
Keywell	**392**
11900 South Cottage Grove Avenue	
Chicago, IL 60628	
312-660-2060	
Peter Kiewit Sons'	**38**
1000 Kiewit Plaza	
Omaha, NE 68131	
402-342-2052	
King Kullen Grocery	**279**
1194 Prospect Avenue	
Westbury, NY 11590	
516-333-7100	
Kinray	**327**
152-35 Tenth Avenue	
Whitestone, NY 11357	
718-767-1234	
Klaussner Furniture Group	**273**
PO Box 220	
Asheboro, NC 27204	
910-625-6175	
Koch Industries	**2**
4111 East 37th Street North	
Wichita, KS 67220	
316-828-5500	
Kohler	**72**
444 Highland Drive	
Kohler, WI 53044	
414-457-4441	

Company	Rank
Jim Koons Management	**362**
2000 Chainbridge Road	
Vienna, VA 22182	
703-356-0400	
Perry H Koplik & Sons	**290**
505 Park Avenue	
New York, NY 10022	
212-752-2288	
KPMG Peat Marwick	**11**
65 East 55th Street, 36th Floor	
New York, NY 10022	
212-909-5000	
Krasdale Foods	**460**
65 West Red Oak Lane	
White Plains, NY 10604	
914-694-6400	
Kraus-Anderson	**440**
525 South Eighth Street	
Minneapolis, MN 55404	
612-332-7281	
Landmark Communications	**409**
150 West Brambleton Avenue	
Norfolk, VA 23510	
804-446-2000	
Lanoga	**251**
PO Box 97040	
Redmond, WA 98073	
206-883-4125	
LaRoche Industries	**464**
1100 Johnson Ferry Road, NE	
Atlanta, GA 30342	
404-851-0300	

Company	Rank
LDI 251 North Illinois Street Indianapolis, IN 46204 317-237-2251	358
Lefrak Organization 97-77 Queens Boulevard Rego Park, NY 11374 718-459-9021	98
Lennox International PO Box 799900 Dallas, TX 75379 972-497-5000	81
Leprino Foods 1830 West 38th Avenue Denver, CO 80211 303-480-2600	158
Levi Strauss & Co 1155 Battery Street San Francisco, CA 94111 415-544-6000	16
Lewis Homes Management PO Box 670 Upland, CA 91785 909-985-0971	403
Lincoln Property 500 North Akard, Suite 3300 Dallas, TX 75201 214-740-3300	148
Little Caesar Enterprises 2211 Woodward Avenue Detroit, MI 48201 313-983-6000	171
Arthur D Little 25 Acorn Park Cambridge, MA 02140 617-498-5000	397

Company	Rank
Phil Long Dealerships 1212 Motor City Drive Colorado Springs, CO 80906 719-575-7100	453
Long John Silver's PO Box 11988 Lexington, KY 40579 606-388-6000	311
Longaberger 95 Chestnut Street, PO Box 73 Dresden, OH 43821 614-754-5000	497
Lupient Automotive Group 750 Pennsylvania Avenue Golden Valley, MN 55426 612-544-6666	284
Lykes Bros PO Box 1690 Tampa, FL 33601 813-223-3981	192
MacAndrews & Forbes Holdings 35 East 62nd Street New York, NY 10021 212-688-9000	18
Maidenform Worldwide 90 Park Avenue New York, NY 10016 212-856-8900	498
Marathon Cheese PO Box 185 Marathon, WI 54448 715-443-2211	471
Maritz 1375 North Highway Drive Frenton, MO 63099 314-827-4000	147

Company	Rank
Mark III Industries	320

PO Box 1868
Ocala, FL 34478
352-732-5878

Marmon Group	20

225 West Washington Street
Chicago, IL 60606
312-372-9500

Maroone Automotive Group	423

8600 Pines Boulevard, PO Box 8480
Pembroke Pines, FL 33024
954-433-3303

Mars	6

6885 Elm Street
McLean, VA 22101
703-821-4900

Mary Kay Cosmetics	201

16251 North Dallas Parkway
Dallas, TX 75248
214-687-6300

Mason	435

2355 Harrodsburg Road
Lexington, KY 40504
606-223-2277

Don Massey Cadillac	247

40475 Ann Arbor Road
Plymouth, MI 48170
313-453-7500

MBM	84

PO Box 800
Rocky Mount, NC 27802
919-985-7200

Sterling McCall Group	484

9400 Southwest Freeway
Houston, TX 77074
713-270-3900

Company	Rank
McCarthy	240

1341 North Rock Hill Road
St Louis, MO 63124
314-968-3300

McCombs Enterprises	151

9000 Tesoro Drive, Suite 122
San Antonio, TX 78217
210-821-6523

McCoy's Building Supply Centers	469

PO Box 1028
San Marcos, TX 78667
512-353-5400

McCrory	332

667 Madison Avenue, 12th Floor
New York, NY 10021
212-735-9500

David McDavid Auto Dealerships	404

3600 West Airport Freeway
Irving, TX 75062
214-790-6000

McJunkin	293

PO Box 513
Charleston, WV 25322
304-348-5211

McKee Foods	263

PO Box 750
Collegedale, TN 37315
423-238-7111

McKinsey & Co	74

55 East 52nd Street
New York, NY 10022
212-446-7000

McWane	410

PO Box 43327
Birmingham, AL 35243
205-991-9888

Company	Rank
MediaNews Group 1560 Broadway, Suite 1450 Denver, CO 80202 303-837-0886	378
Medline Industries One Medline Place Mundelein, IL 60060 847-949-5500	364
Meijer 2929 Walker, NW Grand Rapids, MI 49544 616-453-6711	21
Menards 4777 Menard Drive Eau Claire, WI 54703 715-876-5911	44
Menasha PO Box 367 Neenah, WI 54957 414-751-1000	202
Merit Behavioral Care One Maynard Drive Park Ridge, NJ 07656 201-391-8700	446
Metallurg 27 East 39th Street New York, NY 10016 212-686-4010	333
Metromedia One Meadowlands Plaza East Rutherford, NJ 07073 201-531-8000	73
Micro Electronics PO Box 182323 Columbus, OH 43218 614-850-3000	280

Company	Rank
Mid-Atlantic Cars 10287 Lee Highway Fairfax, VA 22030 703-352-5555	65
Larry H Miller Group 5650 South State Street Murray, UT 84107 801-264-3100	197
Milliken & Co PO Box 1926 Spartanburg, SC 29304 864-503-2020	40
Minyard Food Stores PO Box 518 Coppell, TX 75019 214-393-8700	213
Montgomery Securities 600 Montgomery Street San Francisco, CA 94111 415-627-2000	437
Montgomery Ward & Co 535 West Chicago Avenue Chicago, IL 60671 312-467-2000	14
Montgomery Watson 300 North Lake Avenue, Suite 1200 Pasadena, CA 91101 818-796-9141	477
Benjamin Moore & Co 51 Chestnut Ridge Road Montvale, NJ 07645 201-573-9600	363
Moorman Manufacturing 1000 North 30th Street Quincy, IL 62301 217-222-7100	191

Company	Rank
Morris Communications PO Box 936 Augusta, GA 30903 706-724-0851	478
Ed Morse Automotive Group 6363 NW Sixth Way, Suite 400 Fort Lauderdale, FL 33309 954-351-0055	88
MA Mortenson PO Box 710 Minneapolis, MN 55440 612-522-2100	244
Moyer Packing PO Box 395 Souderton, PA 18964 215-723-5555	379
MTD Products PO Box 368022 Cleveland, OH 44136 330-225-2600	305
MTS 2500 Del Monte Street West Sacramento, CA 95691 916-373-2500	186
Mullinax Management PO Box 280 Amherst, OH 44001 216-984-2431	359
National Car Rental 7700 France Avenue South Minneapolis, MN 55435 612-830-2121	138
National Distributing One National Drive SW Atlanta, GA 30336 404-696-9440	212

Company	Rank
National Wine & Spirits PO Box 1602 Indianapolis, IN 46206 317-636-6092	468
Nesco 6140 Parkland Boulevard Mayfield Heights, OH 44124 216-461-6000	181
Neuman Distributors 175 Railroad Avenue Ridgefield, NJ 07657 201-941-2000	125
Newark Group 20 Jackson Drive Cranford, NJ 07016 908-276-4000	281
Nibco 1516 Middlebury Street Elkhart, IN 46515 219-295-3000	473
Nobody Beats the Wiz 1300 Federal Boulevard Carteret, NJ 07008 908-602-1900	139
North Pacific Lumber PO Box 3915 Portland, OR 97208 503-231-1166	174
NW Transport Service 717 17th Street, Suite 500 Denver, CO 80202 303-312-8000	393
Olan Mills PO Box 23456 Chattanooga, TN 37422 423-622-5141	323

Company	Rank
OmniSource 1610 North Calhoun Street Fort Wayne, IN 46808 219-422-5541	373
Oppenheimer Group Oppenheimer Tower World Financial Center New York, NY 10281 212-667-7000	198
Ormet 1233 Main Street, Suite 4000 Wheeling, WV 26003 304-234-3900	193
Ourisman Automotive Enterprises 4400 Branch Avenue Marlow Heights, MD 20748 301-423-4028	394
Oxbow 1601 Forum Place West Palm Beach, FL 33401 407-697-4300	490
Pacific Coast Building Products PO Box 160488 Sacramento, CA 95816 916-444-9304	461
Pacific Holding 10900 Wilshire Boulevard, 16th Floor Los Angeles, CA 90024 310-208-6055	390
Pacifico Group 6701 Essington Avenue Philadelphia, PA 19153 215-492-1700	496

Company	Rank
Packard Bell NEC One Packard Bell Way Sacramento, CA 95828 916-388-0101	12
Packerland Packing (1995) PO Box 23000 Green Bay, WI 54305 414-468-4000	307
RB Pamplin 900 SW Fifth Avenue, Suite 1800 Portland, OR 97204 503-248-1133	239
Charles Pankow Builders 2476 North Lake Avenue Altadena, CA 91001 213-684-2320	301
Parisian 750 Lakeshore Parkway Birmingham, AL 35211 205-940-4000	296
Parsons & Whittemore Four International Drive Rye Brook, NY 10573 914-937-9009	86
Parsons Brinckerhoff One Penn Plaza, 2nd Floor New York, NY 10119 212-465-5000	385
Parsons Corp 100 West Walnut Street Pasadena, CA 91124 818-440-2000	100
Pathmark Stores 301 Blair Road Woodbridge, NJ 07095 908-499-3000	31

Company	Rank
PC Richard & Son	462
150 Price Parkway	
Farmingdale, NY 11735	
516-843-4300	
Peerless Importers	309
16 Bridgewater Street	
Brooklyn, NY 11222	
718-383-5500	
Penske	47
13400 Outer Drive West	
Detroit, MI 48239	
313-592-5000	
Pepper Cos	482
643 North Orleans Street	
Chicago, IL 60610	
312-266-4703	
Perdue Farms	62
PO Box 1537	
Salisbury, MD 21802	
410-543-3000	
Pilot	131
PO Box 10146	
Knoxville, TN 37939	
423-588-7488	
PMC/SLIC	187
PO Box 1367	
Sun Valley, CA 91353	
818-896-1101	
PNY Electronics	411
200 Andersen Avenue	
Moonachie, NJ 07074	
201-438-6300	
Polo Ralph Lauren	206
650 Madison Avenue	
New York, NY 10022	
212-318-7000	

Company	Rank
Potamkin Cos	120
4675 SW 74th Street	
Miami, FL 33143	
305-665-9600	
Price Waterhouse	26
1177 Avenue of the Americas	
New York, NY 10036	
212-819-5000	
PrimeSource	466
1800 John Connally Drive	
Carrollton, TX 75006	
214-417-3748	
Printpack	355
4335 Wendell Drive SW	
Atlanta, GA 30336	
404-691-5830	
Progressive Tool & Industries	436
2100 Telegraph Road	
Southfield, MI 48034	
810-353-8888	
Prospect Motors	150
PO Box 1360	
Jackson, CA 95642	
209-223-1740	
Publix Super Markets	9
PO Box 407	
Lakeland, FL 33802	
941-688-1188	
Purina Mills (1993)	170
PO Box 66812	
St Louis, MO 63166	
314-768-4100	
Purity Wholesale Grocers	282
6413 Congress Avenue, Suite 250	
Boca Raton, FL 33487	
407-994-9360	

Company	Rank
Quad/Graphics Duplainville Road Pewaukee, WI 53072 414-246-9200	182
Quality King Distributors 2060 Ninth Avenue Ronkonkoma, NY 11779 516-737-5555	195
Queen Carpet PO Box 1527 Dalton, GA 30722 706-277-1900	269
QuikTrip PO Box 3475 Tulsa, OK 74101 918-836-8551	103
Quill 100 Schelter Road Lincolnshire, IL 60069 800-789-1331	416
RaceTrac Petroleum PO Box 105035 Atlanta, GA 30348 770-431-7600	168
Raley's 500 West Capitol Avenue West Sacramento, CA 95605 916-373-3333	69
Ralphs Grocery 1100 West Artesia Boulevard Compton, CA 92020 310-884-9000	28
Rand McNally 8255 North Central Park Avenue Skokie, IL 60076 847-329-8100	430

Company	Rank
Randall Stores PO Box 1200 Mitchell, SD 57301 605-996-7511	463
Randall's Food Markets 3663 Briar Park Houston, TX 77042 713-268-3500	49
Queen Carpet **Rayovac** PO Box 44960 Madison, WI 53744 608-275-3340	330
Red Apple Group 823 Eleventh Avenue New York, NY 10019 212-580-6805	57
Reltec (1995) 5875 Landerbrook Drive, Suite 250 Cleveland, OH 44124 216-460-3600	398
Renco Group 30 Rockefeller Plaza New York, NY 10112 212-541-6000	75
Restaurant Co One Pierce Place, Suite 100E Itasca, IL 60143 708-250-0471	209
Ricart Automotive PO Box 27130 Columbus, OH 43227 614-836-6265	343
Rich Products 1150 Niagara Street Buffalo, NY 14213 716-878-8000	159

Company	Rank
Rickel Home Centers	381
200 Helen Street	
South Plainfield, NJ 07080	
908-668-7000	
Ris Paper	420
7300 Turfway Road, Suite 540	
Florence, KY 41042	
606-746-8700	
Riverwood International (1996)	114
3350 Cumberland Circle, Suite 1400	
Atlanta, GA 30339	
770-644-3000	
CH Robinson	93
8100 Mitchell Road, Suite 200	
Eden Prairie, MN 55344	
612-937-8500	
Rocco	412
PO Box 549	
Harrisonburg, VA 22801	
540-568-1400	
Roll International	123
11444 West Olympic Boulevard	
10th floor	
Los Angeles, CA 90064	
310-442-5700	
Rooney Brothers	413
111 West Fifth Street, Suite 1000	
Tulsa, OK 74103	
918-583-6900	
Roseburg Forest Products	226
PO Box 1088	
Roseburg, OR 97470	
541-679-3311	
Rosen's Diversified	414
1120 Lake Avenue	
Fairmont, MN 56031	
507-238-4201	

Company	Rank
Rosenthal Cos	228
1550 Wilson Boulevard, Suite 700	
Arlington, VA 22209	
703-522-2300	
S&P Co	374
100 Shoreline Highway, Bldg B,	
Suite 395	
Mill Valley, CA 94941	
415-332-0550	
Sammons Enterprises	116
300 Crescent Court, Suite 700	
Dallas, TX 75201	
214-855-2800	
Sansone Auto Network	375
100 Route One	
Avenel, NJ 07001	
908-815-0500	
Santa Monica Ford	353
1230 Santa Monica Boulevard	
Santa Monica, CA 90404	
310-451-1588	
SAS Institute	366
SAS Campus Drive	
Cary, NC 27513	
919-677-8000	
Sauder Woodworking	438
502 Middle Street	
Archbold, OH 43502	
419-446-2711	
Save Mart Supermarkets	146
PO Box 4278	
Modesto, CA 95352	
209-577-1600	
Schneider National	82
PO Box 2545	
Green Bay, WI 54306	
414-592-5100	

Company	Rank
Schnuck Markets 11420 Lackland Road St Louis, MO 63146 314-994-9900	94
Schottenstein Stores 1800 Moler Road Columbus, OH 43207 614-221-9200	129
Schreiber Foods PO Box 19010 Green Bay, WI 54307 414-437-7601	112
Les Schwab Tire Centers PO Box 667 Prineville, OR 97754 541-447-4136	395
Schwan's Sales Enterprises 115 West College Drive Marshall, MN 56258 507-532-3274	51
Schwegmann Giant Super Markets PO Box 26099 New Orleans, LA 70186 504-947-9921	252
Science Applications International 10260 Campus Point Drive San Diego, CA 92121 619-546-6000	56
Scoular 2027 Dodge Street Omaha, NE 68102 402-342-3500	67

Company	Rank
Sealy 1228 Euclid Avenue, 10th Floor Cleveland, OH 44115 216-522-1310	300
Services Group of America 4025 Delridge Way SW, Suite 500 Seattle, WA 98106 206-933-5225	140
Shamrock Foods 2228 North Black Canyon Highway Phoenix, AZ 85009 602-272-6721	232
Shapell Industries 8383 Wilshire Boulevard, Suite 700 Beverly Hills, CA 90211 213-655-7330	500
Sheehy Automotive 12450 Fair Lakes Circle, Suite 380 Fairfax, VA 22033 703-802-3480	339
Sheetz 5700 Sixth Avenue Altoona, PA 16602 814-946-3611	253
Sherwood Food Distributors 18615 Sherwood Avenue Detroit, MI 48234 313-366-3100	257
Shorenstein 555 California Street, Suite 4900 San Francisco, CA 94104 415-772-7000	380

Company	Rank
Sierra Pacific Industries	196
PO Box 496028	
Redding, CA 96049	
916-378-8000	
Silgan	153
Four Landmark Square, Suite 400	
Stamford, CT 06901	
203-975-7110	
Simmons	421
One Concourse Parkway, Suite 600	
Atlanta, GA 30328	
770-512-7700	
JR Simplot	45
PO Box 27	
Boise, ID 83707	
208-336-2110	
Simpson Investment	85
1201 Third Avenue, Suite 4900	
Seattle, WA 98101	
206-224-5000	
Sinclair Oil	107
PO Box 30825	
Salt Lake City, UT 84130	
801-524-2700	
Six Flags	315
400 Interpace Parkway, Building C	
Parsippany, NJ 07054	
201-402-8100	
Skadden, Arps, Slate, Meagher & Flom	310
919 Third Avenue	
New York, NY 10022	
212-735-3000	

Company	Rank
Southern California Auto Group	428
3233 Pacific Coast Highway	
Torrance, CA 90505	
310-370-7401	
Southern Foods Group	485
PO Box 279000	
Dallas, TX 75227	
214-824-8163	
Southern Wine & Spirits	60
1600 NW 163rd Street	
Miami, FL 33169	
305-625-4171	
Southwire	70
PO Box 1000	
Carrollton, GA 30119	
770-832-4242	
Spalding & Evenflo (1995)	285
PO Box 30101	
Tampa, FL 33630	
813-204-5200	
Specialty Foods (1993)	66
9399 West Higgins Road, Suite 800	
Rosemond, IL 60018	
847-685-1000	
Specialty Retailers	288
10201 Main Street	
Houston, TX 77025	
713-667-5601	
Stater Bros Markets	80
21700 Barton Road	
Colton, CA 92324	
909-783-5100	

Company	Rank
Steelcase	46
PO Box 1967	
Grand Rapids, MI 49501	
616-247-2710	
Steiner	347
505 East South Temple	
Salt Lake City, UT 84102	
801-328-8831	
Stevedoring Services of America	283
3415 Eleventh Avenue SW	
Seattle, WA 98134	
206-623-0304	
Stroh Brewery	113
100 River Place	
Detroit, MI 48207	
313-446-2000	
Sullivan Communications	386
100 Winners Circle	
Brentwood, TN 37027	
615-377-0377	
Sunbelt Beverage	294
2330 West Joppa Road	
Lutherville, MD 21093	
410-832-7740	
Sundt	491
4101 East Irvington Road	
Tucson, AZ 85714	
520-748-7555	
Sutherland Lumber	199
4000 Main Street	
Kansas City, MO 64111	
816-756-3000	

Company	Rank
Sverdrup	321
13723 Riverport Drive	
Maryland Heights, MO 63043	
314-436-7600	
Sweetheart Holdings	207
10100 Reisterstown Road	
Owings Mills, MD 21117	
410-363-1111	
Swinerton	495
580 California Street	
San Francisco, CA 94104	
415-421-2980	
Swope Automotive Group	492
10 Swope Auto Center	
Louisville, KY 40299	
502-499-5000	
TAD Resources International	141
639 Massachusetts Avenue	
Cambridge, MA 02139	
617-868-1650	
Tang Industries	118
3773 Howard Hughes Parkway	
Las Vegas, NV 89109	
702-734-3700	
Tasha	387
43285 Auto Mall Circle	
Fremont, CA 94538	
510-252-5050	
Taylor	258
1725 Roe Crest Drive	
North Mankato, MN 56003	
507-625-2828	

Company	Rank
Technical Aid 109 Oak Street Newton, MA 02164 617-969-5100	361
Texas Petrochemicals 8707 Katy Freeway, Suite 300 Houston, TX 77024 713-477-9211	449
Charlie Thomas Dealerships PO Box 34566 Houston, TX 77234 713-948-5700	245
TIC PO Box 774848 Steamboat Springs, CO 80477 970-879-2561	447
Tishman Realty & Construction 666 Fifth Avenue New York, NY 10103 212-399-3600	348
Titan Industrial 555 Madison Avenue, 10th Floor New York, NY 10022 212-421-6700	480
TLC Beatrice International Holdings Nine West 57th Street, 39th Floor New York, NY 10019 212-756-8900	63
Topa Equities 1800 Avenue of the Stars, Suite 1400 Los Angeles, CA 90067 310-203-9199	298

Company	Rank
Toresco Enterprises 170 Route 22 East Springfield, NJ 07081 201-467-2900	479
Towers Perrin 335 Madison Avenue New York, NY 10017 212-309-3400	220
Townsend's PO Box 468 Millsboro, DE 19966 302-934-9221	376
Trace International Holdings 375 Park Avenue New York, NY 10152 212-230-0400	41
Transammonia 350 Park Avenue New York, NY 10022 212-223-3200	48
Transnational Motors PO Box 2008 Grand Rapids, MI 49501 616-949-7570	356
TRT Holdings 500 North Water Street Suite 1100 North Corpus Christi, TX 78471 512-884-1831	183
TTC Illinois 50 Meadowview Center Kankakee, IL 60901 815-935-8100	329

Company	Rank
Tube City 12 Monongahela Avenue Glassport, PA 15045 412-678-6141	415
Turner Industries 8687 United Plaza Boulevard Baton Rouge, LA 70809 504-922-5050	422
Tuttle-Click Automotive Group 14 Auto Center Drive Irvine, CA 92718 714-830-7122	344
UIS 15 Exchange Place Jersey City, NJ 07302 201-946-2600	216
Ukrop's Super Markets 600 Southlake Boulevard Richmond, VA 23236 804-794-2401	426
UniGroup One United Drive Fenton, MO 63026 314-326-3100	104
United Co PO Box 1280 Bristol, VA 24203 540-466-3322	472
United Parcel Service 55 Glenlake Parkway NE Atlanta, GA 30328 404-828-6000	3

Company	Rank
VT 8500 Shawnee Mission Pky, Suite 200 Merriam, KS 66202 913-432-6400	77
Walbridge, Aldinger 613 Abbott Street Detroit, MI 48226 313-963-8000	297
Walsh Group 929 West Adams Street Chicago, IL 60607 312-563-5400	369
Waremart PO Box 5756 Boise, ID 83705 208-377-0110	295
Warren Equities 375 Park Avenue, Suite 2502 New York, NY 10152 212-751-8100	242
Washington Cos PO Box 8182 Missoula, MT 59807 406-523-1300	316
Watkins Associated Industries PO Box 1738 Atlanta, GA 30301 404-872-3841	360
Watson Wyatt Worldwide 6707 Democracy Boulevard, Suite 800 Bethesda, MD 20827 301-581-4600	419

Company	Rank
Wawa 260 Baltimore Pike Wawa, PA 19063 610-358-8000	205
Webb Automotive Group 18700 Studebaker Road Cerritos, CA 90703 310-860-6561	467
Wegmans Food Markets PO Box 844 Rochester, NY 14692 716-328-2550	59
Wesco Distribution (1994) Four Station Square Pittsburgh, PA 15219 412-454-2200	54
Westfield Cos PO Box 5001 Westfield Center, OH 44251 330-887-0101	222
Wherehouse Entertainment 19701 Hamilton Avenue Torrance, CA 90502 310-538-2314	476
Whiting-Turner Contracting 300 East Joppa Road Towson, MD 21286 410-821-1100	265
Wickland PO Box 13648 Sacramento, CA 95853 916-978-2500	227

Company	Rank
Wilbur-Ellis 320 California Street San Francisco, CA 94104 415-772-4000	217
Williamson-Dickie Manufacturing PO Box 1779 Fort Worth, TX 76101 817-336-7201	424
Wirtz 680 North Lakeshore Drive Chicago, IL 60611 312-943-7000	342
WWF Paper Two Bala Plaza Bala Cynwyd, PA 19004 610-667-9210	208
Young & Rubicam 285 Madison Avenue New York, NY 10017 212-210-3000	142
Young's Market 2164 North Batavia Street Orange, CA 92865 714-283-4933	184
HB Zachry PO Box 21130 San Antonio, TX 78221 210-922-1213	246

Company Name Index

Subject Index